LESSONS FROM SUCCESSFUL AFRICAN AMERICAN LAWYERS:
Practical Wisdom for Those on the Path to Lawyerhood

Volume I

Edited by Evangeline M. Mitchell, Esq.

HOPE'S PROMISE
PUBLISHING LLC

Lessons from Successful African American Lawyers:
Practical Wisdom for Those on the Path to Lawyerhood

Copyright © 2020 Evangeline M. Mitchell. All rights reserved.

No part of this material may be reproduced or transmitted in any form or by any means, electronic or mechanical, including photocopy, recording or any information storage or retrieval system, without the prior express written permission of the publisher.

The information contained in this book is for informational purposes only and is not intended as legal advice or any other professional service. Persons seeking legal advice should consult with an attorney licensed in their jurisdiction.

Printed in the United States of America. First Edition.

Attn: Evangeline M. Mitchell, Publisher
Hope's Promise Publishing LLC
770 Massachusetts Avenue, Box #391076
Cambridge, Massachusetts 02139

E-Mail: info@hopespromisepublishing.com
Website: www.hopespromisepublishing.com

ISBN 978-1-7352613-1-7

LESSONS FROM SUCCESSFUL AFRICAN AMERICAN LAWYERS:
Practical Wisdom for Those on the Path to Lawyerhood

Volume I

Edited by Evangeline M. Mitchell, Esq.

HOPE'S PROMISE
PUBLISHING LLC

Dedication

To all of the *future* and *aspiring* African American lawyers, especially those who don't personally know any lawyers and are hungry for advice and mentorship.

Know that there are many, many African American lawyers who have been in your shoes and did not have a soul to go to for advice or support. As a community of professionals, I can confidently say that WE genuinely care and want to see you succeed. Those represented in this book are only a small number, but from what they have to share, you will gain so much. If each of them was able to sit down and have a long meet-up or a series of coffee meetings and meals with you, this is what they would share.

This collective effort is a genuine labor of love and was compiled with love, compassion and care especially for *you*.

We need you and pray that you fight for our people and serve as foot soldiers in our continuing fight for equity and justice.

Table of Contents

About the Editor 6

Disclaimer 7

Acknowledgments 8

Preface 9

Special Notes 15

The 55 Successful African American Lawyers (Names, Photos, Titles and Organizations/Companies) 17

Ricky Armand, Esq. 22

Everett Bellamy, Esq., M.S. 26

David A. Brennen, Esq., LL.M. 29

Jamila Marie Brinson, Esq. 32

Kendra Brown, J.D., LL.M., M.Div. 36

Paulette Brown, Esq. 40

Richard O. I. Brown, Esq. 44

Elizabeth Campbell, Esq. 47

Jessica N. Childress, Esq. 50

Ashley N. Cloud, Esq., M.B.A. 54

Jonathan H. Cox, Esq. 57

Khyla Craine, Esq. 60

Derick D. Dailey, Esq. 63

Charles Robert Davidson, Esq., M.A.L.D., Ph.D. 66

Xavier R. Donaldson, Esq. 70

Linda M. Dunson, Esq., LL.M. 75

Beverly Caro Dureus, Esq., Th.M., D.Min. .. 79

Lacy Durham, Esq., M.B.A., LL.M. 83

Erica Edwards-O'Neal, Esq. 90

Conway Ekpo, Esq. 93

A. Zachary Faison, Jr., Esq. 98

Vanessa Griddine-Jones, J.D., LL.M. 103

Kory Chenault Hawkins, J.D. 106

Yolanda D. Wesley Ingram, Esq. 108

Darrell Duane Jackson, J.D., Ph.D. 112

Shirley A. Jefferson, Esq. 114

Danné L. Johnson, Esq. 117

Shontavia Johnson, Esq. 120

Maurice Lamb III, Esq., LL.M. 123

Akilah Mance, Esq. 126

Adia Z. May, Esq., M.B.A. 130

Joseph Q. McCoy, Esq., A.M. 133

Jeremy McLymont, Esq. 136

Winfield Ward Murray, Esq., LL.M. 141

Danielle M. Nettles, Esq. 144

Scheril Antoinette Murray Powell, Esq. ... 149

Marsha Ross-Jackson, Esq., M.P.A. 152

Theodore M. Shaw, Esq. 158

Reginald Shuford, Esq. 163

Grace E. Speights, Esq. 167

Benjamin Taylor, Esq. 171

David T. Taylor, Esq., M.B.A. 174

Jerome Dennis Taylor, Esq. 178

Nydia D. Thomas, Esq. 182

Orlesia A. Tucker, Esq. 186

Twanda Turner-Hawkins, Esq. 189

Artika R. Tyner, Esq., M.P.P., Ed.D. 192

Gerald L. Walden, Jr., Esq., M.B.A. 195

Asha White, Esq. 199

Paul S. Williams, Esq. 202

Sherry Williams, Esq. 204

Suntrease Williams-Maynard, Esq., M.P.A. 208

Patricia Wilson, Esq. 213

Adrien K. Wing, Esq., M.A. 216

Ruqaiijah Yearby, Esq., M.P.H. 219

About the Editor

Evangeline M. Mitchell, Esq., Ed.M. is a social entrepreneur, documentary filmmaker, and lawyer. She is the founder of Hope's Promise Publishing, the first niche publishing company dedicated to producing books geared specifically to aspiring Black lawyers. She is the author or editor of several books including *The African American Pre-Law School Advice Guide, Profiles & Essays of Successful African American Law School Applicants, The African American Law School Survival Guide, Conquering the Bar Exam,* and *Creating Your Personal Strategic Action Plan for Law School Admission Success* workbook.

She is the founder of the National Black Pre-Law Conference and the National HBCU Pre-Law Summit, the country's only major national information-sharing, networking and empowerment events created especially for aspiring Black lawyers, and for current HBCU students and alumni. She also launched The Bridge Builders Esq. Mentorship Program for Aspiring Black Lawyers with the goal of providing "mentoring circles" for prospective law students to enable them to have law student and lawyer mentors and peer pre-law accountability partners to support them in their journeys to law school. In addition, she is the founder of HBCUPRELAW.com and BLACKPRELAW.com informational resource websites. Further, she is the creator, director and executive producer of the docu-series/web series *Becoming Black Lawyers: African Americans and the Law School Experience.*

Through her self-initiated grassroots programming and other efforts and her ability to bring people together around a common cause, she has helped thousands of Black people across the country with law school aspirations better understand what it takes to get into law school and succeed while there. Additionally, she mentors numerous prospective law students across the country.

Evangeline is the recipient of several awards including the Leadership Empowerment Award from the National Black MBA Association-Houston Chapter, the Roberson L. King Excellence in Education Award from the Houston Lawyers Association, the Sadie T.M. Alexander Service Award from the National Black Law Students Association, the Nation's Best Advocates - 40 Lawyers Under 40 from IMPACT and the National Bar Association, the Top 50 Black Lawyers of Houston and Trailblazer Award, Who's Who in Black Houston, the Houston Bar Association's Houston Volunteer Lawyers Program Equal Access Champion Award, the Legacy of NBLSA Award from the National Black Law Students Association, the CLEO Edge Award for Education, Ms. JD's Road Less Traveled Award, The National Black Lawyers - Top 100, the National Black Law Students Association Pre-Law Division Honoree Award, and the Lawyers of Color Power List 2020.

Evangeline is a graduate of HBCU Prairie View A&M University, the University of Iowa College of Law, and the Harvard University Graduate School of Education. Born in New Orleans, Louisiana and raised in Houston, Texas, she currently resides in Cambridge, Massachusetts.

Disclaimer

The purpose of this book is to share the contributing lawyers' personal and professional profiles, as well as hard-earned lessons learned based on their personal experiences and perspectives. The featured lawyers provide wisdom regarding law school preparation, law school admission, choosing a law school, making the most of the law school experience, passing the bar exam, finding a job and advancing in one's career, creating one's own opportunities and choosing a career path, overcoming the additional challenges of being a Black law student and lawyer, as well as defining success and considering one's legacy.

The editor encourages and recommends the reader of this book to read it with an open, yet critical and questioning mind. If there are things you are not sure about or want to challenge, then you should absolutely do so. You are encouraged to ask law students, lawyers, law school administrators, and law professors their perspectives and take on those things. Questioning and further examining things is what being a truly educated person is about. At the same time, please accept the "spirit" in which the book was assembled - with a compassionate heart and a sincere desire to help the aspiring African American lawyer prepare for what is truly one of the most demanding post-baccalaureate professional programs and career paths one can undertake.

After completing this book, you are encouraged to read as many resources and talk to as many people as possible on law school and the legal profession until you are personally confident that you know all there is to know about the tumultuous journey you are about to embark upon. Choose to take personal responsibility and ownership of your legal education and career. Then, work on your individual plan for success based on your vision and personal definition of what success will look like for you.

The editor, the book's contributors, and Hope's Promise Publishing LLC, shall have neither liability nor responsibility to any person or entity with respect to any loss or damage caused, or alleged to be caused, directly or indirectly, by the information contained in this book.

If you do not wish to be bound by the above disclaimer, you may return this book to the publisher for a full refund.

Acknowledgments

Thanking GOD for the vision for this project. Thank You for ordering my steps, and giving me the strength and courage to run my own race.

Many thanks to ALL of the lawyers who so generously took precious time out of their busy schedules to thoughtfully contribute to this volume all of the many lessons they've learned from their experiences. All for the benefit of future lawyers on the path to lawyerhood. Thank you for helping to make this vision a reality. I couldn't have pulled this off without you.

Thank you to my two beautiful children Nyla and Michael, our "gifts from God", who inspire me daily - to do better and be a better human being. After I began serious work on this book project, I had to stop abruptly due to a devastating health event that happened to my husband Michael, which traumatized and dramatically impacted our family and all of our lives in ways we could not have imagined. The experience and the ongoing aftermath could have broken me but because of the love of and responsibility for our children, I have become stronger and more resilient than I ever thought possible. Because of the strength I've gained from their love and confidence in me, I have been able to pick up the pieces of this project that I temporarily abandoned and complete what I had started. Their love along with coping with that adversity has given me the motivation and greater determination to continue in my life's mission and purpose of serving others and empowering the next generation of Black lawyers.

Special thanks go to the aspiring lawyers (pre-law students and law students) who served as proofreaders and reviewers for this book. Thank you to Jolie Marie Radunich, Shemroy Julien, Thalia Clerveau, Michael Franklin, Kaylin Robinson, Alissa Jacques, Kaia Kirk, Nana Nyantakyi, Zainob Sowunmi, Keith Clark, Brittany Goddard, Moriah Wilkins, and Jasmine Brown.

Preface

What a joy and honor to be able to compile such a significant book! You have no idea what a beautiful gift it is and what a blessing we have in store. This book is especially important to *African American* aspiring lawyers because of our shared history. After the abolition of slavery, due to legally-sanctioned, race-based discrimination, segregation, and inequities, many African Americans did not have the *opportunity* to obtain an equal grade school or secondary education, let alone higher education. Given this, even the "idea" of becoming a lawyer was elusive. However, due to the strategic and hard-fought legal battles of National Association for the Advancement of Colored People (NAACP) lawyers, social justice warriors and pioneers including Charles Hamilton Houston and Justice Thurgood Marshall, doors have been opened to African Americans to attend law schools and other educational institutions that were at one time closed to us simply because of our race. Now, even though all things are still not equal and systemic barriers continue to persist - there are opportunities. Because so many sacrificed, fought and died for our right, as full citizens (as opposed to second-class citizens), to receive any level of education without being shut out simply because of race, it is indeed possible to attend and graduate from any law school, take and pass any bar exam, and become a lawyer.

Although becoming a lawyer is possible, the path to lawyerhood is far from easy. To be blunt, it's HARD. Having mental toughness and the ability to handle the academic rigor is important but it's not necessarily enough. Role models and mentorship remain incredibly important for those who want to stay the course and cross the finish line. However, many African Americans who might consider becoming lawyers don't have a relative, family friend, or neighbor who has achieved this goal. Despite how far we've come, we have a long way to go, so many may *still* not even be able to visualize it as something within reach because they have never *seen* in person a real Black lawyer. Others who might consider it may not have the chance to actually *talk* to one about how they can actually make it happen. The reality is that you can't just approach busy people, even through email or social media like Facebook or LinkedIn, and guarantee that they are willing to take time out with someone they don't know and give you all the critical advice they might have for you or wish they had in wanting to pursue this challenging path. Through this book, we hope to play some role in contributing to solving that problem for many. Those readers with law school aspirations, who otherwise could not find a mentor through their family relationships, social circles, or in their surrounding communities, now have a number of amazing and caring mentors through the featured lawyers' contributions. This work assembles excellent advice from 55 unquestionably successful African American lawyers from across the country.

As you will see in reading the book, all of these lawyers featured do different types of work, went to different law schools, and live in different parts of the country. Based on knowing these individuals and their selfless motivations for wanting to be a part of a project like this, I can tell you that despite their many differences, they all have one thing in common. For them, success is not only about achieving one's own individual goals – but it's more than that. It's not just getting a degree to be able to do work to gain a certain status in order to make a certain amount of money so they can get a certain type of car, live in a certain home, or brag about obtaining certain "things" – as mainstream society would want us to believe. Every single one of the lawyers who contributed to this project fervently believes that it is just as important to "give back", "pay it forward", and to help others achieve their dreams – which essentially means that as a community, many of us believe that success is not individual, but collective. We embrace the spirit of "Sankofa" which is a word in the Twi language from the Akan tribe in Ghana meaning that we must reach back and retrieve the knowledge we have gained from the past and then bring it to the present so that we can make progress and build a successful future. The Sankofa bird as illustrated on the cover is a mythic bird whose head is facing backward while his feet are facing forward. If I have "made it" and I am not doing anything to make sure others from my community make it as well, then I really haven't made it at all. *We* haven't made it. The collective mantra seems to be: I am not successful unless I work hard to help ensure the success of others. This consciousness and collective sense of social responsibility, and an understanding from whence we've come are what makes the African American community so special. Due to the limitations of a book, I was only able to capture a small segment of our community of Black lawyers in this volume, but the good part is that they all share in this deeply-held belief in supporting and helping those who come behind us. We have a genuine desire to serve and lift as we climb. I can assure you that there are more of us than you think.

Most of those who contributed are first-generation college graduates and almost all are the very first in their families to become lawyers. Their stories are your stories. They come from similar backgrounds. They know from firsthand experience how it feels to be trailblazers and to go into uncharted territories. They know it's scary and it's challenging. They were once frightened and unsure - and persevered anyway despite the difficulties. They also know that if they did it, so can you. What you will learn from reading more about them and their success strategies is that these lawyers all have a fierce work ethic, a commitment to excellence, and a strong belief and confidence in themselves. I find all of them to be absolutely remarkable human beings that I greatly admire. Almost all of them have volunteered to speak at one of my annual national conferences aimed specifically at empowering African American prospective law students - either the National Black Pre-Law Conference or the National HBCU Pre-Law Summit. They are all servant leaders. Even though you are hearing from 55 different people, don't think you are simply going to get the exact same advice over and over again. You are being given unique insight, advice, and perspectives from *all* of them, which is really quite interesting. There are many common things, yet every single person has something special to contribute. They provide personal information about themselves and their backgrounds so you can see them as real human beings, and then they share the lessons they've learned - giving recommendations and advice for your future actions based on their past experiences. They don't want you to make the missteps they did because they didn't know any better. They want you to know better so you can do and be better than they are. This is selfless and noble.

As the editor of this volume, I took a lot of notes as there were so many invaluable gems and brilliant takeaways from every single contributor. There is so much that can be taken from each individual lawyer and so before you get started, I will share some thoughts and suggest some ways that you can make the most out of reading this book if you truly believe you want to become a lawyer. I am confident that this book will be one helpful resource particularly to those who are in high school and college, as well as college graduates, and working professionals who have delayed law school and/or who are pursuing it as a second career. It will even be useful to parents, guidance counselors, career and pre-law advisors, and law student and lawyer mentors who are trying to advise and assist those interested in law school. This is key reading particularly for first-generation college graduates, and first-generation law school applicants and law students.

Understand that this is not your typical listing of successful people. I have read the magazines showcasing some of the most successful and influential lawyers. You are able to look at their fancy titles and the companies they work for, the schools they went to, their achievements, and the awards they've won. I think these publications are great in terms of being aspirational, but as proud as I may be of the success of those people when I read about all they've accomplished, there are so many questions I'm left to ask about their *journeys* to get there that are unanswered. I have lots of questions: What kind of background did they come from? Are they from socioeconomically disadvantaged backgrounds or middle or upper-class backgrounds where many others had high educational achievements? Did they have mentors and how did they find them? What obstacles did they have to overcome to get to where they've arrived? If they could give advice, what would they say to others who want to achieve their level of success? What is the best advice that they would give? What is the worst advice they received? How did they prepare for law school, get through law school, and study for the bar exam? How have they achieved success in their post-law school careers? What are their perspectives, as African Americans, on how to handle racism and discrimination and still meet one's goals in spite of it? Can they shed light on some things that the rest of us would not have any idea about in terms of reaching for success because we don't personally know anyone who has gotten as far in their education or career? How do they really define "success"? Of all they have accomplished, what are their greatest accomplishments? Readers, it is all here - and more. And the advice imparted is truly extraordinary.

Read about their favorites. Gain perspective by deeply thinking about their favorite quotes. Put together a list of their quotes. Create your own "reading list" based on the favorite books and the favorite legal cases of these stellar individuals. I would strive to read as many of the books as you can but *at least* five of them. If you are limited on time, get the audiobooks for some of them. Know that they are their favorites for a reason. You would want to read what successful people have read and most treasure. Google and read some of the legal cases that they have noted. Consider how you feel about those cases and get comfortable reading and even re-reading them. Think about where the contributing lawyers featured are from, and when and why they decided to go to law school. Take the time to consider their professional affiliations and work experience, but also look at where they went to college, what they did there, where they went to law school, and what they did in law school. Take a look at the organizations they belong to and their community involvement. Research those things you find interesting but don't know much about. Are these things you might want to aim for or be involved with?

When it comes to the advice they give, read it, reflect on it, and go over it in your mind very carefully. For each and every lawyer, take the time to underline, highlight, and then write out those "pearls" of wisdom that mean something to you. I would suggest that you place them all in a special notebook. In this book, there are so many life-changing pointers and suggestions that can be absolute game-changers. These are the many lessons that you can learn from the lawyers' hard-earned wisdom. You can figure out what actions to take based on what they've learned from their lived experiences.

If I would have had this book while still in high school, college, or even once I had started law school, it would have changed so much for me. I really didn't know much and had to just go and figure things out. I feel like I had to stumble through a dark room - and so I really appreciate the wisdom that is imparted here. I am from a working-class household. I am from a single-parent household for a portion of my childhood. We had the necessities. By the time I was in high school, I knew if I wanted something I would have to go out and do it for myself. My mother didn't have extra money and I didn't bother asking for things I knew could be a burden on her. I didn't grow up around extended family or have a community of support I could go to. Since my mother had not gone away to college and didn't have a four-year college degree, she didn't have any advice for me. Because my mother told me she could not contribute anything to my college education, I chose to attend a Black college less than an hour away from my hometown because I earned a Presidential Academic Scholarship that would fully cover my tuition, room and board, and books for all four years. On the same day that I graduated from high school, I was literally dropped off at my college campus. I participated in a summer institute where I lived in a dorm and took classes prior to the fall semester starting. I had to do things for myself and figure things out for myself. We didn't have social capital. I didn't know college graduates or professionals. When I asked my mom if she knew any lawyers, she let me know that she didn't, aside from her divorce lawyer (and she didn't want to make that introduction). So I made my way throughout my higher education and legal education *without* the benefit of lessons that could have helped me to have achieved even more than what I had by figuring out so much on my own.

Both of my parents grew up in New Orleans, Louisiana (my birthplace), and in poverty. They moved to Houston, Texas seeking better opportunities when I was just a few months old. Although my mother longed for a college education and had dreams of becoming a doctor, she grew up in a different time - in the 50s and 60s. When she shared her hopes, she was told it was not possible because she was poor and Black. When I was growing up, I could actually feel her pain and sense of sorrow from not having opportunities and not being able to pursue her dreams. She didn't give up on her desire to earn a college degree though. She managed to earn her bachelor's degree in political science while I was in law school and then her master's degree in business after I graduated law school - becoming the first of the 10 children in her family to receive a four-year college degree. My father did not get past an eighth-grade education so his lack of education limited him in terms of jobs. All I remember is his working in the printing department of an oil and gas company and his spending almost all of his time on the weekends, when he was at home, working in the garage on parts and motors with dreams of becoming a successful inventor and going to Washington to get his inventions patented - before he left his job and our family after he and my mother divorced.

One thing that both parents gave me that drive and fuel who I am today was a strong desire to not give up on my dreams. From them, I felt what it feels like when a person is unable to fulfill their dreams. I was uncomfortable. I felt on a visceral level that they both were very ambitious people who got married and had children because that was what they were supposed to do - but that they were not happy because they were not living out their dreams and the lives they wanted. They were both filled with unrealized potential but due to poverty, growing up during Jim Crow segregation, and the barrier of race, as well as lack of opportunity and support, they were just working jobs and getting by - but not pursuing the dreams in their hearts that God placed inside of them. They shared their dreams and the fact that they had not realized them. Knowing this and feeling this, I believe that's why I am so passionately devoted to pursuing my dreams *and* why I care so much and want to help people fulfill their dreams - particularly their dreams of becoming lawyers.

Having the dream of becoming a lawyer and not knowing any is tough. I never saw a lawyer growing up. I never saw a Black lawyer either - but I knew they existed. Clair Olivia Hanks Huxtable from *The Cosby Show* was my role model so I knew they were out there somewhere. The few Black lawyers that I encountered towards the end of my college career were like magical unicorns to me and received my automatic respect. Unfortunately, the particular individuals I met shared that they didn't like law school, but did not really take time to talk to me or take an interest in getting to know or mentoring me. Being someone who was the "first" to pursue this path, I didn't know how to ask the ones who were uninterested if they knew other lawyers who might be willing to talk to or help me. In law school, I met some lawyers who were good people but they were not doing anything I had a genuine interest in. They were either working for corporations or in big law firms. They wanted to help if I was interested in those paths. My issue was that I didn't want a traditional path. As I always did, I would figure it out on my own. I was frightened and brave and entrepreneurial. There were options out there for idealistic, social justice-oriented future lawyers but even as a law student I didn't know options existed outside of traditional law firms or corporations. I remember feeling frustrated because I felt that the opportunities that existed did not align with my own reasons for wanting to go to law school. Although I had my own plans, I didn't even realize that I had the power to create and start my own practice, business, or organization at the time. It was probably because I didn't see or know other people who had done it. It turns out, that is exactly what I did. I chose to follow my gut and go against the herd mentality when all I actually *saw* was people trying to get posted jobs. So many of us have similar stories. I went to law school with blind faith and had to find my way. Despite the challenges and roadblocks, I have absolutely no regrets. It does mean something to be a lawyer, to be an African American lawyer. It is one of the accomplishments that I had to work really hard for and that I am most proud of.

There is so much here within the pages of this book that I could have learned from early on which could have helped me become even more strategic and competitive, and make even better decisions in so many ways. There is priceless value in having 55 Black lawyers just pour into you. For them, it is an investment. What is included in these pages is absolute gold that cannot be taken for granted. I would like for you to read this book from cover to cover. Recognize that you need to take note of things here that resonate with you. Think about and carefully ruminate on the advice given. Then, start thinking about how you can put some of the advice into action in your own personal plan of becoming a lawyer. Write down your plan. Afterward, read other books about law school admissions, the law school experience, the legal profession, and non-traditional and alternative career options, networking, relationship building, and life and career success. You can't honestly say you want to be a lawyer if you don't like to or are unwilling to read and research. You know why? Because that's what law students and lawyers do!

In addition to reading, you should absolutely seek out real-life mentors. I informally mentor numerous students throughout the country. Because I have put myself out there as a resource, I get students who approach me all of the time - both the right way and the wrong way. Make sure you make it a point to get mentors - the right way. For starters, you must have a teachable spirit and an open heart. Also, understand that unless you are participating in a formal mentorship program, you can gain mentors and ask people to mentor you but not necessarily directly. Busy people get scared about making commitments and promises they may be unable to keep. Good people care about their word and having integrity and don't want to overcommit. Don't overwhelm the lawyers you meet by making them feel you are putting something else on their plates. Just make your plans of going to law school known, and then ask if you can keep in touch and ask questions from time to time whenever they get a free moment. Make it informal with no pressure, and then take an interest in the "person" who you are seeking out for mentoring help. Send notes and cards, and e-mails to just check-in, stay connected, touch base, and see how they are doing. Work on building a relationship. You should take the lead, and take initiative to keep in touch and maintain the relationship. Don't just go to people only when you want something. Nobody likes that. Think about how it can be a two-way street, and consider asking if you can ever volunteer or be supportive of any projects they might be working on. It may be as simple as sharing information about community events on social media to your friends and connections. Show strength. Don't share sob stories about how you don't think you can do it. Don't show that you are easily discouraged because of people telling you you can't do anything. If you come off as weak and soft, then they may feel that law school will crush you and they are setting you up for failure. You must be intellectually and mentally strong. You have to believe in yourself. Self-confidence is incredibly important. You must show that you want this and will not allow anything or anyone to stop you. Ask how you might serve, even in some small way. When you do reach out with questions, utilize some of the things you learned in this book and from other sources in order to get further clarification. Question pieces of advice that contradict what others are saying, and ask more about the common things that most of the lawyers seem to be saying for confirmation.

Understand that lawyers' time is precious and sacred. They get paid for their time. The worst insult you can give is showing that you don't respect it. Respect their time. Don't ask them to pour out everything to you like you are an empty vessel. Do some research on your own and be proactive about your future. Show initiative and take ownership of your future legal education and career. This book is an incredible start.

People want to help people. Our people really do want to help each other - but especially those who are driven, self-motivated, and doing and willing to do everything within their power to help themselves. We are now living in the "Information Age." There is so much information available. Many of us couldn't go to the Internet or Amazon to find books and resources when we made the decision to pursue law school. If they were not available at our school or the local library, we were simply out of luck. Things have changed dramatically for the better, so please recognize all that is available to you and take full advantage of it - and then reach out and ask about those things you can't find on your own and ask about those things you should be reading and doing.

As a community of lawyers and especially as Black lawyers, we want you to join our ranks and really want to help. Some of us are friendlier than others. There are some who had it very hard and may want you to have to go through what they went through yourself. Ignore the ones who are unfriendly and bitter. Seek out those who are friendly and helpful. And work on building and maintaining warm, mutually-beneficial relationships. However, no matter what, you must also do *your* part and then be respectful and thoughtful in your approach. Maintain a spirit of gratitude, and don't act as if people owe you anything. No one "has to" go out of their way to help you. It is a choice. Your attitude and humility (or lack thereof) and expression of appreciation can impact whether someone chooses to or chooses not to assist you in reaching your goals. Be the person that someone wants to help.

I absolutely wish you the very best of good success whether you continue on the path to lawyerhood - or choose another path entirely. Most of us didn't have any mentors or the warm embrace of support, encouragement, and tough love that lie within these pages - so you have a major advantage. Appreciate the time taken to sow into you through the pages of this book, and the loving and caring spirit with which this volume has been put together. It *does* matter to be an *African American* lawyer, so don't let anyone ever tell you that it doesn't. Race is a social construct that was created in the beginnings of this country to justify the economic necessity of slavery and invent a permanent underclass. Racist ideology continues to be perpetuated so that some people have and maintain power and privilege and others do not. Having the opportunity to learn from *African American* lawyers is vitally important and makes a difference. Your becoming a lawyer, particularly as an African American, matters to me, your family, your community, the legal community, the African American community - and beyond.

Our representation in law school classrooms and in the legal profession matters and our voices are significant. We are the only group of people in this country that shares a unique and special relationship with the American legal system. The law was used to create a racial caste system and social hierarchy; to control every aspect of our lives through slave law; to consider us as property and deny us our humanity; and to refuse to recognize us as U.S. citizens. Then, the law granted us limited "freedom" and rights through the 13th amendment (ended the institution of slavery), the 4th amendment (gave us American citizenship, and due process and equal protection of the law), and the 15th amendment (provided the right to vote to Black men). The law was also used to subjugate us to second-class citizenship through Black codes (after the abolition of slavery, laws created to limit the freedom of Black people and help ensure they would serve as cheap labor) and Jim Crow laws (laws that mandated the segregation of public schools, places, and transportation between Blacks and Whites). Later, the law was used to give us "first-class" citizenship rights - rights that we should have been given as American citizens, but that we had to fight for and that continue to be undermined. These laws included the Civil Rights Act of 1964 (prohibited discrimination in public places and in employment, integrated schools and public accommodations, and made employment discrimination illegal) and the Voting Rights Act of 1965 (prohibited racial discrimination in voting). . . . The struggle still continues.

As this book gets ready to be released, we are in the midst of the coronavirus pandemic, a recession, and national (and international) protests and outcries against the brutality, killings, inhumane treatment, and injustice faced by Black people here in the United States. Amid the unrest, this is actually an exciting time for aspiring Black lawyers to be a part of taking that sense of urgency, energy, anger, frustration, and exhaustion felt about racism and the status quo - to consider how to use the power of the law and any other tools available to us to make change. I can't think of any time during my entire lifetime where I have heard so much talk about systemic racism, structural racism and equity, reparations, changing laws and policies, and dismantling and restructuring the criminal legal system and other systems, and re-defining justice as we now know it. I believe that this pivotal moment and movement and what's happening in our country right now in 2020 makes it an opportune time to want to pursue law school and become a lawyer. There are so many new and innovative ways of considering and re-imagining legal education, the law, and lawyering that didn't exist when I was in law school. There is so much about education and legal education that I rejected and didn't accept - but didn't seem would ever change. I guess I was ahead of my time. Now, it seems that change is on the horizon. This is a time when it would be exhilarating to be a law student. Embrace it, be thoughtful, strategic and courageous, and call for and demand the changes that we may have asked for that fell on deaf ears. People are actually listening now. You can make changes we couldn't make - and changes we didn't know we could make during our lifetime.

A legal education is one that empowers. The law has power. It has the power to harm or to help. Remember that. As you embark on a journey that is difficult and that will be filled with pitfalls, curveballs and pain, you should be prepared for the challenges, understand that it is supposed to be tough so you must be tougher - gritty and resilient. Know that you *have to* keep going *anyway*. When you feel like you want to give up, think about what your ancestors had to go through and the generations of Black lawyers before you. Believe it or not, they had it much harder. Respect them and appreciate the struggle and their desire to open doors for you. You have a role to walk through those doors, and continue the fight to make opportunity even greater for those coming behind you - knocking down new doors.

Take all of the advice in these pages, see what makes sense for you, and act upon it. And when you decide to become a lawyer, commit to it with everything that is within you - knowing it will be tough but it can be done - if you are willing to work harder than you have ever worked and if you want it badly enough. God has given you everything you need to succeed. You have seeds of greatness inside of you and it's your job to do whatever you can to bring that greatness out. Strongly believe in yourself and know that there is nothing you can't do. You just have to remain committed and determined to see it through no matter how hard it gets, and no matter what it takes. You must be "all in" and understand that law school and the bar exam are rites of passage designed to weed out and break the weak. They serve as a means to an end to enter this elite fraternity of "lawyerhood". As Black lawyers, we are eager to welcome you into our fraternity. But make no mistake, you will have to work for it and *earn* it. It will take blood, sweat, and tears. No one is given a law degree. At the end of the day, it is entirely on YOU.

Even though you can't see it, you actually do have a community of support. Know that every single individual who is a part of this book project and the thousands of lawyers out there who could not be are all cheering for your success. We believe in you. If you work incredibly hard, sacrifice, make up your mind that this is what you want, and take the advice inside, you can have J.D. and Esq. behind your name. No matter what some people might try to tell you, those credentials are indeed respected. The journey is worth it. We hope that reading this book plays a small role in helping you to get and stay on the path to becoming a lawyer - if it's truly in your heart to do so. The legal profession is an incredibly important one - yet remains the least diverse major profession. There are more Black doctors than there are lawyers - believe it or not. Your joining our ranks can help change that. We need you. We need you to serve as lawyers and judges in the courtrooms. We need you to represent clients at the negotiation tables.

We need you to advocate for our people. We need you to serve as leaders. We need you to run for office. We need you to open law practices and non-profit organizations. We need you to build schools and businesses in our communities. We need you to invest in real estate and to stop the gentrification of our communities. We need little Black children and adults to see you. And we need little children and grown people of every race and all walks of life to see you. . . . And when you make it, make sure you share your own lessons and help others, especially African Americans, become lawyers too. Now, get ready to learn from these successful lawyers, these successful African American lawyers. To your great and greater success! Happy reading!

Evangeline M. Mitchell, Esq.

Special Notes

What do you have to do to become a lawyer?

For those unfamiliar with the process of becoming a lawyer, it makes sense to explain it briefly before you start reading the book. Gaining admission into law school generally requires earning a bachelor's degree in any subject from an accredited institution and taking either the Law School Admission Test (LSAT) which is accepted by all law schools, or the Graduate Record Examination (GRE) which is accepted by an increasing number of law schools. You must submit an application package which will include your application, test scores, recommendations, a personal statement and a diversity statement. The admissions process is highly competitive. After gaining admission into law school, you would usually attend full-time for three years. However, some people enroll in two to two and a half year accelerated programs, or attend part-time and graduate in four years. Once you graduate from law school, you will earn a Juris Doctor or Doctor of Jurisprudence - the J.D. degree a terminal, professional degree.

With the law degree, you will have legal training and can say that you are trained as a lawyer, but you are not able to practice law, call yourself an "attorney", or put "Esq." or "Esquire" behind your name yet. You still have to pass the bar exam. Most law school graduates study for the bar exam the summer after they graduate from law school. Most people graduate in May and the bar exam is typically administered in July. If you do not pass it in July, you can register to re-take it in February. Most people submit their application to take the bar while still in law school. You must sit for the bar exam for the state where you intend to practice law.

The bar exam is a comprehensive exam that consists of all of the subjects all law students across the country typically take during their first year (i.e., contracts, torts, evidence, civil procedure, constitutional law, real property, and criminal law and procedure). All bar exams will include the Multistate Bar Exam (MBE), a multiple-choice exam, the Multistate Essay Exam (MEE), and the Multistate Performance Test (MPT), which is designed to test lawyering skills. Bar takers must also demonstrate mastery of several state-specific subjects. The bar exam is a two to three-day exam, depending on the state where you take it. In addition, you will also need to take the Model Professional Responsibility Exam or the MPRE. This is a multiple-choice exam testing the rules of professional responsibility. Most law students take this exam while still in law school.

Every state has a minimum score that you will need to achieve in order to pass their bar exam. You may be fortunate enough to pass on your first try. If not, you will have other opportunities to pass. However, given the enormous amount of work required to study for and take the exam, it is suggested that it is something you should aim to do only once. Some states have a discretionary or absolute limit to the number of times you can take the bar exam there, while others do not. Every state sets their own rules. For example, you only have three attempts to pass the bar in the state of Maryland and five attempts in Texas, but most states allow unlimited attempts.

In addition, you will need to pass a "character and fitness" review which involves having people recommend you and attest to your having good moral character. It also involves your revealing any brushes you've had with the law, your being accused of academic misconduct, any disciplinary actions taken against you such as being "written up" for breaking some rule or policy, any lawsuits you may have been a part of, or other potential issue that may put your character into question. You will need to share any debt you have and any blemishes on your consumer credit. So, please make sure you pay your bills on time, communicate with creditors for bills you can't pay and work out a plan, and remain proactive about reviewing your credit reports and knowing your credit score. Further, some states require an in-person interview as a part of your character and fitness assessment. It's a lot, but it's doable. As you can see, there's so many hurdles to jump over, so your becoming a lawyer is indeed a big deal.

Please be aware that there are a few jurisdictions that will allow you to serve as an apprentice under the supervision of a practicing lawyer or judge in place of attending a traditional law school and then you can take the bar exam. These states include California, Virginia, Vermont and Washington. The state of Wisconsin has "diploma privilege" where they will admit you to their state bar if you graduate from a law school in that state. This is the only state that does not require your taking the bar exam. Another exception is in the state of New Hampshire. The University of New Hampshire Franklin Pierce Law School has a program called the Daniel Webster Scholar (DWS) Honors Program. If you are a "Webster Scholar", you do not have to take a traditional bar exam after graduating. Instead, you would take and pass a variant of New Hampshire's Bar Exam during your second and third years of law school. Before law school graduation, you are sworn into the New Hampshire bar and are able to practice law in that state right after you graduate.

It is also possible to attend law school in Canada, the United Kingdom, Australia, New Zealand, or another country that provides the equivalent of the Common Law legal education provided by American Bar Association-approved law schools in the United States. Then, you can return to the states to prepare for the bar exam. Some people who have earned law degrees in foreign countries may have to take a one-year LL.M. course of study in the U.S. before being eligible to sit for the bar exam. If this is your desire, please make sure to do further thorough research. Additionally, contact the Board of Law Examiners in the states you are most interested in practicing law for their specific requirements to become eligible to sit for their state bar exam. Find out what their law school requirements are as this will impact your decision of where you will want to attend law school. New York and California are the two states that offer the most flexibility for those who receive their legal education in foreign countries.

All of the lawyers in this book have followed the "traditional" path to becoming a lawyer by attending an American Bar Association-accredited law school, and almost all have taken and passed a bar exam, and have been admitted to one or more state bars. A "bar" is an organization of licensed lawyers. Once you pass the bar exam, you become a member of that state's bar.

* Visit the websites for the Law School Admission Council (LSAC) www.lsac.org and the National Conference of Bar Examiners www.ncbex.org for further information.

What does 1L, 2L and 3L mean?

When the lawyers in the book mention 1L, they are referring to the first-year in law school. 2L refers to the second year in law school, and 3L refers to the third year in law school.

What does J.D. and Esq. mean and signify?

J.D. stands for Juris Doctor or Doctor of Jurisprudence degree, which is the degree you earn after completing all requirements for law school - usually after three years of study. You can add those letters behind your name after you have graduated from law school. Esq. stands for Esquire and it is an honorary title that you can add behind your full name to signify that you are a practicing lawyer, and/or you have passed a bar exam, have been licensed and you are able to practice law. You should not use this designation until you are officially licensed and a member of a state bar. Until then, you can use J.D. behind your name. Do note that some people who are licensed, have multiple degrees, and do not actively practice law or may serve in an academic role may choose to use J.D. instead of Esq. Therefore, using J.D. does not necessarily mean that someone is not licensed to practice law. Their license may or may not be inactive.

Why do I capitalize the letter "b" in "Black" instead of using "black" when referring to people of African descent?

I have capitalized the "b" for "Black" when referring to Black people or people of African descent throughout the book. I also capitalize the "w" for "White" for White people or people of European descent as well. Style books differ as to whether or not to capitalize. This is my personal preference because we are referring to a group of people and not just a color. (One of our contributors did not agree with this use and I honored his preference by not changing this in his submission.)

What is a legal case citation? How do you find legal cases?

Every lawyer featured in the book was asked to share their favorite legal case(s). Some lawyers only provided the name. For instance, *Brown v. Board of Education*. The first person named is the plaintiff or the person suing, and the second person is the defendant or the person being sued. In other words, Plaintiff v. Defendant. The abbreviation v. stands for versus which means against or opposed to. Other lawyers provided the case name, as well as the legal case citation, which gives you information on the reporter that the specific case is published in. For instance, for *Brown v. Board of Education*, the case citation is 347 U.S. 483 (1954). 347 represents the volume, U.S. represents the reporter, 483 represents the page number, and 1954 was the year the case was decided.

In the past, you would have to physically look for the books to find the cases. However, due to the current technology, you can use a search engine and find the text of all of the cases you want to read. Despite this, understanding the case citations is important. You are encouraged to read actual legal cases and look up the citations so you understand the reporters they are contained in. Also, look up and write down the meaning of any and all legal terminology that you don't understand. Get a hard copy of *Black's Law Dictionary*, or go online to thelawdictionary.org to get and read the definitions for legal words.

The 55 Successful African American Lawyers

Ricky Armand, Esq.
Personal Injury Attorney
Law Offices of Gary, Williams,
Parenti, Watson & Gary, P.L.L.C.
Stuart, Florida

**Everett Bellamy,
Esq., M.S.**
*General Counsel and Executive Vice
President*
Thread Bioscience Inc.
Annapolis, Maryland

**David A. Brennen, Esq.,
LL.M.**
Dean and Professor of Law
University of Kentucky J. David
Rosenberg College of Law
Lexington, Kentucky

**Jamila Marie
Brinson, Esq.**
Partner
Jackson Walker LLP
Houston, Texas

**Kendra Brown, J.D.,
LL.M., M.Div.**
Director, Public Policy
Mastercard
Washington, D.C.

Paulette Brown, Esq.
*Senior Partner and Chief Diversity &
Inclusion Officer*
Locke Lord LLP
Past President
American Bar Association and
National Bar Association
Princeton, New Jersey

**Richard O. I. Brown,
Esq.**
Assistant United States Attorney
United States Department of
Justice
Palm Beach Gardens, Florida

**Elizabeth A. Campbell,
Esq.**
Director, Inclusion and Diversity
Campbell Soup Company
Camden, New Jersey

Jessica N. Childress, Esq.
Managing Attorney
The Childress Firm PLLC
Founder and CEO
Juris Prudence LLC
Washington, D.C.

**Ashley N. Cloud, Esq.,
M.B.A.**
Attorney Advisor
U.S. Small Business
Administration
Washington, D.C.

Jonathan H. Cox, Esq.
Partner
The Cox Pradia Law Firm, PLLC
Houston, Texas

Khyla D. Craine, Esq.
Deputy Legal Director
Michigan Department of State
Detroit, Michigan

Derick D. Dailey, Esq.
Assistant United States Attorney
United States Attorney's Office
District of Delaware
Wilmington, Delaware

Charles Robert Davidson, Esq., M.A.L.D., Ph.D.
Director
Pre-Law Institute
City University of New York
John Jay College
New York, New York

Xavier R. Donaldson, Esq.
Partner
Donaldson & Chilliest, LLP
New York, New York

Linda Marie Dunson, Esq., LL.M.
Presiding Judge
309th Family Judicial District
Harris County
Houston, Texas

Beverly Caro Duréus, Esq., Th.M., D.Min.
Clinical Professor of Legal Research, Writing, and Advocacy
Dedman School of Law at Southern Methodist University
Dallas, Texas

Lacy L. Durham, Esq., M.B.A., LL.M.
Senior Manager
Deloitte Tax, LLP
Dallas, Texas

Erica Edwards-O'Neal, Esq.
Senior Vice President
Diversity, Equity & Inclusion
New York City Economic Development Corporation (NYCEDC)
Founder
EEO Consults
New York, New York

Conway S. Ekpo, Esq.
Executive Director
Morgan Stanley
New York, New York

A. Zachary Faison Jr., Esq.
President & Chief Executive Officer
Edward Waters College
Jacksonville, Florida

Vanessa Griddine-Jones, J.D., LL.M.
Executive Director
Congressional Black Caucus Institute
Washington, D.C.

Kory Chenault Hawkins, J.D.
Associate Director of Admissions, Coordinator for Diversity and Inclusion
Columbia University School of Law
New York, New York

Yolanda D. Wesley Ingram, Esq.
Director of Bar Support and Assistant Teaching Professor
Drexel University Thomas R. Kline School of Law
Philadelphia, Pennsylvania

Darrell D. Jackson, J.D., Ph.D.
Professor of Law
University of Wyoming College of Law
Laramie, Wyoming

Shirley A. Jefferson, Esq.
Associate Dean for Student Affairs and Diversity and Associate Professor of Law
Vermont Law School
South Royalton, Vermont

Danné L. Johnson, Esq.
Constance Baker Motley Professor of Law
Oklahoma City University School of Law
Oklahoma City, Oklahoma

Shontavia Johnson, Esq.
Associate Vice President for Entrepreneurship and Innovation
Clemson University
Founder
Brand+Business Academy
Greenville, South Carolina

Maurice Lamb III, Esq., LL.M.
Mergers and Acquisitions: Indirect Tax Transactions Associate
Ernst & Young LLP
Houston, Texas

Akilah Mance, Esq.
General Counsel
Houston Forensic Science Center
Houston, Texas

Adia Z. May, Esq., M.B.A.
Business Affairs
William Morris Endeavor
Los Angeles, California

Joseph Q. McCoy, Esq., A.M.
Business Transactions Practice Lead
Riley Safer Holmes & Cancila LLP
Chicago, Illinois

Jeremy McLymont, Esq.
Assistant Public Defender
Miami-Dade Public Defender Office
Miami, Florida

Winfield Ward Murray, Esq.
Federal Attorney
United States Department of Labor
Professor
Morehouse College
Atlanta, Georgia

Danielle M. Nettles, Esq.
Attorney
Linebarger Goggan Blair & Sampson, LLP
Beaumont, Texas

Scheril Antoinette Murray Powell, Esq.
Attorney at Law
Doumar, Allsworth, Laystrom, Voigt, Wachs, Adair, and Dishowitz LLP
Miami, Florida

Marsha L. Ross-Jackson, Esq., M.P.A.
Senior Lecturer and Assistant Dean
Diversity, Equity, Inclusion and Student Professional Development
Executive Director
Institute for Law and the Workplace
Chicago-Kent College of Law
Chicago, Illinois

Theodore M. Shaw, Esq.
Julius L. Chambers Distinguished Professor of Law
Director
The UNC Center for Civil Rights
University of North Carolina School of Law
Chapel Hill, North Carolina

Reginald T. Shuford, Esq.
Executive Director
American Civil Liberties Union (ACLU) of Pennsylvania
Philadelphia, Pennsylvania

Grace E. Speights, Esq.
Global Leader
Labor and Employment Practice
Morgan, Lewis & Bockius, LLP
Washington, D.C.

Benjamin Taylor, Esq.
Partner Attorney
Taylor & Gomez Law Office
Phoenix, Arizona

David T. Taylor, Esq., M.B.A.
Trademark Attorney Advisor
United States Patent and Trademark Office
Alexandria, Virginia

Jerome Dennis Taylor, Esq.
Supervisory Attorney
Social Security Administration
Office of Disability Adjudication and Review
Chicago, Illinois

Nydia D. Thomas, Esq.
Attorney and Director
RISE Transformative Justice Program
Lone Star Justice Alliance
Austin, Texas

Orlesia A. Tucker, Esq.
General Counsel
FBD Partnership, LP
San Antonio, Texas

Twanda Turner-Hawkins, Esq.
Director
Global Litigation
Dematic Corp. and KION Americas
Atlanta, Georgia

Artika R. Tyner, Esq., M.P.P., Ed.D.
Founding Director
University of St. Thomas Center on Race, Leadership and Social Justice
Clinical Faculty
University of St. Thomas
St. Paul, Minnesota

Gerald L. Walden, Jr., Esq., M.B.A.
Head of Legal
The Fresh Market, Inc.
Greensboro, North Carolina

Asha White, Esq.
Deputy Chief of the Criminal Bureau
Massachusetts Office of the Attorney General
Boston, Massachusetts

Paul S. Williams, Esq.
Partner Emeritus and Advisor
Major, Lindsey and Africa
Chicago, Illinois

Sherry D. Williams, Esq.
Senior Legal Executive
Former Vice President, Deputy General Counsel & Global Chief Ethics & Compliance Officer
Jabil Inc.
Former Senior Vice President Global Chief Ethics & Compliance Officer
Halliburton Company
Tampa, Florida

Suntrease Williams-Maynard, Esq., M.P.A.
Special Counsel
Adams and Reese LLP
Mobile, Alabama

Patricia Wilson, Esq.
Professor of Law
Baylor University Law School
Waco, Texas

Adrien K. Wing, Esq., M.A.
Bessie Dutton Murray Professor of Law
Associate Dean for International and Comparative Law Programs
France Summer Abroad Program Director
University of Iowa College of Law
Director
University of Iowa Center for Human Rights
Iowa City, Iowa

Ruqaiijah Yearby, Esq., M.P.H.
Professor of Law
Member
Center for Health Law Studies
Co-Founder and Executive Director
The Institute for Healing Justice and Equity
Saint Louis University School of Law
Saint Louis, Missouri

Ricky Armand, Esq.
Personal Injury Attorney
Law Offices of Gary, Williams, Parenti, Watson & Gary, P.L.L.C.
Stuart, Florida

"May God's will be done."
– Ricky Armand

Success is . . . finding peace and helping others find peace.

PERSONAL FAVORITES

Favorite Quotes:

"Be still, and know that I am God. I will be exalted among the nations, I will be exalted in the earth!" - Psalm 46:10

"Whoever restrains his words has knowledge, and he who has a cool spirit is a man of understanding." - Proverbs 17:27

Favorite Books: *Proverbs* by King Solomon; *Ecclesiastes* by King Solomon; *Crucial Conversations: Tools for Talking When Stakes Are High* by Kerry Patterson, Joseph Grenny, Ron McMillan and Al Switzler; *The Millionaire Next Door: The Surprising Secrets of America's Wealthy* by Thomas J. Stanley and William D. Danko; *The Conscious Parent: Transforming Ourselves, Empowering Our Children* by Shefali Tsabary; *The Mis-Education of the Negro* by Carter G. Woodson; *Narrative of the Life of Frederick Douglass* by Frederick Douglass; *Built to Sell* by John Warrillow; *Never Split the Difference* by Chris Voss; *The Spirit of Kaizen: Creating Lasting Excellence One Small Step at a Time* by Robert Maurer; *Invested* by Danielle Town and Phil Town; *Rich Dad Poor Dad* by Robert Kiyosaki; *The Street Lawyer* by John Grisham; *King of Torts* by John Grisham; *The Big Payback: The History of the Business of Hip-Hop* by Dan Charnas

Favorite Movies: *Black Panther*; *Paid in Full*; *The Lion King*; *Coco*; *Django Unchained*; *13th*

Favorite Songs and Musical Artists: Too many to list, and way too many I'm embarrassed to admit.

Favorite Music Genres: Hip-Hop; R&B; Gospel; Christian Contemporary; Baroque; Konpa; Reggae

Favorite Law School Classes: Trial Practice; Sports Law; Race and the Law; Civil Procedure

Favorite Hobbies: Investing and reading about the stock market; Making playlists; Watching interviews and documentaries; Exercising; Traveling; Date nights; Teaching Bible study for the young adults at a local church

Favorite Attorney Role Models: Willie Gary; Lorenzo Williams; Donald Watson; Trent Steele; Michelle Obama; Dean Shirley Jefferson; Evangeline M. Mitchell

FAMILY AND BACKGROUND

Where Born and Raised: Born - Stamford, Connecticut; Raised - Port St. Lucie, Florida

Family (Spouse/Partner and Children): Spouse - Melissa; Children - Russell Patrick and Ryan McArthur

Family Socioeconomic and Educational Background: My grandparents and parents were born and raised in

Haiti. My parents moved to the United States and had me and my little sister. When I was two months old, they sent me to Haiti to live with my grandmother until their situation improved. My mother was in school and had odd jobs before eventually becoming a social worker. My father delivered newspapers, worked at a gas station, and worked at a bakery before eventually becoming a letter carrier for the United States Post Office.

My parents did the best they could to put food on the table and to ensure that me and my little sister received a good education. They emphasized to us that hard work and an education was the only way to succeed.

THE DECISION TO BECOME A LAWYER

When and Why I Decided to Become a Lawyer: My first memory of wanting to be a lawyer was in the fourth grade. My motivation at the time: I just wanted to wear a black suit, carry a black briefcase, and own a black Mercedes. By my senior year in high school, I let go of that dream, because I thought law school would be too hard for someone like me. I loved music and sports and I thought law school was for people who loved reading. After my second year in college, a conversation with a family friend reignited my dream. I reflected on where my family came from, how hard they worked, and how much they sacrificed for me and my sister. I didn't want to grow old and wonder "What if?". I wanted to go big or go home. I wanted to give it my best shot and let God's will be done.

EDUCATIONAL ACHIEVEMENTS

High School: Palm Vista High School (Grades 9-10); St. Lucie West Centennial High School (Grades 11-12) (Port St. Lucie, Florida)

College/University: University of Central Florida (Orlando, Florida)

Undergraduate Degree: Bachelor of Arts (B.A.)

Major: English

College Honors, Achievements and Activities: *Academic Recognition,* Dean's List; *Member,* National Society of Collegiate Scholars; *Member,* Men of Valor

Law School: Vermont Law School (South Royalton, Vermont)

Law Degree and Graduation Year: Juris Doctor/Doctor of Jurisprudence (J.D.) - Class of 2012

Law School Honors, Achievements and Activities: *Student Ambassador,* Vermont Law School; *Vice President,* Brothers and Sisters in Christ; *Mentor,* Academic Success Program; *Pre-Law Student Division Director,* Northeast Black Law Students Association; *Highest Grade in Class,* Trial Practice; *Highest Grade in Class,* Advanced Transactions; *Member,* 2012 Class Gift Fundraiser Committee

PROFESSIONAL ACCOMPLISHMENTS

State Bar Membership (Where Admitted to Practice Law): Florida

Other Legal Work Experience: *Intern*, 19th Judicial Circuit Public Defender's Office; *Intern*, U.S. Attorney's Office Western District of North Carolina; *Litigation Paralegal*, Steele Law Firm

Professional Organizations: *Member,* National Bar Association; *Member,* Cunningham Bar Association; *Member,* Haitian Lawyers Association; *Member,* Martin County Bar Association

Post-Law School Honors, Achievements, Activities, and Community Involvement: *Mentor*, Martin County High School; *Special Guest Speaker,* National Black Pre-Law Conference and Law Fair (2019)

LESSONS LEARNED: MY RECOMMENDATIONS FOR YOUR FUTURE ACTIONS BASED ON MY PAST EXPERIENCE

Advice on Law School Preparation:

Take an LSAT test prep course, if possible, and take plenty of timed practice exams. Once you've been accepted into law school, I actually encourage students to invest in and read bar prep books or course outlines such as Emmanuel Outlines, BARBRI, Kaplan, etc. It's a great way to get a head start into understanding the theories you will learn in law school.

Advice on Applying to and Selecting a Law School:

When applying to law school, make sure you have your whole package finalized early. Before you even receive your LSAT scores, have your resume and personal statement ready. Have someone review and provide feedback on your resume and personal statement. One of my mentors, whom I met at the National Black Pre-law Conference, helped me tremendously with my resume and personal statement. He tore my personal statement up, and I had to revise it numerous times before it came out right. Your personal story is your story. You want to make sure it is well presented and is noteworthy.

When applying to law school, be open-minded. You may have wanted to be in one place, but there might be another school out there that can better complement your needs or personality. Vermont Law School (VLS) wasn't initially on my radar. In my household, Vermont was not a state we even thought about. VLS wound up offering me the best scholarship, and it turned out being the right place for me. The mountains were my backyard, I had very esteemed professors, and I made lifelong friends. Be open-minded. Remember, may God's will be done.

Advice Regarding Academic Success, Co-Curricular and Extra-Curricular Participation, and Social Engagement in Law School:

The first year of law school is usually the toughest. You are learning a new language, a new way of preparing for class, and you're adjusting to a new environment. This will require a lot of focus and leave little room for distractions. Please seek the assistance of your Academic Success Program and even your professors. Schedule appointments with your professors to go over practice exams. It's vital that you understand not only the material (the rule of law), but you also need to understand how your professors want the rule applied.

Co-curricular and extra-curricular activities can sometimes provide a great sense of relief. Look into activities or programs that you are interested in or align with your career goals.

Adjusting to the social challenges can be rough. If you are fortunate enough to find a small circle of friends you can confide in, it can make a huge difference in your experience. Even if you are not in the same class sections as your trusted confidantes and/or cannot study together, the social outlet can be therapeutic. It's comforting to communicate with someone who can relate to the struggles and adjustments you go through in law school. Your circle matters.

Advice on Preparing for and Taking the Bar Exam:

First, I would advise you to become a bar representative at some point during law school. This allows you to have a free bar prep course after law school. Eliminate as many distractions as possible, and take plenty of timed practice exams. Make sure you not only understand the rule of law, but how to efficiently answer essay questions. In the event you are not in a bar prep course, you still want to get your hands on the material. The BARBRI Bar Review book helped me with essays, and the Kaplan Multistate Bar Exam (MBE) book helped with the MBE.

Advice on Choosing a Job and Career Path Inside or Outside of the Legal Profession:

Be open-minded. None of us know what the future holds, and you can't predict how your life will turn out. You may enter into a position because others say it's prestigious, or because you believed it's what you've always wanted. Once you get there, you might realize it's not what you thought it was. Work hard, network, and be open-minded. God has opportunities and plans for you that you've never even imagined.

Advice on Seeking Legal Job Opportunities and/or Creating One's Own Opportunities:

Entrepreneurship may be ideal for some, but it is not for everyone. Running a business requires *a lot*. There are pros and cons. Even if this is your ultimate goal, you should consider timing. Again, be open-minded and flexible.

Advice on Achieving Career Success and Advancement:

Ask a lot of questions, work hard, and search for quality mentorship. In this profession (and in life), you will come across sharks. You want to find mentors that can give you sound advice and guidance. Treat each experience as a lesson. Once you start to work full time in your law career, you should continue to learn as much as you can because that's when the real schooling begins.

Advice on Overcoming the Additional Challenges Black Law Students and Lawyers Face:

I remember being looked down upon by some of my non-Black classmates. They assumed I made it to law school solely because of my race and not my intellect or potential. In the legal field, not only do you receive similar treatment from some non-Black attorneys, but even from your own clients! The majority of our clients are African American, and I still experience certain prejudices and preconceived notions from them. There's a saying and belief that we must do away with: "You need a Jewish attorney to be successful." That couldn't be further from the truth.

My advice on overcoming these challenges is to earn respect by working hard and producing results. Although this does not guarantee to change everyone's opinions on Black lawyers, we should strive for excellence in all that we do. Actions speak louder than words, and your reputation will begin to precede you. "A good name is to be chosen rather than great riches, and favor is better than silver or gold." - Proverbs 22:1

Best Advice I Received Regarding Law School and the Legal Profession:

"As an African-American law student, you have to go by the T.A.G. rule – you have to be twice as good." – My classmate, Kendra Brown, J.D., LL.M., M.Div.

Worst Advice I Received Regarding Law School and the Legal Profession:

"Get into the highest-ranked school, or graduate at the top of your class. Otherwise, it's pointless."

There's nothing wrong with striving for this goal, but this shouldn't be the end-all and be-all in my opinion. Everyone's path is different.

Best Advice I Would Give to an Aspiring Black Lawyer:

Listen attentively, be open-minded, ask tons of questions, seek counsel, pass on the information you learn, work hard, never forget where you came from, and help others along the way.

Thoughts About Why Earning a Law Degree Is a Powerful Credential for African Americans and Why There Is a Need for More African American Lawyers:

A law degree is one of the most powerful degrees you can attain. Most of the individuals who create and enforce the law in our country have law degrees. Not only does a law degree give you an opportunity to provide a better lifestyle for you and your family, but it also affords us the opportunity to provide so much help to others. In the legal community, we can be a voice for the voiceless, regardless of the field in which you practice. At the time of the writing of this book, we are still lacking diversity in the judiciary. We need more representation in every area of law.

Sadly, our country has a history of oppression and injustice towards African-Americans. The more legal voices we have to help serve and protect our community, the better.

Here are a few reasons why African-American lawyers matter:

<u>Trayvon Martin</u> (2/26/12); <u>Eric Garner</u> (7/17/14); <u>Michael Brown</u> (8/9/14); <u>Laquan McDonald</u> (10/20/14); <u>Akai Gurley</u> (11/20/14); <u>Tamir Rice</u> (11/22/14); <u>Rumain Brisbon</u> (12/2/14); <u>Tony Robinson</u> (3/6/15); <u>Eric Harris</u> (4/2/15); <u>Walter Scott</u> (4/4/15); <u>Freddie Gray</u> (4/12/15); <u>William Chapman</u> (4/22/15); <u>Sandra Bland</u> (7/13/15); <u>Sam DuBose</u> (7/19/15); <u>Jeremy McDole</u> (9/23/15); <u>Jamar Clark</u> (11/15/15); <u>Alton Sterling</u> (7/5/16); <u>Philando Castile</u> (7/6/16); <u>Terence Crutcher</u> (9/16/16); <u>Botham Jean</u> (9/6/18); <u>Ahmaud Arbery</u> (2/23/2020); <u>Breonna Taylor</u> (3/13/2020); <u>George Floyd</u> (5/25/2020)

Thoughts About Whether and Why Law School Is Worth the Financial Investment:

Law school isn't for everyone, and that is okay. However, it was a game-changer for me and my family. Graduating from law school has allowed me to practice personal injury law, which has changed my life financially. One of my goals has always been to be debt free and live in financial freedom. These goals are now in sight, and I'm so grateful for God's provision. I have an opportunity to forever change my family tree financially for the better.

LEGACY AND SUCCESS

My Most Outstanding Accomplishments:

Personally: being a husband and a father, and being able to provide for my family.

Professionally: achieving justice for my clients by recovering millions of dollars in settlements for them. I am also grateful and proud to work for the legendary giant killer, Willie E. Gary. It's a privilege to work for a Black-owned company and to contribute to its success.

The Legacy I Hope to Leave:

I hope to leave a legacy that portrays the blessing of living in God's will. When someone looks back on my life, I hope that it helps, encourages, and inspires them, especially those men and women who look like me. I desire to help increase financial literacy in our communities. My aim is to make my children, their children, and my great grandchildren proud.

The Secret to My Success:

Yahweh. There is absolutely no way I would be where I am today without God's grace, protection, and provision. He's also the One who blessed me with an amazing circle of people. Your circle matters and mine includes family, friends, and mentors who continue to motivate and inspire me.

Everett Bellamy, Esq., M.S.

General Counsel and Executive Vice President
Thread Bioscience Inc.
Annapolis, Maryland

There's too much law but not enough justice.

– Everett Bellamy

Success is . . . self-defined. Set high goals for yourself and let your God-given talent and hard work take it from there.

PERSONAL FAVORITES

Favorite Quotes: "In recognizing the humanity of our fellow beings, we pay ourselves the highest tribute." - Thurgood Marshall

"There are no secrets to success. It is the result of preparation, hard work and learning from failure." - Colin Powell

Favorite Books: *Native Son* by Richard Wright; *Simple Justice* by Richard Kluger

Favorite Movies: *Chinatown; The Silence of the Lambs; Lady in the Blue Dress*

Favorite Songs: Any song by Jimi Hendrix

Favorite Musical Artists: Prince; Most of the Motown artists, especially Stevie Wonder

Favorite Law School Classes: Constitutional Law; Media Law

Favorite Legal Cases: *Brown v. Board of Education*

Favorite Hobbies: Traveling to international destinations; Visiting art galleries; Listening to jazz, R&B and classical music

Favorite Attorney Role Model: Charles Hamilton Houston

FAMILY AND BACKGROUND

Where Born and Raised: Chicago, Illinois (South Side)

Family (Spouse/Partner and Children): Spouse - Karen Bellamy

Family Socioeconomic and Educational Background: I am from a working-class background. My father attended Tuskegee College but left after one year to join the Navy during World War II. My mother completed high school and spent most of her career as a nurse's aide. I am the first lawyer in the family. One of my sisters is a medical doctor. The other has a Ph.D. in psychology.

THE DECISION TO BECOME A LAWYER

When and Why I Decided to Become a Lawyer: I decided to become a lawyer after I made the decision not to pursue a Ph.D. after completing my Master's degree in higher education administration. The counseling aspect of being a lawyer is what attracted me to the law. I wanted to help people resolve their differences. After graduating from law school, I combined my interest in higher education with the law to become a dean at Georgetown University Law Center.

EDUCATIONAL ACHIEVEMENTS

High School: Harper High School (Chicago, Illinois)

College/University: University of Wisconsin-La Crosse (La Crosse, Wisconsin)

Undergraduate Degree: Bachelor of Science (B.S.)

Major: Health Sciences

Law School: Cleveland-Marshall College of Law, Cleveland State University (Cleveland, Ohio)

Law Degree and Graduation Year: Juris Doctor/Doctor of Jurisprudence (J.D.) - Class of 1980

Law School Honors, Achievements and Activities: *National Finalist,* The Frederick Douglass Moot Court Competition

Other Graduate or Professional Degree: Master of Science (M.S.), Student Affairs Administration, University of Wisconsin-La Crosse (La Crosse, Wisconsin)

PROFESSIONAL ACCOMPLISHMENTS

State Bar Membership (Where Admitted to Practice Law): Ohio

Other Legal Work Experience: *Senior Assistant Dean,* Georgetown University Law Center (30 years); *Adjunct Professor of Law,* Georgetown University Law Center (Subject Taught: Small Business Law and Entrepreneurship) (28 years)

Other Professional Work Experience: *Advisory Board Member,* Various small businesses and startup companies; *Instructor,* Council on Legal Education Opportunity Program (CLEO); *Instructor,* Charles Hamilton Houston Preparatory Law Institute (CHH)

Professional Organizations: *Member,* National Bar Association; *Member,* American Bar Association

Post-Law School Honors, Achievements, Activities, and Community Involvement: *Awardee,* Lifetime Achievement Award, McDonough School of Business, Georgetown University (2018); *Listed Honoree,* Who's Who in American Law and Black American Lawyers; *Awardee,* CLEO EDGE Award, Council on Legal Education Opportunity (2018); *Honoree,* Washington Bar Association Hall of Fame; *Honoree,* Sadie T.M. Alexander Award, National Black Law Students Association (NBLSA) (2012); *Honoree,* Legacy Builder Award, National Black Pre-Law Conference and Law Fair (2006); *Advisory Board Member*, Several civil boards

LESSONS LEARNED: RECOMMENDATIONS FOR YOUR FUTURE ACTIONS BASED ON MY PAST EXPERIENCE

Advice on Law School Preparation:

Study hard and study smart. Write as much as you can while in college and get critical feedback on your writing from your professors. Practice time management; there's a lot of reading in law school that requires many hours per day preparing for class. Develop your analytical skills through reading, problem solving and participating in classroom discussions. Take courses that require critical thinking and not just memorization.

Advice on Applying to and Selecting a Law School:

Try to match your academic qualifications with the law schools you apply to. However, don't underestimate yourself - apply to some of the top law schools if you think it's a good match. Also, consider the financial aid the schools offer you. Take time to prepare for the LSAT and be positive about doing well on the test.

Advice Regarding Academic Success, Co-Curricular and Extra-Curricular Participation, and Social Engagement in Law School:

I think it's important to participate in co-curricular activities while in law school. Doing so will enhance what you are learning in the classroom. Also, you make important connections with other students and faculty advisers.

Advice on Preparing for and Taking the Bar Exam:

If students work hard while in law school and take most, if not all, of the subjects on the bar exam, they should pass. Take the time to understand the difference between a law school exam and an essay question on the bar exam. Nothing beats preparation - take a bar review course.

Advice on Choosing a Job and Career Path Inside or Outside of the Legal Profession:

Pursue a career in law that you have a passion for and enjoy. Most lawyers have a 30- to 40-year career, so you have to be satisfied with the work you are doing and that you are using your law degree for the good of society, as well as for your clients.

Advice on Seeking Legal Job Opportunities and/or Creating One's Own Opportunities:

Meet as many lawyers as you can while in law school; making connections and finding out about the type of law they practice. Hone the skills that will allow you to stand out from other students.

Advice on Achieving Career Success and Advancement:

Enjoy what you do. Work hard and collaborate with other lawyers. Realize that with your law degree, you have a power tool for making a difference in the world. Determine what type of practice you thrive in and seek those positions.

Advice on Overcoming the Additional Challenges Black Law Students and Lawyers Face:

You must believe you are as qualified as any other student. If you are in law school, that's where you belong. Strive to be the best you can be.

Know your history. Consider the challenges Black lawyers faced in the past and how they overcame those challenges.

Things are much better now and you have an opportunity to make them even better for the next generation of Black lawyers.

Best Advice I Received Regarding Law School and the Legal Profession:

The best advice I received was do the best I can and try to help others along the way.

Worst Advice I Received Regarding Law School and the Legal Profession:

Worst advice - there are too many lawyers. I soon realized they were talking about lawyers for the rich because low-income people who can't afford a lawyer would love to have one when facing legal challenges.

Best Advice I Would Give to an Aspiring Black Lawyer:

You must believe you are as qualified as any other person with a law degree. Look for role models you can emulate.

Thoughts About Why Earning a Law Degree Is a Powerful Credential for African Americans and Why There Is a Need for More African American Lawyers:

A law degree is a powerful credential for anyone. That's why you find lawyers as heads of corporations, non-profits, and countries. This is especially true for African American lawyers because it equips them with the intellect and skills to fight for social justice and other rights.

Thoughts About Whether and Why Law School Is Worth the Financial Investment:

Law school is worth the financial investment over the long run. It's an investment in your future. However, law students should do the best they can to keep law school debt to a minimum. Try not to borrow too much money to finance your law degree. Apply early for financial aid and keep your expenses in check while in law school.

LEGACY AND SUCCESS

My Most Outstanding Accomplishments:

My most outstanding accomplishment, both personal and professional, is my journey from a working-class neighborhood on the South Side of Chicago to the Nation's Capital, where I have been able to meet and work with some of the most distinguished lawyers and judges in the world. I am also proud of having been able to teach, advise and mentor thousands of students over my 44 years in higher education.

The Legacy I Hope to Leave:

I hope my legacy will be all the students I have helped achieve their dream of becoming a lawyer. And they will, in turn, help other people in need.

The Secret to My Success:

My success was due to a strong sense of my place in the world and knowing that God was with me every step of the way.

Practical Wisdom for Those on the Path to Lawyerhood

David A. Brennen, Esq., LL.M.
Dean and Professor of Law
University of Kentucky J. David Rosenberg College of Law
Lexington, Kentucky

"Always keep your feet moving."
"The glass is always half full."
– David A. Brennen

Success is . . achieving both personal and professional goals while leaving a meaningful impact on the world.

PERSONAL FAVORITES

Favorite Quote: "No man is an island entire of himself. Any man's death diminishes me, because I am a part of mankind. Therefore, send not to know for whom the bell tolls. It tolls for thee." - John Donne

Favorite Book: *Biography of Camille Pissarro* by Ralph Sikes

Favorite Movie: *The World According to Garp*

Favorite Songs: Anything sung by Prince

Favorite Musical Artist: Prince

Favorite Law School Classes: Tax Law; Administrative Law

Favorite Legal Case: *Bob Jones v. United States*

Favorite Hobbies: Golf; Running; Home-building shows

Favorite Attorney Role Models: Thurgood Marshall; Mitch McDeere

FAMILY AND BACKGROUND

Where Born and Raised: Gainesville, Florida

Family (Spouse/Partner and Children): Spouse - Kimberly; Children - (son) Clarence, (son) Andrew, and (son) Spenser

Family Socioeconomic and Educational Background: I was a first-generation college student and law school graduate.

THE DECISION TO BECOME A LAWYER

When and Why I Decided to Become a Lawyer: I decided to become a lawyer at high school graduation when my fourth-grade teacher gave me as a gift a copy of *Black's Law Dictionary*.

EDUCATIONAL ACHIEVEMENTS

High School: Twin Lakes High School (West Palm Beach, Florida)

College/University: Florida Atlantic University (Boca Raton, Florida)

Undergraduate Degree: Bachelor of Business Administration (B.B.A.)

Major: Finance

College Honors, Achievements and Activities: *Member,* Inaugural Freshmen Class; *President,* Black Student Union; *Co-Founder,* Brotherhood of Ten (group that brought first Black Greek-lettered organization to Florida Atlantic University)

Law School: University of Florida College of Law (Gainesville, Florida)

Law Degree and Graduation Year: Juris Doctor/Doctor of Jurisprudence (J.D.) - Class of 1991

Law School Honors, Achievements and Activities: *Finalist,* Final Four, Moot Court; *Awardee,* Florida Administrative Law Book Award

Other Graduate or Professional Degree: Master of Laws (LL.M.), University of Florida Levin College of Law (Gainesville, Florida)

PROFESSIONAL ACCOMPLISHMENTS

State Bar Membership (Where Licensed to Practice Law): Florida

Other Professional Work Experience: *Deputy Director,* Association of American Law Schools (AALS)

Professional Organizations: *Board of Directors,* Access Group, Inc. (2014-2017); *Board of Directors,* Hospice of the Bluegrass (2013-2016); *Chair & Executive Committee,* Section on Law School Deans, Association of American Law Schools (2013-2016); *Board of Governors,* Kentucky Bar Foundation (2009-Present); *Co-Founder, Chair & Executive Committee,* Section on Nonprofit and Philanthropy Law, Association of American Law Schools (2006-2011); *Chair,* Budget, Finance & Fundraising Committee, Society of American Law Teachers Board of Governors (2004-2007); *Chair & Executive Committee,* Minority Groups Section, Association of American Law Schools (2002-2007); *Vice President,* Board of Directors, Community Tax Law Project (Richmond, Virginia) (1997-2003); *Member,* Board of Directors, Frank H. Hiscock Legal Aid Society Board of Directors (Syracuse, New York) (1997); *Member,* Tax Section, The Florida Bar (1992-Present); *Member,* Section of Taxation, American Bar Association (1991-Present)

Post-Law School Honors, Achievements, Activities, and Community Involvement: *Pupil,* Institute for Management & Leadership in Higher Education, Harvard University (2013); *Member,* Diversity in the Profession Committee, Kentucky Bar Association (2010-2014); *Elected Member,* American Law Institute (2002-Present); *Adviser,* Principles of the Law of Nonprofit Organizations, American Law Institute (2002-Present)

LESSONS LEARNED: MY RECOMMENDATIONS FOR YOUR FUTURE ACTIONS BASED ON MY PAST EXPERIENCE

Advice on Law School Preparation:

Read as much as possible. When you can, read books or articles that will stretch your vocabulary and general knowledge. Second, develop your writing. In law specifically, being able to write clearly, concisely, and persuasively will serve you well. Take classes that will require you to research and write papers, as well as have them critiqued by your teachers. Next, start to plan for the Law School Admission Test (LSAT) in your junior year so you have plenty of time to study, take the LSAT, and have time to retake the LSAT if desired. Finally, think about which faculty members you would like to ask for letters of recommendation, a required part of almost every law school application.

Advice on Applying to and Selecting a Law School:

What I have found in my 20+ years in legal education is a Juris Doctor degree will open many paths, including opportunities beyond the traditional practice of law. For this reason, I believe there is no better time to attend law school. When selecting a law school, look at the curriculum and the courses that are offered and make sure they align with your specific interests. Make sure there are a variety of clinical and externship opportunities to gain hands-on experience. Find out the ways in which the law school offers support post-graduation and pay close attention to bar passage and employment statistics, as these are important factors in finding success after law school.

Advice Regarding Academic Success, Co-Curricular and Extra-Curricular Participation, and Social Engagement in Law School:

First, expect to feel confused. There are few clear answers in the law, but that is what makes the legal profession exciting and challenging. Embrace that ambiguity. Second, interact with your classmates. Learn from them and be supportive of each other. Third, use the resources available to you and visit your professors on a regular basis. Finally, have a life outside of law school – exercise, eat well, and remember that this is a challenging experience that will result in both personal and academic growth.

Advice on Preparing for and Taking the Bar Exam:

Create a study schedule and follow it. Take practice tests under test-like conditions. This will show you what you actually understand. Also make sure to get plenty of exercise. This will help relax your mind.

Advice on Choosing a Job and Career Path Inside or Outside of the Legal Profession:

When choosing a career path in the legal profession, select a practice area based on your personality and keep lifestyle factors in mind. Some areas have a steadier flow of work and others have a very unpredictable workflow. It's also okay to pursue a non-legal career – the problem-solving skills, analytical skills, organizational skills, writing skills, and knowledge of the law gained in law school can be of value in almost any career.

Advice on Seeking Legal Job Opportunities and/or Creating One's Own Opportunities:

Take advantage of the career resources at your law school. Take part in on-campus interviews, attend legal career fairs and job consortia, search online job postings, and attend career development seminars. Build a powerful alumni network and seek out career and interview advice from alumni who are practicing attorneys.

Advice on Achieving Career Success and Advancement:

Have a good work ethic – strive to work harder than everyone around you.

Go out and build your professional network. Cultivating relationships can help advance your career.

Check out new opportunities often. Stay positive during the search and consider taking a big opportunity when it comes your way.

Advice on Overcoming the Additional Challenges that Black Law Students and Black Lawyers Face:

Do not allow barriers to overwhelm and prevent you from obtaining your desired goals. Remember that your own drive and determination can overcome many challenges. Stay motivated and look for unique opportunities to achieve success.

Best Advice I Received Regarding Law School and the Legal Profession:

Always remain focused on what prompted you to attend law school. Don't be swayed by money or other similar distractions.

Worst Advice I Received Regarding Law School and the Legal Profession:

Follow the money.

Best Advice I Would Give to an Aspiring Black Lawyer:

Pursue your passion to become a lawyer. Understand how your skills and unique experiences create value within the context of any given situation.

Find a good mentor – a professor, a staff member, or a practicing attorney. They are invaluable as you can bounce ideas off them and they can give you tips on how to overcome some common obstacles today's young attorneys face.

Thoughts About Why Earning a Law Degree Is a Powerful Credential for African Americans and Why There Is a Need for More African American Lawyers:

Perspective taking is a part of the maturation process. However, even those that achieve a high degree of understanding the nuances of nature and nurture that impacts our decision making, cannot fully appreciate the nuance of racial experiences. In a profession that stands for justice, fairness and equality, it is more important than ever that African American lawyers inject their perspective into the national conscience.

Thoughts About Whether Law School Is Worth the Financial Investment:

I believe law school is worth the financial investment because the problem-solving skills, analytical skills, organizational skills, writing skills, and knowledge of the law gained in law school can be of value in almost any career.

LEGACY AND SUCCESS

My Most Outstanding Accomplishments:

Personal: Marrying my wife, Kimberly, and being a father to my three sons

Professional: Being chosen as the first African-American dean at the University of Kentucky College of Law, the state's flagship institution.

The Legacy I Hope to Leave:

Never give up, and don't let your pedigree determine your fate.

The Secret to My Success:

Determination, as well as my support system – the family, friends, and coworkers who have been my greatest motivators. They have empowered me to stay committed to reaching my goals and helped me leave a meaningful impact on the law, the profession and the world.

Jamila Marie Brinson, Esq.
Partner
Jackson Walker LLP
Houston, Texas

"Each day is an opportunity to start anew and go after what is for your greatest good."

– Jamila M. Brinson

Success is . . . working diligently toward a goal while remaining open and receptive to a better goal or result and ultimately knowing that it is all about the journey.

PERSONAL FAVORITES

Favorite Quotes: "You must be the change you wish to see in the world." - Mahatma Gandhi

"Happiness is when what you think, what you say, and what you do are in harmony." - Mahatma Gandhi

"I never dreamed about success. I worked for it." - Estee Lauder

Favorite Books: *Jemima J* by Jennifer Green; *The Wedding* by Dorothy West

Favorite Movie: *Coming to America*

Favorite Song: "Golden" by Jill Scott

Favorite Musical Artists: Jill Scott; Ledisi; India Arie

Favorite Law School Classes: Legal Research and Writing; All Health Law classes

Favorite Hobbies: Traveling internationally; Salsa and African dancing; Attending music and international festivals; Spending time with my family

Favorite Attorney Role Models: Chevazz Brown and Bruce Ruzinsky - two Jackson Walker attorneys who love what they do and go out of their way to be the change so that other attorneys can have the best opportunity to develop their skill sets and networks to succeed in the practice of law.

FAMILY AND BACKGROUND

Where Born and Raised: Born - Brooklyn, New York; Raised - Miami, Florida (After reading in a teen magazine about students of color who went away to college preparatory boarding schools and it changed the trajectory of their lives, I completed the application process on my own, obtained a full scholarship and went away to a college preparatory boarding school in Massachusetts when I was 14 years old.)

Family (Spouse/Partner and Children): Spouse - Marcus; Children - (daughter) Noemi and (son) Mekai

Family Socioeconomic and Educational Background: I am a proud first-generation American. My parents were born and raised in Belize, Central America and came to the United States in their late teens in search of better educational opportunities. My father worked full-time while putting himself through college and earning a Master's in Business Administration. My parents divorced, and I lived with my mother in Miami, Florida. One year before I graduated from college, my mother graduated with her bachelor's degree. I am the first person in my family to graduate from law school. I learned from watching both of my parents and the numerous mentors I had growing up how to make the most of every opportunity, visualize what I would like to achieve, and set step-by-step goals to achieve them, regardless of how long it may take.

THE DECISION TO BECOME A LAWYER

When and Why I Decided to Become a Lawyer: I first thought about becoming a lawyer the summer before my senior year of college when I completed a summer program in public health sponsored through the University of Michigan. During that program, I was introduced to someone who had received a law degree and a master's in public health and was fascinated by the combination of the two degrees and the interesting work he was doing. After I graduated from college, I became a United States Peace Corps Volunteer. During my tenure, I noticed a lot of the powerful women I met who were strong community advocates, ran dynamic non-profit organizations or were highly ranked in the government were all trained as lawyers. I decided law school would be a great training ground for me as well.

EDUCATIONAL ACHIEVEMENTS

High School: Northfield Mount Hermon School (Northfield, Massachusetts)

College/University: University of Pennsylvania (Philadelphia, Pennsylvania)

Undergraduate Degree: Bachelor of Arts (B.A.)

Majors: Health and Societies (Concentration: International Health) and Hispanic Studies

College Honors, Achievements and Activities: Dean's List; George Weiss Scholar; Ronald E. McNair Research Scholar; *Member*, CASA (Caribbean American Students Association); *Member,* African Rhythms (African Dance & Drum Troupe); *Participant*, Junior Year-Long Study Abroad, Dominican Republic

Law School: University of Houston Law Center (Houston, Texas)

Law Degree and Graduation Year: Juris Doctor/Doctor of Jurisprudence (J.D.) - Class of 2010

Law School Honors, Achievements and Activities: Completed 12+ credits in Health Law; Dean's Scholar; *Diversity Scholar,* Association of Corporate Counsel (ACC); *Legislative Health Law Fellow,* Texas State Legislature; *Participant,* Law School Foreign Study Program in Australia and New Zealand (Spring 2010)

PROFESSIONAL ACCOMPLISHMENTS

State Bar Membership (Where Licensed to Practice Law): Texas

Other Legal Experience: *Intern,* Chief United States Bankruptcy Judge Marvin Isgur, Southern District of Texas; *Law Clerk,* Civil Division, United States Attorney's Office; *Legal Extern,* Office of General Counsel, Baylor College of Medicine; *Legal Extern,* BP America, Inc.; *Health Policy Analyst,* 81st Texas Legislative Session, Former Texas State Senator Leticia Van de Putte

Other Professional Work Experience: *Volunteer,* United States Peace Corps (HIV/AIDS education, advocacy, care, and support)

Professional Organizations: *Member,* The Downtown Group; *Former Co-Chair and Member*, Houston Bar Association AIDS Outreach Committee; *2020 Fellow*, Leadership Council on Legal Diversity (LCLD); *Member*, HR Houston (affiliate of SHRM); *Member*, Greater Houston Black Chamber

Post-Law School Honors, Achievements, Activities, and Community Involvement: *Awardee,* 2018 President's Award, Houston Bar Association (HBA); *Honoree,* Rising Star – Employment & Labor Law, Super Lawyers – Rising Stars by Thomson Reuters (2019-2020); *Awardee,* Top 50 Women Lawyers Award, National Diversity Council; *Honoree,* Top 40 Under 40, The National Black Lawyers; *Graduate*, Houston Young Lawyers Association (HYLA) Leadership Academy (2013-2014); *Mentor, Guest Speaker and Presenter*, University of Houston Law Center's Pre-Law Pipeline Program; *Volunteer Board Member,* Chinquapin Preparatory School; *Guardian Ad Litem*, State Bar of Texas; *Pro Bono Attorney*, Houston Volunteer Lawyers; *Host Committee Member, Panelist, and/or Moderator*, National Black Pre-Law Conference and Law Fair (2008-Present); *Volunteer Director,* Board of Directors, West Orem Family YMCA; *Firm Coordinator*, Jackson Walker LLP's Houston office participation in HYLA's Annual Adopt-an-Angel Program and HBA AIDS Outreach Committee's Annual Holiday Adopt-a-Family Program

LESSONS LEARNED: MY RECOMMENDATIONS FOR YOUR FUTURE ACTIONS BASED ON MY PAST EXPERIENCE

Advice on Law School Preparation:

I believe it is beneficial to have at least some full-time work or some other life experience before going to law school. It helps you to maintain perspective about exams and grades when others around you in law school are struggling to do the same. It also provides some practical basis for your determination of what you want to do with your law degree and makes you less susceptible to getting into a legal career that is not right for you. From the law school recruiting perspective, it also helps you to stand out when applying to law firms.

After I graduated from college, I served as a United States Peace Corps Volunteer on the island nation of Saint Lucia in the Eastern Caribbean. While other Peace Corps volunteers sometimes joke that placements in the Eastern Caribbean are "Peace Corps Lite," my experience working with the Ministry of Health, schools, community groups and HIV-positive individuals and their families was anything but light. I loved absolutely every opportunity I had to learn, teach and grow all while volunteering on HIV/AIDS education, treatment, care and support initiatives both in Saint Lucia and across the Eastern Caribbean.

I knew after having that experience it would be essential, regardless of the area of law I practice in, to make the time to engage in *pro bono* legal [without charge/free] work and continue to volunteer with community organizations. It is such a privilege to have a skill set and educational training that allows me to help others overcome legal and other obstacles in their lives.

Advice on Applying to and Selecting a Law School:

Do not rush the application process. Take the time to prepare for the law school application process, and to select the best law school program for you. Apply to the best ranked schools you can get into and apply to several tiers of schools-reach and safety schools. Some law schools do provide scholarships so seek out those schools to decrease the amount of law school debt you will have to incur, which will allow you greater flexibility to follow your passion once you have completed your studies.

Advice Regarding Academic Success, Co-Curricular and Extra-Curricular Participation, and Social Engagement in Law School:

Once you get into law school, make friends with like-minded peers, form productive study groups where you study more than you play, tap into unknown resources such as the Law Review outline bank at your school, find a few activities you are genuinely interested in, develop genuine friendships, and seek out leadership positions in those organizations but not at the detriment of your grades. Be strategic about your extracurricular involvement; if you are interested in health law or international arbitration, take courses and get involved with activities that support and develop that interest. Remember that the goal is to identify the area of law you'd ultimately like to practice in and obtain a job in that area so network, network, network.

Advice on Preparing for and Taking the Bar Exam:

Do not worry about preparing for the bar exam until you have graduated from law school; you need to graduate first, and with the best GPA you can obtain so let that be your priority. Register for a recommended bar preparation course, remove all distractions (including family, intimate relationships, jobs, if possible) and study and prepare for the bar exam as if it were a full-time job that required 40+ hours a week. Leave it all out on the court, as they say, and focus only on studying for the exam so that by the time you sit down to take the exam, you know you can focus on crushing the exam, instead of cursing yourself for not having studied more. Also, adopt several affirmations or quotes about success and say those quotes/affirmations several times a day, especially when you are feeling anxious or scared about the exam. It is important to remain positive so that you can focus on preparing for the exam instead of worrying about failing it. Surround yourself with like-minded people who will support and encourage you, with whom you can effectively and efficiently study, and relax a bit during the process.

Advice on Choosing a Job and Career Path Inside or Outside of the Legal Profession:

Hold fast to your dreams. If you went to law school to become a civil rights attorney, do not let the financial allure of big law firms distract you from that path (unless you genuinely change your mind and want to work for a big law firm). There is no amount of money that is worth more than the satisfaction and joy you feel from doing a job every day that you genuinely love and cannot wait to wake up in the morning to go and do. It is much harder to leave a job where you are making a lot of money but hate the work than to have less money but love what you do.

Advice on Seeking Legal Job Opportunities and/or Creating One's Own Opportunities:

At every step of your pre-law school and law school journey, take stock of what areas of the law you are interested in, have enjoyed learning about, and have actually been exposed to (either through classes, internships, shadowing someone in that area, etc.) and guide all of your decisions on classes, extracurricular activities, and internship/job opportunities towards that direction. Throw everything you have at reaching the goal of obtaining a job in the area of law you love until you succeed at obtaining that job - regardless of how long it takes. In the meantime, make sure your "in the meantime" jobs/experiences help you to develop a skill set that will benefit you once you can get into the area of law you love. Lawyers spend way too much time practicing law to do so in an area that they do not enjoy, so make this a priority.

Advice on Achieving Career Success and Advancement:

It is important to set short-term as well as long-term goals so that you can celebrate the small achievements, which will keep you going until you reach each large achievement. Career success and advancement is not worth devastating your personal relationships or familial goals. If you want to get married and have a family, do not let your career prevent you from doing that. You have a lifetime to develop your career and advance; but not quite as long to do other things that are important in your personal life.

Advice on Overcoming the Additional Challenges Black Law Students Face:

Be aware of the challenges that come along with being a minority in a majority institution (if applicable) and profession so that when challenging situations occur, you are not blind-sided by them or allow them to throw you off your path. However, do not go into your law school career fixated on what others may think of you or how they may or may not treat you. Know that you deserve to be in law school just like everyone else, and focus on making your experience the best experience for you so that by the time you are done, you can rest assured that you got what you wanted to get out of it.

Advice on Overcoming the Additional Challenges Black Lawyers Face:

Develop a strong professional and familial network so that you have a support system you can depend on. Do not be surprised when a challenging situation arises but do not allow it to steer you off of your path or to act in a way that you would be ashamed to tell your mother about. As Michelle Obama has said, "When they go low, [you] go high."

Worst Advice I Received Regarding Law School and the Legal Profession:

Once I started working, I was told not to worry about making my hours but focus on learning the law. That is not true in Big Law. Making or superseding your hours is synonymous for most attorneys in Big Law as learning the law. Focus on getting on the largest cases with the most active partners who you enjoy working with that you can, and taking every opportunity to be a contributing member of the legal team. Be courageous, take ownership and initiative, and have an opinion on how to improve what is being done for the client. Become invaluable. And bill all of your hours with clear and descriptive narratives so it is clear the value you have brought.

Best Advice I Would Give to an Aspiring Black Lawyer:

Stay true to the reasons why you wanted to go to law school in the first place or the path you discover you love more, have a plan of action that includes several back-up plans in case challenging situations occur, and do not lose focus on your end goal. Forgo more money for more love and enjoyment in what you will be doing (almost) every day for the rest of your legal career. Remain steadfast in your dreams, your goals, your abilities and keep moving forward.

Thoughts About Why Earning a Law Degree Is a Powerful Credential for African Americans and Why There Is a Need for More African American Lawyers:

Having a law degree and being a licensed attorney is a feather in your cap that no one can ever take from you. There is an urgent need in this profession for more lawyers who look like the population that they serve. Always remember there are others who look like you who need and want mentors and who look up to you.

Thoughts About Whether Law School Is Worth the Financial Investment:

It is definitely possible to establish a fulfilling career without going to law school and becoming a lawyer. Law school is not the path to riches necessarily, as most attorneys do not earn what others believe we do. You have to be clear about what you want to achieve and how going to law school will get you there. Once you do that, and your path directs you to attend law school, it is worth every penny.

LEGACY AND SUCCESS

My Most Outstanding Accomplishments:

Personal - My most outstanding personal accomplishments have been the amazing relationships I have with my family and friends and my supportive husband Marcus as well as the birth of my beautiful daughter Noemi Rose and my handsome son Mekai Robert.

Professional - My most outstanding professional accomplishment has been diligently working my way up from a frightened, clueless first-year associate to becoming a partner at a prestigious law firm.

The Legacy I Hope to Leave:

When I die, I want others to say that I was kind, loving, supportive, and unabashedly dedicated to bettering myself and others.

The Secret to My Success:

Positive thinking, prayer and affirmation, surrounding myself with a positive and supportive familial and professional network, taking the time to routinely take stock of what is important to me, and the steps I need to take to get to where I want to be, and doing something each day that gets me closer and closer to my goal.

Kendra Brown, J.D., LL.M., M.Div.
Director, Public Policy
Mastercard
Washington, D.C.

"Make a difference for as many as you can as often as you can."
– Kendra Brown

Success is . . . making a difference in the lives of as many as possible as often as possible.

PERSONAL FAVORITES

Favorite Quotes: "Change will not come if we wait for some other person or some other time. We are the ones we've been waiting for. We are the change that we seek." - President Barack Obama

"Work hard in silence, let your success be your noise." - Frank Ocean

"It is not enough that we do our best; sometimes we must do what is required." - Winston Churchill

"Dum spiro, spero" (Latin) - "While I breathe, I hope."

"God, grant me the serenity to accept the things I cannot change, courage to change the things I can, and wisdom to know the difference." - The Serenity Prayer by Reinhold Niebuhr

Favorite Books: *Just Mercy: A Story of Justice and Redemption* by Bryan Stevenson; *I Know Why the Caged Bird Sings* by Maya Angelou

Favorite Movies: *Hidden Figures; Black Panther; Selma*

Favorite Musical Artists: Maranda Curtis; Cece Winans; Elevation Worship; Jonathan Butler

Favorite Law School Classes: Constitutional Law; Corporate Law; Employment Law; Civil Rights Seminar

Favorite Legal Case: *Brown v. Board of Education of Topeka,* 347 U.S. 483 (1954)

Favorite Hobbies: Reading; Spending time with my family; Volunteering in the community; Singing

Favorite Attorney Role Models: Dean Shirley Jefferson; Dean Gil Kujovich; Attorney Everett Bellamy; Attorney Donald Temple

FAMILY AND BACKGROUND

Where Born and Raised: Winchester, Virginia

Family (Spouse/Partner and Children): Child - (daughter) Brooklynn

Family Socioeconomic and Educational Background: I am the first person in my family to attend law school. My father was my high school assistant principal and my pastor. My mother worked for a pharmaceutical company and instilled in us the value of ministry while serving with my father.

THE DECISION TO BECOME A LAWYER

When and Why I Decided to Become a Lawyer: For my undergraduate studies, I attended Hampton University. During my matriculation at Hampton, I was a congressional intern for Representative Bobby Scott. On September 11, 2001, I watched as the second plane hit the twin towers. Over the coming days, I reported to my intern role and took call after call from concerned citizens and I remember saying to myself then that I wanted to be in a role where I could help people. I had also always lived a life of serving others being the daughter of a pastor, thus it followed that I wanted to have a role where I could make a difference in the lives of others.

EDUCATIONAL ACHIEVEMENTS

High School: John Handley High School (Winchester, Virginia)

College/University: Hampton University (Hampton, Virginia)

Undergraduate Degree: Bachelor of Arts (B.A.)

Major: Political Science

College Honors, Achievements and Activities: *Recipient,* Academic Achievers Scholarship; *Member,* The Student Leadership Organization; *Member,* The Political Science/Pre-Law Club; *Student Director,* His Chosen Sounds Gospel Choir

Law School: Vermont Law School (South Royalton, Vermont)

Law Degree and Graduation Year: Juris Doctor/Doctor of Jurisprudence (J.D.) - Class of 2012

Law School Honors, Achievements and Activities: *Awardee,* Dean's Leadership Award; *Awardee,* Merit Scholarship; *Awardee,* David Firestone Scholarship for Campus Involvement; *Northeast Regional Chair,* National Black Law Students Association (NBLSA); *Class Senator,* Student Bar Association; *Member,* Board of Directors, Bookstore; *Student Ambassador,* Vermont Law School; *Congressional Liaison,* National Black Law Students Association; *National Chair,* National Black Law Students Association; *Law School Representative,* Vermont Law School, American Bar Association; *Representative,* Honor Code Committee

Other Graduate or Professional Degrees: Master of Laws (LL.M.), The George Washington University Law School (Washington, D.C.); Master of Divinity (M.Div.), Howard University School of Divinity (Washington, D.C.)

Graduate School Honors, Achievements and Activities: *Awardee,* The Justice Thurgood Marshall Civil Liberties Award, The George Washington University Law School (2013); *Awardee,* The Patricia Roberts Harris Award for Excellence, Black Law Students Association, The George Washington University Law School (2013); *Awardee,* Pro Bono Service Award; *Awardee,* The President's Volunteer Service Award

Additional Education: *Member,* Council on Foreign Relations, Congressional Foreign Policy Study Group, Washington, D.C. (2019); *Participant,* The Wilson Center Artificial Intelligence Lab, Washington, D.C. (Spring 2019); *Participant,* The Wilson Center Congressional Cybersecurity Lab, Washington, D.C. (Summer 2017); *Fellow,* Stanford University-The Hoover Institute Congressional Fellowship Program, Palo Alto, California (Spring 2017); *Fellow,* The Wilson Center Foreign Policy Fellowship Program, Washington, D.C. (Spring 2017)

PROFESSIONAL ACCOMPLISHMENTS

Other Legal Work Experience: *Chief of Staff,* Rep. G. K. Butterfield (U.S. House of Representatives); *Senior Director for Diversity, Inclusion and Affinity,* American University Washington College of Law; *Deputy Chief of Staff and Legislative Director,* Rep. Dwight Evans (U.S. House of Representatives); *Policy Director,* The Congressional Black Caucus; *Legislative Counsel,* Earthjustice; *Special Assistant and Counsel,* Rep. Maxine Waters (U.S. House of Representatives); *Legal Extern,* Office of Civil Rights, Department of Education; *Legal Intern,* Upper Valley Land Trust; *Research Assistant,* Professor Liz Ryan Cole; *Legal Fellow,* U.S. House of Representatives; *Scheduler and Executive Assistant,* U.S. House of Representatives; *Executive Assistant,* Kelly Drye & Warren

Other Professional Work Experience: *Analyst,* Protiviti Government Services, U.S. Securities and Exchange Commission

Professional Organizations: *Member,* National Bar Association; *Member,* Congressional Tech Staffer Association

Post-Law School Honors, Achievements, Activities, and Community Involvement: *Listed Honoree,* Washington, D.C. Top Influencers List, Lawyers of Color (2019); *Honorary Chairperson,* Hampton University Forty Under 40 Awards (2019); *Awardee,* Hampton University Forty Under 40 Alumni Award (2019); *Awardee,* Forty Under 40 Award, The Leadership Center for Excellence (2018); *Listed Honoree,* Recognized on the Maryland Daily Record 2018 VIP List (2018); Presidential Award for Outstanding Service, National Bar Association (2017); *Special Recognition,* Recognized as one of the Maryland Daily Record 2016 Leading Women (2016); *Awardee,* Good Citizenship Award, North Atlantic Region, Alpha Kappa Alpha Sorority, Incorporated (2016); *Awardee,* Social Justice Advocate Award, National Black Law Students Association (2015); *Awardee,* The Kim M. Keenan Advocacy & Leadership Award, Washington Bar Association (2015); *Awardee,* Governor's Volunteer Service Award, State of Maryland (2014); *Honoree,* Trailblazer Under 40 Award, National Bar Association (2014); *Awardee,* 35th Anniversary Alumni Award, Northern Virginia Chapter, Hampton University Alumni Association (2014); *Listed Honoree,* One of the Top Ten to Watch, Power 100, On Being a Black Lawyer (2013); *Chair,* Maryland State Advisory Committee, U.S. Commission on Civil Rights; *Executive Board Member,* Young Lawyers Division, National Bar Association; *Chapter President,* Alpha Kappa Alpha Sorority, Inc.; *Member,* The Links, Inc.; *Regional Board Member,* Boys and Girls Club of Greater Washington; *Member,* Leadership

Circle, Street Law, Inc.; *Ministerial Staff Member,* Carter Memorial Church; *Executive Board Member,* Washington, D.C. Chapter, Vermont Law School Alumni Association; *Former Board Member,* Woolly Mammoth Theatre Co.

LESSONS LEARNED: MY RECOMMENDATIONS FOR YOUR FUTURE ACTIONS BASED ON MY PAST EXPERIENCE

Advice on Law School Preparation:

One word of advice I share with those planning to enter law school is to consider a pre-law program the summer before attending law school. These types of programs prepare you for the cadence and rigor of law school, so that it is not such a huge shock to the system when you start your classes. Additionally, some schools have programs where you can come on campus a week or two before your classes start so that you can understand how your classes will operate. These are all helpful programs.

The road ahead is not easy, but come to law school with an open mind understanding some of the basics – 1) You have reading prior to the first day of classes; 2) You MUST work hard; 3) Plan ahead and manage your time wisely; 4) Plan the law school application as early in advance as you can; 5) No one deserves to be in law school more than you. You earned your seat so rock it out!

Advice on Applying to and Selecting a Law School:

Go to the school that is going to be the best fit for you based on the factors that are important to you. If you can, speak to recent graduates of the law school you plan to attend so that they can share their experience with you. (But take it with a grain of salt because everyone's experience is different.)

Advice Regarding Academic Success, Co-Curricular and Extra-Curricular Participation, and Social Engagement in Law School:

Know yourself. If you have a hard time balancing your time, then limit the amount of extra-curricular activities you participate in. Law school is difficult, bottom line. Plan your time every week so that you are structured in how you complete your reading and assignments. Build in down time so that you are not burning yourself out. Map out the extra-curricular activities that are going to help you achieve your academic goals and overall law school professional and learning experience.

Moot Court, Mock Trial, Journals, Clinics – These all require planning and adherence to deadlines, so please take note of the timelines early so that if you are interested in them, you are prepared.

Your classmates are your lifelong colleagues. Remember that. You will be in touch with them for the rest of your lives and you will be resources to each other as well as friends. Treasure the friendships with your classmates as well as the professional relationships with your professors. They are experts in their fields so you will likely be in touch with them post-law school.

Advice on Preparing for and Taking the Bar Exam:

Prepare, prepare, prepare. The bar exam requires your attention and commitment. If possible, utilize the coursework in your matriculation that is geared towards the bar exam. Some schools have Academic Excellence Programs that prepare you for the bar exam through tailored coursework alongside your regular coursework. Utilize these types of programs so that you are fully equipped when it is time for the bar exam.

Advice on Choosing a Job and Career Path Inside or Outside of the Legal Profession:

Not all law school graduates have a role in the field of law, and that is fine. The skill set that you have is one of the most transferable skill sets and trainings that one can have. But, plan, plan, plan. Start the job inquiries and planning early so that you have an understanding of what career path you desire to take.

Advice on Seeking Legal Job Opportunities and/or Creating One's Own Opportunities:

The greatest impact on your career path is you. From networking, meeting with your professors, being diligent and thorough in your career planning outreach – you have to be committed to your legal journey. It will not be easy, but you must be dedicated to your success.

Advice on Achieving Career Success and Advancement:

One critical piece of advice that I can give is that you have to work just as hard to keep your opportunity as you did to get your opportunity. Be thorough. Work with integrity. If you find you are having trouble managing your time and everything on your plate, take a step back and reset. Set your career milestones and goals and develop an action plan to achieve them. Surround yourself with a few people who are on a similar path so that you can check in on each other, because you know the types of situations they face. This is why it is important to be a part of bar associations because you can share best practices and sharpen each other.

Advice on Overcoming the Additional Challenges Black Law Students and Lawyers Face:

For any Black law students or lawyers who may face microaggressions from individuals who may feel they are not deserving of their role in the legal field, please know that there are more who are for you than are against you.

Your ancestors are in your corner and you stand on their shoulders. Hold your head high, walk tall, work hard and be great!

Best Advice I Received Regarding Law School and the Legal Profession:

Law School - On test taking: Analyze, analyze, analyze. Understand the why. Be laser focused.

The Legal Profession - The profession needs you and people need you…your perspective, your experiences, your insight, and your advocacy.

Worst Advice I Received Regarding Law School and the Legal Profession:

Law School - Someone told me once that you must be in a study group. This is simply NOT true for everyone because not all study groups are helpful. Know yourself but also know that there ARE study groups that are extremely helpful. You just must ensure you understand how everyone works together and how you individually learn. This understanding will set the tone for how you study.

Legal Profession - Never let anyone tell you that you can't do something simply because that is not how it is typically done.

Best Advice I Would Give to an Aspiring Black Lawyer:

You are needed in the legal field - your perspective, your experiences, your voice and your skill. The road is not easy but it is worth it.

The difficulties, the sacrifices, the time spent studying, the things that your friends can do and you cannot (at that time) – it is all worth it in the end. Keep your head down and stay focused.

Thoughts About Why Earning a Law Degree Is a Powerful Credential for African Americans and Why There Is a Need for More African American Lawyers:

African Americans are still woefully underrepresented in the legal profession. African American lawyers are needed in order to ensure our perspective and experiences are present in the legal profession.

Thoughts About Whether and Why Law School Is Worth the Financial Investment:

Don't go to law school if you just want another degree. Don't go to law school if you are just looking for something to fill your time. Law school is expensive and what you may not give financially you will give in study time.

LEGACY AND SUCCESS

My Most Outstanding Accomplishment:

Negotiating legislation that became law.

The Legacy I Hope to Leave:

I want people to know me as an advocate, as someone who advocated on behalf of those who needed someone in their corner or as a voice for those who are no longer with us.

The Secret to My Success:

The secret to my success is my faith. It has gotten me through the hills and the valleys. One of my favorite verses also powers me through the difficult times: "For I know the thoughts that I think toward you, saith the Lord, thoughts of peace, and not of evil, to give you an expected end." - Jeremiah 29:11

Paulette Brown, Esq.
Senior Partner and Chief Diversity & Inclusion Officer
Locke Lord LLP
Past President
American Bar Association and National Bar Association
Princeton, New Jersey

"As Black lawyers who have attained any modicum of success, we have an obligation, at every turn, to drop the ladder to ensure that others have the tools to succeed."

– Paulette Brown

Success is . . . using my law degree in service to others and seeing those whom I have mentored doing the same for those coming behind them. Success is also having no regrets concerning how I have used my law degree.

PERSONAL FAVORITES

Favorite Quote: "To whom much is given, much is required." - Luke 12:48

Favorite Books: *The Bluest Eye* by Toni Morrison; *Wake of the Wind* by J. California Cooper; *Let the Lion Eat Straw* by Ellease Southerland; *A Lesson Before Dying* by Ernest Gaines; *The Warmth of Other Suns* by Isabelle Wilkerson; *Left to Tell* by Imaculee Ilibagiza

Favorite Movies: *Thurgood; Just Mercy; Shawshank Redemption; The Color Purple; Black Panther; Back Street*

Favorite Songs: "Send In the Clowns" by Sarah Vaughan with the Count Basie Orchestra; "Do Away With April" by Sarah Vaughan; Almost any and everything by Nancy Wilson; "What a Difference a Day Makes" by Dinah Washington; "Smoke Gets in Your Eyes" by The Platters; "Function at the Junction" by Shorty Long; "Dock of the Bay" by Otis Redding

Favorite Law School Classes: Constitutional Law; Commercial Law

Favorite Legal Cases: *Brown v. Board of Education; Bell v. Maryland; Roe v. Wade; Griswold v. Connecticut*

Favorite Hobbies: Cooking; Walking; Reading

Favorite Attorney Role Models: A myriad of Black lawyers who continue to inspire, encourage and mentor me.

FAMILY AND BACKGROUND

Where Born and Raised: Baltimore, Maryland

Family (Spouse/Partner and Children): Child - (son) Dijaun

Family Socioeconomic and Educational Background: I am from a blue-collar background. My dad was a teamster and drove a truck. Although not a vocation, my mother was an incredible seamstress. She could make anything.

My father always taught us, there were no girl jobs and no boy jobs. He was the primary cook in the family and my mother exposed us to museums and the arts.

Neither of my parents went to college, nor did my older siblings. I am the youngest of four children.

My maternal grandmother graduated from college but did not retire as a professional.

THE DECISION TO BECOME A LAWYER

When and Why I Decided to Become a Lawyer: When I went to college, I thought I would be a social worker. I wanted to save the world. I didn't know any lawyers. Howard University exposed me to so many attorneys. The first was an attorney from New Orleans who was also the law librarian at Howard's Law School. She was the sister of someone who lived on my floor in the dorm, who in turn was very good friends with my two roommates. They came to Howard knowing they wanted to be attorneys. After freshman year, I started taking political science courses with them. Many of these courses were taught by Howard Law School graduates and several of them were also professors at the law school.

It was during this time that I learned about the many great and renowned attorneys who graduated from Howard's Law School. The commitment to civil rights was something I had not previously considered. I decided that while social work is an extremely honorable profession, I thought I could "save" more people with a law degree.

EDUCATIONAL ACHIEVEMENTS

High School: Northwestern High School (Baltimore, Maryland)

College/University: Howard University (Washington, D.C.)

Undergraduate Degree: Bachelor of Arts (B.A.)

Major: Political Science

College Honors, Achievements and Activities: *President,* Junior Class; *Member,* Alpha Chapter, Delta Sigma Theta Sorority, Inc.; *Editorial Team Member,* Hilltop (Newspaper); *Staff Member,* Bison Yearbook; *Academic Recognition,* Dean's List

Law School: Seton Hall University School of Law (Newark, New Jersey)

Law Degree and Graduation Year: Juris Doctor/Doctor of Jurisprudence (J.D.) - Class of 1976

Law School Honors, Achievements and Activities: *Recipient,* Full Scholarship

Other Graduate or Professional Degrees: Honorary Doctorate Degrees - Suffolk University Law School (Boston, Massachusetts); DePaul University College of Law (Chicago, Illinois); Shepard Broad College of Law - Nova Southeastern University (Fort Lauderdale, Florida)

PROFESSIONAL ACCOMPLISHMENTS

State Bar Membership (Where Admitted to Practice Law): New Jersey

Other Legal Work Experience: *Partner,* Duane Morris LLP; *Partner & Chief Diversity Officer,* Edwards Wildman Palmer LLP

* In addition, I have had a number of in-house positions, served as a Municipal Court Judge and had my own law firm for 15 years.

Professional Organizations: *Member,* National Bar Association; *Member,* American Bar Association; *Member,* Garden State Bar Association; *Member,* Association of Black Women Lawyers of New Jersey; *Member,* New Jersey State Bar Association

Post-Law School Honors, Achievements, Activities, and Community Involvement: *President,* National Bar Association (1993-1994), *President,* American Bar Association (first woman of color in its history) (2015-2016); *President,* Association of Black Women of New Jersey; *Chair,* Labor & Employment Section, New Jersey State Bar Association (first person of color in its history) (2015-2017); *Inductee,* Fred David Gray Hall of Fame, National Bar Association; *Honoree,* Distinguished Alumni, Howard University; *Honoree,* Distinguished Alumni, Seton Hall University School of Law; *Listed Honoree,* 50 Most Influential Lawyers in America, National Law Journal; *Listed Honoree,* Best Lawyers; *Listed Honoree,* Super Lawyers; *Awardee,* C. Francis Stratford Award, National Bar Association (highest award bestowed by the National Bar Association); *Awardee,* Inaugural Ronald Brown International Award, National Bar Association; *Awardee,* Equal Justice Award, National Bar Association; *Awardee,* Gertrude Rush Award, National Bar Association; *Awardee,* Sankofa Award, National Bar Association; *Awardee,* Spirit of Excellence Award, American Bar Association; *Awardee,* Margaret Brent Woman of Achievement Award, American Bar Association; *Awardee,* Diversity Award, New Jersey State Bar Association; *Awardee,* Professionalism Award, New Jersey State Bar Association; *Honoree,* Legacy Builder Award, National Black Pre-Law Conference and Law Fair; *Board Member,* New Jersey Institute for Social Justice; *Member,* LSC Leaders Council, Legal Services Corporation (LSC); *Board Member,* Lawyers' Committee for Civil Rights; *Board Member,* Community Trust Foundation of New Jersey; *Member,* Advisory Council, Community Engagement in the State Courts Initiative, National Center for State Courts

LESSONS LEARNED: MY RECOMMENDATIONS FOR YOUR FUTURE ACTIONS BASED ON MY PAST EXPERIENCE

Advice on Law School Preparation:

Preparation begins long before law school. Preparation should begin the moment you decide you want to attend law school or think you may want to attend law school. Admissions is very competitive, but with proper preparation, getting into and succeeding in law school is quite achievable. You must put forth your best effort at all times. There is generally no time to "play catch up".

It may sound overly simplistic but reading and writing and having it critiqued on a regular basis can be key to being successful. It cannot be underestimated the amount of reading necessary to be successful in law school. Additionally, the ability to write very well is not only necessary for law school, but also throughout one's legal career.

Advice Regarding Applying to and Selecting a Law School:

Personally, I selected the law school that provided me with a full scholarship. Selecting a law school is something that is very personal. It depends upon a number of factors: Does the law school offer courses which are in furtherance of your career goals?; Do you want to be close to family?; What is their reputation for employment opportunities?; What is their reputation for the quality education provided and bar passage rates?; What is the law school's commitment (honest) to diversity and inclusion?

Advice Regarding Academic Success, Co-Curricular and Extra-Curricular Participation, and Social Engagement in Law School:

Prior to considering extra-curricular activities, you should ensure that good study habits have been adopted and you have become accustomed to the law school environment. Generally, academic success will lead a student to be invited to various extra-curricular activities including but not limited to being invited to the school's law review. Without regard to the above, it is important to become a member of the Black Law Students Association. It is an opportunity to connect with those who may be of a similar background who have shared experiences.

Advice on Preparing for and Taking the Bar Exam:

Being centered and removing as many outside distractions as possible. One thing I have found is that culturally, sometimes families don't understand the commitment and the undivided attention that is required to taking and passing the bar. They may believe there is disloyalty to family if you are unable to attend family events.

A coach (can be almost anyone you trust), not for substantive matters, but rather for emotional support. It should be someone who will provide constant support, boosting you, and reminding you that you would not have gotten this far if you are not ready, and to remove any stereotype threat.

Give yourself time to relax immediately before the exam - give all of that knowledge you have time to sink in.

During the bar exam preparation period, I meditated (no, it's not a new "thing") twice a day for twenty minutes.

Advice on Choosing a Job and Career Path Inside or Outside of the Legal Profession:

One of the many benefits of having a law degree is that it provides options. Go outside of your natural affinity group and think about things others are considering and then investigate.

Read about what's going on in business (e.g., *Wall Street Journal, Bloomberg Business* and similar publications) to determine trends and what may be next on the horizon.

Understand that merely because you start down one path does not mean you cannot change your mind. Do what makes you happy, what gives you a sense of fulfillment. Determine which path can also give you the flexibility to be in service to others.

Advice on Seeking Legal Job Opportunities and/or Creating One's Own Opportunities:

Don't allow someone, not the school's career counselor or anyone else, steer you in a direction in which you do not wish to go. Research your prospective employer carefully to ensure it is a place where you will be happy.

Advice on Achieving Career Success and Advancement:

Invest in yourself. It's never too early to have a personal and development career plan. It must be in writing and goals with specific time frames must be set. Have an accountability partner to assist you in staying on task.

Advice on Overcoming the Additional Challenges Black Law Students and Lawyers Face:

Be comfortable with who you are. Don't allow anyone to impose beliefs on you, particularly negative or stereotypical beliefs. Know that if you did not have comparable credentials you would not be where you are, either in law school or in your place of employment.

Remain authentic and don't be discouraged, even when you have to engage in PIA-prove it again.

Don't be afraid to ask for help, for mentorship and/or coaching.

Best Advice I Received Regarding Law School and the Legal Profession:

Attending law school is like a jealous lover. Full attention must be given to it.

Worst Advice I Received Regarding Law School and the Legal Profession:

The only real lawyers are litigators.

Best Advice I Would Give to an Aspiring Black Lawyer:

Always try to remain true to who you are; always bring your A game; there are rarely second chances. Never forget the opportunities that have been afforded you and to pay it forward. This is a great and honorable profession and there is so much good you can do with a law license.

Thoughts About Why Earning a Law Degree Is a Powerful Credential for African Americans and Why There Is a Need for More African American Lawyers:

The paucity of the number of African Americans/Blacks is outrageous. The legal profession remains the least diverse profession of all comparable professions. This means that our population is necessarily underserved.

Thoughts About Whether and Why Law School Is Worth the Financial Investment:

Having a law degree provides infinite opportunities. Notwithstanding the rumor that there are too many lawyers, Black lawyers continue to be underrepresented. There is a void in the legal profession that cannot be filled by anyone else.

LEGACY AND SUCCESS

My Most Outstanding Accomplishments:

There have been several and I have been both fortunate and blessed. There are a couple of highlights I would like to reference. As president of the National Bar Association (NBA), leading a delegation to monitor the first free and democratic elections in South Africa where Nelson Mandela was elected president; all of the goals I was able to achieve through my 360 Diversity and Inclusion Commission when president of the American Bar Association (ABA), much of which can still be found on the ABA's website; visiting all 50 States and two U.S. Territories at least once during my one-year term as president of the ABA, and visiting more than 40 Boys & Girls Clubs.

The Legacy I Hope to Leave:

Knowledge is free. Sharing it takes nothing from you.

The Secret to My Success:

When we do something for the benefit of others - that is your first priority, the rewards will come back tenfold.

Richard O. I. Brown, Esq.
Assistant United States Attorney
United States Department of Justice
Palm Beach Gardens, Florida

"Love yourself, as God loves you."
– Richard O. I. Brown,

Success is... doing for others what they cannot do for themselves.

PERSONAL FAVORITES

Favorite Quote: "Be not deceived: God cannot be mocked. A man reaps what he sows."- Galatians 6:7 (New International Version)

Favorite Books: *The Isis Papers* by Frances Cress Welsing; *The Prophet* by Kahlil Gibran; *The Bible* by God

Favorite Movies: *Boomerang*; *The Wizard of Oz*; *Dope*

Favorite Songs: "The Most Beautiful Girl in the World" by Prince; "Adore" by Prince; "Black Butterfly" by Deniece Williams; "Live and Learn" by Joe Public; "God's Been Good to Me" by Crystal Lewis

Favorite Musical Artists: The Temptations; Prince; Public Enemy

Favorite Law School Classes: Real Property; Torts

Favorite Legal Case: *Brown v. Board of Education of Topeka*

Favorite Hobbies: Sports; Reading; Spending time with family

Favorite Attorney Role Models: Thurgood Marshall; Herbert O. Reid; Eric Holder

FAMILY AND BACKGROUND

Where Born and Raised: Born - West Germany; Raised - Boston, Massachusetts and Richmond, Virginia

Family (Spouse/Partner and Children): Spouse - Donise; Children - (daughter) Hannah and (son) Matthew

Family Socioeconomic and Educational Background: I grew up in an upper-middle-class family with four children. I was the youngest. My father was a retired U.S. Army World War II and Korean War veteran. After this, he became an entrepreneur, who owned a grocery or variety store in Boston. At the age of 10, we moved from Boston, Massachusetts to Richmond, Virginia. My sister, who is the eldest, was the first member of my family to attend college.

THE DECISION TO BECOME A LAWYER

When and Why I Decided to Become a Lawyer: I decided that I wanted to become a lawyer in the 11th grade. I have always had a desire to help people and at the time I thought the best way to do so was to become a politician. When I looked at Virginia's General Assembly, the majority of the members were attorneys. Hence, I thought I had to become an attorney to become a politician.

EDUCATIONAL ACHIEVEMENTS

High School: George Wythe High School (Richmond, Virginia)

College/University: Virginia Commonwealth University (Richmond, Virginia)

Undergraduate Degree: Bachelor of Arts (B.A.)

Major: Political Science

College Honors, Achievements and Activities: *Member,* Pi Sigma Alpha; *Member,* Political Science National Honor Society; CLEO (Council on Legal Education Opportunity) Scholar; *Vice President,* League of Black Journalists

Law School: Howard University School of Law (Washington, D.C.)

Law Degree and Graduation Year: Juris Doctor/Doctor of Jurisprudence (J.D.) - Class of 1986

Law School Honors, Achievements and Activities: *First-Year Class Representative,* Student Bar Association; *Second-Year Class Representative,* Student Bar Association; *President,* Student Bar Association; *Research Assistant,* Real Property Professor

PROFESSIONAL ACCOMPLISHMENTS

State Bar Membership (Where Admitted to Practice Law): Pennsylvania; Georgia

Other Legal Work Experience: *United States Attorney,* U.S. Department of Justice, Southern District of Florida, Miami and Fort Lauderdale, Florida (2007-Present); *Attorney (General Practice/Real Estate and Commercial Litigation),* The Law Office of Richard O. I. Brown, LLC, Atlanta, Georgia (2006-2007); *Senior Assistant District Attorney,* Major Narcotics Unit, Office of the Fulton County District Attorney, Atlanta, Georgia (2006); *Assistant United States Attorney,* U.S. Department of Justice, District of New Jersey, Newark, New Jersey (2003-2005); *Assistant United States Attorney,* U.S. Department of Justice, Southern District of Florida, West Palm Beach, Florida (1995-2003); *Active Duty,* U.S. Army (Mechanized Division), Fort Stewart, Georgia (2001-2002); *Chief,* Military Justice, 3rd Infantry Division; U.S. Army Reserves, Sunny Point, North Carolina and West Palm Beach, Florida (1996-2001); *Operational Law Attorney,* 3220th GSU (FS), Florida (2001); *Chief,* Military Justice, 32nd Army Air Defense Command, Germany (1993-1995); *Government Appellate Attorney,* Legal Services Agency, Virginia (1992-1993); *Trial Defense Attorney,* 2nd Infantry Division, South Korea (1991-1992); *Instructor,* Northern Virginia Community College (1993); *Claims Judge Advocate,* U.S. Army, Higher Headquarters, Fort Belvoir, Virginia (1989-1991); *Special Assistant U.S. Attorney,* Eastern District of Virginia, Alexandria, Virginia (1989-1990); *Legal Assistance Attorney,* Higher Headquarters, Fort Belvoir, Virginia (1988-1989)

Professional Organizations: *Member,* National Association of Assistant United States Attorneys; *Life Member,* Veterans of Foreign Wars

Post-Law School Honors, Achievements, Activities, and Community Involvement:

Recipient, Army Airborne Badge; *Recipient,* Army Service Ribbon; *Recipient,* Army Air Assault Badge; *Recipient,* Overseas Service Ribbon; *Recipient,* Army Commendation Medal; *Recipient,* Army Achievement Medal; *Recipient,* National Defense Service Medal; *Awardee,* Army Excellence in Physical Fitness Award; *Awardee,* FBI's Director's Award (2008); *Outstanding Volunteer of the Year,* U.S. Immigration and Customs Enforcement, United States Attorney's Office, Southern District of Florida, Violence Reduction Program (2015); *Awardee,* Contributions and Dedication Award 2005; *Chair,* Black Affairs Committee (2018-2020); *Volunteer,* Violence Reduction Partnership Community Resource Fair and Farm Share Food Distribution (2015-2019); *Participant,* U.S. Attorney's Community Reading Program (2014-2019); *Featured Panelist,* National HBCU Pre-Law Summit and Law Expo, Atlanta, Georgia (2016); *Featured Panelist,* National Diversity Pre-Law Conference and Law Fair, Miami, Florida (2017); *Featured Panelist,* National Black Pre-Law Conference and Law Fair, Cambridge, Massachusetts (2018); *Panelist,* Miami-Dade County State Attorney Katherine Fernandez Rundle's Second Chance Seal and Expunge Event (2016); *Speaker,* National Urban League's 26th Annual Youth Leadership Summit (2015); *Speaker,* Westminster Academy Black History Month (2015); *Speaker,* Ethical Governance Day Speaker (2015); *Speaker,* American High School (2015); *Team Leader/Mentor,* Drug Education for Youth/Violence Reduction Partnership Summer Camp (2015); *Speaker,* Broward Estates Elementary Career Day (2015); *Keynote Speaker,* Veterans Day (2014); *Speaker,* Piper High School (2013)

LESSONS LEARNED: MY RECOMMENDATIONS FOR YOUR FUTURE ACTIONS BASED ON MY PAST EXPERIENCE

Advice on Law School Preparation:

Be tenacious and attempt to get as much exposure to law school as possible.

Advice on Applying to and Selecting a Law School:

The law is a very broad field so have an open mind going into the practice. Be aware that the higher your LSAT score the more opportunities will be present to you. So if you have the ability, I would highly encourage taking an LSAT prep course.

Advice Regarding Academic Success, Co-Curricular and Extra-Curricular Participation, and Social Engagement in Law School:

Stay true to yourself. Many people try to emulate professors and attorneys they interact with during law school. Don't be someone else. Just remember to do you!

Advice on Preparing for and Taking the Bar Exam:

Take a bar prep course. And if possible, study as if it were the only job you have.

Advice on Choosing a Job and Career Path Inside or Outside of the Legal Profession:

Always try to get paid for what you enjoy doing.

Advice on Seeking Legal Job Opportunities and/or Creating One's Own Opportunities:

More often than not, it will be who knows you as opposed to what you know that gets you the job. Try to cultivate a strong network of peers and senior attorneys that can help you on your journey.

Advice on Achieving Career Success and Advancement:

If you do your best, your success might not come as soon as when you want it, nor be exactly what you think you want at the time. However, effort and focus are habits that translate to long-term success. And that praises God.

Advice on Overcoming the Additional Challenges Black Law Students and Lawyers Face:

There will be plenty of distractions, but remember that you are able to control how much and how hard you work. Attempt to do your best work at all times.

Best Advice I Received Regarding Law School and the Legal Profession:

"No one knows all of the law in all of the law books in the library, but a good attorney knows where to find the law."

"A lawyer is either a social engineer or he is a parasite on society." - Charles Hamilton Houston

Worst Advice I Received Regarding Law School and the Legal Profession:

Make as much money as you can.

Best Advice I Would Give to an Aspiring Black Lawyer:

Find what you enjoy doing and do it.

Thoughts About Why Earning a Law Degree Is a Powerful Credential for African Americans and Why There Is a Need for More African American Lawyers:

The law degree establishes your credibility allowing you to do more than many other American professionals. The beauty of a law degree is that it does not pigeon hole you solely into the practice of law.

Thoughts About Whether and Why Law School Is Worth the Financial Investment:

It is extremely important to weigh the financial investment against the return of the degree. Manage your finances so that you are not beholden to debt.

LEGACY AND SUCCESS

My Most Outstanding Accomplishment:

Helping others achieve their goals.

The Legacy I Hope to Leave:

That I was able to help people, leaving them in a better state after meeting me than they were prior to meeting me.

The Secret to My Success:

Being a dutiful servant to the will of God in my life.

Practical Wisdom for Those on the Path to Lawyerhood

Elizabeth A. Campbell, Esq.
Director, Inclusion and Diversity
Campbell Soup Company
Camden, New Jersey

"Find your unique strength and then capitalize on it to reach your fullest potential."

— Elizabeth A. Campbell

Success is . . . knowing that you have performed your very best, given your last ounce of energy, and conducted yourself with the utmost level of professionalism – no matter the ultimate outcome.

PERSONAL FAVORITES

Favorite Quotes: "Faith is taking the first step even when you don't see the whole staircase." - Dr. Martin Luther King, Jr.

"Nothing beats a failure but a try." - R.J. Smith

Favorite Books: *Gone With the Wind*; *The Firm*

Favorite Movies: *Casablanca*; *The Godfather*; *Becoming* (Michelle Obama documentary)

Favorite Songs: "Lift Every Voice and Sing"; "Glory" by John Legend; "Wanna Be Starting Something" by Michael Jackson; "Imagine" by The Beatles; "Yesterday" by The Beatles

Favorite Musical Artists: Stevie Wonder; Prince; Michael Jackson; Aretha Franklin; The Beatles

Favorite Law School Classes: Contracts; Secured Transactions; Administrative Law

Favorite Legal Cases: Two *pro bono* cases (Social Security Disability claim appeal and workers' compensation death claim); participation as counsel for *amicus curiae* in *Fisher v. University of Texas* before the United States Supreme Court (August 2012)

Favorite Hobbies: Watching spectator sports; Playing softball; Traveling; Reading; Listening to music; Exercising

Favorite Attorney Role Models: Perry Mason; Attorney General Eric Holder; Attorney General Loretta Lynch; Benjamin Crump

FAMILY AND BACKGROUND

Where Born and Raised: Bordentown, New Jersey

Family (Spouse/Partner and Children): Children - (son) Claude ("CJ") and (son) Christian

Family Socioeconomic and Educational Background: I am from a professional, middle-class background. Two of my grandparents had college degrees. Both of my parents had college and/or graduate degrees.

THE DECISION TO BECOME A LAWYER

When and Why I Decided to Become a Lawyer: I decided to become a lawyer when I was approximately 11 years old. My first choice was to become a medical doctor – but I could not see myself imposing pain on someone in the name of helping them. Watching *Perry Mason* on TV showed me a great alternative way to help people – with a lot of superficial bells and whistles.

EDUCATIONAL ACHIEVEMENTS

High School: Bordentown Regional High School (Bordentown, New Jersey)

College/University: American University (Washington, D.C.)

Undergraduate Degrees: Bachelor of Arts (B.A.)

Majors: Political Science and Psychology

College Honors, Achievements and Activities: Graduated *cum laude* "with distinction" with Honors in Government; *Participant,* Student Government; *Member*, Organization of African and African American Students at the American University, or OASATAU

Law School: University of Michigan Law School (Ann Arbor, Michigan)

Law Degree and Graduation Year: Juris Doctor/Doctor of Jurisprudence (J.D.) - Class of 1978

Law School Honors, Achievements and Activities: *Active Member,* Black Law Students Association; *Research Assistant,* Family Law; *Legal Research and Writing Assistant* ("Junior Clerk" and "Senior Judge")

Additional Education: Certificate, Leading Effective Decision-Making, Yale School of Management (Spring 2019); Certificate, Fostering Inclusion and Diversity, Yale School of Management (Fall 2019)

PROFESSIONAL ACCOMPLISHMENTS

State Bar Memberships (Where Licensed to Practice): Washington, D.C.; New York; New Jersey; Pennsylvania

Other Legal Experience: *Partner and Chief Diversity Officer,* Andrews Kurth Kenyon LLP; *Assistant General Counsel,* Delaware North Companies Incorporated; *Associate,* Verner, Liipfert, et al. (subsequently acquired by what is now DLA Piper); *Honors Program Attorney,* Solicitor's Honors Program, United States Department of the Interior

Other Professional Work Experience: *Vice President,* Employment Practices and Services, ARAMARK; *Vice President,* Human Resources, GlobeGround North America; *Vice President,* Administration, Sportservice, a Delaware North company

Professional Organizations: *Past Member,* National Bar Association; *Past Member,* Houston Bar Association; *Past Co-Chair,* Gender Fairness Committee; *Past Member,* Houston Lawyers Association

Post-Law School Honors, Achievements, Activities, and Community Involvement: *Chair,* Board of Directors, Council on Legal Education Opportunity (CLEO); *Member,* Board of Directors, National Diversity Council; *Member,* Board of Directors, South Texas College of Law Houston; *Past Member,* Leadership Council, United Negro College Fund (UNCF) Houston; *Past Member,* Board of Directors, National Diversity Council; *Past Member,* Society for Human Resource Management; *Honoree,* YWCA 2015 Outstanding Women in Law and Government, YMCA (Young Women's Christian Association) (May 2015); *Honorary Chair,* 11th Annual Texas Diversity and Leadership Conference (April 2015); *Honoree,* Top 25 Business Women in Houston, National Women's Council (2015); *Awardee,* Texas Women's Foundation Empowerment International Leadership Award (October 2014); *Awardee,* National PTA Life Achievement Award, National PTA (Parent Teacher Association) (June 2014); *Graduate,* Spring 2014 Business/Civic Leadership Forum, Center for Houston's Future; *Awardee,* Trailblazer Award, Texas Diversity Council (April 2014); *Honorary Life Member,* Texas Congress of Parents and Teachers (in Recognition of Distinguished Service to Children and Youth) (July 2013); *Awardee,* ROAR!® 2013 Lioness® Leadership Award; *Awardee,* Leadership Excellence Award, Texas Diversity Council (April 2013); *Honoree,* "Houston's 50 Most Influential Women of 2012," Houston Woman Magazine; *Listed Honoree,* Strathmore's Who's Who (July 2012); *Awardee,* Leadership and Excellence Award, Texas Diversity Council (December 2011); Sutton Who's Who in American Law (2011); *Listed Honoree,* Who's Who in Black Houston (2009); *Member,* Board of Directors, Texas PTA (Parent Teacher Association); *Member,* Board of Directors, Houston Urban Debate League

LESSONS LEARNED: MY RECOMMENDATIONS FOR YOUR FUTURE ACTIONS BASED ON MY PAST EXPERIENCE

Advice on Making the Choice to Apply to and Attend Law School:

One should attend law school if one really wants to practice law. If not, get an MBA (Master of Business Administration).

Advice on Law School Preparation:

Pursue a major and/or work experience that requires a considerable amount of reading, writing and analysis. Prepare for the LSAT with dedicated study and avail yourself of resources such as the National Black Pre-Law Conference and the Council on Legal Education Opportunity.

Advice on Applying to and Selecting a Law School:

Apply to and attend the best ranked law school that you can - if possible.

Advice Regarding Academic Success, Co-Curricular and Extra-Curricular Participation, and Social Engagement in Law School:

You must keep your eye on the prize. The first semester of law school is the hardest - because it is a new and different experience - but it is also the most important. First-semester grades can shape the course of an entire legal career. Therefore, my advice is to eliminate most outside activities and distractions during the first semester and concentrate on classroom preparation, participation, and follow-up (to include visits with professors). Taking practice exams is an excellent tactic - but having your answers reviewed by the appropriate professor is just as important.

During the first semester and beyond, take time to get to know a few of your classmates - to aid in studying and to start building your network.

The second semester of the 1L year brings with it "experience" in classroom preparation and law school examinations. It is the ideal time to research how to get on law review, write for a law journal, and how to participate in other academic opportunities to develop your legal writing and analysis skills. Your grades this semester matter even more than the first semester and contribute to your overall 1L GPA - which is so very important.

Years 2 and 3 create opportunities for scholarly learning, skill development, networking, and participation in law student associations. Keep your eye on the prize at all times.

Advice on Preparing for and Taking the Bar Exam:

- Select the bar prep course that best matches your own individual learning style; BARBRI was a successful choice for me. Then:
- Take practice exams early and often, under exam conditions
- Perfect a memorization technique
- Learn anxiety/panic management techniques
- Get plenty of sleep, exercise, and healthy eating
- If you are a religious person, pray frequently
- Practice!

Advice on Choosing a Job and Career Path In or Outside of the Legal Profession:

- Conduct a personal "SWOT" analysis to identify your professional strengths, weaknesses, opportunities and threats
- Focus on leveraging your strengths in your career pursuits
- Add in your passion
- Strive for excellence
- Be your authentic self

Advice on Seeking Legal Job Opportunities and/or Creating One's Own Opportunities:

Same as above, plus:
- Network with college/law school alums
- Ask colleagues, friends, associates for assistance and job "leads"
- Be creative; be proactive and work to identify opportunities before a "job" is advertised

Advice on Achieving Career Success and Advancement:

- Do not let anyone outwork you
- Be your best authentic self
- Strive for perfection
- Treat everyone with dignity and respect

Advice on Overcoming the Additional Challenges Black Law Students and Lawyers Face:

Nothing succeeds like success. Hard work with a goal of achieving perfection goes a long way to overcoming barriers.

Best Advice I Received Regarding Law School and the Legal Profession:

- Apply to the University of Michigan Law School
- When one career door closes, another (and often a better) opportunity will open for you
- Find a mentor

Worst Advice I Received Regarding Law School and the Legal Profession:

You cannot be a lawyer; do not apply to any top law schools because you will not be accepted.

Best Advice I Would Give to an Aspiring Black Lawyer:

- Do your absolute best academically
- Go to the best law school that you can, under your circumstances
- Work harder and smarter
- Try to distinguish yourself with your unique background and skills
- Get a mentor

Thoughts About Why Earning a Law Degree Is a Powerful Credential for African Americans and Why There Is a Need for More African American Lawyers:

- Earning a law degree is one way that African Americans can be prepared to create a successful career and at the same time contribute to the community at large.
- We need more African American lawyers, and lawyers of other historically under-represented groups, to achieve the benefits that diverse perspectives bring to problem-solving.
- We also need to expand the pool of top diverse attorneys to reflect the changing demographics of our community for the benefit of us all.

LEGACY AND SUCCESS

My Most Outstanding Accomplishments:

Personal: Mother of two sons; Lifetime Membership recognition by the National PTA (Parent Teacher Association).

Professional: Sworn into practice before the United States Supreme Court with Justice Thurgood Marshall on the bench; Submitted an *amicus curiae* brief before the United States Supreme Court in the *Fisher v. University of Texas* case (August 2012).

The Legacy I Hope to Leave:

One of caring, hard work and tireless effort to benefit my family, clients, future lawyers, and the community at large.

The Secret to My Success:

Preparation, perseverance, and prayer.

Jessica N. Childress, Esq.
Managing Attorney
The Childress Firm PLLC
Founder and CEO
Juris Prudence LLC
Washington, D.C.

"Don't ever lose sight of the 'why' behind the results you seek to obtain."

— Jessica N. Childress

Success is . . . the ability to go to sleep at night knowing your work made a difference in someone's life and waking up every morning excited and ready to do that work again.

PERSONAL FAVORITES

Favorite Quote: "The ultimate measure of a man is not where he stands in moments of comfort and convenience, but where he stands at times of challenge and controversy." - Martin Luther King, Jr.

Favorite Books: *Outliers* by Malcolm Gladwell; *Tipping Point* by Malcolm Gladwell; *Little Bee* by Chris Cleave; *Everything I Never Told You* by Celeste Ng; *Their Eyes Were Watching God* by Zora Neal Hurston; *Native Son* by Richard Wright; *The Memory Keeper's Daughter* by Kim Edwards; *The Help* by Kathryn Stockett; *Beloved* by Toni Morrison; *Narrative of the Life of Frederick Douglass* by Frederick Douglass

Favorite Movies: *John Q; The Parent Trap; Annie; Slumdog Millionaire*

Favorite Musical Artists: Lauryn Hill; Bob Marley; Jay-Z; Boyz II Men; Anthony Hamilton; Erykah Badu

Favorite Law School Classes: Employment Discrimination; Criminal Procedure; Police Misconduct

Favorite Legal Cases: *Mapp v. Ohio, Brown v. Board of Education of Topeka, Shelley v. Kramer; Katzenbach v. McClung; Loving v. Virginia*

Favorite Hobbies: Biking; Writing; Journaling; Traveling; Running; Reading

Favorite Attorney Role Model: Thurgood Marshall

FAMILY AND BACKGROUND

Where Born and Raised: Richmond, Virginia

Family Socioeconomic and Educational Background: I am a first-generation law school student from a middle-class background.

THE DECISION TO BECOME A LAWYER

When and Why I Decided to Become a Lawyer: I decided to become a lawyer when I was eight years old and saw the prominent image of Attorney General Janet Reno, on the *Nightly News with Tom Brokaw*. I had no idea what it meant to be an Attorney General. I did know that "Janet Reno" was a name that I heard almost every night, and she seemed important. By the way, she was a woman. I wanted to be her.

As there were no lawyers in my family, let alone even a handful of college graduates, I asked my father how one became a lawyer. His response was to take me to our family's pre-Internet age wealth of knowledge - our set of World Book Encyclopedias. We turned to the "L" section and carefully read the requirements to becoming a lawyer. Janet Reno, *Matlock*, Blair Underwood in *L.A. Law*, and the *World Book Encyclopedia* were the sole insights that I had regarding what it meant to be a lawyer. As an eight-year-old, I would not have a true insight into what it meant to become a lawyer until almost eight years later when I was fortunate enough to secure a summer internship with the Richmond, Virginia City Attorney's Office - an experience that changed my life – not only because this was the first time that I witnessed the practice of law in living color, but more importantly because this was the first time that I saw a woman of color practicing law. Ms. Harris, my intern supervisor, changed my entire worldview, for her mere presence affirmed that someone who looked like me – a female of color - actually existed in the legal field.

EDUCATIONAL ACHIEVEMENTS

High School: Midlothian High School (Midlothian, Virginia)

College/University: University of Virginia (Charlottesville, Virginia)

Undergraduate Degree: Bachelor of Arts (B.A.)

Majors: Government and African American Studies

College Honors, Achievements and Activities: Graduated With High Distinction; *Member,* Phi Beta Kappa (America's most prestigious honor society); *Member,* Omicron Delta Kappa (national leadership honor society); *Member,* National Society of Collegiate Scholars; University of Virginia Lawn Resident; Harvard University Galbraith Scholar Fellow; *Awardee,* University of Virginia Dabney Award

Law School: The University of Virginia School of Law (Charlottesville, Virginia)

Law Degree and Graduation Year: Juris Doctor/Doctor of Jurisprudence (J.D.) - Class of 2010

Law School Honors, Achievements and Activities: *Member,* Editorial Board, Virginia Journal of Law and Social Policy; *National Director,* College Student Division, National Black Law Students Association; *Board Member,* University of Virginia Diversity Advisory Board; *Recipient,* Oliver Hill Scholarship, Awarded by Old Dominion Bar Association; *Student Council Representative,* University of Virginia School of Law Student Bar Association; *Merit Scholarship Recipient,* University of Virginia School of Law; *Alumna,* National Trial Advocacy College

PROFESSIONAL ACCOMPLISHMENTS

State Bar Memberships (Where Licensed to Practice Law): Virginia; Maryland; District of Columbia

Other Legal Experience: *Federal Judicial Law Clerk,* The Honorable Alexander Williams, Jr. (Retired), United States District Court for the District of Maryland; *Associate,* Proskauer Rose LLP; *Attorney,* United States Department of Justice; *Associate,* Morrison & Foerster LLP; *Summer Associate,* McGuireWoods; *Legal Intern,* Legal Aid Justice Center

Other Professional Work Experience: *Intern,* Congressman Robert "Bobby" Scott (U.S. House of Representatives); *Intern,* Maya Angelou See Forever Foundation; *Intern,* Mid-Atlantic Equity Consortium

Professional Organizations: *Member,* American Bar Association; *Member,* Washington Bar Association; *Member,* Washington Bar Association; *Member,* National Bar Association; *Member,* Greater Washington Area Chapter (GWAC), National Bar Association; *Member,* National Association of Professional Women

Post-Law School Honors, Achievements, Activities, and Community Involvement: *Honoree,* National Bar Association 2015 "40 under 40 Nation's Best Advocates"; *Honoree,* The National Black Lawyers 2015 "Top 40 under 40"; *Recipient,* 2015 Bravo Award, Chesterfield County (Virginia) Education Foundation; *Executive Committee Member,* Legal Aid Justice Center Alumni Advisory Council; *2013 Fellow,* National Employment Law Council Academy; *Honoree,* 2013 Lawyers of Color "Hot List"; *Recipient,* 2016 Kim Keenan Leadership and Advocacy Award, Washington Bar Association's Young Lawyers Division; *Honoree,* 2017 Rising Star, Greater Washington Chapter, National Bar Association; *Alumni Board Member,* Congressional Black Caucus Foundation; *Author,* Published Children's Books (*The Briefcase of Juris P. Prudence; Juris Prudence Goes to Law School; Juris P. Prudence's Kindness Contracts; Juris Prudence & Associates Coloring Book; Juris P. Prudence's Holiday Gift; Juris Prudence & Associates Intern Case Kit*)

LESSONS LEARNED: MY RECOMMENDATIONS FOR YOUR FUTURE ACTIONS BASED ON MY PAST EXPERIENCE

Advice on Law School Preparation:

Preparing for law school starts the moment you enter your undergraduate (and possibly graduate) studies. Your grades matter, so do your very best in every course you take.

Advice on Applying to and Selecting a Law School:

When deciding whether to apply to law school, first carefully evaluate why you want to apply. Your choice should be motivated by something more than monetary reasons. Your choice should be purpose driven. Critically ask yourself, "What are my values and goals, and how will being a lawyer help support those values and achieve those goals?"

Start preparing for the LSAT early, taking as many practice exams as you can. If your budget permits, take an LSAT preparation course to learn as many test-taking techniques as possible.

Ask for your recommendation letters early. Meet face to face with your recommenders and let them know why you are applying to law school so that they can have a better understanding of the person you are and your motivation to become a lawyer when they write your recommendation letters.

Ask law school admissions departments if you can sit in on their law school courses to find out how a true law school course is conducted. Try to talk to students at various law schools about their experiences in law school. Ask them candid questions about what they like and dislike about their law schools.

Advice Regarding Academic Success, Co-Curricular and Extra-Curricular Participation, and Social Engagement in Law School:

Study as hard as you can. Keep a very disciplined study schedule. Law school can get overwhelming, so make sure that you have a strong support system and that you are taking care of your physical and emotional health.

Study in study groups, as well as individually. Study groups are a wonderful way to meet your classmates and get a different perspective about the legal issues that you are learning in your legal courses.

Your law school classmates will become lifelong friends, as well as colleagues. Therefore, take time away from your study groups and individual studies to join organizations that have missions that interest you. Joining organizations is not only a great way to meet your law school classmates, but this is also a great way to get a better understanding of the legal causes that interest you, allowing you to make more informed decisions about your career.

Legal clinics are a fantastic way to gain practical experience as a law student. Try to enroll in at least one clinic before you graduate so that when you start practicing you will have an understanding of how the legal principles that you have learned in the classroom are applied in real life.

Advice on Preparing for and Taking the Bar Exam:

Practice, practice, practice. Similar to LSAT preparation, keep a disciplined study schedule, and take as many practice exams as possible.

Studying for the bar can be an all-encompassing experience, so force yourself to take study breaks and incorporate exercise and other healthy habits into your study schedule. Studying for the bar is an exercise in endurance. Accordingly, be sure to adequately fuel your mind and body so that you can make it to the end of the race victoriously.

Advice on Achieving Career Success and Advancement:

As a lawyer, your goal must be perfection. Doing your very best to serve your clients is the only option. If you are not coming to work each day with the intention to do your best, you are in the wrong profession. If you do make a mistake, which is natural, own up to it. You must have integrity in everything you do as a lawyer, and an essential part of having integrity is to be trustworthy and take responsibility for your mistakes, just as you take ownership for your accomplishments.

Treat everyone you meet with respect, regardless of their titles or lots in life. Your character speaks louder than your title as a lawyer.

It is critical to have trusted mentors who can provide sound guidance as you navigate through your career journey. Finding a mentor is not a passive exercise. Actively seek out people who have achieved the goals that you want to achieve in your career and ask them about their journey.

Seek out opportunities; do not wait for them to come to you.

Advice on Overcoming the Additional Challenges Black Law Students and Lawyers Face:

As a Black attorney, it is often going to be the case that you will have very few people in the workplace that look like you because Black attorneys are currently underrepresented in the legal profession. However, some of my greatest mentors have been people who look nothing like me. Do all that you can to seek out mentors and people that will sponsor you. Just because someone does not look like you does not mean that he or she will not be your greatest advocate. Forge friendships and bonds over the work, and you will find that you may have more commonalities than you think with someone from a totally different background than you.

Best Advice I Received Regarding Law School and the Legal Profession:

The best career advice that I have ever received is, "This is your career and no one else's. Take it by the horns." I took that to mean that many career decisions cannot be determined by anyone other than you, even though it is fine to receive career advice from others. You know yourself best, so you know what job you are striving for and what your passions are. Therefore, if you want to be an environmental attorney, do everything you can to make sure that you become an environmental attorney and not a securities law attorney. That is what taking your career by the horns means to me. It means being resourceful and utilizing all opportunities to make your dreams a reality.

Worst Advice I Received Regarding Law School and the Legal Profession:

Lawyers make a lot of money, so be a lawyer.

Best Advice I Would Give to an Aspiring Black Lawyer:

Always remember your journey. If you have applied and been accepted to law school, you likely are hardworking, diligent, and have accomplished high honors. When you face challenges, as you inevitably will, remember the journey that you have taken to get to where you are, and remember that you are the same person who has overcome vast challenges in the past to get to where you are today.

Thoughts About Why Earning a Law Degree Is a Powerful Credential for African Americans:

Lawyers should represent all walks of life and all socio-economic backgrounds. Those backgrounds inevitably influence decisions ranging from policy decisions on a local, state, and federal level to decisions made in corporate boardrooms.

LEGACY AND SUCCESS

My Most Outstanding Accomplishment:

My greatest accomplishment is the publication of my children's books about an eleven-year-old lawyer who fights for children's rights, *The Briefcase of Juris P. Prudence*. The main character is an eleven-year-old African-American lawyer who is resourceful, kind, and generous - qualities that I would like to see in all lawyers. My hope is that the book and its related series will educate and expose children of all backgrounds to the legal profession. I enjoy using literature to teach and mentor.

The Legacy I Hope to Leave:

I hope that the work I've done in my life will be remembered for being impactful.

The Secret to My Success:

I never stop believing in my dreams.

Ashley N. Cloud, Esq., M.B.A.
Attorney Advisor
U.S. Small Business Administration
Washington, D.C.

"Never compromise who you are to reach your goals."

– Ashley N. Cloud

Success is . . . being unapologetically you while positively impacting the world around you.

PERSONAL FAVORITES

Favorite Quotes: "Arise, shine; for your light has come! And the glory of the Lord is risen upon you." - Isaiah 60:1

"Feel the fear and do it anyway." - Susan Jeffers

"Everything you've ever wanted is on the other side of fear." - George Addair

"You miss 100% of the shots you don't take." - Wayne Gretzky

Favorite Movies: *Harriet; Black Panther; Selma; Hidden Figures; Malcolm X; The Color Purple; Eve's Bayou; The Fifth Element*

Favorite Musical Artists: Robert Glasper; Aaliyah; Erykah Badu; Jill Scott; Roy Hargrove; The Internet; Burna Boy; Bilal; Moonchild; Hiatus Kaiyote; Donnie McClurkin; Kirk Franklin; Niniola; Solange; D'Angelo; Ari Lennox; Prince; John Coltrane; Fela Kuti

Favorite Law School Classes: Sustainable Development; Constitutional Law; Trademarks; Trademark Clinic; Environmental Law; Legal Writing

Favorite Legal Case: *Reed v. Reed*, 404 U.S. 71 (1971)

Favorite Hobbies: Serving the community; Traveling abroad; Learning about new cultures; Bike riding; Visiting museums; Practicing yoga; Exercising; Dancing; Cooking; Thrift store shopping

Favorite Attorney Role Model: Anna Pauline "Pauli" Murray

FAMILY AND BACKGROUND

Where Born and Raised: Houston, Texas

Family Socioeconomic and Educational Background: I am a first-generation college student and law school graduate. My parents did very well for themselves and did not let a lack of formal education stop them from being successful.

THE DECISION TO BECOME A LAWYER

When and Why I Decided to Become a Lawyer: I first got the idea from my mother when I was in high school. Growing up, and being the oldest daughter, my mother was very strict. I was always advocating for myself to do simple things like hang out with friends or get out of the house for a few hours. She noticed the passion I had in "fighting for my rights" and thought that I could use that passion, and my natural ability to make sound arguments in furtherance of my interests, to serve the broader community. I realized that I could use my natural gifts and talents to help others. Originally, I thought that this meant I had to become a civil rights attorney. However, being an empath, I felt that the work would be too much for me to handle on a daily basis.

Coming from a family of entrepreneurs, I recognized my passion for entrepreneurship and economic empowerment for Black people. I hope to continue to impact my community in a positive manner by educating and assisting entrepreneurs in their endeavors to become creative, independent, and economically empowered to live out their dreams.

EDUCATIONAL ACHIEVEMENTS

High School: Katy High School (Katy, Texas)

College/University: University of Houston (Houston, Texas)

Undergraduate Degree: Bachelor of Arts (B.A.)

Major: Sociology

College Honors, Achievements and Activities: Merit Scholar; *Participant,* Challenger Program; *Scholarship Recipient,* University of Houston

Law School: Howard University School of Law (Washington, D.C.)

Law Degree and Graduation Year: Juris Doctor/Doctor of Jurisprudence (J.D.) - Class of 2016

Law School Honors, Achievements and Activities: *Recipient,* Merit Scholarship, Howard University School of Law; *Co-founder and Founding President,* Fashion Law Society; *President,* Howard Law Gospel Choir; *Student Representative,* Joint Degree Program Committee; *Certified Student Attorney,* Trademark and Intellectual Property Clinic; *Study Abroad Law Student,* Summer Study Abroad Program in South Africa, University of Western Cape (Cape Town, South Africa)

Other Graduate or Professional Degree: Master of Business Administration (M.B.A.), Howard University School of Business (Washington, D.C.)

PROFESSIONAL ACCOMPLISHMENTS

State Bar Memberships (Where Licensed to Practice Law): New York; Washington, D.C.

Other Legal Work Experience: *Assistant Attorney General,* Office of Consumer Protection, Office of the Attorney General for the District of Columbia; *Law Clerk,* Ashcraft & Gerel, LLP; *Law Clerk,* Legal Aid Justice Center; *Judicial Intern,* Chambers of Errol R. Arthur, Magistrate Judge of the District of Columbia Superior Court; *Judicial Intern,* Chambers of Sheila Tillerson Adams, Administrative Judge of the Maryland Circuit Court

Professional Organizations: *Member,* Fashion Law Committee, Bar of the City of New York; *Pro Bono Attorney,* D.C. Bar; *Member,* Washington Area Lawyers for the Arts; *Member,* Howard University School of Law Alumni Club, Greater Washington, D.C. Chapter

Post-Law School Honors, Achievements, Activities, and Community Involvement: *Speaker,* National Black Pre-Law Conference; *Pro Bono Attorney,* D.C. Bar Small Business Brief Legal Advice Clinic; *Awardee,* "Outstanding Pro Bono Commitment," U.S. Small Business Administration; *Past President,* Howard University School of Law Alumni Club, Greater Washington, D.C. Chapter

LESSONS LEARNED: MY RECOMMENDATIONS FOR YOUR FUTURE ACTIONS BASED ON MY PAST EXPERIENCE

Advice on Making the Choice to Apply to and Attend Law School:

If God put it on your heart to go to law school, then make it happen by any means necessary. Do not let anyone discourage you from following your dreams. Make sure that you are going to law school for the right reasons because it is not for the faint of heart. There will be times that you must remind yourself why you decided to embark on this journey, but know that you will be so happy you stepped out on faith and made your dream come true.

Advice on Law School Preparation:

I highly recommend connecting with mentors who are lawyers. I would suggest finding a mentor that is fresh out of law school, a mentor that has been practicing law for a few years, and a mentor who is a more seasoned attorney. I believe it provides a well-rounded perspective and helps you gain a better understanding of the current challenges faced by new attorneys as well as where your legal career can take you. I know for some people, they don't know one single lawyer. Whether you know a lawyer or not, I highly suggest you create a profile on LinkedIn so that you can begin networking early and making connections. You never know where your help may come from, and you never know who you may be able to help while on your journey.

I suggest taking courses that require you to hone your research, writing, and analytical skills. You may want to join a pre-law organization if your undergraduate has one on campus. I don't believe you need to major in pre-law or criminal justice if you have other interests. Although there is nothing wrong with those majors, law schools want to have a diverse pool of candidates from which to choose, and college is the time to explore other sides of yourself outside of the law. You absolutely must attend the National Black Pre-Law Conference. You should also take a Law School Admission Test (LSAT) preparation course. Start researching and identifying scholarships for every step of your law school journey, from pre-law to bar preparation.

Advice on Applying to and Selecting a Law School:

Determine exactly what you want out of a law school and conduct research to identify the schools that best fit your needs. Some things you may want to consider: school location, student-professor ratio, curriculum, tuition and fees, available scholarships, diversity in students and professors, unique experiences and offerings, bar passage rates, and job placement. I would suggest applying to multiple schools to compare and contrast them based on the aforementioned considerations.

Advice Regarding Academic Success, Co-Curricular and Extra-Curricular Participation, and Social Engagement in Law School:

Make the main focus of your first year performing well in your classes. You will have plenty of time to busy yourself with social and extracurricular activities during the rest of your time in law school. You want to put yourself in the best position possible to be successful and have the maximum opportunities available to you. Be careful and selective about who you seek for advice.

Make sure that you are using study and learning tactics that work best for you. Be sure to attend your professors' office hours at least a few times each semester. Try not to fall into the trap that there is only one way to be successful in law school. Don't allow the stress and competition of law school to cause you to make decisions because they are popular if they do not align with your values and personality. Always stay true to yourself, remain unique, and don't give in to self-doubt. Be sure to have a self-care practice that will keep you grounded and centered. This may include having a faith-based practice, staying in contact with family and friends, keeping your living space clean, eating healthy, working out, and having a social life (after your first year).

Advice on Preparing for and Taking the Bar Exam:

Find out what programs your law school has for bar readiness. If there is a bar preparation course that you can take while in school, be sure to enroll. Absolutely take a bar preparation course. Seek out scholarships for bar preparation if you need to. You should also ensure that you have funds saved to cover living expenses so that you can study for the bar without working. Create an environment that is peaceful while you study for the bar. Stick to a routine and treat bar study like a job. Always practice all aspects of the bar under real time constraints. Limit talking to your classmates about strategies and tactics for bar study, as it most likely won't be very helpful, since you all are embarking on the journey for the first time. Use the study skills that worked for you in law school. Do not reinvent the wheel.

Best Advice I Received Regarding Law School and the Legal Profession:

Networking is key. Do not be afraid to reach out for help and seek guidance from mentors or from someone whose career you admire. Although you can look to others for inspiration, you should try to chart a path for yourself that is uniquely yours. Always stay true to yourself and never believe that there is only one way to achieve or reach a goal.

LEGACY AND SUCCESS

My Most Outstanding Accomplishment:

Establishing the Fashion Law Society at Howard University School of Law. The Fashion Law Society is the first of its kind in the Washington, D.C. area. Through the Fashion Law Society, we were able to educate law students, lawyers, and the broader community about the many legal issues prevalent in the fashion industry including labor and employment rights, intellectual property rights, contract disputes, sustainability, and cultural responsibility. I see this as my most outstanding accomplishment because it took a lot of hard work and dedication to bring the organization to Howard's campus. It also allowed me to broaden the perspectives of my classmates on what they can do as a lawyer.

The Legacy I Hope to Leave:

I hope to leave a legacy that inspires those that come after me to chart their own path and to not sacrifice who God made them to be for any reason. I hope to inspire others to serve their community and to support others. I hope to encourage Black women to never settle in any aspect of their life and to know that they can have it all.

The Secret to My Success:

My faith in God. I do not know where I would be without my faith in God. He has seen me through many challenges in my life and has been my source of encouragement and discipline throughout my life. My support system has been there for me to serve as a listening ear, a shoulder to cry on when I needed it, and my personal cheerleading squad to celebrate my accomplishments.

Jonathan H. Cox, Esq.
Partner
The Cox Pradia Law Firm, PLLC
Houston, Texas

"Set goal. Work in silence. Crush them. Applaud for your own self!"
– Jonathan H. Cox

Success is . . . largely defined by how happy I am with the work that I am doing. I feel most successful when the people who depend on me like my family, my staff and my clients are comfortable and happy.

PERSONAL FAVORITES

Favorite Quotes: "We are what we repeatedly do, therefore excellence is not an act but a habit." - Aristotle

"Every act whatever of man that causes damage to another obliges him by whose fault it happened to repair it." - Louisiana Civil Code Article 2315. (This was embedded in my brain in my first year of law school and has stuck with me since then.)

"All of man's troubles come from his inability to sit still in a room alone." - Arnold Rothstein

"Don't let the taste of success fool you into thinking that you have arrived." - Unknown

Favorite Books: *Journey to Justice* by Johnnie Cochran; *The King of Torts* by John Grisham; *Vernon Can Read* by Vernon Jordan

Favorite Movies: *The Godfather I; The Godfather II; Gladiator*

Favorite Songs: "A Change Is Gonna Come" by Sam Cooke; "Can I Live" by Jay-Z; "Lucky Me" by Jay-Z; "Beach Chair" by Jay-Z

Favorite Law School Classes: Torts; Evidence; Trial Advocacy

Favorite Legal Cases: *Brown v. Board of Education*; *The People vs. O.J. Simpson* (I was in law school during the trial.)

Favorite Hobby: Golf

Favorite Attorney Role Models: Johnnie Cochran; Thurgood Marshall

FAMILY AND BACKGROUND

Where Born and Raised: Houston, Texas

Family (Spouse/Partner and Children): Spouse - Curlyncia; Children - (blended family) Justin, Gia, Amya, Anya and Gabriel

Family Socioeconomic and Educational Background: I was raised in a middle-class home. My mother is a lifelong educator. My father is a career pharmacist who also possesses a law degree from Thurgood Marshall School of Law Texas Southern University. I have several cousins that also practice law across the United States.

THE DECISION TO BECOME A LAWYER

When and Why I Decided to Become a Lawyer: I decided to become a lawyer when I was 15 years old, still in high school. During this time I was intrigued by politics and history. I was reading a lot then about Thurgood Marshall and his work as a lawyer before he became a Supreme Court Justice. I was intrigued by his passion to advocate for people and communities. I knew that this is what I wanted to do.

EDUCATIONAL ACHIEVEMENTS

High School: Madison High School (Houston, Texas)

College/University: Prairie View A&M University (Prairie View, Texas)

Undergraduate Degree: Bachelor of Arts (B.A.)

Major: Political Science

Law School: Southern University Law Center (New Orleans, Louisiana)

Law Degree and Graduation Year: Juris Doctor/Doctor of Jurisprudence (J.D.) - Class of 1997

Law School Honors, Achievements and Activities: *Member,* National Trial Advocacy Team (2nd and 3rd Years)

PROFESSIONAL ACCOMPLISHMENTS

State Bar Membership (Where Licensed to Practice Law): Texas

Other Legal Experience: *Prosecutor,* Galveston District Attorney's Office; *Criminal Defense Attorney; General Counsel,* MS WORLD LLC

Professional Organizations: *Member,* National Bar Association; *Member,* Houston Lawyers Association; *Member,* Texas Trial Lawyers Association

Post-Law School Honors, Achievements, Activities, and Community Involvement: *Listed Honoree,* Rising Star, Texas Super Lawyers Rising Star Edition (2004 and 2005); *Honoree,* Top 50 Black Attorneys in Houston; *Finalist,* Houston Pinnacle Award (2019)

LESSONS LEARNED: MY RECOMMENDATIONS FOR YOUR FUTURE ACTIONS BASED ON MY PAST EXPERIENCE

Advice on Law School Preparation:

The harder you work in college to maintain a high grade point average (GPA), the more options you will have when you begin to apply to law school. Additionally, there are classes that you can and should take to put you in a position to do well on the Law School Admission Test (LSAT).

However, make no mistake. None of that will determine the type of lawyer you will be. Your life experiences and the passion that you have for the betterment of others will have a much greater impact on the type of law you practice and the type of lawyer you will become.

Advice on Applying to and Selecting a Law School:

Shoot for the stars. Don't be afraid to apply to the schools on your wish list.

Advice Regarding Academic Success, Co-Curricular and Extra-Curricular Participation, and Social Engagement in Law School:

I always participated in extra-curricular activities. In my opinion, you have to have some semblance of a social life while in law school. Your classmates will become your colleagues. Get to know them.

Advice on Preparing for and Taking the Bar Exam:

For those three months between graduation and the bar exam, forget about making money. Study, study and then study.

Advice on Choosing a Job and Career Path Inside or Outside of the Legal Profession:

Your first job probably will not be your last job. Gain experience that you will be able to use when you move on. If you want to be a trial lawyer, the sooner you get comfortable in the courtroom, the better.

Advice Regarding Seeking Legal Job Opportunities and/or Creating One's Own Opportunities:

Networking is so important. I interview legal interns every year. What I have learned as an employer is that it is best to be yourself when interviewing. The truth will always come to light.

Advice on Achieving Career Success and Advancement:

As an African American lawyer, the reality is you will have to fight stereotypes from opposing counsel, the bench and even from potential clients. Your reputation is everything.

Advice on Overcoming the Additional Challenges Black Law Students Face:

You can't change the hearts of others. However, you can stand out by focusing on excellence in all that you do. In most jurisdictions, clerkships and internships are competitive and the percentages of Black law students getting the top-tier positions are disproportionate, but don't be discouraged.

Best Advice I Received Regarding Law School and the Legal Profession:

They call it the "practice" of law for a reason. Perfection in law is not reality. Be prepared. Be an advocate for your clients. Avoid mistakes where you can.

Worst Advice I Received Regarding Law School and the Legal Profession:

Your law degree/law license is the ticket to wealth and prosperity. The truth is that there are many, many struggling lawyers in every city.

Best Advice I Would Give to an Aspiring Black Lawyer:

Understand the business of law. Know that if you desire to run your own law firm, you will find yourself doing much more than legal work. Be prepared.

Thoughts About Why Earning a Law Degree Is a Powerful Credential for African Americans and Why There Is a Need for More African American Lawyers:

Your law license is very powerful. The African American community is still in need of skilled, capable, and passionate advocates. Lawyers should be social engineers for justice. There are many issues that directly affect the African American community and who better to advocate for change than those of us that have had the same life experiences as our clients?

Thoughts About Whether and Why Law School Is Worth the Financial Investment:

Law school is definitely worth the financial investment. This profession can be rewarding and yes, even lucrative. It will require hard work and long hours but don't allow the money to be your single focus. Focus on your craft. The money will come.

LEGACY AND SUCCESS

My Most Outstanding Accomplishments:

Personally, my most outstanding accomplishments are my two children. They are both true blessings in my life and they are a major source of motivation in my legal endeavors.

Professionally, my representation of families in their pursuit of justice for the tragic and unnecessary loss of loved ones.

The Legacy I Hope to Leave:

I hope to leave a legacy that I stood for justice. I want to prove that a group of African American lawyers can come together as an entity to provide legal representation at the highest level. I would like my community to know and understand that there are highly-skilled advocates that are products of those same communities and that no one will fight harder for justice than us.

The Secret to My Success:

At Southern University Law Center, we were taught to have seriousness of purpose. That slogan has stuck with me. The secret to success in my opinion is preparation for the task at hand and passion for the cause that individuals have entrusted with you. There is no substitute for hard work.

LESSONS FROM SUCCESSFUL AFRICAN AMERICAN LAWYERS

Khyla D. Craine, Esq.
Deputy Legal Director
Michigan Department of State
Detroit, Michigan

"Use the power you have until you gain some more."

– Khyla D. Craine

Success is . . . achieving both personal and professional goals while leaving a meaningful impact on the world.

PERSONAL FAVORITES

Favorite Quotes: "From everyone who has been given much, much will be demanded; and from the one who has been entrusted with much, much more will be asked." - Luke 12:48

"Success is liking yourself, liking what you do, and liking how you do it." - the late Maya Angelou

Favorite Books: *The Warmth of Other Suns* by Isabel Wilkerson; *April 4, 1968: Martin Luther King, Jr.'s Death and How It Changed America* by Michael Eric Dyson; *Matilda* by Roald Dahl; *What I Know For Sure* by Oprah Winfrey; *The Four Agreements: A Practical Guide to Personal Freedom* by Don Miguel Ruiz; *Year of Yes: How to Dance It Out, Stand In the Sun and Be Your Own Person* by Shonda Rhimes

Favorite Movies: *To Kill A Mockingbird; The Proposal; X; A Time To Kill; Colombiana*

Favorite Songs: "Purple Rain" by Prince; "The Beautiful Ones" by Prince; "Total Praise" by Richard Smallwood; "Great is Your Mercy" by Donnie McClurkin; "Sweet Love" by Anita Baker

Favorite Musical Artists: Anita Baker; Prince; Whitney Houston; Tamia; Kirk Franklin; Daughtry

Favorite Law School Classes: Constitutional Law; Race and Law

Favorite Legal Case: *Briggs v. Elliott*

Favorite Hobbies: Reading; Listening to music

Favorite Attorney Role Models: Charles Hamilton Houston; Jake Brigance; Kim M. Keenan

FAMILY AND BACKGROUND

Where Born and Raised: Ann Arbor, Michigan

Family Socioeconomic and Educational Background: I grew up in a middle-class, single-parent family in a Midwestern college town. My mother was the first in our family to obtain a graduate degree, and I am the first attorney in our family. I am the only person to attend and graduate from an HBCU (historically Black college or university) - two HBCUs in fact.

THE DECISION TO BECOME A LAWYER

When and Why I Decided to Become a Lawyer: I had first thoughts about it when I was a student at South Carolina State University. I was so involved with the National Association for the Advancement of Colored People (NAACP) and thought I could make a better difference as a lawyer than a doctor. I committed while practicing as a nurse and talking with my colleagues.

EDUCATIONAL ACHIEVEMENTS

High School: Ann Arbor Pioneer High School (Ann Arbor, Michigan)

College/University: South Carolina State University (Orangeburg, South Carolina)

Undergraduate Degree: Bachelor of Science (B.S.)

Major: Nursing

College Honors, Achievements and Activities: *Academic Recognition,* National Dean's List; *Parliamentarian and Social Action Chair,* Alpha Xi Chapter, Delta Sigma Theta Sorority, Inc.

Law School: Howard University School of Law (Washington, D.C.)

Law Degree and Graduation Year: Juris Doctor/Doctor of Jurisprudence (J.D.) - Class of 2012

Law School Honors, Achievements and Activities: *Member,* Charles Hamilton Houston National Moot Court Team; *3L Representative,* Student Bar Association

PROFESSIONAL ACCOMPLISHMENTS

State Bar Membership (Where Licensed to Practice Law): Maryland

Other Legal Experience: *Assistant General Counsel,* National Association for the Advancement of Colored People (NAACP); *Legal Intern,* Association of Federal Government Employees (AFGE); *Legal Intern,* U.S. Department of Justice, Civil Rights Division, Special Litigation Section

Other Professional Work Experience: *Registered Nurse,* St. Thomas Health Services (Nashville, Tennessee)

Professional Organizations: *Member,* National Bar Association

Post-Law School Honors, Achievements, Activities, and Community Involvement: *Awardee,* NBA Top 40 under 40 Best Advocates Award; *Awardee,* 2019 National Bar Association Equal Justice Award; *Honoree,* Young Woman Lawyer of the Year, Women Lawyers Division, National Bar Association; *Honoree,* Young Alumni of the Year, Washington, D.C. Alumni Chapter, South Carolina State University Alumni Association; *Chair,* 2020 Census Subcommittee, Delta Sigma Theta Sorority, Inc.; *Member,* National Social Action Commission, Delta Sigma Theta Sorority, Inc.; *Member,* Junior League of Ann Arbor, Michigan; *Chair,* Young Lawyers Division, National Bar Association; *Keynote Speaker,* Citizenship Law Related Education Program's annual Law Day conference; *Co-author,* Returning Citizens: How Shifting Law and Policy in Maryland Will Help Citizens Who Return from Incarceration, University of Baltimore Law School Law Forum; *Keynote Speaker,* The Maryland State Bar Association

LESSONS LEARNED: MY RECOMMENDATIONS FOR YOUR FUTURE ACTIONS BASED ON MY PAST EXPERIENCE

Advice on Law School Preparation:

Be clear that you don't have to major in "pre-law" to attend law school. Law school is much richer when people of varying degree disciplines are in the class. Focus on achieving well in college, gain some experience outside of your studies, and learn from your colleagues and others around you. Lastly, be clear that this is what you would like to do.

Advice on Applying to and Selecting a Law School:

Look at the broad spectrum of schools available to you. If you have an idea of what type of law you would like to practice, then look at those schools that focus on that subject or area. Also look at the cost, the faculty, and students who make up the school.

Advice Regarding Academic Success, Co-Curricular and Extra-Curricular Participation, and Social Engagement in Law School:

Law school is as tough as you make it. It challenges your thought processes and how you have learned to write, up to that point. Remember that generations of people before you have done it with a lot less technology, less financial resources, but with the same determination and resolve to pursue excellence. Take the opportunities that are afforded to participate in clinics and/or moot court – they are important skills and an opportunity to get to know your colleagues.

Advice on Preparing for and Taking the Bar Exam:

If you focus and commit to learn in your first year of law school, then it will be an actual review during the bar exam prep time. When you begin to prepare for the exam, focus on the goal, believe in yourself, and refrain from interacting with negative people. Also remember that if you happen not to be successful in the first attempt, pick yourself up and try again.

Advice on Choosing a Job and Career Path Inside or Outside of the Legal Profession:

My former boss once told me, "Think about the ultimate goal, and then figure out what skills you need to do that." Each job you obtain will place tools and skills and a network in your tool bag. Also, there are many occupations and career paths for someone with this degree. Your potential is limitless.

Advice on Seeking Legal Job Opportunities and/or Creating One's Own Opportunities:

Research. Confidence. Poise.

Advice on Achieving Career Success and Advancement:

Never forget that your brand is everything. Everyone you meet has the potential to help or hurt your career. Treat everyone fairly and with kindness, and that is as important as all of the degrees or lofty positions you may obtain. The legal profession is very small, and the Black lawyer network is even smaller. The degrees of separation are more like three, instead of six. Burning bridges is never an option.

Advice on Overcoming the Additional Challenges that Black Law Students and Lawyers Face:

You are qualified to be right where you are, and don't let anyone tell you otherwise. Stay focused, work hard, and gain the connections you need to be successful.

I encourage you to join the National Bar Association, where you gain a relationship with many Black lawyers of varied practice areas that would welcome the opportunity to help and mentor you. Also, don't limit your connections to only Black lawyers. There are other lawyers of color and White lawyers that have great advice and a willingness to help you.

Best Advice I Received Regarding Law School and the Legal Profession:

This is the practice, not the perfection of law. Making mistakes is how you learn. Own them, but don't repeat them.

Worst Advice I Received Regarding Law School and the Legal Profession:

Follow the money and then follow your passion.

Best Advice I Would Give to an Aspiring Black Lawyer:

Do this work with a seriousness of purpose. There are people who are counting on you.

Thoughts About Why There Is a Need for More African American Lawyers:

Our nation and the world need more Black lawyers. Our varying perspectives on the world allow us to see and apply the law in transformative ways. The African American lawyer has helped pull our nation and the world towards a more inclusive, respectful, and just place to live. That tradition must continue through the new generation of lawyers that will match the wit, passion, and brilliance of our ancestors with the technology, circumstances, and need of this new millennium.

Thoughts About Whether and Why Law School Is Worth the Financial Investment:

Everything worthwhile has a price. Outside of the financial investment to the school, there is one to yourself, your family, and community. While other countries have found a way to make this profession cost much less, it is still worth it because there are so many people who are counting on us to help advance our nation for the better.

LEGACY AND SUCCESS

My Most Outstanding Accomplishments:

Professional: I think working on the Census project with the NAACP. We were able to do a lot of research and raise the issue of undercounting - especially in the Black community.

Personal: That's a hard question for me to answer. Probably when I traveled to South Africa for my birthday in 2018. It was amazing and enlightening.

The Legacy I Hope to Leave:

That Khyla fought to be a change agent wherever she went and that she empowered young people and women to take an active role in becoming the social engineers for our time.

The Secret to My Success:

I am still on my journey to other levels of success within my life. Yet, the success that I have obtained thus far is due to faith in God and in myself.

Derick D. Dailey, Esq.
Assistant United States Attorney
United States Attorney's Office
District of Delaware
Wilmington, Delaware

"Notwithstanding our plight, we mustn't sit on the sidelines, we must engage, we must remain hopeful, and we must fight back against those who seek to undermine the rule of law and thwart justice."

– Derick D. Dailey

Success is . . . having an impact on others, especially those who are systemically marginalized.

PERSONAL FAVORITES

Favorite Quote: "Do justice, love mercy, and walk humbly." - Micah 6:8

Favorite Books: *God of the Oppressed* by James Cone; *Between the World and Me* by Ta-Nesihi Coates; *Doing Justice* by Phreet Bharra; *Their Eyes Were Watching God* by Zora Neal Hurston; *Convictions* by John Kroger

Favorite Movie: *Lean on Me*

Favorite Music Genre: Anything Old School

Favorite Musical Artists: Aretha Franklin, The Temptations, Jackson 5, etc.

Favorite Law School Class: The Law of Race

Favorite Legal Case: *Cooper v. Aaron*, 358 U.S. 1 (1958)

Favorite Hobbies: Playing piano; Traveling; Trying new food; Spending time with family

Favorite Attorney Role Models: Justice Thurgood Marshall; Judge Constance Baker Motley; Bryan Stevenson; Judge Charles Shaw

FAMILY AND BACKGROUND

Where Born and Raised: Little Rock, Arkansas

Family (Spouse/Partner and Children): Partner - (fiancé) Dr. Yalidy Matos

Family Socioeconomic and Educational Background: I am from a working/middle-class background.

THE DECISION TO BECOME A LAWYER

When and Why I Decided to Become a Lawyer: Like many lawyers, I chose to become a lawyer to make a difference. Growing up in Arkansas and serving as a Teach For America Corps Member in the Mississippi Delta, I witnessed first-hand the injustices that many poor families of color contend with in the public schools. I wanted to remedy that injustice and I believed the law would aid in that pursuit.

EDUCATIONAL ACHIEVEMENTS

High School: North Little Rock High School – West Campus (North Little Rock, Arkansas)

College/University: Westminster College (Fulton, Missouri)

Undergraduate Degree: Bachelor of Arts (B.A.)

Majors: Political Science and Religious Studies

College Honors, Achievements and Activities: *Honoree,* Senior of the Year; *Awardee,* E.C. Henderson Award for Public Service; *Awardee,* Leadership and Service Award;

Triple "S" Scholar; Student Ambassador; *Board of Directors,* Callaway County United Way

Law School: Fordham University School of Law (New York, New York)

Law Degree and Graduation Year: Juris Doctor/Doctor of Jurisprudence (J.D.) - Class of 2017

Law School Honors, Achievements and Activities: *National Chair,* National Black Law Students Association; *Stein Scholar,* Stein Center for Ethics; *James E. Johnson Intern,* Brennan Center for Justice, New York University School of Law; *Extern,* United States Attorney's Office, Eastern District of New York; *Student Member,* Legislative Policy and Advocacy Clinic, Fordham University School of Law

Other Graduate or Professional Degree: Master of Arts (M.A.), Yale University (New Haven, Connecticut)

PROFESSIONAL ACCOMPLISHMENTS

State Bar Memberships (Where Admitted to Practice Law): District of Columbia; Missouri

Other Legal Work Experience: *Litigation Associate,* Dowd Bennett LLP

Other Professional Work Experience: *Corps Member,* Teach for America

Professional Organizations: *Member,* American Bar Association; *Member,* National Bar Association

Post-Law School Honors, Achievements, Activities, and Community Involvement: *Board Member,* Yale Club of Philadelphia; *Board Member,* Yale Black Alumni Association; *Board Member,* Bread for the World; *Board Member,* Justice Revival; *Board Member,* Whitney/Strong Foundation; *Merit Selection Panel,* Federal Magistrate Judge

LESSONS LEARNED: MY RECOMMENDATIONS FOR YOUR FUTURE ACTIONS BASED ON MY PAST EXPERIENCE

Advice on Law School Preparation:

Don't try to major in something that you think will prepare you for law school – major in something you enjoy. Study for the Law School Admission Test (LSAT) and do your best, but don't obsess over it.

Advice on Applying to and Selecting a Law School:

Prior to selecting a law school, visit the school. Don't be afraid to contact the professors and current students to get as much of an inside look as you can. Also, if you know where you ultimately want to practice, try to align your law school selection to that state/jurisdiction. It may save you a few headaches when it's bar exam time.

Advice Regarding Academic Success, Co-Curricular and Extra-Curricular Participation, and Social Engagement in Law School:

Don't overdo it. Stay focused on your purpose.

Advice on Preparing for and Taking the Bar Exam:

The bar exam is challenging. Take it seriously. Develop a daily study routine and stick to it. But, don't obsess over it. There is no magic formula to passing.

Advice on Choosing a Job and Career Path Inside or Outside of the Legal Profession:

A more senior lawyer once told me, "Derick, think of your legal career as 40 years long. You don't have to do everything at once. You have time." I commend that advice to you.

Advice on Seeking Legal Job Opportunities and/or Creating One's Own Opportunities:

Take charge of your legal career. It will be what you make it. Do not wait around for opportunities, create them. Ask for assignments that pique your interest. Apply for a job that you think you're not yet qualified for, etc. As my grandmother would say, "Step out on faith."

Advice on Achieving Career Success and Advancement:

Success is varied, and it should never be defined by others. Define it for yourself and pursue it.

Advice on Overcoming the Additional Challenges Black Law Students and Lawyers Face:

Lean in to the challenges you face as a law student, a lawyer, and as a person of color in America, more generally. You'll find strength in your attempting to overcome those challenges. As you face them though, do not allow them to cause you to tear others down – with your words, actions or thoughts. Find ways to overcome your challenges by extending grace to others and doing to others as you'd have them do unto you.

Best Advice I Received Regarding Law School and the Legal Profession:

The law can, and must be, a tool for progress.

Worst Advice I Received Regarding Law School and the Legal Profession:

That there was a right and a wrong way to successfully navigate law school and the legal profession. Not so.

Best Advice I Would Give to an Aspiring Black Lawyer:

Before you begin the journey towards law school and becoming a lawyer, think critically about your motivation for doing so. Reflect on your values and how you intend to pursue those values with a law degree.

Thoughts About Why Earning a Law Degree Is a Powerful Credential for African Americans and Why There Is a Need for More African American Lawyers:

While representation matters at every level of the legal field, we do not need more African American lawyers *per se*, we need more racially-conscious, and justice-oriented lawyers.

Thoughts About Whether and Why Law School Is Worth the Financial Investment:

Not every law school is worth the financial investment. This is why it is important to think seriously about what you want to do after law school before you make the decision to go.

LEGACY AND SUCCESS

My Most Outstanding Accomplishment:

There are many aspects of my professional life that I am proud of. Specifically, in my current role, I am proud to be serving as our office's representative on the District's Re-entry Court, chief of our Financial Litigation Unit, and working with local and state partners to develop a resource hub for the formerly incarcerated, their families, and the community at-large.

The Legacy I Hope to Leave:

I hope to inspire others to dethrone themselves from the center of their reality and center the most marginal.

The Secret to My Success:

God and a loving, supportive village.

Charles Robert Davidson, Esq., M.A.L.D., Ph.D.

Director
Pre-Law Institute
City University of New York
John Jay College
New York, New York

"Plans are good but a vision is even better."

– Charles Robert Davidson

Success . . . is being able to truly believe that your contributions to someone's good - no matter how small - matter greatly.

PERSONAL FAVORITES

Favorite Quote: "And as for you, brothers and sisters, never tire of doing what is good." - 2 Thessalonians 3:13

Favorite Books: *Between the World and Me* by Ta-Nehisi Coates; *The Complicity of Lawyers in the Criminal Injustice System* by Alec Karakatsanis; *Pluie et Vent sur Telumée Miracle* by Simone Schwartz-Bart; *White Rage: The Unspoken Truth of Our Racial Divide* by Carol Anderson; *Nobody: Casualties of America's War on the Vulnerable, from Ferguson to Flint and Beyond* by Mark Lamont Hill

Favorite Movies: *Amazing Grace* (2018); *If Beale Street Could Talk*

Favorite Musical Artists: Césaria Evora; Anita Baker

Favorite Law School Classes: International Law; Antitrust; Administrative Law

Favorite Legal Cases: *Brown v. Board of Education* (and the critiques of it); Supreme Court Fourth Amendment and criminal procedure jurisprudence (again, because there is so much to critique)

Favorite Hobbies: Reading; Speaking and studying foreign languages; Exercising; Watching good television

Favorite Attorney Role Models: Anita Hill; Derrick Bell; Bryan Stevenson; Thurgood Marshall

FAMILY AND BACKGROUND

Where Born and Raised: Born - Baltimore, Maryland; Raised - Columbia, Maryland and Silver Spring, Maryland

Family Socioeconomic and Educational Background: My parents were both born in the early to mid-1920s in rural North and South Carolina, migrated north in the late 1940s. My mother was the eldest in a large family and was the sole member of her family to graduate from college. My father was one of four brothers, all of whom would go on to become doctors. My father's two elder sisters both became well-known educators and community activists. I grew up in an upper-middle class home: my father as mentioned was a successful doctor and my mother was primarily a homemaker during my childhood. Of my two older sisters, one became a physician and the other a dentist. While a lot of my family members became medical professionals, there are many lawyers and judges in the family. Having said that, I am always aware of some of the privilege and access I had because of my family background. At the same time, I am keenly aware of the pervasive nature of American racism that meant that despite these privileges, the extent of our access and even awareness was not like that of many of my White peers. My parents and relatives had grown up in Jim Crow and I always feel that despite their outward success, we still felt the legacy of that in so many ways at home.

THE DECISION TO BECOME A LAWYER

When and Why You Decided to Become a Lawyer: Even though I was a French literature major (and thought that would be my career path), I loved my Constitutional Law and International Law classes in college and really saw myself in a public service career in law. At around the same time, I was profoundly marked by the series *Eyes on the Prize*. I remember being fascinated by the role of federal courts (and state defiance of these courts) in desegregating school systems in accordance with *Brown*. I became fascinated with the power of the courts to effect social change that benefitted Black people based on Constitutional principles even in the face of entrenched, visceral, and massive White resistance. It was mostly my interest in these academic questions that prompted me to think of going to law school.

EDUCATIONAL ACHIEVEMENTS

High School: St. Paul's School (Brooklandville, Maryland); Centennial High School (Columbia, Maryland)

College/University: University of Maryland (College Park, Maryland)

Undergraduate Degree: Bachelor of Arts (B.A.)

Major: French Literature

College Honors, Achievements and Activities: *Academic Recognition,* Dean's List

Law School: The George Washington University Law School (Washington, D.C.)

Law Degree and Graduation Year: Juris Doctor/Doctor of Jurisprudence (J.D.) - Class of 1992

Other Graduate or Professional Degrees: Certificat d' Etudes, Université de Paris III (Paris, France); Master of Arts in Law and Diplomacy (M.A.L.D.), The Fletcher School of Law and Diplomacy, Tufts University (Boston, Massachusetts); Doctor of Philosophy (Ph.D.) in International Relations, The Fletcher School of Law and Diplomacy, Tufts University (Boston, Massachusetts)

Additional Education: Master of Arts (A.M.) in Middle Eastern Studies, Harvard University (Cambridge, Massachusetts) (Working on thesis)

PROFESSIONAL ACCOMPLISHMENTS

State Bar Membership (Where Admitted to Practice Law): Maryland

Other Legal Work Experience: *Attorney,* U.S. Department of Justice Honors Program

Other Professional Work Experience: *Director,* Center for Teaching and Learning, John Jay College (New York, New York); *Adjunct Assistant Professor,* John Jay College (New York, New York); *Assistant Professor of International Law,* American University in Cairo (Cairo, Egypt); *Director,* International Law Concentration, American University in Cairo, Egypt; *Academic Coordinator,* International Law Program, American University in Cairo, Egypt; *Visiting Scholar,* Civic Education Project (Baku, Azerbaijan); *Legal Education Advisor,* American Bar Association (Cairo, Egypt); *Legal Education Consultant,* American Bar Association, New York

Professional Organizations: *Member,* Northeast Association of Pre-Law Advisors (NAPLA); *Member,* National Association of Fellowship Advisors (NAFA)

Post-Law School Honors, Achievements, Activities, and Community Involvement:

Awardee, Outstanding Employee Recognition Award; *Honoree,* Dean's List Students Awards; *Recipient,* Perry Ellis Sutton SEEK Award; *Recipient,* Vielka Holness Award for Outstanding Commitment to Students; *Finalist,* Carnegie Scholars Program in Islam; *Awardee,* Best Undergraduate Professor; *International Fellow,* Soros Foundation/Open Society Institute-Europe; *Faculty Fellow,* Civic Education Project; *Recipient,* Doctoral Funding Award; *Fellow,* U.S. Department of State Democracy Fellows Program; *Recipient,* Eisenhower Dissertation Fellowship; *Honorable Mention,* Ford Foundation Minority Dissertation Fellowship; *Awardee,* Arthur Vining Foundation Award for Future University Professors; *Recipient,* Foreign Language and Area Studies Scholarship

LESSONS LEARNED: MY RECOMMENDATIONS FOR YOUR FUTURE ACTIONS BASED ON MY PAST EXPERIENCE

Advice on Applying to and Selecting a Law School:

While rankings have some meaning, most important in my opinion is *fit*. A top-ranked school may look great on a resumé, but that does not fully take into account that you will be spending three (sometimes grueling) years in an institution. If you do not feel welcome, supported, and seen at an institution, the high rank will be of very little comfort. Moreover, in my experience, the lingering effects of being "othered" and feeling unseen in an environment has impacted my capacity to succeed to the very best of my abilities. While some may thrive in these settings, many students find them discouraging. Find a setting where you can be challenged but where you fit and where you thrive. This holds true for law school, career, relationships, everything really.

Advice Regarding Academic Success, Co-Curricular and Extra-Curricular Participation, and Social Engagement in Law School:

Law school is challenging. I realized that I didn't enjoy it very much at first, and frequently thought about leaving. There were very few Black people in my class and only four Black people in my section (and only one other Black man)

and it was a strange environment and I had spent much of my education in PWIs (Predominantly White Institutions). The teaching style as well as the interactions with classmates was very unfamiliar to me and while I had always been a great and engaged student, I found myself not interested in many of the first-year subjects and I started to really dislike the experience. Fortunately, I had this small circle of friends with whom I could commiserate; we helped each other academically and personally. (It was common then for people to speak about the few Black students as "affirmative action admits.") I connected with the Black Law Students Association (BLSA) and made more friends. As the first year ended, these were my best friends at the school. By the second and third years, I was much more comfortable and began working at the Department of Justice as an intern, which I enjoyed. I would advise all students to overcome any reluctance to connect to peers - especially ones who can relate to the experience of being a Black person/Person of Color (POC) in law school - and to really invest in making these connections. They are academically useful but can also be personally life-saving when the experience proves especially challenging (and I suspect, for most people, law school is challenging at some point).

Advice on Preparing for and Taking the Bar Exam:

I loved the bar exam. Unlike law school assessments, I thought it was straightforward - difficult but straightforward - and quite fair. I had been told by some mentors to take an "easy" bar exam (no such thing) so that I would be sure that I would pass. I disregarded this advice and committed myself to study. Including bar prep classes, I would study eight to ten hours a day. I had a rigorous and pretty rigid study schedule and I practiced on released questions every day. I frankly think I learned more in my studying for the bar than I did in many of my law school classes. Approach the bar exam with the idea that you are only taking it one time (and if that proves false, that's okay). Write off pretty much everything else and use whatever study approach works for you, but put in the time. Practice. Practice some more. Identify weaknesses and attend to those (instead of spending time on areas where you are consistently strong). Understand why you are getting answers right or wrong. Strange as it sounds, I loved studying for and taking the bar exam. It was a great experience of discipline and intellectual challenge.

Advice Regarding Choosing a Job and Career Path Inside or Outside of the Legal Profession:

Be honest with yourself about yourself. You will likely have several options from which to choose, but try not to be seduced by things that actually do not matter to you. It is so important to remember that it is okay not to want what others want. Remember that while most people follow "traditional" pathways, there is always room for you to consider where your own unique path leads. I thought I needed to be practicing law in the way others did and I quickly realized that was not for me. It took a while but I discovered that I loved the law - but I loved *teaching* it to young people. Recognizing that I wanted something different and pursuing that path has led me to a very happy and fulfilling career.

Advice on Seeking Legal Job Opportunities and/or Creating One's Own Opportunities:

As I mentioned above, it is important to think carefully about how you want to use your law degree. There are countless ways that you can put it to good use for yourself and for others. You should certainly seek advice widely from people who are doing the sort of work that interests you. Hopefully, you will have a good mentor and solid support networks who will support and encourage you. Be flexible: it is great to have a plan, but it is far better to have a vision of what you want your career to ultimately look and feel like. Plans will always fall through but a vision will keep you on track when they do. Be willing to gain diverse experience and to deviate from the way you think things "should" be. You will have a more joyful, less stressful, and definitely a more interesting career.

Advice on Achieving Career Success and Advancement:

It is far easier to be successful at something you love to do than it is at something you hate. Money can only motivate you so much. Try to find work that you enjoy and that is meaningful to you and to others. I have found that when you do the work you love, you naturally excel. (It goes without saying that in addition to loving it, you need to be good at it, too!) You do not need to do a lot of performing to come to the attention of others; you are simply noticed because people notice people who are authentically doing what they love to do. Focus on finding that space, honing your skills, staying open to feedback (especially when you don't want to hear it), and being of genuine service to others. Another aspect of career success is helping others to reach where you are. Making it to the top and being alone doesn't strike me as success unless we are helping others - particularly our Black sisters and brothers - get there too. Finally, the most truly successful people that I have met have a deep sense of humility. They recognize that their value does not lie in a title, a job, an office, or a particular income. Their self-worth is constructed of things far more solid and they can hold their success in a way that reflects that solid sense of self.

Advice on Overcoming the Additional Challenges Black Law Students and Lawyers Face: There is a paradoxical tendency in educational and professional settings to both ignore Black people and their needs *and* to be hyper-focused on their conduct/speech/work product. This frustrating dynamic can take its toll if you are constantly seeking the approval and validation of people who may intentionally or unconsciously withhold it. Do your best work because that is *what* you do. Be the consummate professional because that is *who* you are. Be the voice that stands up in the face of injustice and inequity because that's what *we* Black people do.

Always remember that your dream job is still a job. Do not lose sight of what is important to you and your communities.

Worst Advice I Received Regarding Law School and the Legal Profession:

"Just do it." "You are smart, you will be fine." No, I really needed guidance and mentorship. Get all the help you can get from knowledgeable people and credible sources. Do not try to navigate law school and the legal profession on your own.

Best Advice I Would Give to an Aspiring Black Lawyer:

Do not forget - especially in challenging times - that you are the help that someone needs. You. Just as you are with all of your supposed flaws, your faults, with all the mistakes, the lack and hardship you may have experienced - even with all of that - especially because of all of that, you are uniquely able to give someone exactly what she or he needs. You will be the lawyer who can relate to those clients in a way no one else can. You will understand things that will be mysterious to your classmates and colleagues. *Your experience is your expertise*. You can sit at any table, in any room, with confidence when you realize that you bring something to every situation. Don't let yourself be intimidated from speaking up and speaking out, particularly in spaces where you are the only Black person. Your voice, your wisdom, and your insight are exactly what is needed.

Thoughts About Why Earning a Law Degree Is a Powerful Credential for African Americans and Why There Is a Need for More African American Lawyers:

As Black communities continue to be ravaged by racialized violence, poverty, disproportionate death from COVID-19, underfunded and underperforming school systems, overpolicing and mass incarceration, there is no question in my mind that we need Black lawyers who are committed to serving the underserved in an almost unprecedented way. The law has for far too long been a tool of social control for our society's most vulnerable groups - whether those groups are racial minorities, immigrants, women, differently abled individuals, the poor, or trans - and we need lawyers to revitalize law as a tool for transformative social change. And this can be accomplished regardless of where you choose to work: volunteer your time and talent, do *pro bono* work, donate to organizations that support these communities. To be a Black lawyer is to be a member of a small elite group, given that we make up only four percent of the profession (and Black women make up an even smaller proportion) and we must use our privilege to help those who need our help.

Thoughts About Whether and Why Law School Is Worth the Financial Investment:

If you have done the work of thinking with brutal honesty about who you are, what you want, and why you want it, and those answers point toward law school, then I think law school can be an extraordinarily worthwhile and financially sound choice. But it is an investment, and like with any investment opportunity, you must do your due diligence before you hand your money over. Talk to people, visit schools, sit in on classes, do internships in as many legal settings as possible, take advantage of pre-law advisement, and find a mentor. Just as you would be unlikely to buy a home without really investigating whether you really want to spend several hundred thousand dollars on a particular house, explore law school with that same critical and searching approach. Like any investment, there are no guarantees, of course, but you will want to be able to say you made an informed and intelligent decision.

LEGACY AND SUCCESS

My Most Outstanding Accomplishment:

I am most proud of the fact that I made supporting Black people and Black students an organizing principle of my life. I am very proud that I have been able to talk to and reach so many students who might have otherwise not had the guidance of a Black mentor.

The Legacy I Hope to Leave:

I believe my legacy is in every student whom I support. I hope that my legacy will be a cohort of young Black people who will have been encouraged and uplifted and reminded of their brilliance and their innate beauty. That is a legacy I would certainly be proud of.

The Secret to My Success:

The key for me has been to focus on my own personal, intellectual, and spiritual development. I fear that if we fail to take care of ourselves, we can inadvertently bring our wounds to the people that we want to help. Once I have ensured that I am in a place to support others, I put others first. One of my favorite lines of Scripture says it this way: "As for you, brothers and sisters, never tire of doing what is good."

Xavier R. Donaldson, Esq.
Partner
Donaldson & Chilliest, LLP
New York, New York

"Be the best YOU that you can be at whatever you are doing."
— Xavier R. Donaldson

Success is . . . when you are happy doing what you are doing.

PERSONAL FAVORITES

Favorite Quote: "It is not the critic who counts; not the man who points out how the strong man stumbles, or where the doer of deeds could have done them better. The credit belongs to the man who is actually in the arena, whose face is marred by dust and sweat and blood; who strives valiantly; who errs, who comes short again and again, because there is no effort without error and short-coming; but who does actually strive to do the deeds; who knows great enthusiasms, the great devotions; who spends himself in a worthy cause; who at the best knows in the end the triumph of high achievement, and who at the worst, if he fails, at least fails while daring greatly, so that his place shall never be with those cold and timid souls who neither know victory nor defeat." - Teddy Roosevelt

Favorite Books: *Makes Me Wanna Holler* by Nathan McCall; *Soul on Ice* by Eldridge Cleaver; *Their Eyes Were Watching God* by Zora Neale Hurston; *Barracoon* by Zora Neale Hurston; *The Souls of Black Folk* by W.E.B. Dubois; *Songs of Solomon* by Toni Morrison; *Invisible Man* by Ralph Ellison

Favorite Movies: *The Matrix; Shawshank Redemption; Malcolm X; Boyz in Da Hood; Love and Basketball; Dead Presidents; A Soldier's Story; Full Metal Jacket*

Favorite Songs: "What's Going On" by Marvin Gaye; "Redemption Song" by Bob Marley; "That's the Way of the World" by Earth, Wind and Fire; "Me Against the World" by Tupac; "Through the Fire" by Chaka Khan; "I'll Be There" by Michael Jackson

Favorite Law School Classes: Legal Writing; Evidence; Criminal Law; Constitutional Law.

Favorite Legal Cases: *Brown v. Board of Education; Plessy v. Ferguson; Bollinger* line of cases; *Utah v. Strieff* (Judge Sotomayor's dissent)

Favorite Hobbies: Reading; Coaching my kids; Exercising; Playing golf

Favorite Attorney Role Models: Thomas B. Donaldson (brother); O.T. Wells; Anthony Ricco

FAMILY AND BACKGROUND

Where Born and Raised: Born - Queens, New York; Raised - Liberty City neighborhood in Miami, Florida

Family (Spouse/Partner and Children): Spouse - Paula; Children - (son) Malcolm and (son) Xavier II (commonly known as Malcolm and X, or as I like to say "Malcolm X" when we are outside in public)

Family Socioeconomic and Educational Background: My father left high school early and joined the Marines. He was honorably discharged after he lost his leg in the Vietnam War on a mine while attempting to save a fellow soldier. My mother is a registered nurse and has been a nurse for as long as I can remember. My oldest brother, Thomas, is a practicing attorney in New York City.

We were raised during the 1970s and 1980s when Liberty City was being ravaged by severe violence, massive narcotics and two violent citywide race riots. As a family, we experienced serious economic hurdles, and suffered through racism and classism, but my parents "always made it work."

THE DECISION TO BECOME A LAWYER

When and Why I Decided to Become a Lawyer: My brother, Thomas Donaldson, played a pivotal role in me choosing to become a lawyer. While in college, he explained to me that lawyers played prominent roles in ensuring that African Americans were treated fairly. Where we grew up, we experienced improper police conduct on a massive scale. He suggested that I become a prosecutor because a prosecutor's role was to pursue justice and because they had wide discretion to dismiss cases brought to them by corrupt police officers. Because we had personally experienced and observed an enormous amount of police misconduct, I thought that being a prosecutor was the best way to remedy these harms committed in our community, learn the process and then defend those wrongly accused. As a consequence, I decided to go to law school to become a prosecutor, pursue justice and ensure that the right people were being prosecuted and ultimately that justice was in fact being dispensed in a fair and honest way.

EDUCATIONAL ACHIEVEMENTS

High School: Miami Northwestern Senior High School (Miami, Florida)

College/University: St. Augustine's University (Raleigh, North Carolina)

Undergraduate Degree: Bachelor of Science (B.S.)

Major: Criminal Justice

College Honors, Achievements and Activities: Graduated *magna cum laude* "with great distinction"; *Recipient,* UNCF Academic Scholarship; *Listed Honoree,* Who's Who of Colleges and Universities; *Appointee,* Attorney General for the Student Body; *Member and Captain,* St. Augustine's University Track Team; *Winner,* NCAA (National Collegiate Athletic Association) National Track Team Championships (won several); *Qualified Athlete,* United States Olympic Trials (met qualifying standards); *Individual Winner,* NCAA National Track Championships (two championships); *Awardee,* NCAA All-American Award (multiple award winner); *Recipient,* Academic All-American Awards (multiple award winner); *Member,* Alpha Phi Alpha Fraternity, Inc.

Law School: Howard University School of Law (Washington, D.C.)

Law Degree and Graduation Year: Juris Doctor/Doctor of Jurisprudence (J.D.) - Class of 1994

Law School Honors, Achievements and Activities: *Captain,* National Moot Court team; *Attorney General,* Howard University Law School Student Body; *Student Member,* Admissions Committee

PROFESSIONAL ACCOMPLISHMENTS

State Bar Membership (Where Admitted to Practice Law): New York

Other Legal Work Experience: *Adjunct Professor,* Brooklyn Law School (Subject Taught: Trial Advocacy)

Professional Organizations: *Member,* New York State Bar Association; *Member,* New York City Criminal Bar Association; *Member,* New York State Association of Criminal Defense Attorneys; *Member,* Metropolitan Black Bar Association

Post-Law School Honors, Achievements, Activities, and Community Involvement:

Administrator, New York County Supreme Court Judicial Screening Committee; *Member,* Screening Committee, First Judicial Department, Supreme Court of the State of New York, Article 18B Assigned Counsel; *Lecturer,* Criminal Law Section, New York State Bar Exam; *Team Leader and Lecturer,* New York State Bar Association Trial Academy; *Lecturer,* Metropolitan Black Bar Association Trial Clinic; *Lecturer,* New York Association of Criminal Defense Attorneys; *President,* Metropolitan Black Bar Association; *Board Member,* New York City Criminal Bar Association; *Executive Member,* Criminal Justice Committee, New York State Bar Association; *Executive Member,* International Committee, New York State Bar Association; *Member,* Criminal Justice Act (CJA) Federal Panel; *Member;* Homicide Panel for the First Department; *Award Recipient,* New York Attorney General's Office; *Award Recipient,* New York State Black and Hispanic Caucus; *Award Recipient,* Borough Presidents; *Award Recipient,* Mayor of the City of New York; *Award Recipient,* Bronx District Attorney's Office; *Award Recipient,* New York City Council; *Award Recipient,* New York State Legislators; *Regular Speaker* (at high schools, youth programs, community boards and other associations relating to the significance of the law, public policy, business, education and politics)

LESSONS LEARNED: MY RECOMMENDATIONS FOR YOUR FUTURE ACTIONS BASED ON MY PAST EXPERIENCE

Advice on Law School Preparation:

As soon as you know you want to go to law school, you have to begin focusing on your grades. You **MUST** get good grades. Additionally, while you are in college, you must do what you can to ***DISTINGUISH YOURSELF*** amongst your peers by: joining college organizations and becoming active on campus; starting your own clubs or businesses; mentoring youth; volunteering at the courthouse or not-for-profit organization; or joining the ROTC (Reserve Officer Training Corps). But do something.

Furthermore, before you take the Law School Admission Test (LSAT) or Graduate Record Exam (GRE) you **MUST** take a review class. I had great grades in college and because of that, I thought that I could just take the LSAT without utilizing an LSAT review class. Wrong!!! I bombed the first (and second) time I took the LSAT. When I finally swallowed my pride and took the LSAT review class, my score went up dramatically. Getting into law school is a competitive process. You are competing against your classmates and other students from around the country. I can assure you that other students are taking review classes as well. Thus, in order to be on equal footing with them (and equally prepared), **TAKE A REVIEW CLASS**.

Finally, be prepared to tell "your" story. What is it about you that makes a particular law school want "you" to represent them as an attorney? Think about it this way: if you have a 3.6 GPA and scored 169 on the LSAT and another student from a different school has a 3.6 GPA and scored 169 on the LSAT, why should the law school choose you? What is it about you that **DISTINGUISHES** you from the other student? Were you in the Student Government Association (SGA)? Did you start your own company? Did you do volunteer work before law school? What adversity did you overcome? Did you participate in sports or other extra-curricular activities while maintaining high grades? Did you excel at anything else before applying to law school? Be prepared to tell "your" story of how you DISTINGUISH yourself from all others. Law schools like good stories and admission counselors like reading good stories.

Advice on Applying to and Selecting a Law School:

When you are applying to a law school, you should want a few questions answered about that law school before applying: Does this law school waive application fees? Do you want to live in that area where the law school is located? What is the bar passage rate of that law school? What is the employment rate for graduating law students? Is it a national, regional or local law school? What types of jobs do most graduates obtain after graduating from that law school? What is the diversity of the law school? What is the cost of the law school? Do you know anyone that attended that law school and how do they feel about the law school? What is the ranking of the law school and why? Are they offering me a scholarship?

Additionally, you want to submit a pristine application. There must not be any mistakes, typos or improper sentences in your application. Remember, very often, it comes down to two people for one remaining slot in a law school admission class. Don't give the committee a reason to choose the other person because you used spell check instead of re-reading and having a mentor review your application before submitting it.

Advice Regarding Academic Success, Co-Curricular and Extra-Curricular Participation, and Social Engagement in Law School:

The academic rigors of law school will probably be more demanding than your undergraduate work. You will have to read hundreds of pages a week and study several hours per night. In law school, everyone is smart. But you have to do your best to DISTINGUISH yourself amongst your peers. That starts from the first semester. Your first semester grades are critical and you must do your absolute best to acquire the highest grades you can. I would suggest that after the first month of law school, try and find friends or classmates to form a study group comprised of people that genuinely want everyone in the group to do well. Additionally, try and find a 2L or 3L that has taken the same courses you are taking and ask them for strategies on how to get a good grade from certain professors. Furthermore, this is the age of "real time" information. To that end, reach out to a lawyer that you know and bounce questions off of them. Use your resources because I can assure you that everyone else is. In law school, your ultimate goal is to DISTINGUISH yourself from other students at your law school *and* students from law schools on the other side of town. Hence, it is important, if possible, that you participate on a law journal, on a trial advocacy team, on a moot court team, in an organization, intern at a courthouse, intern for a government office, work for a professor or do whatever you believe will DISTINGUISH you from other students while *simultaneously* maintaining good grades.

The law school environment can be an emotionally, psychologically and physically challenging experience. It is unquestionably very draining. As such, I have always believed that law students *must* have "responsible fun" while in law school. It will be difficult to find the time but I truly think it is necessary. I believe that having "responsible fun" will help you achieve higher grades and ultimately perform at a higher level during classroom sessions because it will relieve stress and anxiety. When we were in law school, we formed a law school intramural basketball team that played against many of the undergraduate intramural teams as well as local teams in the surrounding area. This allowed us to relieve some stress, exercise and actually develop lifelong friendships. I would suggest that you make time to exercise, enjoy your pre-law school hobbies, take in a few movies or have an occasional law student gathering at a local restaurant or bar. As long as you are having "responsible fun" and it is not interfering with your goal to DISTINGUISH yourself amongst your peers, you will be fine.

Advice on Preparing for and Taking the Bar Exam:

Bar exam preparation requires two things: time management and smart studying. I have heard many stories about people who have spent an enormous amount of time studying only to fail the bar exam multiple times. Why?

Because, although they studied for long hours, they did not study smart for those long hours.

Studying smart means taking a bar review class and then studying every day/night after class. You then must draft and review your outlines. Do not use someone else's outlines. You must draft your own outline because you learn more as you draft your own outlines. Secondly, you must do as many *timed and simulated* test questions and tests as feasibly possible. After you finish each *timed and simulated* test question and/or test, you must read *all* the answers: the right ones and the wrong ones. During your review of the answers, you should not move on to the next question unless you know exactly why you got the right answers correct and why you got the wrong answers wrong. If you finish all of the test prep questions in your bar review materials, find a friend who is using a different bar review course and do their test questions in a *timed environment*. The goal is to do as many *timed and simulated* test questions as you can.

Time management means organizing your schedule so that you can study a certain amount of hours EVERY DAY and sticking to that schedule. If you have a job, then organize your study schedule around your work schedule. But studying must happen EVERY DAY. And every day before you begin to study, you should take a deep breath and say to yourself "I am gonna pass this bar exam." You have graduated from college. You have graduated from law school. Now comes the easy part. When you sit down to take the bar exam, say "I am gonna pass this bar exam." And guess what? You will pass the bar exam.

Advice on Choosing a Job and Career Path Inside or Outside of the Legal Profession:

By the time you reach your third year of law school, most law students will have chosen a career path. Life, however, does not always cooperate with your well-thought-out plans. Very often family, debt or job location will prevent law students from embarking on a journey of choice. That is fine! I will continue to stress that law school training actually prepares you for a variety of professions. Several of my classmates from law school have never practiced law and are extremely happy and very successful. But remember there is often more than one path to get to the same place. If there is an opportunity outside of the legal profession that you believe will put you on a happiness trajectory, jump on that train and take a comfortable seat.

Choosing a path inside the legal profession is the choice most law students make. As I said earlier, law school trains you for a variety of professions. Practicing law, however, hones skill sets that make you desirable and almost essential to every profession. So, if the opportunity presents itself to begin your career within the legal profession, and if it is something you are comfortable with, do not hesitate. Hone your skills early and often, and be prepared to pivot when the next opportunity presents itself.

Advice on Achieving Career Success and Advancement:

Simple: Master the art of the pivot. In other words, always be able to turn right or left at a moment's notice. During your legal career, you must constantly hone your skills as an attorney and find ways to DISTINGUISH yourself amongst your peers.

You must also continually develop relationships in your chosen concentration and widen your networking circles. You do yourself a disservice by only networking with your colleagues. Don't be afraid to consider other opportunities. Again, you are an attorney and as such, you have multiple skill sets that are useful in banking, marketing, technology, retail, insurance and healthcare.

If you are seeking advancement in your firm or corporation, it goes back to DISTINGUISHING yourself to the decision makers, strategic networking and having a reliable mentor that can help you navigate the often massive yet invisible hurdles that lie within your firm or organization.

Advice on Overcoming the Additional Challenges Black Law Students and Lawyers Face:

It is absolutely true that Black law students and lawyers experience hardships that others do not. It is important that lawyers remember that the legal profession is still one of the least diverse professions in the United States. As such, you will be treated differently. If you are aware of this probability, then you are better equipped to deal with it when it occurs. It is at that moment that you should reach out to your resources. Discuss with your mentors how you should deal with the problem and definitely find a solution. You cannot simply allow the challenges to languish. You must resolve them with a well-thought-out strategic plan. You are an attorney now. You are trained to identify, analyze and solve problems masqueraded as challenges. Personal challenges are no different: identify the problem, analyze it and then find a solution. Your mentors can always provide assistance because they have undoubtedly experienced and overcome the same challenges.

Additionally, be true to thyself. Know who you are and be the best that YOU can be. Have confidence that YOU are just as good as anyone else. You are going to get a lot of advice telling you to be someone other than yourself: resist it! That is the short game. You are in this for the long haul and being the best YOU is more important than trying to be like someone else for someone else.

Best Advice I Received Regarding Law School and the Legal Profession:

The best advice I received regarding law school and the law profession came from my older brother Thomas Donaldson. When I was in college, he would always tell me that the law, if used properly, could make the world a better place. He instilled in me that lawyers were the instruments of justice and fair play and that because we had seen so much hatred and unfair treatment by law enforcement that we needed to use the law to balance the scales.

Worst Advice I Received Regarding Law School and the Legal Profession:

When I was a senior at St. Augustine's University, I was also one of the student ambassadors. In that capacity, anytime a prominent person visited the school, I would meet them and represent the student body. On one occasion, a member of the George Bush family (I think Jon Bush) visited. While in the library conference room sitting at the conference room table, Mr. Bush leaned over to me and asked, "Well, what do you want to do after college?" I looked at him and responded, "I intend to go to law school." He then said to me without hesitation, "Well, don't we have enough lawyers?" And I responded, with the same lack of hesitation, "Not enough good ones." The president of our university and everyone in that room looked at me like I was crazy. I often wondered whether he would have asked a student that question at the University of North Carolina Chapel Hill or Duke University. I don't know whether he was really implying that I shouldn't go to law school or that I wasn't worthy of going to law school. Whatever he was implying, I needed to make it crystal clear to him that not only was I going to law school, but that I was going to be a "good lawyer" thereafter.

Best Advice I Would Give to an Aspiring Black Lawyer:

Keep your eyes open; complacency is your enemy; and DISTINGUISH yourself at whatever you are doing by making yourself relevant and essential.

Thoughts About Why Earning a Law Degree Is a Powerful Credential for African Americans and Why There Is a Need for More African American Lawyers:

At just about every meaningful point in African American history, there was an African American attorney leading the charge. In 1900, two Howard students passed the Virginia Bar Exam proving that Black people had the acumen and intellect to take and pass bar exams. Then, in 1902, an African American attorney, James Hayes, argued against Virginia's 1902 Constitution that disenfranchised African Americans. We can never forget that the renowned Charles Hamilton Houston fought Jim Crow Laws at every turn and laid the framework for Thurgood Marshall to show the world that African Americans deserved an equal place on American soil. Indeed, African American attorneys have been leading the charge to change the laws that affect every aspect of American life since 1900. Being a lawyer is indeed a license that automatically brings a certain level of credibility to every word I say or every line I write.

Today, however, we are facing the rise of a dormant dragon determined to burn down all that people have fought and died for. The federal judiciary is currently being stacked with ultraconservative judges who were specifically trained and selected to re-interpret over 100 years of Constitutional Law. I fear that we have become oblivious to the possibility that there are those out there who are determined to take this country back to a time when certain segments of society feared to walk or speak in public. We have become complacent in our comfort. This country, now more than ever, needs African American lawyers that have the architectural skill to design and build legal walls that will withstand a tsunami of hatred. They must understand that their foe is also well versed in history and knows what has worked against them in the past. So our new lawyers must play chess, not checkers; play the long game rather than the short one; and must be willing to choose methods of victory that have not been utilized in the past.

Thoughts About Whether and Why Law School Is Worth the Financial Investment:

Law school is worth the financial investment because there is so much you can do with a law degree. You can enter the legal profession or embark on a myriad of other pursuits in a variety of industries. Moreover, if you join the law profession (and I hope that you do), the skills you acquire practicing law are skills that are immediately transferrable: organizational skills, analytical skills, writing skills, issue-spotting skills, problem solving skills, and interviewing skills. Once you graduate from law school, you are marketable. If you practice law and hone your skills, you are relevant, necessary and essential to the efficient operation of any organization.

LEGACY AND SUCCESS

My Most Outstanding Accomplishments:

Personally: Becoming a father to two wonderful boys and marrying an outstanding woman.

Professionally: Having a deciding seat at the table where decisions are made relating to who may or may not become judges in the state of New York.

Other: Coaching, teaching, and speaking. Anytime I see the light bulb illuminate in one of my athletes, students or audiences while coaching, teaching or speaking, it feels absolutely magnificent.

The Legacy I Hope to Leave:

That I was a great father and great husband. That I truly believed you should lift as you climb. That I never forgot where I came from. And that because others helped me succeed, I am dedicated to helping others in their paths toward success.

The Secret to My Success:

Preparation, support and being the best ME possible.

Linda M. Dunson, J.D., LL.M.
Presiding Judge
309th Family Judicial District
Harris County
Houston, Texas

"A leader molds its prodigy in a manner which encourages creativity and self-direction as well as ensuring replication of values."

– Linda M. Dunson

Success is . . . being able to balance faith, spirituality and thought process outside of the confines of laws of nature in a manner that maintains inner peace and personal happiness without desecrating the love for, respect for and concern for humanity.

PERSONAL FAVORITES

Favorite Quotes: "The greatest glory in living lies not in never falling, but in rising every time we fall." - Nelson Mandela

"This book of the law shall not depart out of thy mouth; but thou shalt meditate therein day and night, that thou mayest observe to do all that is written therein; for then thy shalt make thy way prosperous, and then thou shalt have good success." - Joshua 1:8

Favorite Books: *I Know Why the Caged Bird Sings* by Maya Angelou; *Makes Me Wanna Holler* by Nathan McCall; *Success Runs in Our Race: The Complete Guide to Effective Networking in the Black Community* by George C. Fraser; *To Kill A Mockingbird* by Harper Lee; *Savage Inequalities* by Jonathan Kozol; *The Souls of Black Folk* by W.E.B. DuBois; *Think and Grow Rich* by Napoleon Hill; *Up From Slavery* by Booker T. Washington; *Jack Reacher Series* by Lee Child; *Yellow Crocus* by Laila Ibrahim

Favorite Movies: *The Jerk; The Green Mile; Forrest Gump; The Color Purple; Eyes on the Prize; Being Black in America; Selma; Long Walk to Freedom*

Favorite Music Genres: Gospel; Blues; R&B; Motown Sounds

Favorite Musical Artists: Michael Jackson; Barry White; Whitney Houston; Anita Baker; Yanni

Favorite Law School Classes: Tax; Contracts; Constitutional Law; Family Law

Favorite Legal Cases: *U.S. v. Fordice,* 505 U.S. 717 (1992); *Ayers v. Musgrove,* I studied this discrimination in higher education lawsuit while in law school and actually got the opportunity to write a brief and a be an appellant's lawyer in the appeal of the case before the Fifth Circuit (*Ayers v. Thompson,* 2004).

Favorite Hobbies: Volunteering in the community; Reading; Traveling; Visiting museums; Watching movies; Watching documentaries on African American history; Observing nature

Favorite Attorney Role Model: Honorable Craig A. Washington, an example of "my brothers' keeper" and former U.S. Congressman

FAMILY AND BACKGROUND

Where Born and Raised: Huntsville, Texas

Family Socioeconomic and Educational Background:

I am the fourth of six children who were raised by a single mother. I am the only child in my immediate family to attend college and the first generation to attend and graduate law school. I grew up in a very "economically poor" and racially segregated community. Most of the homes in my neighborhood were clapboard and unpainted. My mother taught me that being poor was never an excuse to not be at my best. The neighborhood was involved in raising, disciplining and teaching its children. Our role models – teachers, preachers, doctors, businessmen, etc. - lived in our neighborhood (though their homes were often painted and in better condition). Having a constant faith in God, looking out for my brothers and sisters, loving my neighbors, being a person of integrity, having a good work ethic, respecting my time and the time of others, and to always fight on the side of right, were a few of the values instilled in me by my mother and my community.

THE DECISION TO BECOME A LAWYER

When and Why I Decided to Become a Lawyer:

I decided to become a lawyer while attending the University of Houston working on my bachelor's degree in sociology and psychology. There were very few African American students in the classes in which I was enrolled; and the professors openly made racially discriminatory remarks in support of the academic inferiority of African Americans advanced in *The Bell Curve*. (See the book entitled *The Bell Curve: Intelligence and Class Structure in American Life* by Richard J. Herrnstein and Charles Murray (1994).)

I was well aware of the social and psychological constructs which influenced the behaviors of individuals. I had an enlightening moment after listening to several of my professors' derogatory remarks. I concluded that the social and psycho constructs that guided behaviors also provided the foundation for our written laws. If the laws are written in such a way that favors one race over another race, it is clear how the law's legal injustice contributes to social injustice since by its nature of disparate punishment it promotes a message of inferiority of ethnic minorities.

Although I was offered a sociology fellowship by the University of Houston, I decided that I needed to position myself in the best possible place to effect social and perhaps psychological change; hence, I became a lawyer.

EDUCATIONAL ACHIEVEMENTS

High School: Huntsville High School (Huntsville, Texas)

College/University: University of Houston - Central (Houston, Texas)

Undergraduate Degree: Bachelor of Arts (B.A.)

Majors: Psychology and Sociology

College Honors, Achievements and Activities: Graduated *magna cum laude* "with high distinction"; Selected for Honors Biology; *Academic Recognition,* Dean's List; *Internship,* Northwest Assistance Ministries (Homeless Shelter)

Law School: Thurgood Marshall School of Law, Texas Southern University (Houston, Texas)

Law School Degree and Graduation Year: Juris Doctor/Doctor of Jurisprudence (J.D.) - Class of 2001

Law School Honors, Achievements and Activities: *Articles Editor,* Thurgood Marshall School of Law TMSL Law Review; *Awardee,* CALI Excellence for the Future Award® (The Center for Computer-Assisted Legal Instruction) in Legal Research and Writing (earned highest score in class); *Awardee,* American Jurisprudence Award, Consumer Law (earned highest grade in class); *Academic Recognition,* Dean's List; *Treasurer,* Student Bar Association; *Member,* Phi Delta Phi International Legal Honor Society

Other Graduate or Professional Degrees: Master of Laws (LL.M.) in Taxation, University of Houston Law Center (Houston, Texas)

Additional Education: Certification, Basic Mediation; Certification, Advanced Family Law Mediation; *Participant,* State Bar of Texas Evidence Academy; *Participant,* Texas Lawyers Care Trial Academy; *Participant,* Texas Criminal Defense Lawyers Association (TCDLA) Trial Academy; License, U.S. Customs Broker

PROFESSIONAL ACCOMPLISHMENTS

State Bar Membership (Where Licensed to Practice): Texas

Other Legal Experience: *Chief Operating Officer,* Global Ports Solutions, LLC; *Attorney,* Law Offices of Linda M. Dunson; *Director of Legal Programs,* Houston Branch, National Association for the Advancement of Colored People (NAACP); *Contract Attorney,* Donovan Watkins; *Associate Attorney,* Alvin O. Chambliss, Civil Rights Attorney; *Judicial Extern,* Judge Greendyke, U.S. Southern District Bankruptcy Court; *Judicial Extern,* Judge Nancy Johnson, U.S. Southern District Court; *Civil Externship,* U.S. Customs and Border Patrol, U.S. Department of Justice

Professional Organizations: *Member,* Houston Lawyers Association; *President,* Houston Lawyers Association (2007-2008); *Member,* Houston Lawyers Association; *Member,* Association of Women Attorneys; *Member,* National Center for State Courts; *Member,* National Association of Women Judges; *Member,* National Council of Juvenile and Family Court Judges; *Member,* Texas Center for the Judiciary

Post-Law School Honors, Achievements, Activities, and Community Involvement: *Listed Honoree and Community Leader Recognition,* Who's Who Among Black Houston (2010); *Honoree,* President of the Year, National Bar Association (2008); *Member,* Class XXIX, Project Blueprint Leadership Training; *Member,* Law Advisory Board, Children at Risk; *Senior Companion,* Jewish Community Center; *Volunteer,* Houston Volunteer Lawyers Program; *Career Speaker,* Bush High School, Fort Bend Independent School District (Richmond, Texas); *Panelist,* Annual Property Preservation Workshop, Houston Lawyers Association; *Panelist,* Panel Discussion: Election Protection and Voter's Rights, National Bar Association National Convention (2008); *Panelist,* Panel Discussion: Is America Ready for a Black President?: From a Democrat and Republican Perspective, Black Law Students Association (BLSA), South Texas College of Law; *Panelist,* Panel Discussions: Solo Practice; Networking with Lawyers, National Black Pre-Law Conference; *Member,* Law Practice Management Committee, State Bar of Texas; *Keynote Speaker,* Martin Luther King Annual Commemorative Program (Crockett, Texas); *Poster Feature,* Featured on "African Americans & the Vote" Poster (national Black history poster) (2020); *Public Service Announcement (PSA) Feature,* Featured in Public Service Announcement, Houston 19 Video Census 2020, U.S. Census Bureau; *Awardee,* Happy Experience Exemplary Leadership and Outstanding Contributions to the Community Award, She's Happy Hair and She's Happy Foundation (2019); *Featured Speaker,* 2020 South Early High School Graduates Video (Houston, Texas); *Awardee,* Black History Award for Achievement, Mt. Zion Missionary Baptist Church (2020) (Huntsville, Texas); *Special Recognition,* International Women's Day and African American Women Elected to the Judiciary, Fort City Chapter, The Links, Incorporated; *Awardee,* History Maker Award, Epsilon Phi Chapter, Iota Phi Lambda Sorority, Inc. (2019); *Awardee,* Maroon & Gray Heart & Soul Spirit Award, Texas Southern University (2019); *Honoree,* Exemplary Service to Judicial and Legal Community in Family Law, Thurgood Marshall School of Law, Texas Southern University (2019); *Awardee,* Distinguished Alumni Award for Commitment to Fairness and Justice, MLK Jazz Brunch & Award Ceremony (2020)

LESSONS LEARNED: MY RECOMMENDATIONS FOR YOUR FUTURE ACTIONS BASED ON MY PAST EXPERIENCE

Advice on Making the Choice to Apply to and Attend Law School:

As best as you can, make sure going to law school is what you want to do. Do not let your motive be the money you hope to derive from the practice of law, but let your choice be driven by the passion you have to use the skills that you will gain during your study of law, to solve problems in order to enhance the human condition.

Advice on Law School Preparation:

Law school requires a lot of time and focus; therefore, having a good mentor is essential. Law school requires heightened work-life balance skills because it tends to be very stressful for those who may have families. Therefore, it is very important to sit down with your spouse/family before entering law school to discuss your time constraints, financial capabilities and other unforeseen issues, which may impact the family while attending law school; and discuss how you all as a family will face and resolve these issues. Additionally, read a lot and hone your critical thinking skills.

Advice on Applying to and Selecting a Law School:

Thoroughly research several law schools looking at their bar passage rates, diversity, and curriculum among other things. Once it is decided which schools you may want to attend, make sure you meet the school's qualifications, i.e., Grade Point Average (GPA), Law School Admission Test (LSAT) score, etc. If you need a higher GPA, then take college classes to raise your GPA. Also take an LSAT prep course. Finally, I suggest writing a personal statement that is in line with the school's mission and tailored specifically to the instructions in the school's admission packet.

Advice Regarding Academic Success, Co-Curricular and Extra-Curricular Participation, and Social Engagement in Law School:

Always allow time to study. Unlike undergrad, law school doesn't allow for playtime. Mastering the first-year curriculum is crucial to your success. Make sure you read your cases and learn how to brief them; it will help to develop your critical skills. Learn your study style and do not deviate from it. Do not hesitate to use law supplements if they help you grasp and understand the information quicker.

Advice on Preparing for and Taking the Bar Exam:

Take a test preparation course and practice, practice, practice essay writing and taking the multi-state. Prepare a study schedule and stick to it. Learn mnemonic devices to help you learn the information quicker. Take previous bar practice exams under timed conditions.

Advice on Achieving Career Success and Advancement:

It is important that you always know your objective and never lose your focus. Always have a mentor; and, always use every encounter with other persons as an opportunity to advance your endgame.

Advice on Overcoming the Additional Challenges Black Law Students and Lawyers Face:

Most often Black law students may have to become solo practitioners. Know that you have value and you are competent to practice law. Decide which area of law you are interested in practicing and build your niche around that area. Take Continuing Legal Education (CLE) courses on the targeted area and if possible, find opportunities to speak on the legal subject matter at churches, civic centers, etc. Network, Network, and Network – networking provides an opportunity for you to showcase yourself and your product before different genres of professionals who may be in need of your service or who may be able to refer someone else to you for your service.

Best Advice I Received Regarding Law School:

Unfortunately, I received my advice regarding law school after I had entered law school. Nevertheless, I was able to apply the principles of developing my own study style, using my time wisely and asking the professors questions no matter how dumb I think the questions may be.

Best Advice I Received Regarding the Legal Profession:

As for the legal profession, I was advised to:

Always have a mentor to advise you on areas of law which are unfamiliar to you.

Always invest in your profession, buy the best books and attend Continuing Legal Education (CLE) courses.

Always know your worth; the client will not value your time if you don't.

Always answer the phone when a fellow lawyer calls.

Always go to court prepared and dressed professionally.

Always respond promptly to a grievance which has been filed against you. Your license is hard to get, yet it's easy to lose.

Always keep a network of lawyers who you can call on for support and guidance and to be the voice of reason.

Never breach the Rules of Ethics nor compromise your integrity for a client.

The legal profession is changing so always diversify to have several streams of income.

LEGACY AND SUCCESS

My Most Outstanding Accomplishments:

- Being elected in 2018 as one of the history making "Black Girl Magic" Houston 19 African American female judges.

- Serving as the brief writer and appellant's counsel in the famous *Ayer/Fordice* case.

- Hosting a countywide weekend legal clinics and recruiting 60+ volunteer lawyers to low-income individuals on various legal issues including family law.

- Collaborating with multiple organizations and public officials to host an Annual Property Preservation platform whereby panelists inform the low-income community about how to keep or redeem inherited real estate.

- Organizing over 100 attorneys and co-hosting an Election Protection non-partisan effort along with the Lawyers Committee for Civil Rights to protect the rights of voters on election day (2002 -2010).

- Creating a system of taking legal services to the indigent families in underprivileged communities as opposed to having them bear the burden of trying to commute to the legal service providers; See *Empowering the Client Through Knowledge: Legal Services with a Twist - NAACP Legal Redress Program* by Linda M. Dunson (Texas Lawyers Care 2009).

- Mentoring as many young lawyers as I possibly can and providing courtroom internships.

The Legacy I Hope to Leave:

I hope to leave footsteps in the sand just as Christ. I want it to be said that I carried my brother, my sister when they could not carry themselves. I want it to be said that I lived by example; that I was willing to get in the trenches and fight besides the lowly. I want it to be said that my love was reflective. I want it to be said that I respected the time I was given and used it wisely.

The Secret to My Success:

1) My faith - Proverbs 18:16: "A man's gift makes room for him, and bringeth him before great men." I believe that my ability to think critically and my zeal to protect the rights of others are my gift from God and are to be used in fulfilling His purpose for my life. And, without much effort on my part, I have often found myself in places where my gift has been critical to the happiness and safety of others.

2) Seeing myself as a conduit, a vessel used to bless others - I am a link in a chain consisting of my fellow colleagues, my family, my friends whom I need to carry out my purpose. They empower, support and love me in spite of and encourage me to be me and to let my gifts flow to where they are most useful.

3) Humility - staying humble and accessible to others, knowing that although I worked hard I still did not make it to my destination by my hard work alone.

Practical Wisdom for Those on the Path to Lawyerhood

Beverly Caro Duréus, Esq., Th.M., D.Min.
Clinical Professor of Legal Research, Writing, and Advocacy
Dedman School of Law at Southern Methodist University
Dallas, Texas

"Grow up, but never outgrow Jesus or a healthy imagination."
– Beverly Caro Duréus

Success is . . . being the person you were created by God to be and utilizing your gifts and skills in that capacity to the best of your ability.

PERSONAL FAVORITES

Favorite Quotes: "Don't be late for now." – Delores Martin

"If you don't stand for something, you will fall for anything." – Author Unknown

"Trust in the LORD with all your heart and lean not on your own understanding; in all thy ways acknowledge Him and He will make your paths straight." - Proverbs 3:5-6

Favorite Books: I enjoy fiction, and books related to theology and law. I enjoy audio books by wordsmiths – Charles W. Swindoll, Dr. Anthony T. Evans, Bishop T.D. Jakes, and Beth Moore. Other favorites include: *The Holy Bible* (New International Version) – including Greek interlinear; *Saving My Assassin* by Virginia Prodan; *Evidence That Demands a Verdict* by Josh McDowell; *Faces at the Bottom of the Well* by Derrick Bell; *The Power of a Praying Woman* by Stormie Omartian; *The Shack* by William P. Young; *Holiday Island* by Gwendolyn V. Campbell and Dr. Beverly Caro Duréus; *Mother's Notes* by Gwendolyn V. Campbell; *This Present Darkness* by Frank E. Peretti; *Piercing the Darkness* by Frank E. Peretti; *Left Behind* by Jerry B. Jenkins and Tim LaHaye

Favorite Movies: *The Passion; Selma; War Room; One Night with the King; Walking with the Giants; All American; Courageous; The Remaining; Left Behind (2014); 2012; The Book of Eli; Fireproof*

Favorite Songs: "The Blessing" by Kari Jobe; "King of Glory" by the Pentecostals of Alexandria

Favorite Music Genres: Christian contemporary music; Christian jazz; Symphonic music

Favorite Musical Artists: Kirk Whalum; Tom Braxton

Favorite Classes: Torts; Civil Procedure; Juvenile Law

Favorite Legal Cases: *Palsgraf v. Long Island R.R. Co.* (about foreseeability); and *Brown v. Board of Education* and *Plessy v. Ferguson* (as a result of what they have meant to the advancement of African Americans and my home state of Kansas).

Favorite Hobbies: Teaching and preaching *The Bible*; Studying prophecy and apocalyptic literature; Watching apocalyptic movies and videos; Traveling; Bowling; Going to Broadway plays and live theatre productions; Entertaining; Going to our son's basketball games and watching him run track; Writing poetry and short stories; Encouraging and motivating students; Watching the KC Chiefs and Dallas Cowboys

Favorite Attorney Role Models: Real person - H. Ron White (Dallas, Texas); TV character - Perry Mason

FAMILY AND BACKGROUND

Where Born and Raised: Kansas City, Kansas

Family (Spouse/Partner and Children): Spouse - Dr. Edsel Duréus; Child - (son) Edsel II

Family Socioeconomic and Educational Background: I am from a middle/working-class family with a strong sense of community and a strong faith in God. My maternal grandmother was college educated and my mother was a firm believer in education and excellence. My father was a wonderful provider for all of our educational pursuits. I come from a family of overachievers and all of my siblings attended college and as the youngest of five, they set the bar pretty high. It was hard to escape the fact that I was a "Caro," a family well-connected and well-respected in our community.

THE DECISION TO BECOME A LAWYER

When and Why I Decided to Become a Lawyer: I graduated from law school in 1986. It was destiny for me to become a lawyer. The desire to do so has been within me since the 3rd grade. I believe that it was a God-planted desire, and from a young age I enjoyed oral advocacy, mediating disputes, and nurturing, protecting and representing people. Those character traits resulted in me being a litigator, law professor, and most recently, a Christian mediator.

EDUCATIONAL ACHIEVEMENTS

High School: Sumner High School and Sumner Academy of Arts and Sciences (Kansas City, Kansas)

College/University: Drake University (Des Moines, Iowa)

Undergraduate Degree: Bachelor of Arts (B.A.)

Major: Public Administration/Political Science

College Honors, Achievements and Activities: *Listed Honoree,* Who's Who in American Colleges and Universities (1983); *Basileus (President),* Eta Tau Chapter, Alpha Kappa Alpha Sorority, Inc. (1982-83); *Vice President,* Black Students Organization (1981); *Member,* Black Gospel Choir (1979-1983)

Law School: Drake University Law School (Des Moines, Iowa)

Law Degree and Graduation Year: Juris Doctor/Doctor of Jurisprudence (J.D.) - Class of 1986

Law School Honors, Achievements, Activities, and Community Involvement: *Intern,* Chief Judge William Stuart, United States District Court for the Southern District of Iowa (1986); *Academic Recognition,* Dean's List (1983-1986); *Member,* Order of the Barristers (national honor society) (1986); *Vice Justice,* Phi Alpha Delta Legal Fraternity International (1985-1986); *Member,* Phi Alpha Delta Legal Fraternity International (1983-1986); *Chairman,* Moot Court Board (1985-1986); *Awardee,* Rodney L. Hudson Senior Advocacy Award (1986); *Advocacy Finalist,* Iowa Supreme Court Day (1986); *Best Oralist Award,* Midwest Regional Moot Court Competition (1985); *Member,* Frederick Douglass Moot Court Team (1983-1986); *Vice President,* Black Law Students Association (1984-1985); *Member,* Black Law Students Association (1983-1986); *Awardee,* Mediation Award, Iowa Civil Rights Commission (1985); *Criminal Law Intern,* Alfredo G. Parrish, P.C. (1983-1985); *Summer Associate,* Blackwell Sanders Matheny Lombari & Weary (1985); *Listed Honoree,* Who's Who in American Law Schools (1986); *Member,* National Moot Court Team (1985-1986); *Member,* Midwest Moot Court Team (1985-1986)

Other Graduate or Professional Degrees: Doctor of Ministry (D.Min.), Perkins School of Theology, Southern Methodist University (Dallas, Texas); Master of Theology (Th.M.), Dallas Theological Seminary (Dallas, Texas)

Additional Education: Mediator

PROFESSIONAL ACCOMPLISHMENTS

State Bar Membership (Where Licensed to Practice Law): Texas

Other Legal Experience: *Co-Executive Editor,* The International Lawyer; *Co-Executive Editor,* The Year in Review; *Attorney,* Beverly Caro Duréus, Attorney at Law; *Associate Professor of Law,* Drake University Law School; *Shareholder,* Chapman & Reese, PC; *Senior Counsel and Ecclestical Section Chair,* Adorno, Yoss, White & Wiggins, n/k/a White & Wiggins, L.L.P. ; *Associate,* Gardere & Wynne; *Mediator,* Iowa Civil Rights Commission; Founder and President: Katallasso Alternative Dispute Resolutions – Christian Conciliations (K-ADR™)

Other Professional Work Experience: *Founder and President,* Katallasso Ministries International™, a division of Katallasso Enterprises™; *Vice President and Director,* Women's Ministries and Christian Education, Thanksgiving Tabernacle Bible Fellowship

Professional Organizations: *President,* Dallas Association of Black Women Attorneys (1992); *Vice President,* Dallas Association of Black Women Attorneys (1988); *Historian,* Dallas Association of Black Women Attorneys (1991); *Member,* Dallas Association of Black Women Attorneys (1986-1994); *Member,* J.L. Turner Legal Association (1986-1994); *Director at Large,* J.L. Turner Legal Association (1988-1989); *Member,* American Bar Association Section of International Law; *Member,* Dallas Bar Association; *Member,* William Mac Taylor American Inn of Court (1990-1991); *Member,* State Bar of Texas; *Member,* African American Lawyers and Litigation Sections, State Bar of Texas; *Member,* National Bar Association; *Member,* Association of American Law Schools; *Member,* Dallas Bar Foundation

Post-Law School Honors, Achievements, Activities, and Community Involvement: *Honoree,* Marquis Who's Who in America (lawyers) 2020; *Nominee,* Southern Methodist University's Provost's Teacher of the Year Award (2019-2020); *Listed Honoree,* "Leader in Academia" Recognition, Who's Who in Black Dallas, 4th Edition (2018) and 5th Edition (2019); *Member,* Golden Key International Honor Society (2015-2016); *Awardee,* Faithful Servant-Leader Award,

Thanksgiving Tabernacle Bible Fellowship (2015); *Honoree,* Striving for Success Recognition, Black Law Students Association (2016); *Camp Coordinator/Junior Achievement Affiliate Instructor,* Vacation Business and Bible School (2015-2016); *Board Member,* Van Ross Foundation; *Founder and President,* Katallasso Enterprises™; *Founder and President,* Katallasso Ministries International™; *Originator,* Scripture Ware Originals™; *Vice President,* Thanksgiving Tabernacle Bible Fellowship; *Director of Women's Ministries,* Thanksgiving Tabernacle Bible Fellowship; *Director of Christian Education,* Thanksgiving Tabernacle Bible Fellowship; *Pastor of Women's and Children's Ministries,* Thanksgiving Tabernacle Bible Fellowship; *Executive Director,* Taking the Word to the World Ministries, Inc.; *Advisory Board Member,* Stepping Stones Mentoring Ministry; *Board Member,* Troubleshooting for Christ; *Faculty Advisor,* Black Law Student Association; *Faculty Advisor,* Christian Legal Society; *Co-Executive Editor,* ABA/SIL (American Bar Association/Section of International Law) The International Lawyer and The Year in Review; *General Partner,* GB Enterprises: God's Books; *Member,* CAYA (Come As You Are) Mentoring Enterprise; *Board Member,* H.O.P.E. Farm, Inc. (1992-1994); *Volunteer,* Mission Arlington; *Volunteer,* Transformation Prayer Group - Cedar Hill; *Volunteer,* Cedar Hill Police Department Chaplain Team; *Member,* Alpha Kappa Alpha Sorority, Inc.; *Honoree,* Who's Who in American Colleges and Universities (1986); *Awardee,* Up and Coming Trailblazer's Award, Dollar and Sense (1991); *Teacher Appreciation Award,* Black Law Students Association (1990); *Article Contributor,* Gospel Time's Magazine (1994); Who's Who in American Colleges and Universities (1998-1999); *Mediator-Trainee,* Sidney Stahl, Mediator; *Ex officio Member,* Judicial Clerk and Diversity Issues Committees, SMU Dedman School of Law; *Member,* Admissions Committee, SMU Dedman School of Law; *Faculty Advisor,* Black Law Students Association, SMU Dedman School of Law; *Former Member,* Faculty Review and Investigation Committee of the Honor Council, SMU Dedman School of Law; *Volunteer,* North Texas Legal Services (1987-1994); *Volunteer,* Pro Bono Services (1994-Present)

LESSONS LEARNED: MY RECOMMENDATIONS FOR YOUR FUTURE ACTIONS BASED ON MY PAST EXPERIENCE

Advice on Law School Preparation:

Learn the King's English early on! If you can't write what you're thinking, no one will ever know how bright you are! If possible, try to be a CLEO Fellow (Council on Legal Education Opportunity). It's a great opportunity to take a test run at law school. Also, do take a Law School Admission Test (LSAT) prep course. Last, be mindful of your grade point average (GPA). It is calculated along with your LSAT score to yield an index number that will be a determining factor for law school admissions. The higher the index score, the higher the rank of the school to which you will likely be admitted.

Advice on Applying to and Selecting a Law School:

Apply broadly but go to the best school into which you are admitted. You should decide if you want to be a "big fish in a little pond" or a "little fish in a big pond." The size of the school can and likely will have an impact on your ultimate GPA. Once you get admitted, swim to win and don't be distracted by the fact that you are a person of color. You don't have time to deny who you are nor should you. Environments are richer as a result of diversity.

Advice Regarding Academic Success, Co-Curricular and Extra-Curricular Participation, and Social Engagement in Law School:

My favorite quote is from a wise seasoned woman who became a treasured friend in law school. She often said to me, "Don't be late for now." Since I love to multitask and could function on very little sleep, I loved being involved in activities. However, her quote reminded me of the need to make the main thing, the main thing. Do try to get involved in activities that you enjoy and especially those that will build your resume, but not at the expense of being prepared for class or making good grades. It is helpful to look at the table of contents of your textbooks to make sure you at least know where in the larger scheme of things a lecture is going to fall on each particular day so you can keep in mind the bigger picture. If you don't understand, ask for clarification or help. Professors are often different in their offices than you might find them to be in class – many really are approachable. As you outline, keep in mind that normally two cases do not stand for the same proposition. Be able to zoom in on the nuance that each case offers.

Advice on Preparing for and Taking the Bar Exam:

Attend a bar preparation course. It is also helpful to have a study partner. Time management is the key. Decide early on to make studying for the bar your full-time priority if you can. If at first you don't succeed, try again. Many great lawyers are not good test takers.

Advice on Choosing a Job and Career Path Inside or Outside of the Legal Profession:

Find something that you enjoy doing and do it with excellence.

Advice on Seeking Legal Job Opportunities and/or Creating One's Own Opportunities:

Begin planning now for the job that you want by being selective about what you post in cyberspace. Your history will eventually catch up with you. Attend functions hosted by prospective employers and present yourself in the most favorable light. Do your research on a firm before you meet its members, and be interesting and engaging. Do ask questions!!!! Be willing to work as an unpaid intern to gain experience. Offer to fly yourself in for an interview with a firm that does not recruit on your campus; if you land an interview and impress them, you might still get reimbursed. Learn and use great networking skills and follow-up with emails, calls and/or letters. Keep tabs of where your school's alumni are and use them as possible contacts. Use the services provided by your school's Career Placement department.

Advice on Overcoming the Additional Challenges Black Law Students and Lawyers Face:

We are living in a culture where, in many cases, expressing one's microaggression is becoming more acceptable. Thus, decide to be an agent of change and not a victim of another's ignorance. However, choose your fights carefully. It might serve you better to equip yourself with a law degree so that you can make a meaningful change to a system than to try to change the mind of a small-minded person whose opinion about you or an issue really does not matter. Beware of distractions. Like a leopard can't change its spots, a foolish person that you encounter seldom changes his or her mind. You will know when it is time to speak up about an issue, warped mindset, or an event. It's okay not to speak out about everything. In error, some may opine that you are not a voice, but only an echo. However, you will always know the truth is that you're just not interested in their conversations. Only a fool gives full vent to their thoughts.

Lawyers are often born leaders so when the situation calls for it - lead. Even an inarticulate presentation of the right point can lead to victory. Thus, do not let any limitation curtail you from contributing when necessary. There will be disparities in opportunities, so be prepared to be competitive and make it difficult for people to disregard you. If you are disregarded, forge your own path and establish your own practice if necessary. Achieve your dreams. The very organization, firm, or individual that disregarded you may not have the ability to discern a real diamond. People who lack discernment, or who are small-minded, do not make good business partners or associates.

In many cases, there may not be many people of color in your school, classes, or place of employment. If there is a support system where you are, seek it out. If there is not one, create one. Gravitate toward good people regardless of the ethnicity or color. Good character crosses ethnic and color divides. Look for what you have in common with others rather than just focusing on differences.

If sensitivity awareness will help your environment, suggest it to those who are in a position to make it happen. Know what your legal rights are pertaining to hostile environments and other disparities.

Best Advice I Received Regarding Law School and the Legal Profession:

Pray to get in, pray to succeed while in, and pray to be gainfully employed in a fulfilling practice after you finish. Prayer works!

Best Advice I Would Give to an Aspiring Black Lawyer:

Learn to network and get one or two good mentors. It is also good to have a "Nathan" in your life. This is the person who can tell you the truth, when you get off the right path.

After you "arrive" at the top, reach back. The measure of success is not just whether you "make it" but if you have also helped someone else to achieve their dream.

Thoughts About Why Earning a Law Degree Is a Powerful Credential for African Americans and Why There Is a Need for More African American Lawyers:

For too long people of color have been kept away from the table. Once at the table, people of color need to know how to engage properly and to make a contribution and a difference. A law degree can open a lot of doors. It can help a person to empower others by helping to eradicate injustices and to level the playing field. It equips individuals to be the voice for the voiceless. It can equip a person to have a legal answer and strategy when injustices and inequities such as gentrification befall the disenfranchised.

There is a need for more African American lawyers because there really is no longer any such thing as affirmative action. Many thus have to fight in a court of law to get or to keep what is rightfully theirs. We need jurists and law makers of color so that the laws being drafted will keep the playing field level and so that the laws that are in place will be applied fairly and without a disparate impact. As crimes against people of color continue to escalate, the fight for justice should escalate proportionately. Those having a law degree will have the access to the systems that can effectuate change.

A law school experience is definitely worth the financial investment because the skills obtained can be utilized for much more than going to the courthouse. A law student will learn how to analyze problems and to be a problem solver. The information is thus transferable to many different walks of life. While it might be an expensive venture, it is always good to invest in yourself. Material things fade away but what is in your mind is locked away. One only needs to use the information and keep one's mind sharp and active to maximize its effectiveness.

LEGACY AND SUCCESS

My Most Outstanding Accomplishments:

Personal: Marrying God's choice for me, my partner in ministry – Dr. Edsel Duréus, and the birth of our son – Edsel, II

Professional: Leaving my full-time law practice to follow the Lord's command to "feed His sheep".

The Legacy I Hope to Leave:

I hope to encourage my students and others to be the best lawyers they can be without breaking the rules or being unethical. I hope that they will see that faith and the practice of law need not be mutually exclusive.

The Secret to My Success:

Seeking first the Kingdom of God and His righteousness (and all other necessities of life will then be added) (Matthew 6:33); Taking my work seriously, but not always myself or others; Doing the right thing and doing all things in excellence.

Lacy L. Durham, Esq., M.B.A., LL.M.
Senior Manager
Deloitte Tax, LLP
Dallas, Texas

"Dare to operate in the spaces between excellent and extraordinary!"

"You have come a long way chasing your dreams, your hard work will pay off because what you do today determines what you'll get tomorrow."

— Lacy L. Durham

Success is . . . never ending possibilities created by determination, grit, and resilience.

PERSONAL FAVORITES

Favorite Quote: "Excellence is an art won by training and habituation. We do not act rightly because we have virtue or excellence, but we rather have those because we have acted rightly. We are what we repeatedly do. Excellence, then, is not an act but a habit." – Aristotle

Favorite Books: *Becoming* by Michelle Obama; *The Audacity of Hope* by Barack Obama; *Just Mercy: A Story of Justice and Redemption* by Bryan Stevenson; *The Firm* by John Grisham; *Invisible Man* by Ralph Ellison; *Song of Solomon* by Toni Morrison; *Strategize to Win: The New Way to Start Out, Step Up, Or Start Over in Your Career* by Carla Harris; *The Little Black Book of Success: Laws of Leadership for Black Women* by Elain Brown, Marsha Haygood, and Rhonda McClean; *Rebels in Law: Voices in History of Black Women Lawyers* by J. Clay Smith Jr.; *Expect to Win: 10 Proven Strategies for Thriving in the Workplace* by Carla A. Harris; *Earning It: Hard-Won Lessons from Trailblazing Women at the Top of the Business World* by Joann S. Lublin

Favorite Movies: *Black Panther; Malcolm X; The Great Debaters; Inside Man; Night Comes On; Dream Girls; Purple Rain; Marshall; Burning Cane; The Black Power Mixtape; Hidden Figures; Love Jones;* Anything by Marvel

Favorite Music Genres: Smooth R&B; Hip-Hop; Jazz

Favorite Song and Musical Artist: Any and everything by Prince

Favorite Law School Classes: Tax; Contracts; Business Formations; Civil Procedure; Elder Law; Juvenile Justice

Favorite Legal Cases: *Brown v. Board of Education of Topeka* (1954) - Reversed *Plessy v. Ferguson* "separate but equal" ruling and stated that segregation in public education is a denial of the equal protection of the laws.

Loving v. Virginia (1967) - The Court strikes down all state miscegenation laws which ushered in a civil rights movement because it found that people of any race, anywhere in the U.S. could get married.

Dred Scott v. Sandford (1857) - Ruled that Scott would remain a slave because as such he was not a citizen and could not legally sue in the federal courts. Subsequently, the *14th Amendment* overturned the Dred Scott decision by granting citizenship to all those born in the United States, regardless of color.

The Heart of Atlanta Motel, Inc. v. United States (1964) - Reasoned that discrimination by businesses had a big impact on Black people traveling, even when it was a small business, since negative effects could be far-reaching when added up. It fueled the Civil Rights Act that dismantled many forms of discrimination.

Matthew Shepard and James Byrd Jr. Hate Crimes Prevention Act (2009) - Birthed from two tragic criminal cases, the subsequent legislation held that federal authorities, including the Federal Bureau of Investigation, can investigate and prosecute hate crimes motivated by a victim's actual or perceived gender, sexual orientation, gender identity, or disability.

Gideon v. Wainwright (1963) - Held that state courts were required to appoint attorneys for those who could not afford their own counsel stating that "lawyers in criminal courts are necessities, not luxuries".

Reynold v. Sims (1964) - Ruled that the right to vote is a fundamental right, and equal participation is crucial. This decision made the government more democratic in nature.

Miranda v. Arizona (1966) - Held that law enforcement must advise suspects of their rights (to remain silent, to an attorney, and that anything they say can and will be used against them in a court of law) and failure to do so would prevent evidence obtained from being used in a trial unless the warnings had been given and expressly waived.

Favorite Hobbies: Traveling the world to explore history and culture; Enjoying the arts; Listening to live music; Theater; Cinema; Frequenting museums and festivals; Collecting art by Black artists and African masks

Favorite Attorney Role Models: Michelle Obama; Barack Obama; Lucy Terry Prince; Claire Babineaux Fontenot; Dr. Sadie Tanner Mossell Alexander; Barbara Jordan; Jane Bolin; Justice Thurgood Marshall; Justice Ruth Bader Ginsburg; Constance Baker Motley; Dennis Archer; Paulette Brown; Eric Holder, Jr.; Lorretta Lynch; Frank Muse Freeman; Elijah Eugene Cummings; Bryan Stevenson; Constance Baker Motley

FAMILY AND BACKGROUND

Where Born and Raised: Minden, Louisiana

Family Socioeconomic and Educational Background: In many aspects, I don't think my story is much different than your average kid from the deep south. I am the product of two people who somehow met at Grambling State University, fell in love, and married at the ripe age of 23. Both of my parents were college-educated and my mother held a master's degree. To their union two girls were born, me being the oldest.

My mother, a lifelong educator, specialized in providing innovative instruction to students with severe mental, physical, social and/or emotional delays. She encouraged me to run wild with my imagination and dream big; so, I did! I first dreamed of being a lawyer in elementary school. In fact, I would tell anyone who would listen that one day I was going to be a big-time lawyer and most importantly help others in need and be a voice for those that otherwise have no representation. My father started his career in the oil industry working for big-named companies and later retired as a corrections officer. He made sure we were protected and provided for at every turn.

Then, tragedy struck when my mother left school one day to get supplies for her students. She was in a car accident and died instantly; our family dynamics drastically changed. I can remember my grief-stricken father telling me soon thereafter that the only thing he wanted me to do was to fulfill my mother's wishes and "get a good education and be somebody." As a child, I had no idea what would result, but I knew that my father meant business; and who doesn't want to fulfill their mother's wishes.

The absence of a mother and one income created a dynamic in which we were now considered poor, disadvantaged, at risk and more. Society will have you labeled as anything but a success. However, my father refused to let his children become negative statistics and didn't want any of those labels for us. He recognized the challenge of a widowed, young, Black male raising two daughters and heroically faced it head on. Thankfully, my father was not a man of chance and knew right away that he needed assistance to help raise his two girls. He specifically sought out opportunities for educational advancement, leadership development, and mentorship. He knew that he would need the support of an entire village to help raise girls to be successful women. The investment of a village of educators, community leaders, and mentors during my educational endeavors has yielded unimaginable results. My mother's wish for me to earn a top education, my father's persistence, and the assistance of a village has allowed me to achieve my wildest dreams.

THE DECISION TO BECOME A LAWYER

When and Why I Decided to Become a Lawyer: I became a lawyer because at a very young age I knew my purpose and passion was to help people. In middle school, my father switched careers and became a corrections officer. One of his responsibilities was to transport inmates to their court proceedings. He came to know more than a few judges very well and would share my grand dreams of being a lawyer. As a result, a few judges allowed me to shadow them, tour chambers, candidly interview them and even sit at their benches. Those firsthand experiences solidified my desire to be a lawyer. I knew the law was the best avenue to acquire transferable skills to advocate for others, influence the change I wanted to see, and be a resource to uplift my community.

EDUCATIONAL ACHIEVEMENTS

High School: Minden High School (Minden, Louisiana)

College/University: University of Louisiana at Monroe (Monroe, Louisiana)

Undergraduate Degree: Bachelor of Business Administration (B.B.A.)

Majors: Accounting; Finance

College Honors, Achievements and Activities: *Listed Honoree,* Who's Who Among Students at American Universities and Colleges; *Academic Recognition,* President's/Dean's List; *Awardee,* National Founder's Award, Pi Sigma Epsilon; *Recipient,* Student Involvement Scholarship, University of Louisiana at Monroe; *Member,* Phi Eta Sigma; *Member,* Alpha Lambda Delta; *Member,* Omicron Delta Kappa; *Member,* Phi Kappa Phi; *Member,* Mortar Board; *Member,* Student Government Association; *Member,* Beta Alpha Psi; *Member,* Institute of Internal Auditors; *Member,* Strategies Targeting African American Retention and Transition (STAART); *Member,* Interdenominational Ensemble; *Member,* Residential Housing Association; *Member,* ULM 31

Law School: Southern University Law Center (Baton Rouge, Louisiana)

Law Degree and Graduation Year: Juris Doctor/Doctor of Jurisprudence (J.D.) - Class of 2006

Law School Honors, Achievements and Activities: *Treasurer,* Student Bar Association; *Participant,* Elder Law Clinic; *Participant,* Thurgood Marshall Mock Trial; *Pupil,* SULC Southern University Inn of Court; *Member,* Black Law Students Association (BLSA); *Member,* Women In Law; *Member,* Christians in Law; *Member,* Delta Theta Phi Law Fraternity; Bar Study Representative

Other Graduate or Professional Degrees: Master of Business Administration (M.B.A.), Louisiana Tech University (Ruston, Louisiana); Master of Laws (LL.M.) in Taxation, Southern Methodist University School of Law (Dallas, Texas)

Additional Education: Certificate, Mediation

PROFESSIONAL ACCOMPLISHMENTS

State Bar Memberships (Where Admitted to Practice Law): Louisiana; Texas

Other Legal Work Experience: *Managing Attorney*, Durham Law & Consulting (ERISA, Employee Benefits, Executive Compensation, Tax, Estate Planning)

Other Professional Work Experience: *Employee Benefits Advisor,* Employee Benefit Security Administration, U.S. Department of Labor; *In Charge Auditor,* Little and Associates, CPAs

Professional Organizations: *Member,* American Bar Association; *Member,* National Bar Association; *Member,* Louisiana Bar Association; Member, State Bar of Texas; *Member,* National Association of Black Accountants (NABA); *Member,* National Black MBA Association (NBMBAA); *Member,* Society of Human Resource Professionals (SHRM); *Member,* World Wide Employee Benefit Network (WEB)

Post-Law School Honors, Achievements, Activities, and Community Involvement: *Member,* Mayor's Star Council (2019-2020); *Cohort Member,* Emerging Leaders in Philanthropy (ELP), Communities Foundation of Texas (2019-2020); *Program Graduate,* Women Empowered to Lead in the Legal Profession (WE LEAD) (Leadership program), Dallas Bar Association (2018); *Awardee,* National TRiO Achievers Award, Council for Opportunity in Education (2019); *Alumni Spotlight,* University of Louisiana at Monroe University (Fall 2018); *Awardee,* Distinguished Alumnus Award, Southern University Law Center (2018); *Awardee,* History Makers Award, Southern Methodist University Black Alumni Association; *Listed Honoree,* Who's Who in Black Dallas (2017); *Awardee,* Athena Award, Dallas Regional Chamber Young Professionals Leadership (YPL) Program (2017); *Leadership Class Graduate,* Leadership Dallas (2017); *Awardee,* TRiO Achievers Award, Louisiana Association of Student Assistance (LASPA) (2016); *Awardee,* Young Leader Award, Dallas Women's Foundation (2016); *Magazine Feature,* Extraordinary Minorities in Texas Law, Texas Lawyer Magazine (2015); *Listed Honoree,* 40 Under 40, Dallas Business Journal (2013); *Honoree,* National Bar Association (NBA) and IMPACT Nation's Best Advocates, *40 Under 40* (2013); *Awardee,* Humanitarian Award, Young Lawyers Division, National Bar Association (NBA) (2013); *Honoree,* Outstanding Woman of Tomorrow, Altrusa International (2012); *Honoree,* Star of the Year, American Bar Association Young Lawyers Division (2013); *Scholar,* Young Lawyers Division, American Bar Association (2009–2010); *Honoree,* Star of the Quarter, Young Lawyers Division, American Bar Association (2012); *Fellow,* Business Law Section, American Bar Association (2010-2012); *Awardee,* Joseph M. Pritchard Inn Outstanding Director Award, Texas Young Lawyers Association (2011-2012); *Awardee,* President's Award of Merit, Texas Young Lawyers Association (2010–2011, 2012-2013); *Special Recognition,* "One to Watch," Dallas Bar Association (March 2010); *Leadership Class Graduate,* Dallas Bar Association (2008–2009); *Awardee,* Outstanding Young Lawyer Distinguished Career Award, Southern University Law Center (2011); *Leadership Class Graduate,* Business Council for the Arts (North Texas) (2009–2010); *Member,* Board of Directors, ChildCare Group; *Member,* Board of Directors, Dallas Theater Center; *Member,* Board of Directors, Diverse Attorney Pipeline Program (D.A.P.P.); *Member,* Board of Directors, Pipeline to Possibilities; *Member,* Advisory Council, National Diversity Council, *Advisory Council*; *Member,* Board of Directors, University of Louisiana at Monroe Alumni Association; *Member,* Junior League of Dallas; *Member,* Delta Sigma Theta Sorority, Inc.

LESSONS LEARNED: MY RECOMMENDATIONS FOR YOUR FUTURE ACTIONS BASED ON MY PAST EXPERIENCE

Advice on Law School Preparation:

Think carefully about your undergraduate major and how it will potentially relate to your future law school foundation and ultimate professional practice area. Focus on taking courses, participating in organizations, and activities that allow you to strengthen certain skills such as: reading comprehension, writing, advocacy, and communication.

In addition, spend the time talking to local lawyers to explore different practice areas and potential work environments. Never underestimate how real connections can influence and assist with future recommendations and/or employment references so be intentional about developing a network of professors, mentors, and others that you trust to provide guidance.

Advice on Applying to and Selecting a Law School:

Seek out opportunities to take Law School Admission Test (LSAT) prep classes and simulate practice tests in advance of the actual exam. Understand the financial impact of the next 3 to 4 years (during matriculation and one year after graduation) and consider how to prepare financially. Understand the timeline and deadlines for scholarships, grants, and free financial aid which are typically very early. Research to understand the different types of law schools, how grades are earned, the school's bar passage rates, what type of work graduates go on to do, etc. and select which aligns most based on your criteria. Update your resume and work on any items that are questionable (i.e., frequent job changes, gap years, lack of volunteer work, etc.). Get very comfortable telling your story even if it's tragic or less than desirable; being authentic will help you both fine-tune your application essays and help you solidify why you want to be a lawyer. Think about doing something fun for yourself the summer before law school starts because life changes drastically after day one. Seek out information about whether the law school offers pre-law summer courses to introduce you to basic legal concepts such as case briefing, outlining, IRAC (Issue-Rule-Analysis-Conclusion) methods, basic law school jargon and concepts. Check your ego and change your mindset because everyone that applies to law school is competitive and very intelligent; you will need to distinguish yourself.

Advice Regarding Academic Success, Co-Curricular and Extra-Curricular Participation, and Social Engagement in Law School:

Students should both strive to master academic success and demonstrate leadership qualities. Your academic achievements will initially get the attention of potential employers, but your ability to be a leader will give you credibility.

Law school is a great time to get involved with activities that will allow you to stand out but there is a balancing act to avoid burnout, overcommitting and compromising other aspects of your life. Students should look for opportunities and experiences both related to law school and in their respective communities that demonstrate the following: teamwork, navigating through challenge, and individual contribution to aid others. This time also allows you to develop interpersonal and soft skills that are critically important in the legal profession. This is the time to demonstrate personal integrity and showcase relevant skills such as commitment, loyalty, and respect for others, empathy, etc.

Your participation in activities is completely what you make of it. The more effort you put in, the more value you will get out of it. Use this time to get involved in areas that may be outside of your comfort zone which will give you experiences but also give you a sense of purpose in addressing social injustices that you are passionate about. Master these qualities and you will be sure to stand out amongst your peers and experience self-satisfaction.

Advice on Preparing for and Taking the Bar Exam:

The first step is making sure your mental fortitude is up for the challenge. You must understand the importance of the bar exam; passage sooner (rather than later) will build your confidence, get you into the job market faster – take this seriously! Take the time to know the testing rules, criteria, grading methodology, and score needed to pass in your jurisdiction. Select a bar prep provider that aligns with your studying style (e.g., read and memorize, highlight, live course instruction, self-study, flashcards, outlines, combination, etc.). Know your test-taking strengths and weaknesses and focus on the weaknesses more. Look for test patterns and be familiar with what subjects are tested most frequently and master those first. Form a small study group of three to four people to test your knowledge and collect feedback from others but also reserve individual study time. Secure two alternative study areas where you can concentrate (other than the library and your home). Keep your bar prep bag ready to go with all your needed tools (e.g., dictionary, prep books, highlighters, timers, snack bars, etc.). Don't cheat yourself by giving it a half effort - create a study routine and schedule and stick to it. Schedule breaks and at least one day of the week off to do something fun and rest. Eliminate as many distractions as possible (i.e., change your voicemail to let people know [that you are studying] during certain hours, remove social media distractions, set expectations with family, create a study uniform and meal schedule so you don't consume valuable time with deciding what to wear or eat, etc.). Simulate the actual timed exam at least three times with your study group and grade the results. Stay the course and get a good night's sleep the day before and leave it all on the exam.

Advice on Choosing a Job and Career Path Inside or Outside of the Legal Profession:

Dare to be different! The most important decision to make in choosing your career path is really doing the work to find what type of roles align with your purpose and passion. This is especially true because whatever you decide, you must show up to that career every day. It's also worthy to mention that you don't have to get it right the first time; you can keep trying until you find the right fit for you. That fit may also change as your life changes. If you know upfront that you desire a non-legal career right out of law school, make sure to take the classes or gain additional skills that you think are needed for that career. Whether it's private practice, public service, business related, being a social change agent or political in nature, being a lawyer is still a noble profession.

The attractiveness of law school is that you acquire so many transferable skills that you can leverage in many different careers. The education you receive will provide foundational skills, such as analytical thinking and persuasion capabilities, effective communication, research and public speaking that easily translate and provide value to many different career paths, both legal and nonlegal. You can easily use the tools that you have to reposition your strengths to meet the requirements of many other options.

If you don't do what you love, then you won't love what you do. You deserve both! You are the only one that is vested in your career. Be open and receptive to different opportunities.

Advice on Seeking Legal Job Opportunities and/or Creating One's Own Opportunities:

There is no one-size fits all approach. The legal profession is filled with experienced and capable attorneys, that sometimes make it challenging for Black lawyers to stand out. In addition, there are fewer jobs available in the traditional sense, which makes the ones available highly coveted and sought-after. In order to best position yourself for job opportunities, you should not underestimate the power of networking. Talk to people about what they do and how they achieved their success. Let other people be an advocate for you; the wider you cast your net, the better the chance you will find that legal opportunity. This networking should start your first year and continue throughout your career.

Whatever you choose, don't be deterred from opportunities that don't exactly match your background or skill set. Most employers are very interested in people with legal backgrounds because of the valuable skill set [they possess]. Learn to be clear about what you have learned and how those skills are trackable to the job opportunity at hand and advocate for yourself. Don't limit yourself to just Big Law. Think about other work environments such as boutique firms, legal aid, state or federal government, and in-house roles. Also be flexible in your approach to practice areas and industries; think about areas that overlap and try to find opportunities there.

Creating your own opportunities and business is exciting. However, don't let fear drive you to launch your business without being properly equipped. Successful entrepreneurs understand business. You will know the law, but the business of law is something totally different. Find mentors and other business owners that you can shadow and teach you the pitfalls to be successful. Don't try to do everything and surround yourself with other experts to fill in the gaps that you may have. Another way to create your own opportunities and build a solid business is to determine a niche practice area that you can excel at and create demand. Don't be afraid to do what no one else is doing. When making the choice, consider a niche that is in an area that you can fully immerse yourself in for the duration of your career. You will become the go-to person for that practice area over time.

Advice on Achieving Career Success and Advancement:

Your career is a marathon, so you must prepare for career success and advancement. You've trained a very long time enduring undergraduate studies, law school, and the bar exam. You have sacrificed time, finances, relationships, and more, but you can't let up. Getting the job is just the beginning; you must plan and be persistently dedicated to turn your collective experiences into a long and fulfilling career. You own your career at every turn and cannot expect anyone else to do the work for you. I recommend that every couple of years, you spend some time evaluating where you are in your career and asking questions that are most important to you. These questions might include: Does this path still meet my financial needs?; Is the amount of time I spend at work satisfactory?; Am I able to balance the demands with my personal life?; Is there a next level or upward growth opportunity?; Can I imagine myself here in the future? etc.

Take calculated risks and explore options. Network with people (other professionals and headhunters) that are in the practice area or environment that you aspire to work in. Develop your elevator speech and tell people what you want to do in a clear and concise manner while highlighting the skills that you already possess. Study the people that already have the career that you want to determine where the gaps are in your skillset. Practice taking criticism and feedback and learn from what is offered. Move on when necessary. Learn the art of promoting yourself and what you do well. Be a lifelong learner and focus on becoming a subject matter expert to be the go-to person for results in that practice area. Leverage industry information and technology, perform salary comparisons, learn the art of negotiation. Don't negotiate your deal breakers with yourself or anyone else; stand firm. Most importantly, ask for what you want. You should not play small when it comes to developing and advancing your career. You advocate for others, learn to be a zealous advocate for yourself first.

Advice on Overcoming the Additional Challenges Black Law Students and Lawyers Face:

Heavy is the head that wears the crown. Your responsibilities are likely intensified as a Black law student and attorney. Your achievements will make you the go-to person for many, whether you like it or not. You may be the only highly-educated person and/or attorney some people know, so your opinion, thoughts, and actions will matter more now than it ever did before. Stay patient and humble. You can be a resource to people without giving your time and knowledge away for free.

On the other hand, your achievements will be challenged and questioned relentlessly because race, ethnic, and culture prejudice and biases still exist. You may be directly challenged or stereotyped by others based on your credentials, capabilities, choice of law school, work environment, and more. It's critical to remember that you have the same credentials as them. Don't be stigmatized by rhetoric. Know that your degree and bar card are just as good. You must believe in yourself and have confidence. Don't pretend that those microaggressions don't exist, but don't dwell on them either.

You will inevitably make mistakes and lots of them. You may feel like those mistakes are intensified or that you suffer from the imposter syndrome. Don't be tempted to let anyone or even you, keep you down because of those mistakes. Take every opportunity to learn from your mistakes, recover fast, anticipate problems and solutions, ask for help from a trusted advisor and move on. Try to avoid the same mistake twice and give yourself some grace if you did everything that you could because things happen even to the most prepared.

Create a toolbox to navigate stress. You will need to learn effective tools to minimize your stress and create a balance. Learn early what works for you and make a habit to practice it routinely. When you stray or feel yourself getting stressed and you will, remember to dig back in your toolbox for some points to help you get back centered. In order to be successful in taking care of your well-being, you have to study and practice it - just like the law is learned.

Best Advice I Received Regarding Law School and the Legal Profession:

"There will be times when the critics will be louder than people cheering for you. Keep going. There will be people who will intentionally try to tarnish your reputation. Let your character shine. There will be people who will do everything to discredit your skills and challenge your abilities. Take it with a grain of salt and let your work speak for itself. You must remember to rise above the occasion. You will have more knowledge than most people you encounter and the fact that you are Black, young, and a woman will make a lot of people uncomfortable. Stay humble and do good things." - My Daddy

"You never have to go at anything alone. There is a vast network of Black lawyers that have come before you and many that will come after you. You are not expected to know it all, but you are expected to be a reasonable attorney and use your resources to find out who does know it. You should never walk alone." - Attorney Mentor

"We have prepared you to be the best. Represent us well and never forget your "seriousness of purpose."" - Southern University Law Center Chancellor

Worst Advice I Received Regarding Law School and the Legal Profession:

"Take the job that pays the most. Go with the opportunities that will yield the greatest financial increase." - Law Firm Recruiter in response to me entertaining another offer

"Just work hard. You don't need to be concerned with advancing in your career. Just keep your head down and work hard in order to get ahead." - Majority Law Partner

Unfortunately, I've learned that both pieces of advice are misconceptions. There is nothing wrong with wanting to be financially secure, but also recognize what sacrifices come with the financial increase. It's often long hours, working six to seven days a week, and other sacrifices. Yes, you absolutely must work hard and be excellent, but you also must be strategic and visible. You must learn to highlight your accomplishments or someone else will take credit for your hard work.

Best Advice I Would Give to an Aspiring Black Lawyer:

Your word and your brand are everything! You've worked exceptionally hard to make it to this point so never compromise your character, value or integrity – for anyone or anything. Develop the grit to say "no" to things that don't align with your goals and priorities and stand firm on it. There is no distinction from your personal and professional brand; it is all a reflection of you. We are not afforded the luxuries of being haphazard in our efforts, so you must always sign your work with excellence. You are no stranger to working harder than others and that won't stop now, but you will become more efficient and effective because you have been shaped by the fire; use that to your advantage. At some point you're going to feel incompetent, maybe even suffer from the imposter syndrome; push through those difficult times and use your network to prop you up. Find several mentors and at least one sponsor in your organization that has capital and is willing to spend it on you. Never forget the reasons why you chose law or the oath that you took; it keeps you centered. Always pay it forward and remain humble.

Thoughts About Why Earning a Law Degree Is a Powerful Credential for African Americans and Why There Is a Need for More African American Lawyers:

Representation matters! Black lawyers matter. It is no secret that there is an overwhelming shortage of Black lawyers. This shortage causes people of color to be underrepresented in every aspect of access to justice; from the courtrooms, among elected officials, law firms, and legal organizations and it trickles over to lack of representation outside of the legal profession in other aspects of corporate America. The number of Black lawyers does not coincide or reflect the percentage of the Black population. The lack of diversity prevents adequate representation and a missing voice in America.

People tend to make stronger connections when they can see someone who looks like them or who comes from a similar ethnic/cultural background. This greater sense of relatability is what builds trust and allows for better representation. Absent more Black representation, our communities that are often rural and socioeconomically challenged, continue to be particularly underserved. The privilege of being a Black lawyer provides our communities access to more resources and helps better connect our communities. It is the answer to who will fill a void and is focused on making a difference in the lives of those who need their assistance the most in Black communities.

Thoughts About Whether and Why Law School Is Worth the Financial Investment:

Law school is the best financial investment and the best investment I made in myself. The journey has taught me skills that are transferable to so many other areas and allows me the opportunity to be in places to affect the type of change that benefits my community in a meaningful way. In addition, I also made a conscious and informed decision to select an affordable law school for my budget. I am personally fulfilled by my choice.

The analysis to determine if you should proceed with financial investment in law school is personal and should be tailored to include both a financial component and personal goals evaluation. You must consider the cost of law school and the expected salary you will earn in return once you have completed all the requirements. However, you should also weigh in other factors such as geographical location, tier school, job outlook, type of practice area and more. Some of these factors will greatly influence your decision. Likewise, you must determine the reason you want to go to law school and consider whether those reasons can be fulfilled without having a law degree. The answer will of course depend on each individual and whether you're willing to contend with many challenges along the way. I highly recommend anyone considering law school to ask some tough questions and weigh the pros and cons first. If the value of attending law school is greater than not attending, then I would proceed to creating a plan to tackle the financial investment.

LEGACY AND SUCCESS

My Most Outstanding Accomplishments:

Personally - The ability to be in a position, have a platform, and the power to be a change agent. Knowing that I have used my time, talent, and treasures to pay it forward and represent those who have long been ignored and who otherwise might not be heard, seen, or given their just due respect. I have made an impact to change the community where my family and I live, work, and play.

Professionally - My prior role as chair of the American Bar Association Young Lawyers Division - representing the voice of 180,000 young lawyers and serving as the international ambassador for young lawyers. I was able to build coalitions and meaningful pacts with young lawyers in Canada, Europe, and Africa.

The Legacy I Hope to Leave:

Every day I live as if my legacy will be that as a social engineer and an upstander. "A social engineer [is] a highly skilled, perceptive, sensitive lawyer who [understands] the Constitution of the United States and [knows] how to explore its uses in the solving of problems of local communities and in bettering conditions of the underprivileged citizens." An upstander is someone who recognizes when something is wrong and acts to make it right. I want to be someone who stood up for what is right and did my best to help support and protect others by being socially responsible.

The Secret to My Success:

Stay firm in your faith, family, and friends. Keep a diverse personal and professional solid tribe of people that keep you grounded, serve as your critics and your cheerleaders, [help you] think through ideas and talk to challenges, and keep you grounded. Do exceedingly good things in public and in private and expect no accolades in return. Stay eager to do what is right. Always remain humble. Dare to dream big!

Erica Edwards-O'Neal, Esq.

Senior Vice President
Diversity, Equity & Inclusion
New York City Economic Development Corporation (NYCEDC)
Founder
EEO Consults
New York, New York

"Lead from wherever you land."
– Erica Edwards-O'Neal

Success is . . . defined by you.

PERSONAL FAVORITES

Favorite Quote: "These mountains that you are carrying, you were only supposed to climb." - Najwa Zebian

Favorite Books: *Having Our Say: The Delany Sisters' First 100 Years* by Amy Hill Hearth, Annie Elizabeth Delany, and Sarah Louise Delany; *Fire Next Time* by James Baldwin; *Girl on a Train* by Paula Hawkins; *The Color of Water* by James McBride

Favorite Movies: *The Five Heartbeats; Beaches; A Soldier's Story; Remember the Titans*

Favorite Musical Artists: Thurston O'Neal; Bill Withers; The Winans; Andraé Crouch; Bob Marley; Sade; Prince; The Clark Sisters; Tupac

Favorite Law School Classes: Criminal Law; Torts

Favorite Legal Case: *Boynton v. Virginia*

Favorite Hobbies: Watching stand-up comedy; Researching anything; Reading biographies; Sitting in the sun; Taking Africa dance classes

Favorite Attorney Role Models: Michele Coleman Mayes; Edgar Cahn; Johnnie Cochran

FAMILY AND BACKGROUND

Where Born and Raised: Wakefield, Virginia

Family (Spouse/Partner and Children): Spouse - Thurston; Children - Brittney, Jada, Jaidyn and Jordyn

Family Socioeconomic and Educational Background: I come from a large working-class family with my mother, father and five siblings. I am the youngest of six children (three girls and three boys) that grew up in Wakefield, Virginia - a very small town.

THE DECISION TO BECOME A LAWYER

When and Why I Decided to Become a Lawyer: In junior high, I was asked to learn and recite Dr. Martin Luther King, Jr.'s "I Have a Dream" speech. No young man volunteered so I was asked. The first few times that I read through the speech they were just words, and then something clicked and I was moved to tears. I began to research the movement and those words became alive for me and I wanted to understand the fight. The March on Washington was an amazing demonstration but the heavy lifting was done on the local level by lawyers and local activists.

EDUCATIONAL ACHIEVEMENTS

High School: Sussex Central High School (Sussex County, Virginia)

College/University: College of William and Mary (Williamsburg, Virginia)

Undergraduate Degree: Bachelor of Arts (B.A.)

Major: Government

College Honors, Achievements and Activities: *Recipient,* Mamie Stringfellow Academic Merit Scholarship; *Recipient,* Bucktrout-Braithwaite Academic Merit Scholarship; *Member,* Ebony Expressions Gospel Choir; *Trainer,* Sports Medicine; *Member,* Black Student Organization; *Volunteer,* Housing Partnerships

Law School: Touro Law Center (Huntington, New York)

Law Degree and Graduation Year: Juris Doctor/Doctor of Jurisprudence (J.D.) - Class of 1999

Law School Honors, Achievements and Activities: *Research Assistant,* Professor Peter Zablosky (Torts); *Public Service Law Fellow,* Touro College Law Center; *Public Interest Law Fellow Intern,* Nassau/Suffolk Law Services Housing Rights Project; *Law Intern,* New York State Office of the Attorney General; *Legal Mentor/Youth Court Coordinator (Law Intern),* Time Dollar Institute

PROFESSIONAL ACCOMPLISHMENTS

State Bar Membership (Where Admitted to Practice Law): New York

Other Professional Work Experience: *Founder,* EEO Consults; *Director,* Diversity & Career Services, Touro Law Center; *Director,* Fight for Families Coalition, Health and Welfare Council; *Americorp Volunteers In Service To America VISTA,* Housing Rights Project

Professional Organizations: *Member,* Metropolitan Black Bar Association; *Member,* Amistad Bar Association; *Member,* National Urban League; *Member,* National Association for the Advancement of Colored People (NAACP); *Member,* New York State Bar Diversity Committee; *Member,* National Association of Law Placement Professionals (NALPP); *Member,* Society for Human Resource Management; *Member,* Committee on Diversity and Inclusion, New York State Bar Association; *Member,* Diversity Pipeline Initiatives Committee, New York City Bar Association

Post-Law School Honors, Achievements, Activities, and Community Involvement: *Member,* Tri-State Diversity Council; *Awardee,* Diversity Leadership Award, National Diversity Pre-Law Conference and Law Fair; *Awardee,* Legal Access and Diversity Champion Award, National Black Pre-Law Conference and Law Fair; *Member,* State of Black Long Island Equity Work Group; *Advisory Board Member,* Girls, Inc.; *Advisory Board Member,* Fred Schaufeld Scholarship; *Honoree,* 2016 Babylon Women of Distinction

LESSONS LEARNED: MY RECOMMENDATIONS FOR YOUR FUTURE ACTIONS BASED ON MY PAST EXPERIENCE

Advice on Law School Preparation:

Take a Law School Admission Test (LSAT) preparation course and if you cannot afford one, reach out to your local bar association and research free resources. Read more and take courses that will allow you the opportunity to hone your analytical and writing skills.

Advice on Applying to and Selecting a Law School:

Be open to locations beyond your local state. Research and visit the law school before you make a final decision. Look for diverse representation on the student body, staff and faculty, and request to speak to some of those folks. Ask what the school is doing to ensure the cultural competence of the faculty and staff. Additionally, ensure that the school offers a range of support services. Finally, when offered a financial package, compare and contrast with other offers and ask for more.

Advice Regarding Academic Success, Co-Curricular and Extra-Curricular Participation, and Social Engagement in Law School:

Balance is the key. You want to be a well-rounded student. Focus on the course work and choose one or two activities/organizations to be involved with. The organizations that you connect with should help you to grow your network, present an opportunity for growth and bring some joy. It is okay to say "no" and to say "no" without explanation to the extras.

At some point, someone will do or say something to cause you to doubt yourself, but please remember you belong… you belong in the classroom, the courtroom and the boardroom. You deserve the seat that you are in.

Advice on Preparing for and Taking the Bar Exam:

Eliminate distractions, try to set aside some savings, and if you are employed, make every effort to save as many days/hours as possible so that you can have ample time for dedicated bar focus. If you are unable to take time off, use recommended study schedules and pace yourself. Recognize that it is a stressful time. Be diligent, but be kind to yourself.

Advice on Choosing a Job and Career Path Inside or Outside of the Legal Profession:

Be open. Seek informational interviews from attorneys and law graduates that are doing the type of work that you are interested in. An informational interview is a meeting that allows potential job seekers to gain insight on career opportunities or a specific industry from an employed professional. People love to talk about themselves and there is no stress of actually having to offer a job. They are often fun and informative with the added bonus of building your network.

Advice on Seeking Legal Job Opportunities and/or Creating One's Own Opportunities:

Before your last year, join your state, city and diverse bar associations as a student member. These organizations often offer or advertise internship, scholarship, mentorship and employment opportunities. Get hands-on experience through clinics, internships or limited volunteering. I have had previous students participate in hands-on clinical programs, gain valuable experiences and launch their own law practices immediately after the bar.

Advice on Achieving Career Success and Advancement:

Find mentors and sponsors. Sponsors typically advocate on your behalf. For example, inside of an organization, a sponsor might bring you along to meetings, highlight your work/accomplishments or recommend you for an assignment. Mentors advise and counsel. You should have long-term mentorship relationships but also participate in speed mentoring opportunities.

Advice on Overcoming the Additional Challenges Black Law Students and Lawyers Face:

Don't be afraid to advocate for yourself and to raise your hand for the new sometimes scary opportunity.

Join affinity groups to get and give support and strategies for thriving.

Be honest with yourself about your strengths and weaknesses. Highlight your strengths and work to gradually improve in other areas.

Best Advice I Received Regarding Law School and the Legal Profession:

Ask questions when you don't understand and show up for office hours.

Worst Advice I Received Regarding Law School and the Legal Profession:

Big Law is the only way to be successful.

Thoughts About Why Earning a Law Degree Is a Powerful Credential for African Americans and Why There Is a Need for More African American Lawyers:

The study of law is a powerful tool and a value add for any career choice. Law school helps to further hone your critical thinking, advocacy and writing skills. The truth is African Americans are still underrepresented in the field of law, and yes the world still needs another lawyer.

LEGACY AND SUCCESS

My Most Outstanding Accomplishments:

Personally - Being a loving and supportive wife and mother makes me the most proud. I am proud to say that our home is not perfect but it is a home filled with love and laughter.

Professionally - Launching my own consulting firm and creating the first diversity role at Touro Law Center.

The Legacy I Hope to Leave:

I have a passion for creating pipelines for new career and employment opportunities. I want it to be said that I helped and inspired people to pursue a better life, even if you have to do it afraid.

The Secret to My Success:

Trusting in God and doing my part to put action to my faith. Doing the work.

Practical Wisdom for Those on the Path to Lawyerhood

Conway S. Ekpo, Esq.
Executive Director
Morgan Stanley
New York, New York

"Make time to invest in others because you never know when something as simple as an encouraging word can make all the difference in allowing someone to get through a difficult time in their lives and achieve greatness."

— Conway S. Ekpo

Success is . . . building meaningful relationships, moving the needle and lifting as you climb.

PERSONAL FAVORITES

Favorite Quote: *"Make visible what, without you, might perhaps never have been seen."* - Robert Bresson

Favorite Books: *All Deliberate Speed: Reflections on the First Half Century of Brown v. Board of Education* by Charles Ogletree; *Becoming* by Michelle Obama; *Between the World and Me* by Ta-Nehisi Coates; *Crash of the Titans* by Greg Farrell; *Dreams From My Father* by Barack Obama; *Game Change* by John Heilemann and Mark Halperin; *Outliers* by Malcolm Gladwell; *The Associate* by John Grisham; *Things Fall Apart* by Chinua Achebe; *We Were Eight Years in Power* by Ta-Nehisi Coates; *What's the Matter with Kansas?* by Thomas Frank; *Why Should White Guys Have All the Fun?* by Reginald Lewis

Favorite Movies: *12 Years a Slave; Color Purple; Coming to America; Contact; The Godfather; The Godfather Part II; Inception; Margin Call; Ocean's 11; The Big Short; The Dark Knight; The Shawshank Redemption; Too Big to Fail; Trading Places*

Favorite Musical Artists: Biggie Smalls; Childish Gambino (Donald Glover); Daniel Caesar; Drake; Eminem; Erykah Badu; Frank Ocean; India Arie; Jay-Z; Jill Scott; John Coltrane; Lauryn Hill; Migos; Miles Davis; Michael Jackson; Mos Def; Pharrell Williams; Tupac; Travis Scott

Favorite Law School Classes: Civil Procedure; Constitutional Law; Evidence

Favorite Legal Cases: *Brown v. Board of Education; Hamdan v. Rumsfeld; Loving v. Virginia; McCleskey v. Kemp; Obergefell v. Hodges*

Favorite Hobbies: Cryptocurrency; Exercising; Mentoring Black attorneys; Venture capital investing

Favorite Attorney Role Models: Charles Hamilton Houston; Barack and Michelle Obama

FAMILY AND BACKGROUND

Where Born and Raised: Lawrence, Kansas

Family (Spouse/Partner and Children): Spouse - Martha Joanah; Children - (daughter) Langston and (son) Ellison

Family Socioeconomic and Educational Background: I am the oldest of six children raised in my early years by my father, mother and step-mother, and subsequently, during my teenage years and beyond, by only my mother and step-mother. We grew up poor. My father passed away and both my mother and step-mother have a high school education.

THE DECISION TO BECOME A LAWYER

When and Why I Decided to Become a Lawyer: After I graduated from college with an engineering degree and had worked a few years as an engineer, I soon discovered that I was most passionate about the legal aspects of my job as opposed to the engineering ones. I soon registered for the LSAT and the rest, as they say, is history.

EDUCATIONAL ACHIEVEMENTS

High School: Lawrence High School (Lawrence, Kansas)

College/University: University of Kansas (Lawrence, Kansas)

Undergraduate Degree: Bachelor of Science (B.S.)

Major: Architectural Engineering

College Honors, Achievements and Activities: *Member,* Black Student Union; *Member,* National Society of Black Engineers (NSBE); *Member,* Kappa Alpha Psi Fraternity, Inc.; *Member,* National Pan-Hellenic Council; *Member,* Student Senate; *Participant,* Upward Bound

Law School: Rutgers Law School (Newark, New Jersey)

Law Degree and Graduation Year: Juris Doctor/Doctor of Jurisprudence (J.D.) - Class of 2007

Law School Honors, Achievements and Activities: *Member,* Law Review; *Participant,* Minority Student Program; *Member,* National Black Law Students Association; *Member,* Student Bar Association

PROFESSIONAL ACCOMPLISHMENTS

State Bar Memberships (Where Admitted to Practice Law): New Jersey; New York; United States Patent and Trademark Office

Other Legal Work Experience: *Adjunct Law Professor,* Rutgers School of Law; *In-House Counsel,* Bank of America; *In-House Counsel,* Merrill Lynch; *Senior Associate,* Hogan Lovells LLP; *Associate,* Riker Danzig LLP; *Associate,* Heller Ehrman LLP; *Judicial Extern,* United States District Court for the Southern District of New York; *Judicial Extern,* United States District Court for the District of New Jersey; *Legal Intern,* Prudential Financial

Other Professional Work Experience: *Founding Member,* Savantus Venture Fund (a venture capital fund)

Professional Organizations: *Secretary,* In-House Counsel Committee, New York City Bar Association; *Vice President of Finance,* Metropolitan Black Bar Association

Post-Law School Honors, Achievements, Activities, and Community Involvement: *Founding Member,* 1844 (group of Black male law firm associates in New York City); *Founding Member,* Black BigLaw Pipeline, Inc. (non-profit that provides substantive support for Black junior law firm associates); *Member,* Board of Directors, My Brother's Keeper/My Sister's Keeper (non-profit organization that provides support and programming for Black attorneys); *Member,* Board of Advisors for Legal Outreach (non-profit organization that prepares underprivileged minority youth for college); *Member,* Board of Advisors, National Black Law Students Association; *Fellow,* Council of Urban Professionals (2016); *Member,* Board of Directors, Roosevelt Island Operating Corporation (appointed by New York Governor Andrew Cuomo and approved by the New York State Senate); *Volunteer,* City Bar Justice Center's COVID-19 Small Business Legal Clinic

LESSONS LEARNED: MY RECOMMENDATIONS FOR YOUR FUTURE ACTIONS BASED ON MY PAST EXPERIENCE

Advice on Law School Preparation:

Familiarize yourself with law school supplements such as *Examples & Explanations* during the summer before 1L, but don't overdo it. Your law school grades will be determined solely by law professors who you haven't met yet, so you don't know which areas of the law they will stress on their exams before you get to law school. The most important thing before law school is to score as high as possible on the LSAT and, if you are still in college, increase your GPA as much as possible.

Advice on Applying to and Selecting a Law School:

Rankings are an unfortunate reality in legal education, so seek to attend the highest ranked law school that you can afford. We'll circle back to this later.

Advice Regarding Academic Success, Co-Curricular and Extra-Curricular Participation, and Social Engagement in Law School:

During your first year, treat law school like a full-time job. Much of where you will end up as an attorney is determined by your first-year grades, so eliminate as many distractions as possible. Meaning, if you have a significant other going into law school, hold onto them. If you don't, then don't start any new relationships. You can and should join organizations like the National Black Law Students Association (NBLSA) for example, but your membership in these organizations should take a back seat to your studies. Keep your eye on the prize, which should be attaining as high of a GPA by the end of your first year as possible. Also aim to make law review or one of the other journals at your school as well as moot court. All of these accomplishments will provide you with employment options after you graduate.

Your grades will be determined by your performance on your exams. For many of you, this will boil down to your performance on **one exam** offered at the end of the semester for each class you're taking. In order to distinguish yourself from your classmates, you should know that there is a significant difference between knowing the law and knowing how to write an effective law school exam answer. Legal writing is formulaic (e.g., start by stating the issue, then the rule that applies to the issue, then provide your analysis, and then briefly conclude). Unless your

A. Zachary Faison Jr., Esq.

President & Chief Executive Officer
Edward Waters College
Jacksonville, Florida

"Inspect what you expect. Choice, not chance will determine your ultimate destiny!"

– A. Zachary Faison, Jr.

Success is . . . best measured by the strength of your desire, the size of your dream; and how you handle the inevitable failures and disappointments along your journey.

PERSONAL FAVORITES

Favorite Quote: "Being confident of this very thing, that He who hath begun a good work in you shall complete it until the day of Jesus Christ." - Philippians 1:6

Favorite Books: *The Sacred Call: A Tribute to Donald L. Hollowell—Civil Rights Champion* by Louise Hollowell & Martin C. Lehfeldt; *Stamped From The Beginning: The Definitive History of Racist Ideas in America* by Dr. Ibram X. Kendi; *The Crisis of The Negro Intellectual* by Harold Cruse; *The Debt: What America Owes To Blacks* by Randall Robinson; *Between the World And Me* by Ta-Nehesi Coates; *The New Jim Crow: Mass Incarceration in the Age of Colorblindness* by Michelle Alexander; *A Testament of Hope: The Essential Writings and Speeches* by Dr. Martin Luther King Jr.; *From Here To Equality: Reparations For Black Americans In The Twenty-First Century* by Dr. William A. Darity and Dr. A. Kirsten Mullen; *Black Radical: The Life and Times of William Monroe Trotter* by Kerri K. Greenridge; *Who's Holding Your Ladder?: Leadership's Most Critical Decision—Selecting Your Leaders* by Samuel R. Chand; *The Color of Law: A Forgotten History of How Our Government Segregated America* by Richard Rothstein; *The Color of Money: Black Banks and The Racial Wealth Gap* by Mehrsa Baradarian; *Slavery by Another Name: The Re-Enslavement of Black Americans from the Civil War to World War II* by Douglas A. Blackmon; *The Half Has Never Been Told: Slavery and The Making of American Capitalism* by Edward E. Baptist

Favorite Movies: *Rocky I-IV; Belly; Malcolm X; Glory; Django; Get Out; Hoop Dreams; Do The Right Thing; Boyz N The Hood*

Favorite Music Genres: Traditional and contemporary gospel music; R&B; 90's and 00's era; Hip-Hop; Southern trap music

Favorite Musical Artists: The Winans; John P. Kee; Richard Smallwood; Hezekiah Walker; Kirk Franklin; Georgia Mass Choir; Mississippi Mass Choir; OutKast; Goodie Mob; Cameo; Earth, Wind, and Fire; The Commodores; Michael Jackson; Whitney Houston; Lauryn Hill; Erykah Badu; Boyz II Men; Jodeci; 112; Jagged Edge; T.I.; Nas; Ludacris; Jeezy; Gucci Mane; 2 Chainz; Kendrick Lamar; J. Cole

Favorite Law School Classes: Criminal Defense Clinic; Race in the Law; Criminal Procedure; Education Law

Favorite Legal Cases: *Dred Scott v. Sandford; Brown v. Board of Education; Plessy v. Ferguson*

Favorite Hobbies: Attending sporting events especially college football and basketball games (Edward Waters College, The University of Georgia, and Albany State University); Traveling domestically and abroad with my wife; Reading and listening to lectures concerning past and contemporaneous issues of race in America; Watching documentaries; Movie watching with my wife; Writing; Working out in the gym; Engaging in robust debates and conversations; Politics our intelligence and technical proficiency in the law. I can't tell you how many Black attorneys I have mentored who are unable to gain access to certain legal jobs because of the low ranking of the law school on their resume. Many legal job postings will literally include language in the job description that the employers are only interested in hiring graduates from top law schools. Keep in mind I'm telling you this as somebody who wholeheartedly disagrees with the law school ranking system's ability to predict good lawyers. I would love to see the rankings dismantled. But unfortunately the rankings exist and I wouldn't be doing my duty if I didn't warn you about their significance.

Best Advice I Would Give to an Aspiring Black Lawyer:

Reach out to your village. I am a part of a number of non-profit organizations and professional organizations created specifically to support other Black lawyers in the profession. Many of us suffer in isolation simply because we don't know or are too embarrassed to ask for help. Don't do that. Use your resources and do not reinvent the wheel. There are numerous senior Black attorneys in this profession who are ready and willing to invest in you and your success. Use us.

Thoughts About Why Earning a Law Degree Is a Powerful Credential for African Americans and Why There Is a Need for More African American Lawyers:

As I mentioned above, there are roughly one million attorneys practicing law in America, and of that one million only 3% (roughly 30,000) are Black. We are severely underrepresented in all legal practice areas as well as the judiciary. We need more Black judges, more Black prosecutors, more Black mergers and acquisitions attorneys, more Black employment law attorneys, more Black entertainment and intellectual property lawyers, more Black financial services attorneys, etc. Representation matters.

Thoughts About Whether and Why Law School Is Worth the Financial Investment:

If law school did not come at such a high cost, I would encourage all Americans to attend law school because quite frankly this country was set up by lawyers for lawyers. An understanding about what your legal rights and obligations are is crucial for understanding how to navigate so many different aspects of our society such as signing a lease for an apartment, being stopped by the police, starting a business, running for office, organizing a protest march, etc.

The fact of the matter, however, is that law school does come at a cost. And that is a very real factor that you will have to weigh for yourself given your financial situation. For me, it was well worth the investment because it has provided me with access to a world that quite literally would not have been possible without my law degree. It has increased my lifetime earning potential, allowed me to fully understand how to accumulate wealth for my family and, most importantly, has given me satisfaction and a sense of purpose in helping others. If any of those aspects are appealing to you, I would give law school a hard look.

LEGACY AND SUCCESS

My Most Outstanding Accomplishment:

In 2016, I was awarded with the New York City Bar Association's Diversity & Inclusion Champion Award. This is an award that is typically reserved for judges, general counsels and other senior attorneys who have dedicated years of their lives towards moving the needle for diverse lawyers. As an attorney who had only been practicing law for nine years at the time I was recognized, I was one of the youngest award recipients in the history of the New York City Bar Association.

I received the award in recognition for the work that I and several others had done in founding a group called 1844, which is a group of 60 Black male lawyers who primarily practice in BigLaw and in-house legal departments in New York. The group's name "1844" is in reference to the year that the first Black person, Macon Bolling Allen, was admitted to practice law in America. The group's purpose is to build genuine relationships between its members and leverage those relationships to help them develop personally and professionally and give back to our communities.

As part of 1844's many community outreach initiatives, we have hosted an annual panel discussion aimed at helping Black law firm summer associates navigate the rigors of BigLaw, conducted "know your rights" seminars helping minority youth successfully and safely navigate police encounters, lobbied local and state legislators to change the laws impacting how law enforcement engages with the community, held fundraisers in support of the DREAMChasers Foundation which helps minority teenagers who lack financial and academic resources enter specialized New York City high schools, and founded a venture capital fund which has invested in several minority-owned tech startups.

The Legacy I Hope to Leave:

The legacy I hope to leave is one of empowering others to uplift themselves and our community. By way of example, in 2019 I and several others founded a non-profit, the Black BigLaw Pipeline, Inc. which has served as a powerful and unique resource for reshaping diversity and, specifically, the experience of Black attorneys in the legal profession. The organization is comprised of senior Black attorneys, including law firm partners, senior associates, in-house counsel, government lawyers, and consultants. It provides substantive and soft skills training to junior Black attorneys in large law firms, and empowers them to, in turn, train others to do the same. This is representative of the type of legacy I hope to leave behind.

The Secret to My Success:

First and foremost, God's grace. Second, I deliberately make time for what is important and I refuse to waste my time on what is not.

jump over the hurdles between first year and third year, but that's as far as the third-year associate's experiences go. That's why it is important to keep two sets of mentors: (i) attorneys who are a few years ahead of you; and (ii) senior lawyers (e.g., law firm partners or senior government or in-house lawyers) who are at least a decade ahead of you. Try to have multiple mentors within each cohort, and constantly check in with both cohorts for guidance on your short-term and long-term career goals. Think of your mentors as your own personal board of directors; you want as many voices as possible to weigh in and help you navigate the rigors of the legal profession.

Let's turn to sponsors. Although it is possible for a single person to simultaneously serve as both your mentor and sponsor, these are typically two separate and distinct types of individuals. As we discussed, mentors can be slightly older confidants who provide a safe space within which to guide you along your career path. Sponsors, by contrast, are exclusively senior attorneys who are cloaked with a significant level of authority that allows them to call the shots in places where you do not currently have access. In a word, a sponsor is an advocate. They lend their voice in a room full of decision-makers to advocate for you to receive a new opportunity and, by virtue of their status, they can actually influence others to make the opportunity happen. The latter part of this definition is key.

Whereas a mentor could be somebody like a senior associate from your law firm practice group, a sponsor is going to be somebody more along the lines of the head of the group or the managing partner at your firm. While a senior associate at a law firm may be able to tell you how to become a successful senior associate, they do not, for example, have the ability to make you into a law firm partner. A sponsor, on the other hand, has the ability to open doors and provide concrete opportunities and will do so on your behalf - but only if they know you are somebody worthy of investment.

Unlike a mentor, a sponsor is not someone to whom you would typically confide your day-to-day highs and lows. Not only is their time likely to be severely limited (by virtue of their senior status), but it's also important that your sponsors always see you in your best light, which is why personal branding is critical for securing sponsors. Be thoughtful about what you share with, and display to, potential sponsors. Establish your brand as an attorney who is not only technically proficient in the law, but is also mindful of the big picture when it comes to servicing the client (e.g., what are the client's long-term objectives and how does the current matter you are working on play into that broader strategy?). That kind of branding will catch the attention of potential sponsors.

Advice on Overcoming the Additional Challenges Black Law Students and Lawyers Face:

With respect to the unique experience of Black law students, the first thing to note is that there are roughly one million attorneys practicing law in America, and of that one million only 3% (roughly 30,000) are Black. As most of you know, the Black community constitutes approximately 12% of the U.S. population, thus, by that metric, we are severely underrepresented within the legal profession. The second thing to note is that law school is one of those educational environments where you will likely be the only Black person in the classroom while your White classmates boldly articulate in great intellectual detail why certain criminal procedure laws against Black people are necessary or why affirmative action for Blacks is unconstitutional. In other words, you will be challenged daily on an intellectual, emotional, spiritual and professional level.

Despite these challenges, I would encourage any Black student who is genuinely interested in the law to consider law school (provided they have considered the financial concerns, of course) simply because Black lawyers are desperately needed in the community. There are many legal issues facing the Black community (the prison industrial complex, public educational system, Black consumer protection, opportunity zones, health care, etc.) that demand that we have a seat at the table when these issues are being decided.

Best Advice I Received Regarding Law School and the Legal Profession:

The best advice I received regarding law school was to prepare myself mentally for how challenging it was going to be. It sounds simple, but you'd be surprised how many people burn out mentally once they get there. The best advice I've received regarding the legal profession, as I've mentioned above, is the importance of building genuine relationships.

Worst Advice I Received Regarding Law School and the Legal Profession:

The worst advice I received about law school and the legal profession was to accept an offer to attend an unaccredited or extremely low ranked law school (I did not take that advice and instead sat out for a year and increased my LSAT score). The reason why that's bad advice is because, as I mentioned above, whether we agree with it or not, the ranking of your law school is directly proportional to the opportunities that will become available to you upon graduation.

Unfortunately, the legal profession is not the type of profession where you can instantly be successful irrespective of where your law school happens to be ranked. Even if your goal is to bypass legal employers altogether and become a solo practitioner hanging your own shingle, you still have to keep in mind that potential clients will also cast judgment, fairly or unfairly, upon where you receive your law degree from.

This is particularly important for Black attorneys who unfortunately do not receive the benefit of the doubt regarding professor tells you otherwise, stick to the formula on your exams. Avoid common pitfalls like using words such as "obviously" and "clearly," or mistakenly thinking that you are "arguing both sides" when only pointing out the issues on both sides and then moving on to spot the next issue before performing any analysis on the issues you have just raised. Legal analysis is complicated and has to be wrestled with, so "show your work" to your professors.

Most professors reward quality analysis over the quantitative exercise of pointing out as many issues as possible, but it will depend on the professor. So your number one goal should be to know your professor's preferences and do as many of their practice exams as possible and have the professor review your answers prior to exam day.

Advice on Preparing for and Taking the Bar Exam:

A common reason why many Black law students tend to fail the bar exam is because they have to work during the months leading up to the exam. If you can, eliminate the financial challenge of sustaining yourself for those two or three months while you are preparing. One way to help eliminate that burden is to volunteer as a student representative for a bar prep course that is being offered at your school; this will ensure you take the prep course for free. While students should be hesitant to take on any more loan debt than absolutely necessary, if you must take out a bar loan then do it. Certain legal employers such as law firms will offer to provide you with a stipend while you prepare for the bar, so look into that as well.

Once you've eliminated as many distractions as possible, the key to passing the bar exam tends to lie with mastering the 200 multiple-choice questions on the Multistate Bar Exam (MBE). After three years of writing law school exam answer essays, most students are able to construct a satisfactory essay answer for any given bar exam question, but the same does not hold true regarding the multiple-choice questions. You either know the answer or you don't. My advice is to practice at least 50 MBE questions each day and review the answers to understand why you got each question correct or incorrect. Over time, this will build up your familiarity with the way in which the MBE questions are tested, and it will allow you to develop a quick sense of which answer choices can be eliminated as well as which answers are likely the correct choice. This is important because you will only have 1 minute and 48 seconds per question on the MBE. Thus, familiarity with the MBE format is key.

Advice on Choosing a Job and Career Path Inside or Outside of the Legal Profession:

I went into "BigLaw" (i.e., large law firms) after law school so I will speak to that career path. For those of you interested in entering BigLaw, there are a few things you should be aware of. First, BigLaw places a premium on law school rankings. Meaning, the higher your law school is ranked, the higher your chances of being hired. Second, BigLaw applies strict scrutiny to law school GPA, so if this is a career path you want to pursue, make sure you are doing all that you can to increase and maintain a high GPA. Law review or moot court will be helpful, but GPA is paramount. Last, but not least, relationships are extremely important in BigLaw. A vouch from somebody who has a relationship with a partner at a law firm that you're applying to can go a long way and, in some instances, can even be more important than where you went to law school or what your GPA is (within reason of course). So start developing relationships with your classmates, recent graduates, professors, etc. as soon as you arrive at law school. If you wait to get to know somebody until you need a favor, it's already too late.

Advice on Seeking Legal Job Opportunities and/or Creating One's Own Opportunities:

I would reiterate here that personal relationships are probably the most valuable credit you can build during your time as both a law student and as an attorney. Developing genuine relationships and providing help to others without expecting anything in return will open the doors you need to create your own opportunities going forward.

Advice on Achieving Career Success and Advancement:

In my mind, there are two sources of advice and guidance that are critical to helping you successfully navigate your career: mentors and sponsors. While both are essential to your development and career advancement, there are significant distinctions between mentors and sponsors that dictate how you should approach, build, and maintain these different relationships.

A mentor is somebody senior to you who you can confide in. As Black attorneys, many of us are the first in our families to graduate from college, let alone practice law. Thus, it is that much more important that we seek out those who can help us navigate the legal profession.

Ideally, a mentor is somebody who has already walked the path that you're about to travel and who is willing to share, in great detail, how you can sidestep common obstacles that they themselves experienced along that same path. The more honest and open the communication, the more likely the mentor-mentee relationship is to be successful, which means you will need the freedom to be completely transparent - and even vulnerable - with your mentors (a critical difference from your sponsor relationships, as we'll discuss below). In my experience, the most successful mentor-mentee relationships are often established by proactively seeking out fellow Black attorneys who come from similar backgrounds. These potential mentors tend to be particularly motivated to invest in you because they can see themselves in you and want you to succeed as they have.

When seeking mentors, keep in mind that mentors essentially act as guides, meaning that they can show you how to get from where you are to where they are, but not much further. For example, a third-year associate mentor at a law firm can tell a first-year associate how to successfully

Favorite Attorney Role Model: Dr. Norman C. Francis, President Emeritus of Xavier University of New Orleans (a legendary lawyer, HBCU President, and recipient of the U.S. Presidential Medal of Freedom in 2006)

FAMILY AND BACKGROUND

Where Born and Raised: Atlanta, Georgia

Family Socioeconomic and Educational Background: I am a third-generation graduate of a HBCU (Historically Black College or University) with a grandmother who was a graduate of Morris Brown College in Atlanta, Georgia. Both of my parents are HBCU graduates of Spelman College and North Carolina A&T State University respectively and my mother also earned a master's degree and Ph.D. from Emory University. I have a younger sister who is also a Spelman College graduate who later earned a master's degree from the University of Pennsylvania and a Ph.D. from Emory University. I attribute any measure of professional or academic success I have been blessed to achieve directly to the high emphasis upon which my parents placed on education and high academic achievement. My academic success was always THE foremost priority and expectation in my upbringing as the expectation was never whether I would attend college or graduate school, but which one I would attend and my ability to earn a scholarship through my academic performance. Relatedly, through observation of both of my parents' ascension in their professional careers, I learned the value of hard work, perseverance, and the tremendous need to ground my own aspirations in a foundation undergirded by a strong formal education.

THE DECISION TO BECOME A LAWYER

When and Why I Decided to Become a Lawyer: I decided that I wanted to become a lawyer after my sophomore year in college. As an English major with initial aims towards becoming a journalist, I was blessed to have developed some formidable skills as a writer and I was also known to be a skilled orator around campus who was particularly passionate about matters of race, the racial history of African Americans in America, and further how that history directly impacted our current place in American society. Towards that end, I began being mentored by a professor of political science at Albany State University (ASU) who unbeknownst to me at the time was literally a trailblazing legal and civil rights heroine and woman to earn a law degree from the University of Georgia School of Law - the State of Georgia's flagship institution of higher education. She planted the initial seed in my mind that I could become a lawyer and potentially excel as an advocate for justice particularly for African Americans within our state. Per her mentorship, she recommended me for selection in the Donald J. Weidner Summer Law Program for Undergraduate Students at Florida State University College of Law where I spent the summer in Tallahassee on the law school campus after my sophomore year at ASU and the totality of the experience (i.e., a legal writing memo project; mock first-year Socratic method style classes; a mock moot court competition, visiting lectures from then current lawyers including Attorney Benjamin Crump) convinced me that I wanted to pursue a legal career. In particular, post that experience I knew that I wanted to utilize the law and the advocacy opportunities afforded by the legal profession as a tool in advancing the posterity plight of African Americans.

EDUCATIONAL ACHIEVEMENTS

High School: Henry W. Grady High School (Atlanta, Georgia)

College/University: Albany State University (Albany, Georgia)

Undergraduate Degree: Bachelor of Arts (B.A.)

Major: English

College Honors, Achievements and Activities: Graduated *magna cum laude* "with high distinction"; Albany State University Presidential/Foundation Scholar; Albany State University Velma Fudge Grant University Honors Program Graduate; National Merit Scholar Graduate; U.S. Department of Transportation Dwight D. Eisenhower National Fellow; *Member,* Alpha Kappa Mu National Honor Society; *Member,* Sigma Tau Delta National English Honor Society; Albany State University National Merit Scholar; *Listed Honoree,* Who's Who Among Students in American Colleges and Universities; *Awardee,* Highest Ranking English Major Award (Junior & Senior Year); *Awardee,* Albany State University Velma Fudge Grant Honors Council Award

Law School: University of Georgia School of Law (Athens, Georgia)

Law Degree and Graduation Year: Juris Doctor/Doctor of Jurisprudence (J.D.) - Class of 2006

Law School Honors, Achievements and Activities: *Executive Board Member,* Moot Court (2005-2006); *Team Member,* Moot Court (2004-2006); *Semi-Finalist,* Top Four Teams, Georgia Intra-State Moot Court Competition (2005); *Runner-Up,* Best Brief Award, Georgia Intra-State Moot Court Competition (2005); Top Eight Teams, Herman Talmadge Moot Court Competition Quarterfinalist (Fall 2004); *Competitor,* Richard B. Russell Moot Court Competition (Round of 16, Spring 2004); *Law Student Participant,* Criminal Defense Clinic, University of Georgia School of Law

Additional Education: *Participant,* Harvard University Graduate School of Education Institute for Educational Management; Certification in Fundraising Management (CFRM), Indiana University-Purdue University at Indianapolis (IUPUI); *Participant,* American Association of State Colleges and Universities (AASCU) New President's Academy (San Diego, California); *Fellow,* American Association of State Colleges and Universities (AASCU) Millennium Leadership Institute

PROFESSIONAL ACCOMPLISHMENTS

State Bar Membership (Where Licensed to Practice Law): Georgia

Other Legal Experience: *General Counsel and Vice President of External Affairs,* Tuskegee University; *Assistant District Attorney,* Prosecuting Attorneys Council of Georgia; *Special Assistant to the President for Legal & Legislative Affairs,* Mississippi Valley State University

Other Professional Work Experience: *Chief of Staff and Vice President for Institutional Advancement,* Mississippi Valley State University; *Vice President for Enrollment Management & Student Affairs,* Virginia Union University; *Adjunct Professor,* Albany State University (Subject Taught: Business); *Adjunct Professor,* Mississippi Valley State University (Subjects Taught: Criminal Justice; Political Science)

Professional Organizations: *Member,* National Bar Association; *Member,* National Association of College and University Attorneys (NACUA); *Member,* American Bar Association; *Board of Directors,* United Negro College Fund (UNCF); *Member,* Rotary Club International; *Trustee Member,* Jacksonville Chamber of Commerce; *Board of Directors*, Jacksonville Electric Authority (JEA); *Council of Presidents Member,* Gulf Coast Athletic Conference; *Member,* Jacksonville Civil Council

Post-Law School Honors, Achievements, Activities, and Community Involvement:

Listed Honoree, The Business Journal's Influencers: Rising Stars 100; *Honoree,* Top 40 Business Leaders Under 40, Jacksonville Business Journal; *Honoree,* Top 40 Attorneys Under 40, National Bar Association; *Honoree,* Top 40 Alumni Under 40, The University of Georgia; *Honoree,* Top 50 Alumni Under 50, Albany State University

LESSONS LEARNED: MY RECOMMENDATIONS FOR YOUR FUTURE ACTIONS BASED ON MY PAST EXPERIENCE

Advice on Making the Choice to Apply to and Attend Law School:

First, and very frankly speaking, it is an absolute imperative that aspiring law school attendees take the opportunity to visit law school campuses (i.e., not during the regular law school open house events or the minority accepted student days) during a regular operating day of the law school. Walk around. Sit in a 1L class or classes. Identify a recent alumnus who might be willing to speak with you concerning their law school experience at the particular school you are considering. Speak with the students and faculty. Take note of the number (or lack thereof) of African Americans that have earned membership on law review, other school sponsored legal journals, and the school sponsored moot court teams. Ask yourself (and be honest) concerning whether you see African-American law students experiencing academic and/or professional success (as alums) at that particular school. Second, it is critical that you shadow an actual lawyer(s) and observe the actual "practice of law" before you make the decision to apply and attend. Attending and successfully graduating from law school and later becoming a licensed member of the bar will be perhaps the most harrowing and academically and personally challenging experience of your life. It is not for the faint of heart and you need to be fully invested and have the highest level of conviction that this is in fact the career goal that you want to invest a very significant amount of your life and resources towards achieving. I've found law school and the actual "practice of law" to be very different and I believe aspiring law students should make sure and explore their acumen and fit for both BEFORE deciding to attend.

Advice on Law School Preparation:

I would very strongly recommend seeking a mentor who is a lawyer and observing the day-to-day functions of a lawyer in the particular area of law that you think you may want to practice. Almost everyone I initially met wanted to be some variance of a "corporate lawyer" and work in a large national or international firm. Accordingly, however, very few of us actually knew what that truly entailed in terms of lifestyle (i.e., billable hours and work/life balance, cultural expectations and competencies, etc.). In addition, I would also recommend taking undergraduate courses that will equip you with the opportunity to develop needed applicable legal skills and competencies such as reading dense/lengthy materials and analytical research and writing. While I have observed persons from literally every undergraduate background experience academic success in law school, my experience has divulged that the students who experience the most academic success in law school are those who are gifted in their ability to synthesize large amounts of information through critical analysis and then clearly articulate that analysis (undergirded by critically examined and/or well researched facts) in a succinct and persuasive way. Also, taking a Law School Admission Test (LSAT) preparation course is an absolute no brainer. Do it.

Advice on Applying to and Selecting a Law School:

FIT is **very** important. It is not inaccurate that the legal profession is (at least initially) very credential conscious and so there is absolutely something to be said about law school rankings and your making an earnest attempt to apply, earn admission, and attend the most highly ranked law school that your grades, LSAT score, and co-curricular/leadership profile will allow you to attend. However, just because a school is highly ranked and you earn admission to that school does not mean that it is the right environmental, ideological, or cultural fit for you. These considerations DO MATTER and will absolutely impact your experience and ultimately your success. Do your homework beyond your review of law school rankings. Again, visit law school campuses (i.e., not during the regular law school open house events or the minority accepted student days) during a regular operating day of the law school. Walk around the law school campus and observe the settings. Sit in a 1L class(es). Identify a recent alumnus who might be willing to speak with you concerning their law school experience at the particular school you are considering. Speak with the students and faculty. Take note of the number (or lack thereof) of African Americans that have earned membership on law review, other school sponsored legal journals, and the school sponsored moot court teams. Ask yourself (and be honest) concerning whether you see African American students experiencing academic and/or professional success (as alumni) at that particular school. These aforementioned analyses should be critical components in your law school selection process.

Advice Regarding Academic Success, Co-Curricular and Extra-Curricular Participation, and Social Engagement in Law School:

Co-Curricular? Extra-Curricular? Social experiences? During your first year? Nope. I learned the hard way that while these are indeed "normal" quality of life expectations in almost every other sense and setting - they are best placed on hold during your first year in law school. You should be fully prepared to focus singularly and exclusively on your academics during your first year of law school study. You will have plenty of time for the co-curricular, extra-curricular, and socializing as a 2L and 3L. However, I can't over emphasize enough that your 1L academic demands will take second seat to nothing and no one, and your academic performance as a 1L - good, bad, or indifferent - will in many ways set the course for the rest of your law school experience in some sense and the beginnings of your legal career post-law school in a much greater sense. Academically, you must remember that law school is a marathon, and not a sprint. Even more, the legal principles and lessons that you should be deriving from your class readings represent dependent building blocks that are inextricably linked. Case in point, if you don't fully grasp the concept of "mens rea" (Latin word meaning "guilty mind"), it will be nearly impossible for you to determine the difference between murder and manslaughter. As such, you must develop a focus towards mastering each individual "building block" concept If you ever hope to develop a high mastery of the subject area on the whole. It is a very methodical learning process that takes extraordinary focus and a very significant commitment of time. Relatedly, I found that a great way to visualize and better understand the unfolding academic process for law school study in each legal subject area was to simply review the table of contents of the casebook as it typically illustrates the building block concept areas that must be mastered.

Advice on Preparing for and Taking the Bar Exam:

Wow. Deep breath. My advice is first to know YOUR learning style and stick with what YOU KNOW will lead to YOUR optimum exam performance. This is YOUR bar exam experience and no one else will be responsible for your success or failure. The outcome is on YOU! Indeed, the stakes are very high and I would resolve (as I did) that if I'm going to be unsuccessful it WILL NOT be because I did it how everyone else was doing it when I KNEW I needed to approach this exam differently than the status quo. So more specifically, there are bar exam prep companies that are the "industry standard" companies that EVERYONE will swear by as THE KEY to bar study and preparation. Towards that end, if those boilerplate outlines and materials made by those companies worked for you throughout your law school experience then by all means have at it. However, I never thrived with the industry standard materials and methodologies and I quickly realized that I wouldn't thrive with 200 folks in a warehouse like class setting watching hours-long droning lectures with a professor whizzing through Black Letter Law concepts and bar exam tips on a television screen.

No, I needed a more methodical, self-paced, individually responsive kind of study plan and process and I further needed an opportunity to actually get away from the seemingly unending and almost sickening curiosity of how I was performing in my practice exams relative to everyone else. As such, I broke away from "the pack" and invested in a, at the time, much lesser-known bar preparation course that focused on self-paced real-time interactive/responsive feedback on the Multistate Bar Exam (MBE) and utilized a money-back guarantee that I would pass the exam if I completed the requisite bar prep requirements. I made my own study schedule, developed my own daily study plan by subject, drilled over 3000 MBE questions incessantly, self-administered numerous three-hour increment session practice exams, self-administered about 10 fully-timed practice exams, and finally killed all the outside noise embodied in the "strategies, tactics, best practices, tips, and secrets" that my classmates and their industry standard companies embraced. I took the road less traveled - and it worked. I passed. Bottom line: Do what works best FOR YOU to perform at your highest level!! DO YOU!!!

Advice Regarding Career Success and Advancement:

Where you start is not always where you'll finish. Grades are important. They are in fact VERY important. However, your grades don't always reflect your tenacity, grit, resilience, and/or doggedness to succeed despite formidable challenges. I didn't graduate anywhere near the top of my law school class and I would venture that the great majority of my classmates are absolutely shocked when they learn all that I have been able to accomplish as a lawyer over the course of the last nearly 15 years in my professional career. They wrongly miscalculated the grade quotient. As you build your career. It will take much more than good law school grades for you to become and remain successful. You must be resilient because disappointment and failure are inevitable junctures for essentially everyone. You must KNOW WHO YOU ARE and not reduce your value and your potential to be great to a single academic year in a particular setting at a particular time in your life. Lastly, always hold EVERYONE in high regard by remaining humble and treating everyone with dignity, respect, and with a spirit of kindness. The law school classmate who at 25 had it all together with the six-figure BigLaw salary in the palatial confines of the immaculate downtown skyscraper can be unemployed and barely scraping by at 40. Conversely, the classmate who no one regarded as ever being capable of becoming anything remotely significant in the legal profession at 25 can become a multimillion-dollar litigator with clients from around the world literally begging her to represent them by 40. I've seen it happen. Again, where you start is not always where you'll finish. Be humble; be respectful; be kind.

Advice on Overcoming the Additional Challenges Black Law Students and Lawyers Face:

FACT: You will inevitably face challenges of blatant and insidious racism and discrimination as an African American law student and lawyer at some point in your legal career. This is an inescapable reality as the profession has been and remains overwhelmingly White and male in American law schools around the country and in all of our nation's state legal bars. As a law student, you can in some measure work to reduce your exposure to these realities by again thoroughly vetting the law schools you are considering (i.e., visit law school campuses you are considering, identify and speak to a recent African American alumnus; note the number - or lack thereof - of African Americans that have earned membership on law review, other school-sponsored legal journals, and the school-sponsored moot court teams, etc.). However, your vetting in no way means you will be fully insulated from mistreatment on account of your race.

Nevertheless, the old African American adage of being three times as prepared, professional, and competent once again rings true. Control the things you CAN control which are those aforementioned characteristics: Always be prepared. Always be professional. Always be ultra-competent. Lastly, know your worth and don't let others and their assessments and evaluations of you define who you are, your ability, and your potential for greatness as a lawyer. Define success for yourself and hold true to that definition despite what may come to try and shake your success standard and steal your confidence.

Best Advice I Received Regarding Law School and the Legal Profession:

Remember why you first wanted to be a lawyer and go to law school. Think back to the injustice or mistreatment that motivated you to want to become an advocate for others in seeking justice and equal protection under the law. When disappointments and failures come, as they inevitably will, hold fast to that seminal inspiration.

Remember, law school and in many respects the legal profession is a marathon not a sprint. Pace yourself accordingly and don't judge your own outcome or the outcomes of others based upon a one-mile time in a twenty-six-mile race.

LEGACY AND SUCCESS

My Most Outstanding Accomplishments:

Professional: Being named general counsel and vice president for external affairs at Tuskegee University, one of the nation's most historic and distinguished Historically Black Colleges or Universities (HBCU).

At 37 years of age, being selected as the youngest serving president or chancellor of a Historically Black College or University (HBCU) in America.

The Legacy I Hope to Leave:

My legacy is embodied within the lives of the students I am blessed to serve and support at Edward Waters College - the State of Florida's FIRST independent institution of higher learning and FIRST Historically Black College or University (HBCU). Every single day I have the enviable privilege of enabling primarily young, primarily African American, primarily first generation, and primarily socioeconomically challenged students to literally break the generational chains of illiteracy, poverty, and degradation off of their and the lives of their families. Their individual and our collective success towards that end is the greatest legacy I could ever hope to leave.

The Secret to My Success:

There is no secret. Quite simply:

"…..And the government will be upon His shoulder.

And His name shall be called

Wonderful, **Counselor**, **Mighty God**,

Everlasting Father, **Prince of Peace.**

Of the increase of *His* government and peace

There will be no end,

Upon the throne of David and over **His** kingdom,

To order it and establish it with **judgment** and **justice**

From that time forward, **even forever**." - Isaiah 9:6

His name is **JESUS**.

Vanessa Griddine-Jones, J.D., LL.M.
Executive Director
Congressional Black Caucus Institute
Washington, D.C.

"Stay started; stay determined; stay evolving."

– Vanessa Griddine-Jones

Success is . . . where aspiration meets determination.

PERSONAL FAVORITES

Favorite Quote: "The test of our progress is not whether we add more to the abundance of those who have much, it is whether we provide enough for those who have little." - Franklin D. Roosevelt

Favorite Books: *The Autobiography of Malcolm X* by Alex Haley; *The Souls of Black Folks* by W.E.B. DuBois; *The 48 Laws of Power* by Robert Greene

Favorite Movies: *The Color Purple; The Wiz; The Green Mile*

Favorite Song: "Adore" by Prince

Favorite Musical Artists: I'm a music lover; too many to name.

Favorite Law School Classes: Criminal Law; International Criminal Law; Trial Practice

Favorite Legal Cases: *Reynolds v. Sims; Dred Scott v. Sandford; Roe v. Wade*

Favorite Hobbies: Reading; Traveling; Cooking

Favorite Attorney Role Models: Barack Obama; Michelle Obama; Charlotte E. Ray

FAMILY AND BACKGROUND

Where Born and Raised: Born - Atlanta, Georgia; Raised - Columbia, South Carolina

Spouse and Children: Spouse - Retired Colonel Shannon Jones; Children - (son) Shannon and (daughter) Olivia

Family Socioeconomic and Educational Background: I grew up in a single-parent home filled with a plethora of love and encouragement by my grandparents, aunts, uncles and cousins. Both parents earned college degrees. However, my mom did so while working two jobs. She personified hard work, focus and determination. She encouraged me to explore and experience new things even if that meant the discovery only led to reveal what I didn't like or want.

THE DECISION TO BECOME A LAWYER

When and Why I Decided to Become a Lawyer: There have been several epiphanic moments in my life that facilitated my decision to be a lawyer. I wanted to be an anthropologist, prima ballerina, writer, politician and fashion designer. However, when I was in the eighth grade, my civics teacher played the 1976 clip of Barbara Jordan's keynote speech at the Democratic National Convention. I was captivated by her brilliance, the force of her words and her commanding presence. I wholly believed and declared that to be a force in this world, I had to be a lawyer like she was. I believed that to effectuate real change a law degree was the first step.

EDUCATIONAL ACHIEVEMENTS

High School: Richland Northeast High School (Columbia, South Carolina)

College or University: Columbia College (Columbia, South Carolina)

Undergraduate Degree: Bachelor of Arts (B.A.)

Major: Public Affairs

Law School: Southern University Law Center (Baton Rouge, Louisiana)

Law Degree and Graduation Year: Juris Doctor/Doctor of Jurisprudence (J.D.) - Class of 2014

Law School Honors, Achievements and Activities: *Certified Student Attorney,* Southern University Law Center Mediation Clinic; *Study Abroad Law Student,* Southern University Law Center Study Abroad Program, University College London (London, England); *Intern,* Texas Legislative Internship Program; *Member,* International Law Association; *Member,* Black Law Students Association (BLSA)

Other Graduate or Professional Degree: Master of Laws (LL.M.) in International Law, University of Houston Law Center (Houston, Texas)

Additional Education: *Participant,* Harvard Kennedy School Executive Education Program

PROFESSIONAL ACCOMPLISHMENTS

Other Legal Work Experience: *Student Attorney,* Felony Trial Division, Harris County Public Defenders' Office

Other Professional Work Experience: *Senior Policy Advisor,* U.S. House of Representatives; *Legislative Aide,* South Carolina House of Representatives; *Founder/Principal,* Evolved Agenda Consulting, LLC

Professional Organizations: *Member,* American Bar Association; *Member,* National Bar Association; *Member,* Washington Government Relations Group; *Member,* National Council of Negro Women (NCNW)

LESSONS LEARNED: MY RECOMMENDATIONS FOR YOUR FUTURE ACTIONS BASED ON MY PAST EXPERIENCE

Advice on Applying to and Selecting a Law School:

From the Law School Admission Test (LSAT) to your state's bar exam, entering this profession is a weeding out process. Your application is a paper audition to convince admissions that you are academically capable, educationally mature and mentally and emotionally strong enough to focus and endure the rigors of law school. Law school deans want to know that you are worthy to join the ranks of the profession they have worked hard to be and stay a member of.

I always tell those interested in law school to choose a school where your needs are met and nurtured. I remind them that the law being taught is the same at Harvard as it is at Howard. And at the end of this journey, the bar exam is the great equalizer and if you're not prepared, then where you matriculated won't matter.

Advice Regarding Academic Success, Co-Curricular and Extra-Curricular Participation, and Social Engagement in Law School:

Accept the old adage that "the law is a jealous mistress." Embrace the fact that for three years your social life and extra-curricular activities will be slowed to an almost standstill. However, the reward for the sacrifices made are worth every event and gathering missed.

Advice on Choosing a Job and Career Path Inside or Outside of the Legal Profession:

A law degree is an amazing foundation for any profession. It prepares you to think on a more critical and analytical level. That knowledge and skill set is beneficial in any profession. Incorporate your legal education into what fulfills you most.

Advice on Achieving Career Success and Advancement:

Be anxious for nothing. Plan your work and work your plan. Decide where you want to be and lay out everything from the people to the places that will help you achieve the success and advancement you seek. What you know and who you know are important, but who knows you, your work ethic and abilities is also paramount.

Worst Advice I Received Regarding Law School and the Legal Profession:

I was told by many lawyers/judges not to go [to law school]. They said that most practicing lawyers were unhappy and unfulfilled in their profession. They said I would regret the time and money spent in pursuit of a legal education.

Best Advice I Would Give to an Aspiring Black Lawyer:

Choose your own path. Establish your own time frame. Set your own goals. Don't fall victim to preset ideals and goals that others try to impose upon you because they will try. There are times when being a Black lawyer will be both a benefit and a burden. You must bear the weight of both. Do so with great pride and confidence.

Thoughts About Why Earning a Law Degree Is a Powerful Credential for African Americans and Why There Is a Need for More African American Lawyers:

Having a keen knowledge of the law and understanding the purpose for which the law and lawyers exist is a noble aspiration and noble profession in which one can enter. Whether you practice or not, the abilities and skills you've acquired have the potential to preserve liberty and save lives in ways not imagined.

Thoughts About Whether and Why Law School Is Worth the Financial Investment:

My J.D. and LL.M. were investments in me and my future. Their worth to me - priceless!

LEGACY AND SUCCESS

My Most Outstanding Accomplishment:

Being able to lead an organization with the trust, respect and support of the most powerful African Americans in the country (i.e., Congressional Black Caucus members) has been my most outstanding accomplishment and one of my greatest honors.

The Legacy I Hope to Leave:

Authenticity and genuineness. I want the transparency of my journey, my faith, my focus and my determination to be a guiding post to those who want to enter this profession but have myriad obstacles that seem unsurmountable. Find comfort in knowing that what God has for you is for you. Nothing or no one can block or stop that.

The Secret to My Success:

"For I know the plans I have for you," declares the Lord, "plans to prosper you and not to harm you, plans to give you hope and a future." - Jeremiah 29:11

Kory Chenault Hawkins, J.D.

Associate Director of Admissions Coordinator for Diversity and Inclusion
Columbia University School of Law
New York, New York

"Don't tell me, show me!"
– Kory Chenault Hawkins

Success is . . . measured in small increments over time, such that I can look back over a period and feel confident that I have taken whatever steps possible towards achieving my goals. As the saying goes, it's about the journey just as much as the destination.

PERSONAL FAVORITES

Favorite Quote: "Some moments in life, and they needn't be very long or seem very important, can make up for so much in that life; can redeem, justify, that pain, that bewilderment, with which one lives, and invest one with the courage not only to endure, but to profit from it." - James Baldwin

Favorite Books: *Another Country* by James Baldwin; *Dharma Bums* by Jack Kerouac; *Savage Detectives* by Roberto Bolaño; *The Brothers Karamazov* by Fyodor Dostoyevsky; *Losing My Cool: Love, Literature, and a Black Man's Escape from the Crowd* by Thomas Chatterton Williams

Favorite Movies: *City of God; Black Orpheus*

Favorite Musical Artists: Sarah Vaughan; Ella Fitzgerald; Miles Davis; Sade; John Legend; Common; Frankie Ruíz

Favorite Law School Classes: Contracts; International Law

Favorite Hobbies: Traveling internationally; Reading; Playing tennis

Favorite Attorney Role Model: Former President Barack Obama

FAMILY AND BACKGROUND

Where Born and Raised: Indianapolis, Indiana

Family Socioeconomic and Educational Background: I am a second-generation college student and first-generation law school graduate. I grew up in a working, middle-class household and was raised by a single mother, grandmother, and supportive family.

THE DECISION TO BECOME A LAWYER

When and Why I Decided to Become a Lawyer:

I was actually about twelve years old, watching television and I heard the term "corporate lawyer". Prior to that, I thought lawyers only worked in courtrooms, which I did not want to do. Ever since then I started saying I wanted to be a lawyer and it just stuck with me.

EDUCATIONAL ACHIEVEMENTS

High School: Pike High School (Indianapolis, Indiana)

College/University: Morehouse College (Atlanta, Georgia)

Undergraduate Degree: Bachelor of Arts (B.A.)

Major: Spanish

College Honors, Achievements and Activities: Graduated *magna cum laude* "with high distinction"; *Member,* Phi Beta Kappa (America's most prestigious honor society); *Participant,* Honors Program; *Recipient,* Merrill Scholarship for Study Abroad (Spain and Dominican Republic)

Law School: Emory University School of Law (Atlanta, Georgia)

Law Degree and Graduation Year: Juris Doctor/Doctor of Jurisprudence (J.D.) - Class of 2004

Law School Honors, Achievements and Activities: *Participant,* Semester Abroad, University College London Faculty of Laws (London, England)

PROFESSIONAL ACCOMPLISHMENTS

Other Legal Experience: *Case Clerk,* Alston & Bird, LLP; *Latino Justice Corporate Legal Intern,* IBM Americas

Other Professional Work Experience:

Assistant Dean of Recruitment and Admissions, Morehouse College; *Assistant Director of Admissions,* University of California Hastings College of the Law; *Deputy Director for Education Pipeline Programs,* Office of Diversity and Engagement, University of California Office of the President

LESSONS LEARNED: MY RECOMMENDATIONS FOR YOUR FUTURE ACTIONS BASED ON MY PAST EXPERIENCE

Advice on Making the Choice to Apply to and to Attend Law School:

Visit a first-year lecture course at a local law school (even one you're not interested in attending). The experience provides a great insight into the life of a law student.

Advice on Law School Preparation:

Choose an undergraduate major based on what you like, not one that you think most closely mimics law school content. Law schools want scientists, philosophers, sociologists, linguists, economists, and many other disciplines to fill their classes. It's this multitude of experiences that makes for an engaging classroom discussion and prepares lawyers to represent our diverse country.

Advice on Applying to Law School:

Apply early, follow the application instructions carefully, and make your application documents (e.g., personal statement, letters of recommendation, resume, etc.) fit together like pieces of a puzzle that tell your personal story.

Advice Regarding Academic Success, Co-Curricular and Extra-Curricular Participation, and Social Engagement in Law School:

Make friends and study groups with people from different backgrounds than your own. Not only will this help you in your professional relationships, but it will also help you to understand things from a different perspective.

Advice on Preparing for and Taking the Bar Exam:

Treat bar prep like a full-time job with mandatory overtime.

Advice on Choosing a Legal Job and Career Path Inside or Outside the Legal Profession:

You can really do a lot with a law degree. But if you seek a non-traditional career path (not practicing law), it can be challenging for the first few years out of law school. Many jobs will deem you overqualified because of your J.D. So, it's important to at least be open to practicing or doing some legal-related job for a while to get experience. Eventually, more opportunities will come if you pursue them.

Advice on Achieving Career Success and Advancement:

Be a mentor! Opportunities come with helping others.

Thoughts About Why Earning a Law Degree Is a Powerful Credential for African Americans and Why There Is a Need for More African American Lawyers:

It's extremely important for African American and other underrepresented groups to participate in the legal profession. Lawyers interpret law and advocate policies that lead to new laws. Historically, these groups have been left out of the conversation and disproportionately affected by unfair rules. A legal education allows us to be part of the conversation and work to effectuate change.

LEGACY AND SUCCESS

My Most Outstanding Accomplishments:

My most outstanding accomplishments are the relationships I have made over time, both professional and personal. I believe that everything we endeavor to do in life is somehow related to fostering and maintaining mutually fulfilling connections with other people.

The Legacy I Hope to Leave:

I hope to impact each individual with whom I have had the pleasure to know in a unique and personal way.

The Secret to My Success:

I strive to live a unique life and to do things that make me and those around me happy. Success for me comes as a result.

Yolanda D. Wesley Ingram, Esq.
Director of Bar Support and Assistant Teaching Professor
Drexel University Thomas R. Kline School of Law
Philadelphia, Pennsylvania

"You can give out, but don't give up!"
"Sometimes Plan B means Better!"
— Yolanda D. Wesley Ingram

Success is . . . being able to enjoy your professional career as well as your personal life; being able to do the work you love and support others in their career and life goals; being the change that you want to see in the world.

PERSONAL FAVORITES

Favorite Quotes: "In all thy ways acknowledge Him, and He will direct thy path." - Proverbs 3:6

"For I know the plans I have for you," declares the LORD, "plans to prosper you and not to harm you, plans to give you hope and a future." - Jeremiah 29:11

Favorite Books: *Flyy Girl* by Omar Tyree; *Your Blues Ain't Like Mine* by Bebe Moore Campbell; *Makes Me Wanna Holler* by Nathan McCall; *The Rage of the Privileged Class* by Ellis Cose; *Envy of the World on Being a Black Man* by Ellis Cose

Favorite Movies: *Hunger Games*; *Bram Stoker's Dracula (1992)*; *Aliens*; *The Joy Luck Club*; *It's a Wonderful Life*; *Imitation of Life (1969)*; *Dawn of the Dead (2004)*; *Underworld*; *Resident Evil*; *The Road*; *Reign of Fire*

Favorite Songs: "I Need Love" by LL Cool J; "When Doves Cry" by Prince; "Whatever You Want" by Tony! Toni! Toné!

Favorite Musical Artists: Prince; Angie Stone; Marvin Gaye; Whitney Houston; Aretha Franklin; Michael Jackson; Mary J. Blige

Favorite Law School Classes: Torts; Bioethics; Worker's Compensation

Favorite Legal Cases: *Brown v. Board of Education*; *Grutter v. Bollinger*; *Fisher v. University of Texas*

Favorite Hobbies: Reading; Traveling; Fishing; Horseback riding; Playing tennis; Bowling; Playing board games; Writing; Running 5Ks

Favorite Attorney Role Model: Johnnie Cochran

FAMILY AND BACKGROUND

Where Born and Raised: Born - Mound Bayou, Mississippi; Raised - Renova, Mississippi

Family (Spouse/Partner and Children): Spouse - Kevin; Children - (daughter) Kassidy and (son) Kellen

Family Socioeconomic and Educational Background:

My mom finished high school and two years of community college. I don't know my father. I was a first-generation college and first-generation law school graduate. I am the only lawyer in my family but most of my first cousins have college degrees now. I was the first to finish at a four-year college.

THE DECISION TO BECOME A LAWYER

When and Why I Decided to Become a Lawyer: I decided to become a lawyer in middle school because I saw the powerful impact that the law could have on someone's life when I was the witness and victim in a sexual assault case.

EDUCATIONAL ACHIEVEMENTS

High School: Cleveland High School (Cleveland, Mississippi) (Cleveland High School doesn't exist anymore. It has been merged with another high school and is now Cleveland Central.)

College/University: University of Mississippi (Oxford, Mississippi)

Undergraduate Degree: Bachelor of Arts (B.A.)

Major: English

College Honors, Achievements and Activities: *Inductee,* Ole Miss Hall of Fame; Graduated *summa cum laude* "with highest distinction"; *Member,* Phi Kappa Phi (honor society); *Listed Honoree,* Who's Who Among American Colleges and Universities; *Member,* Omicron Delta Kappa (leadership honor society); *Member and Officer,* Alpha Kappa Alpha Sorority, Inc.; *Academic Recognition,* Chancellor's Honor Roll

Law School: Washburn University School of Law (Topeka, Kansas)

Law Degree and Graduation Year: Juris Doctor/Doctor of Jurisprudence (J.D.) - Class of 1995

Law School Honors, Achievements and Activities: Dean's Honors; *Member,* Washburn Law Journal; *Academic Support Tutor and Student Director,* Washburn University School of Law; Patricia Roberts Harris Fellow; *Member,* Black Law Student Association; *Member,* Phi Alpha Delta Law Fraternity, International

PROFESSIONAL ACCOMPLISHMENTS

State Bar Memberships (Where Licensed to Practice Law): Missouri; Kansas

Other Legal Experience: *Assistant Dean of Admissions,* Washburn University School of Law; *Dean of Students and Legal Research and Writing Instructor,* University of Memphis Cecil C. Humphreys School of Law; *Attorney,* Unnamed Large Law Firm; *Account Manager,* Thomas Reuters (Formerly West Group); *Legal Research and Writing Instructor,* Temple University School of Law; *Assistant Dean for Student Services,* Penn State's Dickinson School of Law

Professional Organizations: *Member,* Association of Academic Support Educators; *Member,* Law School Admissions Association; *Member,* Keystone Bar Association

Post-Law School Honors, Achievements, Activities, and Community Involvement: *Member,* Penn State Commission on Racial/Ethnic Diversity (CORED) (2015-2019); *Panelist and Moderator,* National Diversity Pre-Law Conference and Law Fair (2014); *2015 Discover Law Speaker,* Why Pipeline Programs Matter; *Washburn BLSA Panelist,* Minority Student Access to Higher Education (2014); *Member,* Law School Admission Council (LSAC) Forum Workgroup Subcommittee (2013-2015); *LSAC Site Chair,* Academic Assistance Topical Workshop; *Panelist and Planning Committee,* Annual Law School Diversity Professionals Conference (2012); *Diversity & Admissions Panelist,* Law School Admissions Council (2009-2012); *Member,* Board of Directors, Ben F. Jones Chapter, National Bar Association (2009-2011); *Diversity Committee Member and Summer Law Intern Program Coordinator,* Memphis Bar Association; *Board of Directors,* Tennessee Alliance for Black Lawyers; *Access & Diversity Committee,* The University of Memphis; *Featured Panelist,* National Black Pre-Law Conference and Law Fair (2005 and 2010); *Awardee,* President's Award, Memphis Bar Association (2008); *Awardee,* President's Award, National Bar Association (2011); *Honoree,* Woman of the Year in Education, Epsilon Epsilon Chapter, Alpha Kappa Alpha Sorority, Inc. (2005); *President,* The University of Mississippi Black Alumni Advisory Council (2011-2012); *Fellow,* Memphis Bar Foundation (2009-2010)

LESSONS LEARNED: MY RECOMMENDATIONS FOR YOUR FUTURE ACTIONS BASED ON MY PAST EXPERIENCE

Advice on Law School Preparation:

If you are planning to go to law school, you should take college seriously. First and foremost, keep your Grade Point Average (GPA) up as high as possible. Second, get involved in extra-curricular activities and community service that interests you. Do not let the extra-curriculars interfere with the classroom. Choose a major based upon your interests and what will prepare you for law school. Do not pick criminal justice because it will not prepare you for the rigors of law school. Criminal justice prepares you for a career in the criminal justice field, not law school. Follow your passion.

Advice on Applying to and Selecting a Law School:

Do your research before applying to law school. Compare the cost and the scholarship offers carefully. Sometimes the rankings do not matter as much as the amount of debt that you incur. Find a school that is a good fit for your personality. Go to the law school that makes you feel comfortable. You will learn better in an environment where you feel like you belong. Keep your debt down to a minimum to allow you more flexibility in choosing your first legal position after law school. Also, consider where the law school is located. Other than the top 14 law schools, there are no national schools and you will likely end up practicing in the same state (or surrounding states) where the law school is located. Be sure that you are mobile and willing to relocate where the best opportunities are.

Advice Regarding Academic Success, Co-Curricular and Extra-Curricular Participation, and Social Engagement in Law School:

Law school can be a very isolating, competitive challenge. Many schools only give exams one time per year and the grades are ranked. Only 10% of the class can be in the top 10%. Just because you are not in the top 10% does not mean that you will not get a job after law school. Make sure that you pursue moot court or law review and extra-curricular activities in law school that match your interests and passions. Remember why you went to law school. Do you want to serve underrepresented communities, save the planet, help the elderly or help children? Remind yourself often of why you are in law school. Make a few friends who you can trust and rely on during your law school journey.

Advice on Preparing for and Taking the Bar Exam:

Take as many bar exam courses as you can during law school. Take as many writing courses as you can in law school. Sign up for a reputable bar prep program and find out what your law school has to offer in terms of support. Don't wait until the last minute to prepare for the bar exam. Be aware of what you need to study from the first year of law school.

Advice Regarding Choosing a Job and Career Path Inside or Outside of the Legal Profession:

Keep your options open regarding your legal job career path. Your first job may not be your dream job, but you will get great experience for the next position. Be willing to be flexible and willing to relocate to get your foot in the door. Everyone has to pay dues to get to the place that you want to be in the long run. Remember short-term sacrifice equals long-term rewards.

Advice on Seeking Legal Job Opportunities and/or Creating One's Own Opportunities:

The people in the career services office can't help you if they don't know you. Make sure that you visit them for resume review, mock interviews and take advantage of all of the resources that they provide. Use the people in your network to make connections and don't be afraid to ask for help, advice and guidance from other attorneys and law professors.

Advice on Career Success and Advancement:

Find at least two mentors, one personal and one professional, to help guide you through your career path. Ask questions of people who are where you would like to be. Invite them to coffee or lunch and gain insight. Read and keep reading books and articles about navigating corporate America.

Advice on Overcoming the Additional Challenges Black Law Students Face:

Recognize that the legal profession is a conservative profession and slow to change. You will have to conform to a certain extent regardless of your background. As a Black person, when you are sometimes the only face that looks like yours in the room, it can be exhausting. Self-care is important. Surround yourself with other like-minded individuals to maintain your sanity. You will need a strong support system to battle prejudice on a daily basis. Many middle-class, White students have a very narrow, limited world view. It is not your job to educate them but be aware that you will be astonished and shocked at the lack of exposure some of them have had to other cultures. Despite social media, we still have a very insular and isolated society when it comes to race, ethnicity, religion and sexual orientation. Just be aware of and appreciate that most people come from the perspective that their life experience is NORMAL, and everyone else's is abnormal, just because it is different.

Advice on Overcoming the Additional Challenges Black Lawyers Face:

Black lawyers, especially, women and those who look young tend to encounter racism, ageism and sexism regularly. Often clients and judges and other attorneys assume that you are not an attorney. They will think that you are a secretary, law student, paralegal or anything other than an attorney. Seeing a Black lawyer is not what most people are accustomed to thanks to the image that is portrayed by the media. The stereotypical lawyer is White, male and middle-aged. You will need to deal with this, and it will bother you sometimes and other times it won't. Pick your battles wisely and mentally prepare a response.

Best Advice I Received Regarding Law School and the Legal Profession:

The best advice I received was to get to know my law professors when I was in law school. They are your best allies and best mentors. They can help guide your legal career for decades. Also, they can help you improve your exam performance. The best advice that I ever got from a law professor was to take as many seminar classes as I could to become a better writer.

Worst Advice I Received Regarding Law School and the Legal Profession:

The worst advice that I ever got was to take a job at a big law firm when I did not like the practice area.

Best Advice I Would Give to an Aspiring Black Lawyer:

I would tell aspiring Black lawyers to not give up on their dreams, no matter what. Set goals and have a plan. Plan your work and work your plan. Seek out supporters and allies to help guide you and listen to their advice. Ask questions and keep asking questions until you find a way to achieve your dreams and goals. Remember a goal is a dream with a deadline.

Thoughts About Why Earning a Law Degree Is a Powerful Credential for African Americans and Why There Is a Need for More African American Lawyers:

Lawyers are the people who can fight the system when it is unjust and corrupt. Every movement in our society has been led by lawyers. Without African American lawyers, we would not have the right to vote or attend integrated schools. Laws control every aspect of our society from the moment we are born until the day that we die. Without understanding how the legal system works, then we are defenseless against those who would abuse the laws put in place to protect citizens.

Thoughts About Whether Law School Is Worth the Financial Investment:

Law school can be very affordable if you choose the best financial offer. Law school enrollment is down which makes it easier to get in and less competitive for scholarships. Prepare well for the Law School Admission Test (LSAT) and find law schools where you meet or exceed the minimum to gain admission and free money. Keep your loans to a minimum until the legal job market improves. Investing in an LSAT prep course is a sound investment to help reduce your debt in the long run.

LEGACY AND SUCCESS

The Legacy I Hope to Leave:

I hope that my legacy will be that I helped as many people who dreamed to become attorneys achieve that dream. I am only one person, but I have helped hundreds of others attain the goal of becoming a lawyer. This means that for all of the lives that they will change, I will have played some small part in helping the people who they have helped. This is my life's legacy - to be a dream merchant.

The Secret to My Success:

The secret to my success is faith, God first and family. My family has always been my biggest cheerleaders. My mom sacrificed a lot to help me achieve my dream of being a lawyer. My grandmother and grandfather supported me and so did my mom's sisters and brothers. I stand on their shoulders. I am here because they prayed for me and paved the way for me to get an education and pursue my dreams. They never gave up on me. But they would say that I was always self-motivated and driven to achieve academically. They would say that I would not accept defeat or "no" for an answer when it came to being the best that I could be. They instilled hard work and work ethic in me when I was young and for that, I am eternally grateful. Also, for instilling in me a faith in God and hope for the future that could not be seen when I was growing up below the poverty line in the rural Mississippi Delta. On my hardest day, I remember that it could be worse, I could be picking cotton. My grandparents were sharecroppers who picked and chopped cotton before I was born. With God, all things are possible. Now, I am an attorney and administrator for a top university. I am beyond blessed and highly favored.

Darrell D. Jackson, J.D., Ph.D.
Professor of Law
University of Wyoming College of Law
Laramie, Wyoming

"Respect all ... fear none!"
– Darrell D. Jackson

Success is . . . defining what you want to accomplish and accomplishing it, no matter how long it takes or how much pain it requires.

PERSONAL FAVORITES

Favorite Quote: "You cannot tell the story of the fish from the fisherman's mouth." - Anonymous Indigenous Proverb

Favorite Books: *And We Are Not Saved* by Derrick Bell; *The Miner's Canary* by Lani Guinier and Gerald Torres; *Racism on Trial: The Chicano Fight for Justice* by Ian F. Haney Lopez; *The Education of Blacks in the South, 1860-1935* by James D. Anderson; *Racial Formation in the United States* by Michael Omi and Howard Winant; *Racism Without Racists* by Eduardo Bonilla-Silva; *Pedagogy of the Oppressed* by Paulo Freire; *Discipline & Punish: The Birth of the Prison* by Michel Foucault

Favorite Movies: *Black Panther; Creed; Boomerang; 300; Strictly Business*

Favorite Musical Artists: Prince; Queen; Boyz II Men; Ludacris; NF; Regina Carter; Miles Davis; John Coltrane

Favorite Law School Classes: Criminal Law; Criminal Procedure; Secured Transactions

Favorite Legal Cases: *Brown v. Board of Education; Mapp v. Ohio; Marbury v. Madison*

Favorite Hobbies: Playing golf; Working out; Reading; Watching movies; Racing motorcycles; Practicing martial arts

Favorite Attorney Role Models: Charles Hamilton Houston; Derrick Bell; Douglas Wilder; Barack Obama

FAMILY AND BACKGROUND

Where Born and Raised: Born - Cleveland, Ohio; Raised - Reston, Virginia

Family (Spouse/Partner and Children): Spouse - Kristine; Child - (son) Dre

Family Socioeconomic and Educational Background: As a child, my father worked for the federal government and my mother had a variety of jobs. Before I entered college, both of my brothers had completed college and one had gone on to earn a M.D./Ph.D. As a family, we were far from wealthy but definitely had everything we needed.

THE DECISION TO BECOME A LAWYER

When and Why I Decided to Become a Lawyer: During the winter break of my senior year in college, one of my high school teachers (Mrs. Lee Cox), who served as my "second mom", opined that I should go to law school and set me on the path.

EDUCATIONAL ACHIEVEMENTS

High School: South Lakes High School (Reston, Virginia)
College/University: College of William & Mary (Williamsburg, Virginia)
Undergraduate Degree: Bachelor of Arts (B.A.)
Major: Spanish

College Honors, Achievements and Activities: *Team Member,* Varsity Football; *Team Member,* Varsity Men's Track & Field

Law School: George Mason University School of Law (Arlington, Virginia)

Law Degree and Graduation Year: Juris Doctor/Doctor of Jurisprudence (J.D.) - Class of 1990

Law School Honors, Achievements and Activities: *Editor-in-Chief and Co-founder,* George Mason University Civil Rights Law Journal; *Editor-in-Chief,* George Mason University School of Law's publication of the National Black Law Journal (1988-1989); *Associate Justice,* Moot Court Board; *Editorial Board Member, The Docket* newspaper; *Member,* Phi Delta Phi Legal Fraternity

Other Graduate or Professional Degree: Doctor of Philosophy (Ph.D.) in Education Foundations, Policy, and Practice, University of Colorado School of Education (Boulder, Colorado)

PROFESSIONAL ACCOMPLISHMENTS

State Bar Membership (Where Admitted to Practice Law): Virginia

Other Legal Work Experience: *Fellow,* University of Colorado Law School; *Assistant Dean,* George Mason University School of Law; *Faculty Member,* National Advocacy Center; *Adjunct Professor,* Marymount University; *Assistant United States Attorney,* Washington, DC; *Assistant County Attorney,* Fairfax, Virginia; *Law Clerk,* Judge Marcus D. Williams, 19th Judicial Circuit of Virginia; *Law Clerk,* Judge L.M. Brinkema, United States District Court for the Eastern District of Virginia

LESSONS LEARNED: MY RECOMMENDATIONS FOR YOUR FUTURE ACTIONS BASED ON MY PAST EXPERIENCE

Advice on Law School Preparation:

Start the second you decide you're going to law school. Read books about the 1L experience. Research the first-year classes and get study aids that will provide you with a foundation. Law school is a sprint! Don't wait until you're halfway through to wake up and figure out that you're in the game.

Advice on Applying to and Selecting a Law School:

Apply to "stretch" schools, "most likely" schools, and "for sure" schools. To put a name with a face, visit as many schools as you can. Be in contact so that the school understands your level of interest but make sure you do not get obnoxious with the level of contact.

Advice Regarding Academic Success, Co-Curricular and Extra-Curricular Participation, and Social Engagement in Law School:

During your 1L year, focus on academics. Network with intentionality. Find people doing what you hope to do, go to them, and ask them for suggestions, guidance, and direction.

Advice on Preparing for and Taking the Bar Exam:

Take a bar preparation course and take practice exams in settings that mirror the actual exam until you can no longer count how many practice tests you've taken.

Advice on Choosing a Job and Career Path Inside or Outside of the Legal Profession:

You know who you are and what you enjoy. As you take classes, find people doing what intrigues or excites you most and ask what they did to get there. Use that information to guide what is best for who you are.

Advice on Achieving Career Success and Advancement:

A career is made up of a lot of individual days. Make a plan for 1, 3, 5, 10, 20, and 30 years out but pay attention to each individual day and that you're progressing one step at a time.

Advice on Overcoming the Additional Challenges Black Law Students and Lawyers Face:

Remember that you are not alone and that those who paved the path before us succeeded under a much heavier yoke.

Best Advice I Received Regarding Law School and the Legal Profession:

Work to be number 1, but, always remember what they call the student who graduated last in their class … a lawyer.

Worst Advice I Received Regarding Law School and the Legal Profession:

Just rely on the casebook and class time.

Best Advice I Would Give to an Aspiring Black Lawyer:

Be who you are (that's what got you here so far). Focus on your academics. Get out and meet all the people that you can who are doing what you aspire to do.

Thoughts About Why Earning a Law Degree Is a Powerful Credential for African Americans and Why There Is a Need for More African American Lawyers:

Most everything is connected to or led by the law. Historically marginalized communities NEED people who understand the nuances of the legal language. Finally, research the percentage of the population, nationally and internationally, that has a law degree and you will further understand your uniqueness.

LEGACY AND SUCCESS

My Most Outstanding Accomplishment:

Professionally, my students as well as my books and articles published to date.

The Legacy I Hope to Leave:

The professional legacy that I hope to leave is being built through two groups: One, the students who continually join with me as part of my educational community. Two, the researchers who glean some bit of wisdom or knowledge from my articles and books.

The Secret to My Success:

Faith, family, and focus!

Shirley A. Jefferson, Esq.

Associate Dean for Student Affairs and Diversity and **Associate Professor of Law**
Vermont Law School
South Royalton, Vermont

"Quality is the result of doing ordinary things extraordinarily well."
– Shirley A. Jefferson

Success is . . . having a career or a job that you look forward to and enjoy every morning when you wake up.

PERSONAL FAVORITES

Favorite Quotes: "Law is nothing but common sense and reasoning. Once it ceases to be that, it ceases to be law." - Thomas Paine

"Do unto others as you would have them do unto you." - Matthew 7:12

Favorite Book: *Having Our Say: The Delany Sisters' First 100 Years* by Sarah L. Delany and A. Elizabeth Delany with Amy Hill Hearth

Favorite Movie: *The Good, the Bad and the Ugly*

Favorite Song: "No Charge" by Rev. Shirley Caesar

Favorite Law School Classes: Property; Tax; Wills & Trusts; Sales; Constitutional Law

Favorite Legal Case: *Brown v. Board of Education*

Favorite Attorney Role Model: Attorney Wilhelmina J. Rolark, President and CEO Emeritus, United Black Fund

FAMILY AND BACKGROUND

Where Born and Raised: Selma, Alabama

Family (Spouse/Partner and Children): Child - (son) Jamaal

Family Socioeconomic and Educational Background:

I am from a poor/working class family. My mother earned a high school diploma. My father earned a sixth-grade education. I am the first in my family to attend law school.

THE DECISION TO BECOME A LAWYER

When and Why I Decided to Become a Lawyer: I decided to be a lawyer when I was about 10 years old. I grew up in Selma, Alabama under the Jim Crow laws and saw the injustice shown toward Black people. And that's when I decided to dedicate my life to fighting injustice.

EDUCATIONAL ACHIEVEMENTS

High School: Selma High (Selma, Alabama)

College/University: Southeastern University (Washington, D.C.)

Undergraduate Degree: Bachelor of Science (B.S.)

Major: Public Administration

College Honors, Achievements and Activities: Graduated *summa cum laude* "with the highest distinction"; *Academic Recognition,* Dean's List; *Member,* Delta Sigma Theta Sorority, Inc.

Law School: Vermont Law School (South Royalton, Vermont)

Law Degree and Graduation Year: Juris Doctor/Doctor of Jurisprudence (J.D.) - Class of 1986

Law School Honors, Achievements and Activities: *Recipient,* Juris Doctor Alumni Association Award; *Recipient,* Debevoise Family Scholarship; *Founder,* Minority Student Group

PROFESSIONAL ACCOMPLISHMENTS

State Bar Membership (Where Licensed to Practice Law): District of Columbia

Other Legal Experience: *Title IX Officer,* Vermont Law School; *General Counsel,* United Black Fund, Inc.; *Associate Counsel,* Law Office of Wilhelmina J. Rolark; *Legislative Assistant,* Committee on Judiciary to Council Member Wilhelmina J. Rolark

Professional Organizations: *Member,* District of Columbia Bar Association; *Member,* National Bar Association; *Member,* American Bar Association; *Member,* American Law School Association; *Member,* Vermont Law School Alumni Association

Post-Law School Honors, Achievements, Activities, and Community Involvement: *Member,* Vermont State Police Advisory Commission; *Commencement Speaker,* South Royalton High School; *Commencement Speaker,* Sharon Academy; *Commencement Speaker,* Tunbridge Elementary & Middle School; *Awardee,* Staff Service Award, Student Bar Association, Vermont Law School; *Awardee,* Phenomenal Woman Award, Women's Law Group, Vermont Law School; *Awardee,* General Counsel Award, United Black Fund, Inc.; *Awardee,* Outstanding Award, Black Law Students Association, Vermont Law School; *Honoree,* Legal Education Access and Diversity Champion, National Black Pre-Law Conference and Law Fair; *Panelist and Moderator,* National HBCU Pre-Law Summit & Law Expo; *Panelist, Moderator and Special Guest Speaker,* National Diversity Pre-Law Conference and Law Fair; *Panelist and Moderator,* National Black Pre-Law Conference and Law Fair

LESSONS LEARNED: MY RECOMMENDATIONS FOR YOUR FUTURE ACTIONS BASED ON MY PAST EXPERIENCE

Advice on Law School Preparation:

Start reading *The New York Times, The Quarterly Journal of Economics* and *The Economist.* A lot of Law School Admission Test (LSAT) questions are taken from these articles. Take as many practice exams as you can and review your answers.

Advice on Applying to and Selecting a Law School:

Apply to schools that are looking for diverse applicants and are outside of your comfort zone.

Advice Regarding Academic Success, Co-Curricular and Extra-Curricular Participation, and Social Engagement in Law School:

Limit your involvement in co-curricular and extra-curricular activities. Use that time to study and take practice exams.

Advice on Preparing for and Taking the Bar Exam:

Take as many practice exams as possible under the time allowed. Review all of your answers.

Advice on Choosing a Job and Career Path Inside or Outside of the Legal Profession:

Follow your heart and not what others might want you to do.

Advice on Seeking Legal Job Opportunities and/or Creating One's Own Opportunities:

Before going on an interview, do several mock interviews. Apply for as many jobs as possible. If you put nothing out, nothing will come back.

Advice on Achieving Career Success and Advancement:

Work hard, study hard, be self-motivated and think outside the box for career opportunities. Prepare yourself for a lot of career networking.

Advice on Overcoming the Additional Challenges Black Law Students Face:

Law school requires effective communication, organization and analytical skills and you must demonstrate aptitude for problem-solving and decision-making. Start preparing yourself today.

Best Advice I Received Regarding Law School and the Legal Profession:

Go to a small, quiet, rural law school and use its isolation to excel in the study of law.

Best Advice I Would Give to an Aspiring Black Lawyer:

Cultivate relationships and work collaboratively with other Black and White lawyers. Find a diverse group of lawyers and keep communication open and free.

Thoughts About Why Earning a Law Degree Is a Powerful Credential for African Americans and Why There Is a Need for More African American Lawyers:

A law degree will provide you with great knowledge, leadership skills, and experience that will lead you into positions of power and responsibility, and your influence can be felt throughout the U.S. and in countries around the world. The legal profession needs more dedicated African American lawyers. The legal profession is 77% White and only 23% People of Color.

Thoughts About Whether and Why Law School Is Worth the Financial Investment:

Law school is worth the money. Your law degree is worth five or six times what you will be paid as a lawyer. Also, no one can take away the knowledge you received by attending law school.

LEGACY AND SUCCESS

My Most Outstanding Accomplishment:

Being a Black woman lawyer is my most outstanding accomplishment – both personally and professionally!

The Legacy I Hope to Leave:

To know that I opened the Vermont Law School door for many students who ordinarily would not have been given the opportunity to attend law school.

The Secret to My Success:

I am a highly motivated individual and love to learn. I am always open and looking for new ideas and opportunities.

Practical Wisdom for Those on the Path to Lawyerhood

Danné L. Johnson, Esq.
Constance Baker Motley Professor of Law
Oklahoma City University School of Law
Oklahoma City, Oklahoma

"Just do your part."

— Danné Johnson

Success is . . . doing your part to make the world a great place and waking to do it again and again.

PERSONAL FAVORITES

Favorite Quote: "I am the dream and the hope of the slave." – Maya Angelou, "Still I Rise"

Favorite Book: *Their Eyes Were Watching God* by Zora Neale Hurston

Favorite Movie: *Gladiator*

Favorite Songs: "Fragile" by Sting; "I Hate You" by Prince

Favorite Law School Class: Civil Procedure

Favorite Legal Case: *Brown v. Board of Education* (subject matter and litigators)

Favorite Hobbies: Watching movies; Cooking

Favorite Attorney Role Models: Constance Baker Motley; Thurgood Marshall; Ruth Bader Ginsburg

FAMILY AND BACKGROUND

Where Born and Raised: Detroit, Michigan

Family (Spouse/Partner and Children): Spouse - Reginald; Children – (daughter) Layla and (son) Ahmad

Family Socioeconomic and Educational Background: I come from a working-class family and was the first to attend college. I was raised by a single mother.

THE DECISION TO BECOME A LAWYER

When and Why I Decided to Become a Lawyer: My mother sued her employer and I fell in love with the wording of the affidavit.

EDUCATIONAL ACHIEVEMENTS

High School: University Liggett School (Grosse Pointe Woods, Michigan)

College/University: University of Pennsylvania (Philadelphia, Pennsylvania)

Undergraduate Degree: Bachelor of Arts (B.A.)

Major: African American Studies

College Honors, Achievements and Activities: *Member,* Black Student Association; *Member,* Nominations and Elections Committee, Black Student Association; *Participant,* Semester at Sea, University of Pittsburgh; *Study Abroad Student,* University of Ibadan (Ibadan, Nigeria)

Law School: The George Washington University Law School (Washington, D.C.); Tulane University Law School (New Orleans, Louisiana) (Spent 1L Year at Tulane Law and then transferred)

Law Degree and Graduation Year: Juris Doctor/Doctor of Jurisprudence (J.D.) – Class of 1994

Law School Honors, Achievements and Activities:
Participant, Minority Clerkship Program**;** *Law Student Clinic Participant,* Small Business, Consumer Mediation, and Bankruptcy Clinics; *Member,* Phi Alpha Delta Legal Fraternity, International; *Member,* Black Law Students Association (BLSA)

PROFESSIONAL ACCOMPLISHMENTS

State Bar Membership (Where Admitted to Practice Law): New York

Other Legal Work Experience: *Hearing Officer,* Oklahoma Department of Securities; *Arbitrator,* Dispute Resolution, Financial Industry Regulatory Authority; *Counsel,* Securities and Variable Annuities Sections, MetLife; *Branch Chief,* U.S. Securities and Exchange Commission; *Division of Enforcement/Branch Chief,* U.S. Securities and Exchange Commission; *Senior Counsel,* U.S. Securities and Exchange Commission; *Attorney Recruitment Coordinator,* U.S. Securities and Exchange Commission; *Summer Associate,* Hughes Hubbard & Reed

Other Professional Work Experience: *Corporate Trainer,* Oklahoma Center for Nonprofits; *Diversity Trainer*

Professional Organizations:

Member, Section on Women in Legal Education, American Association of Law Schools (AALS); *Member,* Finance and Legal Committee, Law School Admissions Council (LSAC)

Post-Law School Honors, Achievements, Activities, and Community Involvement:

Awardee, Lifetime Achievement Award, Oklahoma City University School of Law Alumni (2020); *Honoree,* Breakfast for MiLady, Oklahoma City Alumnae Chapter, Delta Sigma Theta Sorority, Inc.); *Awardee,* Ada Lois Sipuel Fisher Award for Diversity, Oklahoma City Association of Black Lawyers (2019); *Listed Honoree,* Selected among the "50 Making a Difference", The Journal Record (2012, 2018); *Law Student Volunteer Coordinator,* Make a Will and Financial Planning Program (2010-Present); *Church Coordinator,* Make a Will and Financial Planning Program (2010-2013); *Member,* The Links, Inc., Oklahoma City Chapter (2010-Present); *Strategic Committee Chair,* The Links, Inc., Oklahoma City Chapter (2019); *Co-Chair,* National Trends Facet, The Links, Inc., Oklahoma City Chapter (2017-2019); *Co-Chair,* International Trends and Services, The Links, Inc., Oklahoma City Chapter (2013-2015); *Appointed Interim Parliamentarian,* The Links, Inc., Oklahoma City Chapter (2011-2012); *Parliamentarian,* Jack and Jill of America, Inc., Oklahoma City Chapter (2015-2016); *Bylaw Revision Chairman,* Jack and Jill of America, Inc., Oklahoma City Chapter (2014-2016); *Member of the Bench,* Ruth Bader Ginsburg Inn of Court (2016-2018); *Member,* Board of Directors, Young Women's Christian Association - Oklahoma City (YWCA-OKC) (2014-2017); *1st Vice Chair,* Board of Directors, YWCA-OKC (2016-2017); *Executive Committee,* Young Women's Christian Association - Oklahoma City (YMCA-OKC) (2016-2017); *Governance Committee,* Young Women's Christian Association - Oklahoma City (YMCA-OKC) (2014-2017); *Finance Committee,* Young Women's Christian Association - Oklahoma City (YMCA-OKC) (2015-2017); *Member,* Zeta Phi Beta Sorority, Incorporated; *Member,* Sisterhood and Inclusion Committee (National Service), Zeta Phi Beta Sorority, Incorporated (2017-2018); *Member,* Legal Advisory Council, Zeta Phi Beta Sorority, Incorporated (2015-2018); *Midwestern Regional Representative*. National Constitution and Bylaw Committee (Regional Service) Zeta Phi Beta Sorority, Incorporated (2015-Present); *Midwestern Regional Phylacter (Parliamentarian),* (Regional Service) Zeta Phi Beta Sorority, Incorporated (2013-2016); *Oklahoma State Director,* (State Service) Zeta Phi Beta Sorority, Incorporated (2018-Present)**;** *Membership Intake Coordinator,* (Chapter Service) Zeta Phi Beta Sorority, Incorporated (2019-2020); *President,* (Chapter Service) Zeta Phi Beta Sorority, Incorporated (2017-2019); *Phylacter (Parliamentarian),* (Chapter Service) Zeta Phi Beta Sorority, Incorporated (2015-2017); *Honoree,* Black Girls Rock Award, Alpha Kappa Alpha Sorority, Inc. (2012); *Member,* Board of Directors, Community Youth Outreach; *Program Committee Chair,* Community Youth Outreach (2011-2012); *Member,* Community Youth Outreach (2011-2012); *Member,* Board of Directors, The Miracle Makers, Inc.; *Chairman,* The Miracle Makers, Inc. (1999-2002); *Member,* The Miracle Makers. Inc. (1995-2003)

LESSONS LEARNED: MY RECOMMENDATIONS FOR YOUR FUTURE ACTIONS BASED ON MY PAST EXPERIENCE

Advice on Law School Preparation:

Time management is the key to law school academic success. The focus of school is learning and networking. Remember to build your network. It is possible that you have never given it 100%. This is the time to try it. Go all in. Also, this is the time to check in with your mental health provider, if you have one. This type of stress and anxiety needs to be managed.

Advice on Applying to and Selecting a Law School:

Consider geographic mobility. The higher the rank the more geographic mobility. If this is not important and you desire a local practice, then ranking is less important.

Advice Regarding Academic Success, Co-Curricular and Extra-Curricular Participation, and Social Engagement in Law School:

You should engage in one academic and one social activity or club, think of spreading your wings, meeting new people and trying new things.

Advice on Preparing for and Taking the Bar Exam:

By this time you have studied hard. This is not the time to take a break. Make a schedule and stick to it. Follow your plan to the bitter end. You will take a bar prep course, get your money's worth, follow those classes step by step.

Advice on Choosing a Job and Career Path Inside or Outside of the Legal Profession:

If you are in law school following a dream, stay focused. Look at the resumes and career paths of those who occupy the positions that you desire, network, and be fearless. What do you want from a job? Define this, write it down. How do you want to feel at the end of the week? How do you imagine spending your time each day? All important questions.

Advice on Seeking Legal Job Opportunities and/or Creating One's Own Opportunities:

This is where your network comes in and your years of networking skills … 1. What to wear? Look it up. You need to look like a lawyer, a job seeker, a trusted person. 2. What to say? You should do mock interviews and actually write out your answers so that you will be prepared. 3. What to ask? You are looking for certain things in an employer. What are these things? Prestige, experience, geography, influence. Let these matters guide your inquiry.

Advice on Achieving Career Success and Advancement:

Consider entering an official mentoring relationship with a senior person. You need peers (listen and offer suggestions), mentors (offer guidance about life and career), and a sponsor (requires you to do things and opens doors for you, places you in the path of opportunities with intention).

Advice on Overcoming the Additional Challenges Black Law Students and Lawyers Face:

You are excellent but often misunderstood before you can get a word in. You need to always be prepared to point to the value that you bring, dress the part, and be well studied. People work with and give things to other people. There is bias but there is very little that you can do to change people. So, do your part.

Best Advice I Received Regarding Law School and the Legal Profession:

Stay focused and set yourself up to do your best.

Worst Advice I Received Regarding Law School and the Legal Profession:

It is not as hard as they say, you don't have to do all of the reading. Don't worry about law review. #Lies

Best Advice I Would Give to an Aspiring Black Lawyer:

Are you sure that you want to go to law school? Why? Be careful. There are many ways to help people; being a lawyer might not be the right avenue.

Thoughts About Why Earning a Law Degree Is a Powerful Credential for African Americans and Why There Is a Need for More African American Lawyers:

The world needs African American lawyers because African Americans are the standard-bearers for the world. We are in some ways able to hold the mirror to America. African Americans are disproportionately negatively impacted by laws and legal systems. We need to be trained and present to combat these systems on every level including, but not limited to, legislation, policy-making, enforcement, prosecution, defense, board-rooms, the judiciary, and all other sectors where we can exercise influence.

Thoughts About Whether and Why Law School Is Worth the Financial Investment:

This is a highly personal question, particularly in a down economy, where legal outsourcing is possible and high caliber counsel is a Zoom call away. Take care not to assume so much debt that you will be required to abandon the goals that motivated you to start law school in the first place.

LEGACY AND SUCCESS

My Most Outstanding Accomplishment:

I am most proud of my tenure as a law school professor and the awards since that time. I could have never imagined this level of success or fulfillment as a young person.

The Legacy I Hope to Leave:

I hope that people will remember that I stood up and spoke honestly to all the haters.

The Secret to My Success:

Work really hard and stay focused. I may not be the brightest but I am able to outwork everybody in the room.

Shontavia Johnson, Esq.

Associate Vice President for Entrepreneurship and Innovation
Clemson University
Founder
Brand+Business Academy
Greenville, South Carolina

"Be purpose-driven in all things, and life will reward your efforts."
– Shontavia Johnson, Esq.

Success is . . . knowing and living your purpose each and every day.

PERSONAL FAVORITES

Favorite Quotes: "Bloom where you are planted."

"For I know the plans I have for you," declares the Lord, "plans to prosper you and not to harm you, plans to give you hope and a future. Then you will call on me and come and pray to me, and I will listen to you. You will seek me and find me when you seek me with all your heart." - Jeremiah 29:11-13

Favorite Books: *Their Eyes Were Watching God* by Zora Neale Hurston; *The Richest Man in Babylon* by George Samuel Clason

Favorite Movie: *The Neverending Story*

Favorite Song: "Someday We'll All Be Free" by Donny Hathaway

Favorite Musical Artist: Donny Hathaway

Favorite Law School Class: Trademark & Unfair Competition Law

Favorite Legal Case: *Thomas Edison v. Granville T. Woods*. Woods was one of the most prolific African American inventors in history, and he was twice sued by Thomas Edison, who saw Woods as a threat. Woods was successful in both lawsuits against Edison.

Favorite Hobbies: Reading; Traveling

Favorite Attorney Role Models: When I was growing up, I did not know any lawyers in real life. The closest people I had to attorney role models as a child were Claire Hanks Huxtable (from *The Cosby Show* television show) and Maxine Shaw (from *Living Single* television show).

FAMILY AND BACKGROUND

Where Born and Raised: Born - Raleigh, North Carolina; Raised - Augusta, Georgia and Aiken, South Carolina Area

Family Socioeconomic and Educational Background: I was an engineering major and literally did not know the difference between a plaintiff and a defendant when I began law school. I did not know any lawyers and had never seen the inside of a courtroom. I think this actually helped me because I did not have any preconceived perceptions about my knowledge base. During the first few days of law school, I felt a bit out of place because many of my classmates were pre-law majors with several generations of lawyers in their immediate familial and/or social circles. Because I knew that I knew nothing and had no attorney mentors at the time, I would hang on to each word that my professors said in class and take copious notes. I also spent quite a bit of time in my professors' offices asking questions, believing that I was merely "catching up" with my classmates. In reality, many of my classmates were overreliant on their undergraduate knowledge and the advice, outlines, and notes given to them by family members or friends who were lawyers. I outperformed many of my fellow classmates because of the extra hours I spent taking notes, making my own outlines, and visiting with my professors.

THE DECISION TO BECOME A LAWYER

When and Why I Decided to Become a Lawyer: I do not have a deep reason for choosing the legal profession. As a child, I always believed that successful careers revolved around doctors, lawyers, and engineers. I was an engineering major who thought I'd be going to medical school. But, after completing an internship in the medical field, I knew that career path was not for me. Law was the only option left from the trifecta, though it turned out to be the right decision for me.

EDUCATIONAL ACHIEVEMENTS

High School: South Carolina Governor's School for Science and Mathematics (Hartsville, South Carolina)

College/University: Clemson University (Clemson, South Carolina)

Undergraduate Degree: Bachelor of Science (B.S.)

Major: Biosystems Engineering

College Honors, Achievements and Activities: Palmetto Fellows Scholar; Jackie Robinson Foundation Scholar; National Society of Black Engineers Scholar; Coca-Cola Clemson Scholar; *Executive Board Member,* Student Government Association; *Member,* National Society of Black Engineers

Law School: University of Arkansas School of Law (Fayetteville, Arkansas)

Law Degree and Graduation Year: Juris Doctor/Doctor of Jurisprudence (J.D.) - Class of 2006

Law School Honors, Achievements and Activities: Graduated Top 15% of Class; Voted Graduation Class Speaker by 2006 Graduating Class; *Academic Recognition,* Dean's List (Each Semester); Vincent W. Foster Scholar; Jim G. Ferguson Scholar; Harold Flowers Law Society Scholar; Phi Delta Phi Balfour Scholar; *Recipient,* W. B. Putman American Inn of Court Scholarship; *Associate Editor,* Arkansas Law Review; *Member,* National Criminal Procedure Moot Court Team; *Awardee,* Best Brief Award, National Criminal Procedure Moot Court Team; *Research Assistant,* Professor Carlton Bailey, University of Arkansas School of Law; *Study Abroad Law Student,* International Law and Legal Studies, University of the Western Cape (Cape Town, South Africa)

PROFESSIONAL ACCOMPLISHMENTS

State Bar Memberships (Where Licensed to Practice Law): Iowa; South Carolina; United States Patent and Trademark Office (USPTO)

Other Legal Experience: *Professor of Law and Kern Family Chair in Intellectual Property Law,* Drake University Law School; *Westerfield Fellow,* Loyola University New Orleans College of Law (Subjects Taught: First-Year Legal Writing, First-Year Appellate Advocacy/Moot Court, Intersection Between Intellectual Property and Human Rights Seminar) (2008-2010); *Intellectual Property Associate,* Nelson Mullins Riley & Scarborough (2006-2008); *Summer Intellectual Property Associate,* Fredrikson & Byron (Summer 2005); *Summer Intellectual Property Associate,* Nelson Mullins Riley & Scarborough (Summer 2005); *Summer Commercial Litigation Associate,* Butler Snow O'Mara Stevens & Canada (Summer 2004); *Summer Health Law Associate,* Friday, Eldredge & Clark, LLP (Summer 2004)

Other Professional Work Experience: *Engineering Research Associate,* National Science Foundation (Summer 2002)

Professional Organizations: *Regular Panelist,* VentureNet Iowa; *Member,* American Intellectual Property Law Association; *Member,* International Trademark Association; *Member,* American Bar Association; *Member,* National Bar Association; *Member,* Order of the Coif (honorary scholastic society)

Post-Law School Honors, Achievements, Activities, and Community Involvement: *Listed Honoree,* 200 Black Women In Tech to Follow on Twitter (2018); *Honoree,* Top 40 Young Lawyers Award, American Bar Association (2016); *Magazine Recognition,* Inspiring Women in STEM, INSIGHT Into Diversity Magazine (2016); *Fulbright Specialist Roster Candidate,* Designated by the U.S. Department of State Bureau of Educational and Cultural Affairs and the Institute of International Education Council for International Exchange of Scholars (2016); *Awardee,* A. Leon Higginbotham, Jr. Fellowship, American Arbitration Association (2016); *Honoree,* The National Black Lawyers Top 100 Designation (2016); *Awardee,* Ladas Memorial Award, International Trademark Association (2014); *Awardee,* First and Third Place Gertrude Rush Award, Iowa Organization of Women Attorneys (2014); *Awardee,* Outstanding Alumnus Award, South Carolina Governor's School for Science and Mathematics (2014); *Awardee,* 42 Under 40 Alumni Award, Jackie Robinson Foundation (2014); *Honoree,* Nation's Best Advocates: 40 Lawyers Under 40 Award, National Bar Association and IMPACT (2013); *Certificate of Appreciation & Support,* "Most Supportive Law Professor", Loyola University College of Law Black Law Students Association (2009)

LESSONS LEARNED: MY RECOMMENDATIONS FOR YOUR FUTURE ACTIONS BASED ON MY PAST EXPERIENCE

Advice on Law School Preparation:

Go in with an open mind and without preconceptions. Build not only personal friendships, but also professional ones. And, stay focused on your own path. There's a reason that race horses wear blinders.

Advice on Applying to and Selecting a Law School:

Research, research, research. When researching, have in mind what is important to YOU (not just what popular rankings services have identified as important). Choosing a law school is a personal decision. Of course, rankings are important, but this all depends on your personal aspirations and career goals. Ask any and every unanswered question, particularly when it comes to admissions, financial aid, and scholarships.

Advice Regarding Academic Success, Co-Curricular and Extra-Curricular Participation, and Social Engagement in Law School:

Knowing who you are, and your purpose on this earth, can help you navigate the sometimes-treacherous law school experience. It can be easy to fall into the "everybody does it this way" trap. Success can have many different meanings - as many different meanings as there are people on this planet. If you know your purpose and goals, you will not get caught up as easily in a version of success that is not your own. The legal profession can be incredibly rewarding if you follow your own path, and incredibly frustrating if you're on someone else's. In addition, practice true servant-leadership. Always look for opportunities to be of service to others, even if (and perhaps especially when) there's no apparent benefit in it for you.

Advice on Preparing for and Taking the Bar Exam:

I'd provide the same advice I shared regarding applying to law school. Stay focused on your path.

Advice on Choosing a Legal Job and Career Path Inside or Outside of the Legal Profession:

Like many things in life, you get out of something what you put into it. Law school has been criticized in recent years because a growing number of graduates are having difficulty finding employment. I believe some of this is attributable to an inability of some newly-minted lawyers to be creative and think beyond the traditional pathways of success in the legal profession. The world is changing, and the profession is changing. It only makes sense that the way we cultivate careers must also change. Be creative in thinking about employment opportunities. Chart your own path.

Best Advice I Received Regarding Law School and the Legal Profession:

Bloom where you are planted.

Worst Advice I Received Regarding Law School and the Legal Profession:

Go for the money.

LEGACY AND SUCCESS

My Most Outstanding Accomplishment:

Professional - Having my 2014 article, Trademark Territoriality in Cyberspace: An Internet Framework for Common Law Trademarks, 29 Berkeley Tech. L. Rev. 1253 (2014), be named the best article in the world on a trademark law topic by the International Trademark Association.

The Legacy I Hope to Leave:

My legacy will be that I (1) honored the purpose God had for my life; (2) positively impacted the lives of other people; and (3) created opportunities and financial freedom for myself and my family.

The Secret to My Success:

I don't believe this is a secret, but my faith and true belief that the Creator put me in every situation I've been in because of a divine plan for my life. As a law student, I made sure to regularly read the Bible even when I had a mountain of work to do for class. I actually read the entire Bible during my first year of law school. This kept me going when I felt like I couldn't see the light at the end of the tunnel.

Maurice Lamb III, Esq., LL.M.
Mergers and Acquisitions: Indirect Tax Transactions Associate
Ernst & Young LLP
Houston, Texas

"Our experiences are life's camera and our eyes take the best pictures."
— Maurice Lamb III

Success is . . . creating a lasting legacy that not only impacts my family but also my local community.

PERSONAL FAVORITES

Favorite Quotes: "What lies behind you and in front of you pales in comparison to what lies inside of you." - Ralph Waldo Emerson

"Success is not the key to happiness. Happiness is the key to success. If you love what you are doing, you will be successful." - Albert Schweitzer

Favorite Books: *A Testament of Hope: The Essential Writings and Speeches* by Martin Luther King Jr. and Edited by James M. Washington; *The Art of War* by Sun Tzu

Favorite Movies: *Inception; Malcolm X*

Favorite Songs: "Song for You" by Donny Hathaway; "A Change is Gonna Come" by Sam Cooke

Favorite Musical Artists: Usher; Michael Jackson; Tupac; Notorious B.I.G.; Outkast

Favorite Law School Classes: Constitutional Law; Federal Income Taxation

Favorite Legal Case: *Brown v. Board of Education of Topeka Kansas*

Favorite Hobbies: Playing basketball; Singing; Painting; Being outdoors

Favorite Attorney Role Models: Thurgood Marshall; Johnnie Cochran

FAMILY AND BACKGROUND

Where Born and Raised: Houston, Texas

Family Socioeconomic and Educational Background: I am a first-generation law school graduate. I come from a lower middle-class background. My dad is a truck driver and my mother was a respiratory therapist. They are extremely hardworking spiritual people that instilled the power of education at an early age. They often reminded me that "an excuse is a skin of a reason stuffed with a lie". If I didn't get an A on a test or a quiz the first time, I would have to retake another test until I did. I realized very quickly that the best option was to get an A the first time.

THE DECISION TO BECOME A LAWYER

When and Why I Decided to Become a Lawyer: I've always wanted to be a lawyer from an early age. My family and friends always encouraged me to become a preacher, but I wanted to be a civil rights attorney like Thurgood Marshall. As I have matured, my passion has shifted to empowering our community economically through spreading financial literacy, financial planning, and tax assistance.

EDUCATIONAL ACHIEVEMENTS

High School: The Kinkaid School (Houston, Texas)

College/University: The University of Texas at Austin (Austin, Texas)

Undergraduate Degree: Bachelor of Arts (B.A.)

Major: Political Science

College Honors, Achievements and Activities: *Member,* Tau Sigma Honor Society (national honor society for transfer students); *Academic Recognition,* Dean's List

Law School: South Texas College of Law Houston (Houston, Texas)

Law Degree and Graduation Year: Juris Doctor/Doctor of Jurisprudence (J.D.) - Class of 2017

Law School Honors, Achievements and Activities: *Vice President,* Black Law Students Association; *Community Outreach Chair,* Federal Tax Law Society; *Participant,* Pro Bono Honors Program

Other Graduate or Professional Degree: Master of Laws (LL.M.) in Taxation, University of Florida Fredric G. Levin College of Law (Gainesville, Florida)

Additional Education: *Certified Mediator,* South Texas College of Law Houston

PROFESSIONAL ACCOMPLISHMENTS

State Bar Membership (Where Admitted to Practice Law): Texas

Other Legal Work Experience: *Law Clerk,* The Pierre Firm PLLC; *Legal Intern,* The Cloud Law Firm; *Volunteer,* Volunteer Income Tax Assistance (VITA)

Other Professional Work Experience: *First Grade Teacher,* Wesley Elementary; *Teacher/Testing Coordinator/Health/Physical Education Teacher,* Dominion Academy Charter School

Professional Organizations: *Member,* National Association for the Advancement of Colored People (NAACP)

Post-Law School Honors, Achievements, Activities, and Community Involvement: *Volunteer,* Good Gang Scholarship Committee; *Volunteer,* Loving Kids Foundation; *Volunteer,* Community in Action; *Volunteer,* Walk Right for Christ

LESSONS LEARNED: MY RECOMMENDATIONS FOR YOUR FUTURE ACTIONS BASED ON MY PAST EXPERIENCE

Advice on Law School Preparation:

Developing relationships with your professors is essential. Don't be afraid to talk to your professors. They are all friendly and their doors are open. Professors want students to drop by during their office hours. Professors prefer to write recommendation letters for students with whom they have a rapport. Find a mentor who can guide you through the process. A mentor will give pearls of wisdom and simplify the entire process from mission statements to essays. Take a Law School Admission Test (LSAT) course to help achieve your highest score possible.

Advice on Applying to and Selecting a Law School:

Find a school with a support system. Focus on location, value, specialized programs, and opportunities. Location is key because if you live in the same area as the school more job opportunities will arise. The alumni network will be larger as well. Every student wants to receive the best quality of education for the price. If you already know your area of expertise, choose a school that has a specialized program. This will suit you best. Extra-curricular opportunities such as clinics, externships, and journals are not only superb resume builders but also offer invaluable experience.

Visit the campus more than once. Ask lots of questions to different faculty members. Speak to representatives from the registrar's office to financial aid because you will need their help in the future. Talk to a dean about the school's support system. My school has a great support system of professors, Langdell scholars, and academic seminars. South Texas College of Law Houston also provides massages and therapy sessions to cope with the stress of finals.

Advice Regarding Academic Success, Co-Curricular and Extra-Curricular Participation, and Social Engagement in Law School:

Remember it's a marathon, not a sprint. Pace yourself so you don't become overwhelmed and break down at the end of semester. Procrastination when it comes to studying, outlining, and doing practice exams and trying to cram at the last two months of law school is not a sure path to success. You would not even be giving yourself a fair chance to see how you measure up this way. Very seldom are there any do-overs. Your grades your first semester affect your internships and opportunities for the first summer and this creates a domino effect. Take it seriously and pace yourself.

Don't undervalue the power of maintaining a lifestyle balance. Try to keep a routine so that you remember to take care of yourself. It will keep your mind sharp. Please get enough sleep. In order to thrive in law school and make it through the entire semester successfully, discipline in academic studies is only one type of required discipline you will need. Lifestyle balance and wellness is another discipline you will need to maintain. If you're not already in a regimen where you're practicing this, start now. Craft and hone a schedule that recharges you.

Prepare for the final from day one. Don't wait until the last few weeks of class. You have only one opportunity to show what you have learned throughout the entire semester. Review weekly so that you are refreshing your memory when it is time to study for finals instead of trying to learn the law. Do not waste time. The earlier you start the more successful you will be on your exam.

Life will go on while you are in school. Lawyers are extremely busy people because our work is never done. Do not forget about personal and family time. My half-day to relax is on Sunday so that I can enjoy my friends and family while watching football or basketball. There are only 24 hours in a day. Maximize your time; it is your most valuable asset.

Advice on Preparing for and Taking the Bar Exam:

Eliminate as much stress as possible from your life by avoiding distractions from family, friends, and social media. Implement a strict daily study schedule. Your top priority is bar preparation. Maintain a good sleep regimen to remain energized. Take a bar prep course that suits your needs. Take practice exams under actual time constraints. Focus on your most challenging practice areas. Get a massage the day before the exam to help you relax.

Advice on Choosing a Job and Career Path Inside or Outside of the Legal Profession:

Choose an area of expertise that suits your individualized skills and goals.

Advice on Seeking Legal Job Opportunities and/or Creating One's Own Opportunities:

Never underestimate the power of networking. Opportunities can come from the most unexpected relationships. Invest in maintaining healthy relationships by following up with handwritten "thank you" cards or sharing interesting articles on social media. Take the time to cultivate these connections so that they are mutually beneficial for all parties involved. Find a mentor at your company or in the same area of practice. Your mentor will assist you in identifying the office culture and politics.

Advice on Achieving Career Success and Advancement:

Seek mentor relationships early on in your career because they can identify talents that you didn't recognize in yourself and help guide your career path. Don't be afraid to take an unconventional career path because only you can determine what success means to you.

Advice on Overcoming the Additional Challenges Black Law Students Face:

I encourage everyone to join the Black Law Students Association (BLSA), but also don't be afraid to join different organizations and clubs of your interest because some of my strongest relationships in law school began when I stepped outside of my area of comfort. Develop strong relationships with your professors by asking questions in and outside of the classroom.

Best Advice I Received Regarding Law School and the Legal Profession:

Focus your attention on problems that are within your control like your grades. Unfortunately, racism, sexism, and discrimination exist in various forms. There are enough issues in your life; do not add to your stress. Do not become distracted and miss your ultimate goal. Have a friend or classmate whom you can express your anger and frustration to. Surround yourself with similar peers such as the Black Law Students Association (BLSA).

Worst Advice I Received Regarding Law School and the Legal Profession:

Do not go to law school because it is not worth it. I am glad that I did not take his advice.

Best Advice I Would Give to an Aspiring Black Lawyer:

You are blessed with the privilege and honor to be a part of the legal community; it is not a right. Do not take it for granted. Treat it with the respect that it deserves. You have sacrificed too much and worked too hard to waste this opportunity.

Thoughts About Why Earning a Law Degree Is a Powerful Credential for African Americans and Why There Is a Need for More African American Lawyers:

Law school is a powerful credential because it teaches students an entirely new way of thinking. Over time, lawyers develop a unique perspective. A law degree offers options unlike any other career; it can be applied in a myriad of ways. The possibilities are endless especially in our communities. African American lawyers are equipped with the requisite skills to uplift and empower our neighborhood by protecting their civil, legal, and financial rights. Black lawyers can start firms that help create and nurture businesses in our areas. We owe our neighborhoods, so it is imperative that we give back any way possible.

Thoughts About Whether and Why Law School Is Worth the Financial Investment:

Is law school worth it? Law school is worth the financial sacrifice because it teaches you a new way of thinking that changes your perspective on how you approach and view the world. You will improve critical and analytical thinking, communication and problem-solving abilities that can be applied in areas outside of legal practice that you can use for the rest of your career.

LEGACY AND SUCCESS

My Most Outstanding Accomplishment:

My greatest accomplishment was telling my parents that I passed the Texas Bar Exam.

The Legacy I Hope to Leave:

I plan to leave a legacy of professionalism, excellence, and overachieving. I want my life to look like a visible manifestation of the power of God in the presence of people for His glory. My plan will show others how to properly invest their resources. My plan is to educate the public on building wealth that lasts for future generations.

The Secret to My Success:

My support system of mentors, family, and church community are the secret to my success. They inspired me to believe in myself even when I could not. They shared their wisdom. My pastor often says that exposure expands expectations. They invested in my education by giving me opportunities: from running a business, to directing and writing plays, to singing for President Bill Clinton. They would not let me fail. They prayed and spoke prophetically into my life, and I am forever grateful.

Akilah Mance, Esq.
General Counsel
Houston Forensic Science Center
Houston, Texas

"Stay humble and thankful to God for blessing you with opportunities and giving you the tools to be successful. In that humility, understand that life will not always reward you with the success you want or deserve, but God's purpose for your life is still intact, just stay the course."
– Akilah Mance

Success is . . . using the talents you were blessed with, to positively impact the world around you. For me, success is finding a way to live a life of purpose, excel on my own terms, maintain positive relationships, and provide opportunities for those who come after me.

PERSONAL FAVORITES

Favorite Quotes: "If I can help one person along the way, then my life will not be in vain."

"For we know that all things work together for the good of them who love God, to them who are called according to his purpose." - Romans 8:28

Favorite Book: *Song of Solomon* by Toni Morrison

Favorite Movie: *Coming to America*

Favorite Musical Artists: Marvin Gaye; Machel Montano; Lecrae

Favorite Law School Classes: Criminal Law; Children and the Law; Clinics/Externships - Family Violence Clinic; Special Education Practicum; Department of Family & Children Services

Favorite Legal Case: My first murder trial conviction as a prosecutor.

Favorite Hobbies: Watching basketball and football; Having dinner parties with my best friends.

Favorite Attorney Role Models: I've been so blessed to have lawyers throughout my career who have supported me and taught me how to be a great lawyer, particularly amazing Black attorneys like Art Pertile III, Jamila Mensah, Alia Adkins, and Leah Hayes.

FAMILY AND BACKGROUND

Where Born and Raised: Born - Lithonia, Georgia; Raised - Stone Mountain, Georgia (suburbs of Atlanta)

Family Socioeconomic and Educational Background: I come from a family of educators, including my parents, grandmother, and great grandmother. My grandparents went to college and so did my parents, even though both of my grandmothers were single mothers in segregated south Georgia. Fortunately, they both had a lot of support from their families to raise my parents and their siblings. I grew up in a middle-class family. However, my parents were public school educators and as young parents, they certainly weren't "middle class" back then. They lived in mobile homes and small apartments in rural Georgia as they both finished college and started teaching. They stuck with it, advanced in the school system, moved to Atlanta, and eventually got to a financial place where I (as the youngest child of three), could grow up in a middle-class suburb in a home my parents owned. I am now the first and only lawyer in the family on either side.

THE DECISION TO BECOME A LAWYER

When and Why I Decided to Become a Lawyer: I just wanted to help people. I didn't really know any lawyers growing up. I'm pretty sure people started telling me I should be a lawyer when I was a young kid because I could read, speak, and write well. So, I wanted to be a lawyer from the time I was in elementary school. As I got older, I decided to become a lawyer because I wanted to help people, especially during a time of challenge and adversity in their lives. This decision was rooted in my sense of obligation to my community; to serve and help the people around me by using my talents.

EDUCATIONAL ACHIEVEMENTS

High School: Lithonia High School (Lithonia, Georgia)

College/University: Rice University (Houston, Texas)

Undergraduate Degree: Bachelor of Arts (B.A.)

Majors: English and Political Science

College Honors, Achievements and Activities: *Study Abroad Participant,* Hessen Summer International University at Philipps Universität, Marburg, Germany (Summer 2004); *Student Presenter,* National Conference on Race & Ethnicity in Higher Education (2004); *Member,* Rice University President's Council on Minority Affairs (2003-2004); *President,* Black Students Association (2003-2004); *Recipient,* Athletic Department Scholarship; *Student Worker Award,* Office of Academic Advising for Athletics (2002-2005): *Recipient,* Roy Trustee Distinguished Scholarship (2001-2005); *Honoree,* Who's Who Among Students in American Universities and Colleges®

Law School: University of Georgia School of Law (Athens, Georgia)

Law Degree and Graduation Year: Juris Doctor/Doctor of Jurisprudence (J.D.) - Class of 2008

Law School Honors, Achievements and Activities: *Law Student,* Comparative International Law Program, University of Oxford; *Member,* Oxford Blues Women's Varsity Basketball Team

PROFESSIONAL ACCOMPLISHMENTS

State Bar Membership (Where Licensed to Practice Law): Texas

Other Legal Experience: *Felony Assistant District Attorney,* Harris County District Attorney's Office (Houston, Texas); *Attorney,* Olson & Olson LLP

Other Professional Work Experience: *Intern,* Texas House of Representatives; *Intern,* DeKalb County (GA) Board of Commissioners' Office; *Intern,* Harris County District Family Court

Professional Organizations: *Member,* International Municipal Lawyers Association; *Member,* Texas District and County Attorneys; *Member,* Houston Young Lawyers Association; *Member,* Katy Bar Association; *Member,* Texas Municipal League

Post-Law School Honors, Achievements, Activities, and Community Involvement: *Honoree,* Moot Court & Mock Trial Judge of the Year, Board of Advocates, Thurgood Marshall School of Law (2011-2012); *Magazine Feature,* Featured in "Local Heroes" article, The Houston Lawyer Magazine (May/June 2012 Edition); *Recipient,* Rice University Young Alumni "Builder's Award" (2016); *Appointee,* Rice University President's Council on Minority Affairs (2015-2016); *Member,* Board of Directors, Association of Rice Alumni (2015-2018); *Alumni Interviewer and College Fair Representative,* Rice Alumni Volunteers for Admission (2006-Present); *President,* Association of Rice University Black Alumni (2014-2016); *High School Mentor,* Leaders of Tomorrow (2012-2018); *Competitions Judge,* Board of Advocates, Thurgood Marshall School of Law (2012-Present); *Girls Basketball Head Coach,* YMCA (2011-2012 Season); *Recipient,* Rice Young Alumni Award (2016); *Appointee,* Rice University Taskforce on Segregation, Slavery and Racial Injustice (2019-Present); *Community Placement Chairman and Member,* The Junior League of Houston (2017-Present); *Class Member,* Leadership Houston Class XXXVIII (2019-Present)

* Presenter at numerous legal and government conferences including state-wide and international conferences.

LESSONS LEARNED: MY RECOMMENDATIONS FOR YOUR FUTURE ACTIONS BASED ON MY PAST EXPERIENCE

Advice on Law School Preparation:

I wouldn't worry about what you study in undergraduate; just do well and get as many educational opportunities and life experiences as possible. Develop the intangibles that will help you succeed in law and any other fields including leadership, how to overcome obstacles, maintaining work-life balance, and constantly learning. Also, take time to see what it's like to actually be a lawyer and what a law school class is actually like so that you know what you are getting into.

Advice on Applying to and Selecting a Law School:

This is your first big lesson in the real-life challenges you will need to balance. Finances matter. Do NOT go into an insane amount of debt that you will literally spend the rest of your life trying to get out from under. You will absolutely regret it. If you do so, you better be able to guarantee that you will walk out of that school and immediately be making a significant amount of money for a long time. To do the work we do as attorneys, with the constant stress and pressure it brings, and then to add a mountain of debt where you feel like you can barely make ends meet, is the worst circumstance to be in. Find a balance between cost and the educational environment you want to have. Also, if you go to a school that has a reputation for one area of practice, you better be sure that you have no desire to practice outside of that area. If you have any doubt, make sure you go to a school where the overall education is respected and valuable no matter what you practice afterwards. Also, know yourself and pick a law school community and location where you give yourself the best chance to focus on your education and succeed. For instance, I loved being close to home, but I did not go to a school in my hometown because I knew I would be distracted by family obligations and activities.

Advice Regarding Academic Success, Co-Curricular and Extra-Curricular Participation, and Social Engagement in Law School:

During your first year, you should literally do nothing but study. Anything you do socially or as an extracurricular activity should be infrequent and not require much commitment. Lean on family and friends outside of law school to keep you motivated and encouraged. There will be many days where you need a break, don't want to see anybody from law school, and need to be reminded of who you are and why you will be successful. Be sure to schedule something that you love to do so that you aren't overwhelmed by the law school experience. Keeping a schedule and repetition is absolutely imperative. After the first year, pursue those things that you are interested in and make sure you explore all the practice areas you may want to pursue. It's much easier to do this as a student rather than trying to switch practice areas after practicing law. Remember, this is only a brief moment in time to set yourself up for life. If you have other obligations outside of school (like family, children, a need to work), then just make sure you stick to a schedule and routine; get the most out of your time.

Advice on Preparing for and Taking the Bar Exam:

Shut out the rest of the world, be actively engaged in your prep class and stick to your study schedule. It's only for a short time and it is the most important step in starting your legal career; everything and everyone else can wait. Also, schedule mental breaks and a little fun here and there, but stick to the time you have allotted for it so that you don't lose focus.

Advice on Choosing a Job and Career Path Inside or Outside of the Legal Profession:

Follow your passion and don't be afraid to try new practice areas. A legal degree is a wonderful tool because it allows you to be a qualified applicant for so many different careers and industries. Never feel like you have to be a traditional lawyer. Just pursue that which makes you passionate and intellectually challenged. Lawyers spend too much time, effort, and energy at work for you to constantly be miserable.

Advice on Seeking Legal Job Opportunities and/or Creating One's Own Opportunities:

It's all about networking. It's so difficult to get a job just by applying to an open call for applicants. Use your connections or the connections of others to get your resume seen by the hiring committee or staff member. Again, having a legal degree means you can always be an entrepreneur and open your own practice if needed or if that's what you really want to do. Be confident knowing you can hustle and provide for yourself as your own boss.

Advice on Achieving Career Success and Advancement:

Stay humble and hungry. Understand that the legal field is as much about relationships and reputation as it is about competency and ability. It's very easy to get caught up in the traditional milestones you are supposed to achieve (becoming partner, becoming lead counsel or a chief/director in governmental agencies), but make sure you are striving for those goals because they matter to you. Don't be stagnant and always re-evaluate your career to make sure you are progressing towards the success that you value. So many lawyers look up after 20 to 30 years and wonder: "Where did the time go?" "What happened to my relationships with my family and friends?" "What happened to my mental and physical health?" Don't have (too many) regrets.

Advice on Overcoming the Additional Challenges Black Law Students Face:

Know who you are and be comfortable in your own skin knowing that you are capable, you bring a unique value to the law school community, and you will be successful. Many law schools try to force you into a certain value system about what success means as a law student and a future lawyer. Keep an open mind and always listen to see what advice the school and professors may have, but then go and make your own decision about what's right for you. Knowing the law is one thing but having the common sense and life experience to understand what the practical effect will be is very important. I think we have to be ready to share our views and interpretations because they are valuable as well. Also, know that your class rank has nothing to do with your success as a lawyer. Do your best obviously, but know that when you become an attorney, it's so different from a law school class and you can really hone your skills to be as successful as any other classmate, if you work hard for it.

Advice on Overcoming the Additional Challenges Black Lawyers Face:

Stay confident in who you are and what you bring to the table. So often, you come into a situation where you don't fit the "traditional" mold, but it doesn't matter. If you made it through law school and the bar, you belong. The law affects every facet of our society, so your presence is always of value because you will understand a case or client when other lawyers will not. Also, many of us feel intimidated by attorneys because they seem to have attended the right schools, know the right attorneys and judges, come from a family of lawyers, or are revered as the best in their profession, but your skill can overcome all of that. They don't have to know you or respect you, but if you succeed, they will have no choice but to fear you in the courtroom.

Best Advice I Received Regarding Law School and the Legal Profession:

Work hard; every day try to learn more about the law profession; stay the course through the ups and downs (there will be many); be confident; and stay true to who are you. Regarding law school, stick to a schedule; regarding the legal profession, your reputation and relationships are everything; once you lose them, you will never get them back.

Worst Advice I Received Regarding Law School and the Legal Profession:

"If you leave this job, what are you going to do?" I just remember when many of my colleagues were leaving our office to pursue other opportunities, the nay-sayers acted as if this one job was the only job any of us could hope to have. They presumed that we, as individuals and as attorneys, were not smart enough or hardworking enough to find another legal career that we could succeed at.

Best Advice I Would Give to an Aspiring Black Lawyer:

I reiterate, stay true to your passions and talents; know your worth. Find a mentor in the legal field to just talk to and get insight from. You may have a rough start or transition as a young lawyer, but don't worry about it; just stay focused and keep learning as much as you can. Every lawyer has gone through this process and made mistakes, so don't think your first years will define your career forever; if you don't start off the way you would like. Keep re-evaluating your career and personal life. So many of us end up with financial problems, mental and physical health issues, or family relationship problems because of how brutal this profession can be. Don't be so engrossed in this profession that you lose everything else in your life.

Thoughts About Why Earning a Law Degree Is a Powerful Credential for African Americans and Why There Is a Need for More African American Lawyers:

We need Black lawyers so very much these days. So many of the problems and challenges we see in our communities or disproportionately affecting our community, is because we've allowed other people to make the laws, with no consideration of their effect on us. It also speaks to the need for more of us to be involved in politics and becoming elected officials. I've always felt a commitment to being involved in the law and politics because I've always understood that one law, one court decision, can change an individual's life in an instant. There's no greater power than that, absent perhaps the ability to decide life and death. So, to that point, we need to be fully integrated into every facet of the law so that when these issues arise, we can affect change immediately.

Thoughts About Whether and Why Law School Is Worth the Financial Investment:

Law school is definitely worth the financial investment, if you treat it as such. That means look at the risk versus the reward, have a plan and several back up plans on how to make the most use of your degree. Understand the economy and trends in the legal profession so that you can be prepared to deal with the ebbs and flows of your career. Don't take on more debt than necessary. When you find out the potential cost of attendance, including living expenses, find out how long it will take to pay it off and at what monthly payment. Prepare for the worst-case financial scenario and count it as a success if you end up making a lot of money and you pay it off in just a few years. There's a huge difference between $500 per month for 10 years versus $1,500 for 20 years. Make a decision you can live with in 10 years or 20 years.

LEGACY AND SUCCESS

My Most Outstanding Accomplishment:

Planning and chairing the celebration for Rice University's "Celebrating 50 Years of Black Undergraduate Life".

The Legacy I Hope to Leave:

I hope people will regard me as a woman of faith who loves her family; who is smart, passionate, and hardworking; genuine, good and decent towards everyone; and who really tried to make a change in this world for the better.

The Secret to My Success:

God and my faith. I can list off all the practical things I try to do, but I'm imperfect and on paper, I'm probably not much different from other people who have been unsuccessful. So, in all I do, I stay humble and thankful to God for blessing me with opportunities and giving me the tools to be successful. In that humility, I understand life will not always reward you with the success you want or deserve, but God's purpose for my life is still intact. It makes you constantly pursue greatness and know that when you fail or fall short, you can still get up and keep going, pressing towards His purpose for me.

Adia Z. May, Esq., M.B.A.
Business Affairs
William Morris Endeavor
Los Angeles, California

"Stay the course and don't look back...that's how you crash."

– Adia Z. May

Success is . . . being able to get up and do work that you love that makes our world better than you found it.

PERSONAL FAVORITES

Favorite Quote: "I love to see a young girl go out and grab the world by the lapels. Life's a bitch. You've got to go out and kick ass." - Maya Angelou

Favorite Books: *The Four Agreements* by Don Miguel Ruiz; *Becoming* by Michelle Obama

Favorite Movies: *The Wiz; Pretty Woman*

Favorite Song: "Believe in Yourself (Dorothy)" by Diana Ross (from *The Wiz* movie)

Favorite Musical Artist: Stevie Wonder

Favorite Law School Class: Corporations

Favorite Legal Case: *Lynum v. Illinois*

Favorite Hobbies: Vintage shopping; Playing tennis

Favorite Attorney Role Models: My father and uncle; Bonnie Berry; Debra Martin Chase is someone I greatly admire for her nontraditional path to becoming a very successful film and TV producer.

FAMILY AND BACKGROUND

Where Born and Raised: Chicago, Illinois

Family Socioeconomic and Educational Background: My father and uncle both practiced law. My parents always told me I could do anything I wanted to do. I had a very supportive environment.

THE DECISION TO BECOME A LAWYER

When and Why I Decided to Become a Lawyer:

I was inspired by watching my dad and always had a natural curiosity for information, words and asked questions constantly. I knew I was going to be a lawyer at 9 years old.

EDUCATIONAL ACHIEVEMENTS

High School: Whitney M. Young Magnet High School (Chicago, Illinois)

College/University: Howard University (Washington, D.C.)

Undergraduate Degree: Bachelor of Business Administration (B.B.A.)

Major: Finance

College Honors, Achievements and Activities: *Member,* Alpha Kappa Alpha Sorority, Inc.

Law School: University of Iowa College of Law (Iowa City, Iowa)

Law Degree and Graduation Year: Juris Doctor/Doctor of Jurisprudence (J.D.) - Class of 2002

Law School Honors, Achievements and Activities: *Graduate Assistant,* Office of Admissions, University of Iowa College of Law

Other Graduate or Professional Degree: Master of Business Administration (M.B.A.), University of Iowa Tippie School of Management (Iowa City, Iowa)

Graduate or Professional School Honors, Achievements and Activities: *Co-founder,* Catapult

PROFESSIONAL ACCOMPLISHMENTS

State Bar Membership (Where Admitted to Practice Law): Illinois; New York

Other Legal Work Experience: *Owner,* Law Office of Adia Z. May, P.C.; *Business and Legal Affairs Consultant,* BBC Studios; *Of Counsel,* Maker Studios Inc. – A Walt Disney Company; *Producer,* Zuri Entertainment; *Senior Vice President, Business & Legal Affairs,* Brown Paper Dolls; *Director of Business and Legal Affairs,* Codeblack Entertainment; *Advisor,* Entertainment Contracts, Screen Actors Guild; *Associate,* Wildman Harrold Allen and Dixon

Professional Organizations: *Member,* Langston Bar Association; *Member,* American Bar Association

Post-Law School Honors, Achievements, Activities, and Community Involvement: *Board Member,* Stuntwomen's National Association; *Executive Board Member,* Howard University Alumni Association of Greater Los Angeles; *Co-Founder,* Collegewood; *Honoree,* National Bar Association and IMPACT's 40 Under 40 Lawyer and Excellence in Innovation Award (2011)

LESSONS LEARNED: MY RECOMMENDATIONS FOR YOUR FUTURE ACTIONS BASED ON MY PAST EXPERIENCE

Advice on Law School Preparation:

Ask lawyers questions because there are so many paths you can take. Also, take classes that allow you to strengthen your reading, writing and communication skills. Be as well-rounded as possible showing that you're also leading on campus and serving your community.

Advice on Applying to and Selecting a Law School:

Aim to get in the best law schools…name and network matters. I went to a regional school, not a national school so I had to work that much harder especially to break into the entertainment law field.

Advice Regarding Academic Success, Co-Curricular and Extra-Curricular Participation, and Social Engagement in Law School:

Get your bearings first because the first year of law school is tough. I had a hard time with Civil Procedure.

Additionally, adjusting from my undergrad experience at Howard University was challenging because I went from an urban city in Washington, D.C. to a smaller college town in Iowa City.

I highly recommend a study abroad experience after the first year. I went to South Africa with the Howard University School of Law and loved it.

Advice on Preparing for and Taking the Bar Exam:

It's mental. Enroll in a good prep course and stay committed to the marathon. It's a marathon not a sprint. If you fail it, take it again.

Advice on Choosing a Job and Career Path Inside or Outside of the Legal Profession:

Choose a path that you love, otherwise it will always just be "a job".

Advice on Seeking Legal Job Opportunities and/or Creating One's Own Opportunities:

Think outside the box. I have worked for law firms, had my own firm, and worked in-house. There are phases to your career and you should always be assessing what works best for you depending on where you are in your career.

Advice on Achieving Career Success and Advancement:

Failure is not final. Success is fleeting. Do not attach to situations because you will have no peace.

Advice on Overcoming the Additional Challenges Black Law Students Face:

"When they go low, we go high." - Michelle Obama

Always do your best and when you are tired, rest.

Advice on Overcoming the Additional Challenges Black Lawyers Face:

You will be tested but do not fear challenges. Be authentically you and speak up even if your voice shakes.

Best Advice I Received Regarding Law School and the Legal Profession:

You can have it all but not at the same time.

Worst Advice I Received Regarding Law School and the Legal Profession:

"Do not leave a big law firm."

"Do you know how many lawyers try to be entertainment lawyers?"

Best Advice I Would Give to an Aspiring Black Lawyer:

Be prepared. Ask questions. Send handwritten "thank you" notes.

Thoughts About Why Earning a Law Degree Is a Powerful Credential for African Americans and Why There Is a Need for More African American Lawyers:

A law degree has many paths to success. It is powerful because it teaches you how to problem solve, be a leader as well as get your point across.

I am still the only one in the room. I sit behind the scenes in Hollywood; we need our voices in the room but in order to do this, we have to open the door whenever we can.

Thoughts About Whether and Why Law School Is Worth the Financial Investment:

Absolutely worth it. It's an investment that you'll see dividends from throughout your career.

LEGACY AND SUCCESS

My Most Outstanding Accomplishment:

Personal: Family.

Professional: Completing my joint J.D./M.B.A. Leading business affairs for commercials and endorsement groups at the largest talent agency in the world.

The Legacy I Hope to Leave:

I hope that others who meet me or see me living my dream, believe that theirs can come true too.

The Secret to My Success:

Keep on going…if you can look up, you can get up.

Joseph Q. McCoy, Esq., A.M.
Business Transactions Practice Lead
Riley Safer Holmes & Cancila LLP
Chicago, Illinois

"Excellence is not an accident. Effort, sacrifice, and faith are necessary for excellence."
– Joseph Q. McCoy

Success is ... manifested through the creation of opportunities for others who then create opportunities for others. Success cannot be individual; it must be about advancing the community.

PERSONAL FAVORITES

Favorite Quotes: "I can do all things through Christ which strengtheneth me." - Philippians 4:13

"My grace is sufficient." - 2 Corinthians 12:9

Favorite Books: *The Bible - King James Version*; *The Good Black* by Paul M. Barrett

Favorite Movies: *Love Jones*; *The Notebook*; *The Wiz*; *Bourne Series*; *Oceans Series*; *Coming to America*; *In Too Deep*

Favorite Songs: "I Will Always Love You" by Whitney Houston; "Can You Stand the Rain" by New Edition; "All in Love is Fair" by Stevie Wonder; "With You I'm Born Again" by Billy Preston and Syreeta Wright; "Lady" by Commodores; "I Never Loved a Man" by Aretha Franklin

Favorite Musical Artists: Whitney Houston; Marvin Gaye; Stevie Wonder; Donny Hathaway; Aretha Franklin; Jennifer Hudson; New Edition; Jamie Foxx; Sean Carter; Tupac Shakur; Michael Jackson; Prince; Luther Vandross

Favorite Law School Classes: All classes that were not litigation focused.

Favorite Legal Case: *Brown v. Board of Education*

Favorite Hobbies: Attending family gatherings; Playing bid whist; Attending concerts (R&B and Hip-Hop); Watching movies

Favorite Attorney Role Models: Many lawyers have had an impact on my career to date in various ways. I have borrowed a little from a lot of individuals to help me navigate the last several years.

FAMILY AND BACKGROUND

Where Born and Raised: Born - Inglewood, California; Raised - Little Rock, Arkansas

Family (Spouse/Partner and Children): Spouse - Jamenda; Children - Quentin and Jordyn

Family Socioeconomic and Educational Background: My family's socioeconomic status was sometimes lower class, sometimes middle class. It depended on the year growing up.

THE DECISION TO BECOME A LAWYER

When and Why I Decided to Become a Lawyer: A year after graduating from college, I wanted to be a sports agent. I realized that a lot of sports agents at that time were also lawyers. I also made an assumption that I could do a lot of things with a law degree given that lawyers do everything versus obtaining a graduate degree in education.

EDUCATIONAL ACHIEVEMENTS

High School: J.A. Fair High School (Little Rock, Arkansas)

College/University: University of Chicago (Chicago, Illinois)

Undergraduate Degree: Bachelor of Arts (A.B.)

Major: Public Policy (with emphasis on Education)

College Honors/Achievements/Activities: Graduated with Honors; Graduated with two degrees including a graduate degree in four years; *Honoree,* University of Chicago Athletic Hall of Fame (Three-sport letterman)

Law School: Northwestern University School of Law (Chicago, Illinois)

Law Degree and Graduation Year: Juris Doctor/Doctor of Jurisprudence (J.D.) - Class of 1998

Law School Honors, Achievements and Activities: *Inductee,* Northwestern University Wall of Fame

Other Graduate or Professional Degree: Master of Arts (A.M.) in Educational Institutional Policy Studies, University of Chicago (Chicago, Illinois)

PROFESSIONAL ACCOMPLISHMENTS

State Bar Memberships (Where Admitted to Practice Law): Texas; Illinois; New York

Other Legal Work Experience: *Managing Partner* and *Chair, Airport Concessions Practice,* Bryan Cave (Chicago Office); *Partner,* Perkins Coie LLP; *Partner,* Schwartz Cooper Chartered; *Associate,* Katten Muchin Rosenman LLP

Other Professional Work Experience: *Adjunct Professor,* Northwestern University School of Law (2010-2019); *Adjunct Professor,* Canisius College

Professional Organizations: *Member,* American Bar Association; *Member,* National Bar Association; *Member,* Commercial Law Section, National Bar Association; *Member,* Chicago Bar Association; *Member,* Cook County Bar Association; *Member,* Airport Minority Advisory Council; Airport Revenue News; *Member,* International Council of Shopping Centers (ICSC); *Member,* Airport Council International

Post-Law School Honors, Achievements, Activities, and Community Involvement: *Listed Honoree,* 2020 LawDragon 500 Leading Lawyers; *Member,* The Economic Club of Chicago (2017-Present); *Board Member,* Cleveland Avenue Foundation for Education (2018-Present); *Board Member,* Partnership for College Completion (2015-2017); *Listed Honoree,* Crain's Chicago, Notable Gen X Leaders in Law (2019); *Listed Honoree,* Most Influential Minority Lawyers in Chicago (2017); *Listed Honoree,* "Most Influential Black Lawyers" Savoy Magazine (2015); *Honoree,* 2013 Chicago United Business Leader of Color; *Listed Honoree,* Illinois Super Lawyers; *Fellow,* Legal Council on Legal Diversity (LCLD) (2011-2012); *Listed Honoree,* Forty Under 40, Law Bulletin Publishing Company (2009); *Board Member,* Illinois Equal Justice Foundation (2010-2017); *Law Board Member,* Northwestern University School of Law (2009-2017); *Fellow,* Leadership Greater Chicago (2007); *Co-Chair,* Selection Committee, Leadership Greater Chicago; *Board Member,* Leadership Greater Chicago (2008-2015); *Board Chairman,* Urban Prep Academies (2005-2017); *Annual Benefit Committee Member,* Cabrini Green Legal Aid (CGLA) (2010); *Board Member,* Big Brothers Big Sisters of Metropolitan Chicago (2007-2010); *Adjunct Professor,* Canisius College (2009); *Chairman,* Sixth Annual My Hero Awards Luncheon, Lawyers Lend-A-Hand (2009); *Board Member,* Chicago Committee (formerly known as Chicago Committee on Minorities in Large Law Firms) (2010-2017)

LESSONS LEARNED: MY RECOMMENDATIONS FOR YOUR FUTURE ACTIONS BASED ON MY PAST EXPERIENCE

Advice on Law School Preparation:

Take it seriously. Lock in for the first year, but especially for the first semester. Now is not the time to be a party animal.

I have advised folks for the last 20-plus years that law school is about the first semester. It's a new kind of learning and a new terminology. By the time you get to your second semester, you revert to what got you through undergraduate and what has worked for you in life to date. You begin to understand that with the exception of the few folks that just pick it up - everyone is pretty much in the same boat. Read, and begin something you will need to do for the rest of your career - begin to develop relationships - with your peers, the administration, and your professors.

If your first-semester grades are lower than you would like, double down, meet with your professors, figure out what went wrong and make sure you are on point in your second semester so that you can begin to create a narrative around improvement, work ethic and commitment.

Never stop building those relationships - with your peers, your professors and your administration.

Advice on Applying to and Selecting a Law School:

This is always interesting. I advocate applying where you want to go to school after doing some research on schools and figuring what you think will be best for you as an individual. Selection is a different animal. Once you get into multiple schools, you need to begin to compare the schools, the economic burden and the expected job prospects. I have advised students to go to a lower-ranked school (depends on the school) where they are getting a lot of money/free ride. I have also advised students to forgo scholarship money at some schools and attend a higher-ranked school. It really depends on the schools on the table, what the individual thinks they want to do and if paying for school makes sense. If you get into multiple schools and you are not getting money, I would lean to the higher-ranked school unless there is some other compelling reason to attend the lower-ranked school. I would always encourage the applicant to negotiate to get money once they get into any school - even if it means deferring school for a year in exchange for a meaningful financial package.

Advice Regarding Academic Success, Co-Curricular and Extra-Curricular Participation, and Social Engagement in Law School:

Once you get through the first semester and find your groove, it's about what you want your experience to be. Get as much exposure as possible when you are in school. Internships, externships, mock trials, volunteering, mentoring younger students, relationship building. Also if you are going to school in a city that you did not grow up in, then get out and learn the city and where you live beyond the campus.

Advice on Preparing for and Taking the Bar Exam:

Study. Study. Then study some more. It's a lot of information, but certainly manageable. But in my experience - most people do have to study. I have told people forever that when the Fourth of July hit, I did not even talk to my mom. I called her and let her know I would call her after I was finished with the bar. Many folks that I have mentored have adopted this practice and really locked in post July 4th. Bar prep is not something that you can do a cram prep for. Use the time allotted and study and then study some more. Treat bar prep like a job and put the time in. Don't stress and don't get caught up in the hype and stress of other people's activity.

Advice on Choosing a Job and Career Path Inside or Outside of the Legal Profession:

If you are not going to practice law, I'm against folks going to law school.

Advice on Seeking Legal Job Opportunities and/or Creating One's Own Opportunities:

You can never build too many relationships. You never know who you will meet and in what circumstance and where that may lead to an opportunity.

Advice on Overcoming the Additional Challenges Black Law Students and Lawyers Face:

There are additional challenges. Know this going in. Embrace it. Find a community to support you - whether you are in a firm, working for the government, having your own firm, etc. Find a community and a support system. Don't go it alone. Despite the challenges, know that there is a lot of success out here waiting for you. So come on and get it - and then create some new opportunities for others.

Best Advice I Received Regarding Law School and the Legal Profession:

Protect your reputation at all costs. All we have is our reputation. Best advice I have ever received.

Worst Advice I Received Regarding Law School and the Legal Profession:

I did not do great on a practice exam during bar prep and an instructor and practicing attorney told me that I would never pass the bar. I remember it like it was yesterday and it was 22 years ago this month. While there may have not been any "advice" attached to this statement, it has stuck with me since then as a guiding principle. Our job is to build up our next generation of lawyers, to encourage them, to support them, to teach them, to guide them. That's not what this particular "instructor" did. And I would add that the practice exam was on a topic that we had not yet covered in bar prep. Bottom line - encourage somebody.

Best Advice I Would Give to an Aspiring Black Lawyer:

Be all in. If this is what you want - go get it. There is plenty of opportunity out here for us. I would also say - talk to practicing attorneys of every generation. Find out what it means to practice law and educate yourself on the arena that you are looking to get into. Talk to folks in your peer group to understand what the first one to three years of practicing look like. Find folks that can translate everything going on in your work environment. Talk to lawyers.

Thoughts About Whether and Why Law School Is Worth the Financial Investment:

I think it depends on what you plan to do with your law degree. This should influence where you apply and where you ultimately attend and what you spend should make sense given your plans for law school. If you are not going to practice law, I would not make the financial investment in going to law school.

LEGACY AND SUCCESS

My Most Outstanding Accomplishment:

Marriage and my two kids. If my wife and I can continue to have more happy days than not for years to come and continue to mold our kids into contributing members of society, that will be my most outstanding accomplishment – which to be clear, I seek to accomplish with and through the partnership of my wife.

The Legacy I Hope to Leave:

Importance of helping others - sometimes even to your personal detriment. I impress on each person that I try to mentor or influence that my expectation is that they do the same thing with others that they will come in contact with. Do not sit back and wait for folks to come to you - extend yourself. I also try to impress on folks that we have to be more open today to difference than ever before when we try to support opportunities for a generation of folks that may view the world a little bit differently.

The Secret to My Success:

There is no secret and plus everyone defines success differently. One thing I would recommend is that an individual define what success means to them and then pursue their definition of success. Nothing is going to come easy and you have to put the time in. If your definition of success is still being formulated, I would say to consider your ability to create other opportunities for success of others in your definition.

To the extent I have had any success, my success hinges on my faith and I am powered by God to do the things that I have been able to do through His Grace and His Mercy.

Jeremy McLymont, Esq.
Assistant Public Defender
Miami-Dade Public Defender Office
Miami, Florida

"Be dedicated to your passion and your passion will lead you to success."

– Jeremy McLymont

Success is . . . demonstrating a consistent commitment to excellence.

PROFESSIONAL ACCOMPLISHMENTS

PERSONAL FAVORITES

Favorite Quote: "Remember, hope is a good thing, maybe the best of things, and no good thing dies." - Stephen King

Favorite Books: *Just Mercy: A Story of Justice and Redemption* by Bryan Stevenson; *A Lawyer's Life* by Johnnie Cochran; Harry Potter Collection by J.K. Rowling

Favorite Movies: *The Dark Knight; The Shawshank Redemption*

Favorite Musical Artists: J. Cole; Nas; Kodak Black; Michael Jackson; Buju Banton; Popcaan

Favorite Law School Classes: Advanced Trial Advocacy; Death Penalty; Criminal Procedure; Race and the Law

Favorite Legal Cases: *Gideon v. Wainwright; State of Florida v. Eric Watson* (my first felony trial)

Favorite Hobbies: Organizing my community around social justice issues; Bettering myself through the acquisition of knowledge

Favorite Attorney Role Models: Bryan Stevenson; H.T. Smith; Charles Hamilton Houston; Johnnie Cochran

FAMILY AND BACKGROUND

Where Born and Raised: Born - Rome, New York; Raised - Tampa, Florida

Family Socioeconomic and Educational Background:

My mother and father emigrated to this country from the Caribbean islands. They met as young teenagers, got married and had three children. I was the second child. My parents divorced shortly thereafter, and my mother raised the three of us as a single mother. That is not to say that my father was not there for us. My father was very present in my life and he and my mother were able to provide for us financially. My mother graduated high school and took some college classes. My father graduated from the University of South Florida with a bachelor's degree. When I was 12 years old, my father was arrested and sent to prison for 78 months. My mother tried her best to manage without his financial support, so our socioeconomic status began to fluctuate. We lived in houses that got foreclosed on, to tiny apartments, to town homes. We experienced a range of financial seasons, some rainy and some sunny.

THE DECISION TO BECOME A LAWYER

When and Why I Decided to Become a Lawyer: At 11 years of age, I knew that I wanted to be a criminal defense attorney. My experiences with the criminal justice system led me to this career. I witnessed the pain that mass incarceration inflicted on so many of my family and friends, and their pain had secondary effects on me because I was helpless. I was four years old the first time I saw my father get arrested. Over the years, every male in my family would eventually get arrested and spend time in jail or prison - every uncle, cousin, and brother. No specific experience with the criminal justice system sparked my desire to become an attorney, but with every arrest and every sentence, my desire grew stronger.

My father's experience with the criminal justice system had the greatest effect on me. By the age of 12, my father had been arrested again. However, this time he was sentenced to 78 months in federal prison for conspiracy to sell marijuana; I was sentenced to 78 months without a father. The judge sentenced my father, who had no previous convictions, at the top of the sentencing guidelines. I resented the judge, and I remember wondering whether the judge cared enough to consider the damage her sentence inflicted on me and my siblings.

My father's sentence had a domino effect on me that exposed me to jail and prison, that is why I believe it had the greatest effect on my decision to become a criminal defense attorney. An indirect result of my father being in prison was me being falsely arrested three times at the age of 16. I knew I wanted to be an attorney early on, but I could not be more certain of that after I spent 21 nights in a juvenile detention center.

EDUCATIONAL ACHIEVEMENTS

High School: Alonso High School (Tampa, Florida)

College/University: University of South Florida (Tampa, Florida)

Undergraduate Degree: Bachelor of Arts (B.A.)

Major: Criminology

College Honors, Achievements and Activities: *Member,* Executive Board, Black Student Union

Law School: Florida International University College of Law (Miami, Florida)

Law Degree and Graduation Year: Juris Doctor/Doctor of Jurisprudence (J.D.) - Class of 2018

Law School Honors, Achievements and Activities: *Recipient,* Eric Garner Memorial Police Brutality Scholarship, National Black Law Students Association (NBLSA); *Recipient,* Dr. Fidel Goldson Sr. Memorial Scholarship, Jamaican American Bar Association; *Recipient,* Henry Latimer Scholarship, T.J. Reddick Bar Association; *Recipient,* Wilkie D. Ferguson Jr. Bar Foundation Scholarship, Wilkie D. Ferguson Jr. Bar Association; *Academic Recognition,* Dean's List; *Awardee,* Book Award, Death Penalty Law; *National Director of Social Action,* National Black Law Students Association (NBLSA) (2016-2017); *National Attorney General,* National Black Law Students Association (NBLSA) (2017-2018); *Social Justice Chair,* H.T. Smith Black Law Students Association, Florida International University College of Law; *President,* H.T. Smith Black Law Students Association, Florida International University College of Law

PROFESSIONAL ACCOMPLISHMENTS

State Bar Membership (Where Admitted to Practice Law): Florida

Other Legal Work Experience: *Intern,* Public Defender Office, Tampa Florida; *Intern,* Older & Lundy Law Firm; *Clerk,* Public Defender Service, District of Columbia

Other Professional Work Experience: Licensed Barber

Professional Organizations: *Vice President,* Jamaican-American Bar Association; *Member,* Wilkie D. Ferguson Bar Association; *Member,* Caribbean Bar Association; *Board Member,* Kalief Browder Foundation

Post-Law School Honors, Achievements, Activities, and Community Involvement: *Volunteer,* Dream Defenders; *Volunteer,* Nation of Islam; *Volunteer,* The Circle of Brotherhood in Miami; *Volunteer,* Miami Dade Branch, National Association for the Advancement of Colored People (NAACP); *Board Member,* Kalief Browder Foundation

LESSONS LEARNED: MY RECOMMENDATIONS FOR YOUR FUTURE ACTIONS BASED ON MY PAST EXPERIENCE

Advice on Law School Preparation:

I was accepted into law school the Thursday before the first day of classes. No one in my family had been to law school so I had no idea what to expect. I had no idea law school would be so drastically different from an undergraduate education. Because of my late admittance, I did not get to go through law school orientation. I honestly did not know there was an orientation. I walked into the class on the first day, not knowing that students had been given first week assignments a week prior to the first day of class. As you could imagine, I was behind the curve in a major way and I was never quite able to catch up during my first semester. Learn from my mistake. My mistake was that I waited until June to take the Law School Admission Test (LSAT), hence why I was admitted into law school so late.

Apply to law school early. In order to apply early, that means you need to take the LSAT early. Do not wait until the last minute to take the LSAT. It is never too early to begin preparing for the LSAT. Your LSAT score will open many doors for you if you take it seriously. I cannot stress enough the importance of obtaining a good LSAT score. Your LSAT score determines which school will accept you, and how much money schools will give you in financial aid. Take an LSAT class. It will help you in the long run. The money you spend on the LSAT class will come back to you in financial aid when you do well on the LSAT. I did not understand the importance of taking timed practice LSAT exams. The best way to increase your LSAT score is to take practice tests under exam-like conditions. You get little value from reading LSAT books; the real score increase comes from taking practice tests.

Your Grade Point Average (GPA) is as important as your LSAT score. If you play to your strengths, a high GPA should be easier to obtain than a great LSAT score. Law schools do not require a specific college major. That means you can pick any major in undergraduate school. My strength was criminal law. It was what I knew I wanted to do and it came very easy to me. However, you do not need to choose a "traditional" law school major. You can major in art or dance. Law schools are not looking at your major, they just want to know that you have the required GPA. For the most part, as long as you have the target LSAT score and GPA, a law school will admit you.

Some people will advise you to choose a major that they think properly aligns with law school. The most common suggestions will likely be pre-law, political science, psychology, English and criminal justice. I think all of these majors are great. However, I personally do not believe any of them are necessary. The purpose of law school is to break you down and completely alter the way your mind is wired. Learning how to write or think in college can disappoint you because law school has a way of making you feel like everything you have ever known is a lie. Law school will change the way you think, write, analyze, and approach issues. Several schools are creating pipelines for potential law students. If your undergraduate school has one of these pipelines, you should get involved.

Advice on Applying to and Selecting a Law School:

It just so happened that one of my professors became someone I look up to. It just so happened that he was Black and he practiced criminal defense and civil rights in the same way that I aspire to do. I was lucky to stumble up Professor H.T. Smith at Florida International University College of Law. My advice is: don't allow yourself to be lucky.

When you are applying to law schools, research the professors who teach at the law school. Reach out to these professors. See how they respond to your emails. Google the name of the law school and its professors and find out what you can expect to come across at the school. Look for the good and bad attributes of the law school and weigh them. One of the most important deciding factors should be the law school's bar passage rate. The entire purpose of going to law school is to pass the bar exam so that you can become a practicing attorney. Thus, you want to go to a school that has a history of their graduates passing the bar. Law school will be a culture shock to you because the people in your class will not look like you. Get in contact with a member of the Black Law Students Association and ask them tough questions about how the school deals with social and racial justice.

All of these things should be considered when selecting a law school.

Advice Regarding Academic Success, Co-Curricular and Extra-Curricular Participation, and Social Engagement in Law School:

During my 1L summer, another student at the school posted a picture of herself and two other men posing with the caption "Niggas in Seville". They were in Seville, Spain for a study abroad program and they thought it would be humorous to post such a photograph. They were not Black students, and they were blatantly disrespectful for posting such an image. It was offensive and I spoke out about it. I lost friends and I gained enemies at the law school for voicing my opinion. Social challenges are real in law school because most of the students and professors will not look like you. They will not come from the same background or zip code as you. Therefore, they will not understand you and they will oftentimes do things that offend you. At times, you may feel the need to escape. The only way to deal with these social challenges is to acknowledge that they are coming and be ready to deal with them as they come. Find support through your BLSA chapter and the faculty who will speak up for Black students. While social challenges exist in law school, there are good people in every law school who will fight for your right to be treated with respect.

If you can, you should get involved in extra-curricular activities. It will be difficult at first to manage your schedule but as you get comfortable with your workload you should try to implement exercise and self-care into your routine. It will feel like you don't have the time to participate in extra-curricular activities, but once you start you will realize that it is possible.

Advice on Preparing for and Taking the Bar Exam:

The bar exam is the most important test of your life. Studying for the bar should be treated as a full-time job. If you put in the work and the time through bar prep, you should pass. Follow the schedule given to you by your bar prep company and try your best not to fall behind. There will be days where you feel like nothing you are doing is working. That is all a part of the process. You can minimize that stress by getting rid of all the additional weights that life will have placed on you at this point. Ask your family to give you space and to respect that you have to study. Go on a hiatus. Let family and friends know that you will not be available for the next couple of months as you study. It is best to save money throughout law school so you have savings that will allow you to take off from work during bar prep. Bar prep is too exhausting to have to work a job in addition to the 10 to 12-hour library sessions that you will put in.

Many people wait until the last minute to secure a post graduate job. The earlier you secure a job the better. Try to find post-bar employment long before bar prep starts. It is not a good feeling to have to study for the bar exam and seek future employment at the same time. Your 3L year should be spent looking for post-graduate employment. Bar prep should be spent preparing for the bar. People will wait until the last minute to find employment, and they will live with stress during bar prep for it. While others are drafting resumes and cover letters to submit job applications, you can spend that time studying or relaxing.

You will need the proper tools to study for the bar. Outside of your bar prep program, I believe there is one other program you should consider purchasing. That program is called Adaptibar. Adaptibar is a program with thousands of bar-like questions that will get you ready for the exam like no other multiple-choice practice tests. Adaptibar provides analytics allowing you to see which subjects are your strengths and weaknesses. With that being said, it is important to limit the amount of bar prep resources you utilize. Don't purchase so much material that you overwhelm yourself. Use what you have and trust your system.

In the beginning, you will work long hours and nothing will seem to stick. Your practice test score will be low and you will wonder if you are in trouble. That is normal. It is part of the process. But keep in mind, just like with the LSAT, the way to pass the bar is to practice, practice, practice.

You should know whether you are ready to pass the bar roughly two to three weeks before the exam. If you have put in the necessary work and time, fear and anxiety will turn into confidence and hunger. Be confident when you take the bar. Success on the bar is found among the takers who know they can pass.

Advice on Choosing a Job and Career Path Inside or Outside of the Legal Profession:

I am of the belief that a person should know, early on, what they want to do in life. The earlier, the better. Law is such an expansive field which means the career paths are limitless. Try to find something that interests you. Something that you feel very passionate about. Your interests and passions should lead you to a few legal career options. For example, if you are passionate about ending systemic racism through the acquisition of land, real estate can be your lane. If you are interested in the way businesses are developed and grown, business law can be your niche. I was very passionate about criminal law, so I knew there was nothing else that I wanted to do. I found out what my passions were early on in life because I was deeply affected by the criminal justice system. However, some people have not developed their passion yet and it makes them indecisive, but that is okay. Just understand what you should be looking for, and that is your passion.

For those people who are undecided, the best way to figure out what you want to do is to gain practical experience through internships. Internships are valuable because they allow you to experience different aspects of the law. If you can intern or shadow as a young undergraduate student, do so. That practical experience will open your eyes to what goes on behind a law firm's closed doors. You will be able to witness different attorneys' workloads. You will be able to gauge the workplace environment. In doing so, you should quickly be able to determine whether you enjoy the type of work you experience.

Believe it or not, there is an entire population of law school graduates who never go on to practice law. Some of these people go to law school knowing they don't want to practice law. Others find out that they don't want to practice law while they are in law school. Many employers value a Juris Doctor degree more than other professional degrees because of the way lawyers are taught to analyze issues. Thus, if you decide not to practice law, you will have a lot of other job opportunities to choose from. Lawyers who don't practice law can be found in the boardrooms of big businesses, in Congress, and in the White House like Barack Obama.

Advice on Seeking Legal Job Opportunities and/or Creating One's Own Opportunities:

Whether you are creating your own opportunity by opening your own business, or you are looking for a job at a law firm, you will need to network to be successful. I cannot stress the importance of networking enough. Rarely does a paper application get you a job at a law firm. Employers are looking for people they can trust. When looking to employ someone, they will first look to their immediate circle of friends and acquaintances. If the employer cannot find an employee in their immediate circle, they will try to find someone that their immediate circle can vouch for. Without creating your own network, you will not be in any of these circles. The last resort for an employer is the paper application that was submitted in a vacuum. Likewise, if you want to open your own firm, you are going to need people to know you exist. Unless you network and build your brand, people will not refer cases to you and potential clients won't even know you exist.

Advice on Achieving Career Success and Advancement:

Once you journey down the road of success and career advancement, it seems to become a never-ending road. As attorneys, we always strive to be more successful - to win more trials; to publish more articles, notes, and books; to achieve more financial security. You have to define what success means for you and know that it is achievable with hard work and a consistent commitment to excellence.

Advice on Overcoming the Additional Challenges Black Law Students and Lawyers Face:

I overcame challenges by surrounding myself with the Black Law Students Association on a local and national level. National Black Law Students Association (NBLSA) led me to my first summer internship working in D.C. at the Public Defender Services. NBLSA introduced me to successful Black law students all over the nation. If it were not for NBLSA, I would not be sharing knowledge through this book. I was not just a member of NBLSA, I engaged NBLSA. That engagement is necessary. There were six Black law students in my incoming 1L class. I had never been so outnumbered. It wore me out and I don't know if I would have made it past my first year if I didn't experience the National Black Law Students Association (NBLSA) Convention during the spring of my 1L year. A student mentor of mine pushed me to join her at the convention. I had no idea what NBLSA was, but I listened.

Best Advice I Received Regarding Law School and the Legal Profession:

I received two pieces of advice in law school that I want to reiterate: 1) Join NBLSA and 2) Network.

Worst Advice I Received Regarding Law School and the Legal Profession:

I did not receive any bad advice regarding law school and the legal profession. I surround myself with people who gave me nothing but good advice and you should do the same.

Best Advice I Would Give to an Aspiring Black Lawyer:

Make sure you network! Being a lawyer has a lot to do with who you know and who you can call on for help. They say your network is your net worth and for attorneys that statement could not be more accurate. Networking will introduce to you mentors who want to see you succeed. I may not have made it past my first year of law school if I had not networked. I met people who opened doors for me and provided me with resources that I did not know existed. Networking can be awkward, it can be uncomfortable - but as a lawyer, you need to get used to it. Embrace it.

Thoughts About Why Earning a Law Degree Is a Powerful Credential for African Americans and Why There Is a Need for More African American Lawyers:

Earning a law degree is powerful because lawyers control every aspect of society. With so few Black lawyers in our profession, we can see why Black people are locked out of so many important spaces. Lawyers draft legislation and then they interpret that legislation to their liking. Lawyers engage in real estate transactions that benefit themselves and their people. When you think about why slave owners did not allow Black people to read, you understand how important it is to be able to use the English language to your benefit. Lawyers are wordsmiths. A mastery of the English language is so important to the development of community. That is why English is spoken all over the world. A law degree can be used for righteous purposes but it can also be used to take advantage of people. We need more Black attorneys who will use their degrees for righteous purposes.

Thoughts About Whether and Why Law School Is Worth the Financial Investment:

When you invest in the stock market, you can watch it grow. You can sit by and do nothing. The same is true when you invest your money into high yield savings accounts. Going to law school is surely a financial investment, but it is not a passive investment. If you want the investment to work for you, you are going to have to work for it. If you are willing to work very hard, you can watch the investment flourish. The possibilities with law are endless. The business opportunities that you can create for yourself will give you a return on your law school investment if you work for it.

LEGACY AND SUCCESS

My Most Outstanding Accomplishment:

My most outstanding accomplishment has to be passing the bar exam. Without passing the bar exam, my legal career would be non-existent. It's an accomplishment I will never forget the details of. I remember countless nights I spent up studying. I remember the friends who studied with me. I remember the struggles. I remember the exam and most importantly, I remember reading my results. When the results came out, I laid down on the floor praying for the best. I scoured through thousands of test results until I got to mine. As I read the results, I was numb from shock, joy and relief. Knowing that I passed the bar exam and that I could go on to become everything that I dreamed of has no equal. I have never worked harder for anything in my life and I am most proud of that accomplishment.

The Legacy I Hope to Leave:

Despite all of the great Civil Rights victories that Johnnie Cochran had, he is widely known for defending O.J. Simpson. Johnnie Cochran paved the way for these million-dollar police brutality settlements. Johnnie Cochran made entire police departments change their policies. Johnnie Cochran struck fear in the hearts of those who violated human rights. I want my legacy to be that which Johnnie Cochran's should be. I want my legacy to be that of Charles Hamilton Houston and Bryan Stevenson. People who spent their lives fighting to make this system acknowledge that Black people have inalienable rights just like everyone else. I want my legacy to be that I changed the structure of the American criminal justice system for the better. I want to leave behind a legacy of opening doors for Black people who have been denied justice. I want to leave behind a legacy that can be carried on by generations of Black lawyers to come.

The Secret to My Success:

Success should be measured by your own goals and ambitions. Success should not be measured by society's standards because society does not have realistic expectations for success. The secret to success is finding out what success means for you. You have to know what you want out of this profession. Once you know what you want, you have to create a pathway to get there. Great mentors will light the path for you. Experience will show you the way, but a consistent commitment to excellence will get you to your final destination.

Practical Wisdom for Those on the Path to Lawyerhood

Winfield Ward Murray, Esq.
Federal Attorney
United States Department of Labor
Professor
Morehouse College
Atlanta, Georgia

"Choose to never give up, choose to outwork your peers, and choose to deliver your best work product everyday and there will be no obstacle you cannot tackle."
— Winfield Ward Murray

Success is . . . giving this world, this country, your state, your city, or your community something that no one else could have given and the recipient is in a better position than before because of your contribution.

PERSONAL FAVORITES

Favorite Quote: "The pen is mightier than the sword." - Edward Bulwer-Lytton

Favorite Books: *Gideon's Promise: A Public Defender Movement to Transform Criminal Justice* by Jonathan Rapping; *Hillbilly Elegy* by J.D. Vance; *Shattered: Inside Hillary Clinton's Doomed Campaign* by Jonathan Allen and Amie Parnes; *Master of the Game* by Sidney Sheldon

Favorite Movies: *The Last Dragon*; *Under the Tuscan Sun*; *Crown Heights*

Favorite Musical Artists: Jill Scott; Erykah Badu; Notorious BIG; Whitney Houston

Favorite Law School Classes: Property; Alternative Dispute Resolution

Favorite Legal Case: *Holmes v. Atlanta*, 350 U.S. 879 (1955)

Favorite Hobbies: Biking; Anything with my dog

Favorite Attorney Role Model: Jon Rapping, the founder of Gideon's Promise, which provides training and resources to public defenders across the country to better equip them to represent individuals in the criminal justice system.

FAMILY AND BACKGROUND

Where Born and Raised: Born and Raised - Atlanta, Georgia (I also spent my summers in Brownsville, Tennessee on my maternal grandparents' working farm.)

Family (Spouse/Partner and Children): Child - (daughter) Grayson

Family Socioeconomic and Educational Background: I am a sixth-generation Atlantan. Four generations of my family have attended Morehouse College and Spelman College. They each attended graduate schools as well. My father was the chief of obstetrics and gynecology at Southwest Hospital in Atlanta and he was one of the financial founders of Morehouse Medical School.

THE DECISION TO BECOME A LAWYER

When and Why I Decided to Become a Lawyer: I grew up hearing wonderful stories about how the legal system could be utilized to make the lives of others better especially for African Americans. My great uncle and his friends filed suit against the City of Atlanta in the 1950s to end segregation on Atlanta golf courses. They were represented by Thurgood Marshall and the United States Supreme Court ultimately ended segregation on Atlanta golf courses in the historic decision from *Holmes v. Atlanta*. Armed with that information, I knew I wanted to dedicate myself to service early on.

EDUCATIONAL ACHIEVEMENTS

High School: Frederick Douglass High School (Atlanta, Georgia)

College/University: Morehouse College (Atlanta, Georgia)

Undergraduate Degree: Bachelor of Arts (B.A.)

Major: English

Law School: Howard University School of Law (Washington, D.C.)

Law Degree and Graduation Year: Juris Doctor/Doctor of Jurisprudence (J.D.) - Class of 2001

Law School Honors, Achievements and Activities: *Awardee,* CALI (The Center for Computer-Assisted Legal Instruction) Excellence for the Future Award, Alternative Dispute Resolution (Highest-scoring student in class)

Other Graduate or Professional Degree: Master of Laws (LL.M.) in Litigation and Alternative Dispute Resolution, The George Washington University School of Law (Washington, D.C.)

PROFESSIONAL ACCOMPLISHMENTS

State Bar Membership (Where Admitted to Practice Law): Georgia

Other Legal Work Experience: *Judicial Clerk,* Chief Judge of the United States Virgin Islands

Other Professional Work Experience: *Deputy Chief of Staff,* Mayor Keisha Lance Bottoms, City of Atlanta; *Vice Chair,* Board of Directors, Gideon's Promise

Professional Organizations: *Member,* Leadership Atlanta; *Member,* 100 Black Men of Atlanta

Post-Law School Honors, Achievements, Activities, and Community Involvement: *Founding Team Member,* Atlanta's Community Court (sought to reduce the rate of recidivism through alternative sentencing; rate of recidivism declined three-fold)

LESSONS LEARNED: MY RECOMMENDATIONS FOR YOUR FUTURE ACTIONS BASED ON MY PAST EXPERIENCE

Advice on Law School Preparation:

If you had good study habits in undergrad, continue to use those skills. You do not need to reinvent the wheel when you go to law school. You may need to tweak it, but you do not need to reinvent it. If you do well studying independently, continue to do so in law school. If you prefer to study in groups, continue to do so in law school. A mistake that students often make is subscribing to the methods other law students employ when in actuality it is best to stick to the methods that fostered your admission to law school in the first place. Law school may require you to study longer and harder, but if you arrive at law school with good study habits you should only modify those habits to match the demands found in law school.

Advice on Applying to and Selecting a Law School:

My advice is simple. Go to the best law school you can that gives you financial assistance. While it is true that there is something to be gained by attending law school in the state where you intend to practice, it is far more important to limit the educational debt you carry into your legal practice. This is especially true if you intend to practice public interest law. Also. students often will go to a law school simply because it is highly ranked. That is a mistake. For instance, if you are admitted to a law school that is ranked No. 3, but they provide you with no scholarship money while also securing an admission and full ride to a law school ranked No. 6, my advice is to go to the No. 6 ranked school. You will work at the same law firm at the No. 3 ranked student, but will not have to pay back $250,000 in educational debt.

Advice Regarding Academic Success, Co-Curricular and Extra-Curricular Participation, and Social Engagement in Law School:

The first year of law school should be exclusively focused on giving 100% to your courses. Your second and third year, you should join moot court, mock trial, or law review. Absolutely do not leave law school without taking a clinic!

Advice on Preparing for and Taking the Bar Exam:

Study like there is no tomorrow. If your law school offers additional courses in legal writing, take those courses. Learn to write well! Then study as much as you possibly can because no one wants to repeat the bar exam. Forego friendships, parties, and any element of a social life until you cross that hurdle!

Advice on Choosing a Job and Career Path Inside or Outside of the Legal Profession:

Be flexible. Go into law school with an open mind. Consider practice areas that may be new to you. African American attorneys are needed in every practice area!

Advice on Seeking Legal Job Opportunities and/or Creating One's Own Opportunities:

Make sure you use social media platforms like LinkedIn. Post often about your career successes, panels you spoke on, and training that you have attended. Continuously update your connections.

Advice on Overcoming the Additional Challenges Black Law Students and Lawyers Face: Know that you WILL face additional challenges. Know that you must be better than your peers who are not Black. Take opportunities when they are offered. Continue to hone your skills by taking additional training. Network as much as possible.

Best Advice I Received Regarding Law School and the Legal Profession:

Law school is a game; learn how to play it.

Worst Advice I Received Regarding Law School and the Legal Profession:

Be a part of a study group and use outlines to prepare for exams. I never worked well in study groups, because it never seemed as though we accomplished as much as when I studied alone. After I went back to studying independently and stopped attempting to use outlines as suggested, my grades increased tremendously.

Best Advice I Would Give to an Aspiring Black Lawyer:

Find a mentor that is willing to tell you the things you do not want to hear and willing to take the time to tell you. And when you do, never let that mentor go.

Thoughts About Why Earning a Law Degree Is a Powerful Credential for African Americans and Why There Is a Need for More African American Lawyers:

We need more African American attorneys because African Americans have still not received equity in the country. Lawyers make great strides to securing equity for those that are marginalized and disenfranchised. We need more attorneys to take up the challenge. Furthermore, criminal justice reform is this generation's new civil rights movement. Who better to lead the movement than those that are being targeted and victimized.

Thoughts About Whether and Why Law School Is Worth the Financial Investment:

Law school is absolutely worth the financial investment. However, be wise! Try to minimize your debt. Look for scholarships before you begin your law school career and continue to do so after you are in law school, including in your 3L year.

LEGACY AND SUCCESS

My Most Outstanding Accomplishment:

My most outstanding accomplishment was leading the Morehouse Moot Court team to the 2015 American Collegiate Moot Court Association's National Championship as the director/coach. Morehouse became the first historically Black College or University (HBCU) to win the Nationals. Our team became the first African American team to win, and I became the first African American coach to win.

The Legacy I Hope to Leave:

My hope is twofold. As a professor, I hope to foster as many African Americans into the practice of law as possible. As a legal practitioner, I hope to provide more equity to African Americans, persons of color, women, and those on the lower end of the socioeconomic rung.

The Secret to My Success:

Building a brand that is known for an unyielding work ethic. Networking with a broad bandwidth of people both inside and outside of the legal community. Never giving up. Receiving an ounce of luck, and a heap of blessings.

Danielle M. Nettles, Esq.
Attorney
Linebarger Goggan Blair & Sampson, LLP
Beaumont, Texas

"I am my own competitor! Instead of competing with others, my greatest competition comes from within."

— Danielle M. Nettles

Success is . . . seeing your dreams and making them happen. This not only means that you have to visualize it, but write it down, create a plan, make it plain and work hard each day to execute your plan. Success essentially is making your life look like your dreams.

PERSONAL FAVORITES

Favorite Quote: "I can do all things through Christ who strengthens me." - Philippians 4:13

Favorite Books: *The Holy Bible; How to Win Friends and Influence People* by Dale Carnegie

Favorite Movies: *Money Heist; The Equalizer; Pretty Woman; Coming to America*

Favorite Songs: "I'm Kissing You" by Des'ree; "All of Me" by John Legend

Favorite Law School Classes: Secured Transactions; Commercial Paper; Civil Procedure; Consumer Law, and Bankruptcy

Favorite Legal Case: *Palsgraf v. Rhode Island Railroad Co.*

Favorite Hobbies: Working out; Traveling; Spending time with my son and family

Favorite Attorney Role Model: Johnnie Cochran

FAMILY AND BACKGROUND

Where Born and Raised: Beaumont, Texas

Family (Spouse/Partner and Children): Child - (son) Micah

Family Socioeconomic and Educational Background: I was raised in a working-class, single-parent family of four. My mom did her best to expose us to opportunity and what it means to give back by serving and volunteering in our church, school and local community. My mother attended some college, but I am a first-generation college graduate and attorney in my family.

EDUCATIONAL ACHIEVEMENTS

High School: Clifton J. Ozen High School (Beaumont, Texas)

College/University: Clark Atlanta University (Atlanta, Georgia) (Graduated); Morris Brown College (Atlanta, Georgia) (Attended 2001-2002)

Undergraduate Degree: Bachelor of Arts (B.A.)

Major: Criminal Justice

College Honors/Achievements/Activities: Valedictorian; Graduated *summa cum laude* "with highest distinction" from Clark Atlanta University; *Academic Recognition,* Dean's List, Morris Brown College (2001-2002); *Academic Recognition,* Dean's List, Clark Atlanta University (2002-2005); *Awardee,* Student Life Award, Clark Atlanta University; *Recipient,* Scholarship as Highest Honors Female with the Highest GPA of College Class (4.0); *President,* Criminal Justice Club; Morris Brown College/Morehouse Melon Honors Scholar

Law School: Thurgood Marshall School of Law, Texas Southern University (Houston, Texas)

Law Degree and Graduation Year: Juris Doctor/Doctor of Jurisprudence (J.D.) - Class of 2010

Law School Honors, Achievements and Activities: Graduated *magna cum laude* "with high distinction"; Graduated in Top 10%; *Academic Recognition,* Dean's List (2008-2010); *Awardee,* American Jurisprudence Award (Highest grade in class), Wills, Trusts, & Estates; *Recipient,* Environmental Law Scholarship; *Member,* Black Law Student Association; *Law Student Representative,* State Bar of Texas

THE DECISION TO BECOME A LAWYER

When and Why I Decided to Become a Lawyer:

I always dreamed of becoming an attorney and I was told quite often that I had the demeanor of an attorney since I was a child. However, as I entered high school, I wanted to find out more about the daily work of an attorney. During my high school matriculation, I volunteered in a community program called the Evelyn M. Lord Beaumont Teen Court Program. I participated in the program from ninth through twelfth grade. The program was twofold in that it offered first-time juvenile offenders a chance to go through a less harsh and penal juvenile justice system by allowing them to receive community service as the punishment for their offenses to society from a jury of their peers. Secondly, it also afforded volunteer students like myself who were not involved in the criminal justice system to participate in the court process by serving as defense attorneys, prosecuting attorneys, and jurors. This program gave me the ability to work with licensed practicing attorneys on real cases and learn the trial skills of an attorney at an early age. The experience of winning cases and learning the nuances of the criminal justice system spurred my desire to become an attorney.

PROFESSIONAL ACCOMPLISHMENTS

State Bar Memberships (Where Admitted to Practice): Texas and North Dakota

Other Legal Experience: *Assistant County Attorney,* Orange County District Attorney's Office; *Assistant District Attorney,* Harris County District Attorney's Office; *Academic Advisor,* Thurgood Marshall School of Law, Texas Southern University; *Associate Attorney,* Banks & Associates; *Intern,* Jefferson County District Attorney; *Intern,* Harris County District Attorney; *Law Clerk,* Banks & Associates; *Summer Associate,* Quarles & Brady LLP; *Intern,* Houston NAACP; *Legal Researcher,* Earl Carl Institute for Legal & Social Policy, Thurgood Marshall School of Law, Texas Southern University

Professional Organizations: *Member,* American Bar Association; *Member,* Jefferson County Bar Association; *Member,* Jefferson County Young Lawyers Association; *Member,* Orange County Bar Association; *Member,* Southeast Texas Young Professionals; *Member,* Beaumont Chamber of Commerce;

Post-Law School Honors, Achievements, Activities, and Community Involvement: *Listed Honoree,* Named to 40 Under 40 List of Southeast Texas Professionals, Texas Beard Company; *Magazine Feature,* Featured among Black Female Lawyers of the Area (Beaumont/Golden Triangle), January/February Edition, Nubian Magazine; *Member,* Alpha Kappa Alpha Sorority, Inc.; *Participant,* Leadership Beaumont, Beaumont Chamber of Commerce

LESSONS LEARNED: MY RECOMMENDATIONS FOR YOUR FUTURE ACTIONS BASED ON MY PAST EXPERIENCE

Advice on Making the Choice to Apply to and Attend Law School:

The decision to attend law school is a life-changing experience. My best advice is to make sure that it is your own personal choice and that you have a passion to work in the legal profession for a lifetime or that you have an idea as to how you can use a law degree as a tool or key to opening doors to endless opportunities. The decision to pursue law school is not something that you should do simply because someone told you to do it, (i.e., your mother, father, wife or husband). You have to want it with a passion because it will help you get out of bed each day to go to class and work hard to make it through the process. Passion equals perseverance. Additionally, do not make the decision based on a false belief of personal financial gain. I believe that you have to really examine your goals, desires, family and financial obligations in life because it is an expensive investment. This is especially true for those who choose to attend law school as a second career option.

Advice on Law School Preparation:

It is crucial that you learn good study habits while attending high school and college. Make sure that you are working to obtain good grades no matter what your major or area of discipline is while in school. Having good grades demonstrates to prospective law schools and the admissions board that you are committed to working hard if accepted into their program. I would advise aspiring students to take a course on critical thinking and/or logical reasoning if your undergraduate institution offers these types of courses. This will help with the logic and games section of the Law School Admission Test (LSAT).

The commitment to attending law school begins with your preparation for the LSAT. This means that one should set aside adequate time to prepare. If you are still in college, plan to begin your studies no later than the fall of your senior year or earlier and sign up for an LSAT preparatory course. These courses normally cost around $1,000 or more (due to inflation), but if you plan properly you can budget for this during your junior or senior year of college. If you have already graduated you can plan to take a preparatory class and purchase books such as Barron's LSAT Prep or Princeton Review LSAT Prep book and go through the entire book from cover to cover. Learn how to take the test and understand each section. As time gets closer to the exam, make sure to take timed tests under simulated exam conditions. Fine tuning your ability to test under pressure and exam conditions not only prepares you for the LSAT, but also for testing conditions in law school.

Advice on Applying to and Selecting a Law School:

Make sure that you start early (i.e., no later than the spring of your junior year of college) so that you can visit the schools that you wish to attend. Try to visit the schools that you are interested in while the law school is still in session for the academic year so that you can have an opportunity to observe law students in class and learn about the Socratic method. Make sure you have researched the law schools that you would like to attend. Understand their LSAT and GPA requirements.

Understand their early admissions deadlines, waiting lists, acceptance dates, etc. Plan to take the LSAT early (i.e., spring of your junior year or summer) so that you can have a better understanding of where you stand before you decide to submit your application for early submission. If you are not certain of your scores, you may have to cast your net wide. Many people have their eyes set on one school and may not be able to get into their first school of choice because they did not know the deadlines for early submission, or they did not have the LSAT scores that they ultimately hoped for. (If you are struggling with the LSAT, you must come to understand the science behind the LSAT and that taking multiple LSAT exams may or may not move your score up or down.) This is exactly the reason why you want to study and plan to take the test early so that you can get your scores back in enough time to determine if you should take additional LSAT exams.

Advice Regarding Academic Success, Co-Curricular and Extra-Curricular Participation, and Social Engagement in Law School:

Academics - Make sure that you are adequately prepared for class, which means that you have read the material assigned, briefed your cases and understand enough to engage in an intelligent and informed discussion with your professor(s). It is very challenging to read all of your assignments (i.e., pages assigned for each subject), but if you start early you can get through it. Understand that for every three-hour class you should be prepared to study six hours outside of class. General rule is that you are expected to study double the amount of time you spend in class. Remember, law school is a full-time job!

You will come to learn whether you prefer study groups and/or whether you are more productive studying alone. This is really important and will determine how you perform on exams, therefore, you must conduct a hard self-examination to determine what is best for you. You must be completely honest with yourself or your grades could suffer. I would suggest trying both ways and you will eventually figure out what works best for you.

In law school, you will also gain a thorough understanding of how you learn and consume information. You will understand that law school is not about memorization like many courses in college, but it is about processing the information and applying the concepts that you have learned to other scenarios.

Additionally, in law school you will come to learn whether you are an audio learner, visual learner, or both. This is extremely important. NOTE: You may learn by writing things down and putting them in an outline format. Conversely, you may have a friend that may learn by putting things down on flashcards or listening to audio CDs. Do not become overwhelmed, or in essence, freaked out if your friend uses flashcards and you prefer to study your outlines. You have to learn that what works for you may not work for others and vice versa.

Law school is an opportunity to tailor your resume for potential employers. It can be fun, but one must remember that it is not high school nor is it college. Law school is a very self-disciplined environment depending on the institutional culture. A law student must be able to balance a tight schedule and simultaneously maintain a strict focus on their studies while making a well-rounded career and experience for oneself.

My observation – students who performed well in law school were on law review, law journal, moot court, mock trial and participated in one to two social organizations. However, I found that students who were involved in too many social organizations had a difficult time maintaining stellar grades. Again, I believe that it is all about balance. I suggest being involved in a few organizations, but they should be organizations that count towards employment or show that you are well-rounded. During your first year of law school, it can be difficult to be active in multiple organizations and balance your commitment to studying for class and exams. However, as you matriculate through law school it becomes more manageable due to the experience of being a law student and learning how to meet the demands of a study schedule.

Advice on Preparing for and Taking the Bar Exam:

Not only have I had the opportunity to take the Texas Bar Exam and pass the first time, but I have also had the opportunity to teach a bar exam-writing course as an academic instructor at Thurgood Marshall School of Law. This course focused on Day Three of the Texas Bar Exam, which covers 12 essay subjects. As an Instructor, it became apparent to me that students must realize that studying for the bar exam begins on the first day of law school. The more effort, time, and energy you put into preparing for law school exams over the course of attending law school for three years, the more it will help ease the anxiety of actual bar preparation after graduation.

Actual Bar Preparation: Rid yourself of distractions. Do not make any new life changes or decisions (i.e., get married, quit your job, get divorced, start a new relationship or end a relationship). If you have children, make adequate arrangements for childcare, or pet care for pet parents. You should be prepared to devote a 40-hour workweek in studying and preparing for the exam. Set a schedule for the days that you will study the Multistate Bar Exam (MBE) questions, the Civil Procedure and Criminal Procedure and Evidence questions and essay questions. (Due to recent changes in the Texas Bar Exam and Uniform Bar Exam, this suggestion may or may not apply.) Study past bar exams from the last five years for the essay portion, and if you have more time, go back 10 years so that you can see the pattern for the most tested rules. After learning all of the material, as stated before, you should practice taking exams under simulated testing conditions to get better as time goes on.

Advice on Choosing a Job and Career Path Inside or Outside of the Legal Profession:

Go to seminars and continuing legal education sessions that your law school offers through the career services office and talk to attorneys in different practice areas. Ask attorneys about their daily life as a lawyer in the courtroom, office, and/or at home.

Ask about internship and volunteer opportunities, especially in 1L or 2L year (see below for more). At this stage, try not to become discouraged when you find out that some internships do not pay. Remember that the goal here is to get experience. Sometimes volunteer projects and internships lead to paid positions. Additionally, sign up for legal clinics at your law school. Legal clinics are a great way to work in an area of interest and earn hours toward graduation at the same time.

Advice on Seeking Legal Job Opportunities and/or Creating One's Own Opportunities:

Start early during your law school career interning in various law offices or government agencies. It is imperative to apply for jobs when the career services office allows 1Ls to start applying for jobs. (See your law school's career services office for 1L restrictions.)

The more internships, clerkships, or jobs that you have during law school the better you will be able to narrow down the area of law that you would like to work in if you have not already chosen an exact field. Doing these things will help you determine if you would like to work in a big firm, small firm, in-house, government agency, clerk for a judge, or help you determine if you would like to become a solo practitioner.

Each law school has an On-Campus Interviews (OCI) Season, which is a time when various firms and other legal employers visit the law school campus.

When applying for the OCI, make sure you have a packet of the following: Your business card, updated resume, cover letter, writing sample and transcript (if you are a 1L you may not have grades back yet in time for OCI, but most employers understand this). Stay on top of your career services office about any database, email blasts for jobs, career fairs, or any other modern-day career opportunities.

Make sure to always show up early for interviews, and be neatly and conservatively dressed. (Women's hair should be pulled back in a bun or worn neatly over the shoulders. Wear pearls or no jewelry.) Professional attire should be worn: black, grey or navy blue suit with white blouse or shirt with collar.) Avoid extravagant dress, jewelry or colors.

Carry a simple black portfolio or folder with your documents organized nice and neatly inside. Make sure that you have enough copies of your packet to hand out to each person present at your interview. (There can be one to three or more people from the company. Therefore, bring extras including a copy for yourself.) Also, it is important to know your resume and tailor your resume toward the firm that is interviewing you if you have a particular skill set (i.e., include your immigration experience if you are interviewing with an immigration firm).

Research the firm and know fun and interesting facts about the firm and/or the person that is going to interview you. This will help you stand out from other interviewees.

Have pre-written questions that you would like to ask the potential employer to help demonstrate your interest in their firm, company, or agency. Also practice your responses to sample interview questions, which you can obtain from your institutions' career services office. Do not be shy and try not to be nervous. Relax and be yourself!

Advice on Achieving Career Success and Advancement:

Set goals and obtain them. Give your best at whatever path you choose. Think of each job as a building block no matter how big or small. Learn as much as you can about the area of law that you are practicing in and the function of the law office or agency that you are with so you can understand the process. Practicing law is about understanding the process no matter what area you decide to practice in such as criminal law, civil litigation, entertainment, oil and gas, tax law, or family law. Each area of the law is about process. Become an expert on the process in your practice area. This will allow you to advance and achieve great career success throughout your practice of law.

Advice on Overcoming the Additional Challenges Black Law Students and Black Lawyers Face:

I attended two institutions: Thomas M. Cooley in Lansing, Michigan, which was the largest law school in the United States, and Thurgood Marshall School of Law at

Texas Southern University in Houston, Texas. There was a diverse group of students and everyone wanted to work hard to get through law school. I joined the Black Law Student Association to be a part of a group that was active within the institution and helped with study materials. I then transferred to Thurgood Marshall School of Law, which was noted for being one of the most diverse schools in the nation. I experienced a very warm welcome from the student body, faculty, staff and administrators.

Due to the history and culture at Thurgood Marshall School of Law and the large population of African American students and lawyers in the Houston community, I noticed the challenges later during clerkships and more so when I became an attorney. You may experience difficulty and some challenges, however, you have to align yourself with those who are willing to help. Therefore, it is good to seek mentors within the profession, workplace or even reach out to other family and friends who have had experience navigating the corporate world. Always ask questions if you do not understand, always be polite, ethical, and remain professional. Finally, give it your 100% best each day, be confident and stand by your work!!!!!! Never sacrifice your integrity or ethics and you will gain the respect of your colleagues and those around you!

Best Advice I Received Regarding Law School and the Legal Profession:

Always look for the big picture in each class and throughout the whole law school process.

Worst Advice I Received Regarding Law School and the Legal Profession:

Most lawyers told me not to go to law school and suggested that I go to medical school instead.

Best Advice I Would Give to an Aspiring Black Lawyer:

Accept that attending law school is a full-time job. Once you get into law school, get to know your professors and other support staff. Your professors will ultimately be great resources for letters of recommendation for your bar applications, scholarships while in law school and future jobs. Also keep in mind that they will eventually become your colleagues when you graduate. Stay focused and begin studying early in the semester (i.e., no later than week five if your school administers exams only once each semester per course). Look for the big picture, learn the material, test and retest. Do not be afraid to ask questions, but make sure you take time to understand or seek help if you do not understand.

Also, the Professor is the King of His or Her Court (Class). Learn the law the way your professor teaches the material. This is helpful to understand because this translates to the real world and how judges operate in their courtroom.

One must understand that law is a "one-man, one-woman show". Therefore, your success depends on what you know and what you took the time to study. You cannot depend on your friend for the answer or information during tests or during the bar exam. You must conquer the material and become an expert on each area of the law. If you do well in one subject versus others, you have to give the others just as much time and attention. If you find that you do well in one subject as opposed to other subjects, apply that same study technique to other subjects that you find more challenging.

Thoughts About Why Earning a Law Degree Is a Powerful Credential for African Americans:

A Doctor of Jurisprudence law degree is an extremely powerful credential, but you just have to know how to use it. It not only opens doors for African Americans, but it allows you to sit at the table and engage in conversations and discussions, which are opportunities that some people may not otherwise have. A law degree equals exposure!

Thoughts About Whether and Why Law School Is Worth the Financial Investment:

In the wake of the social climate in America, there is a need for African American lawyers in the legal community so that we can help others better understand the things that are happening within various communities.

However, as a whole, African American attorneys are needed in the legal community because we offer a different perspective. It is clear that our world and country are diverse. Therefore, every sector of the law should be diverse so that we can offer our insight on various issues and also expose our children to more opportunities and so many discussions that are taking place, politically, professionally, and socially around the world.

LEGACY AND SUCCESS

My Most Outstanding Accomplishment:

Being named as one of the Top 40 Under 40 Young Professionals in Southeast Texas List within my local community as a top leader who gives back to the community both personally and professionally.

The Legacy I Hope to Leave:

I hope to bring people of color together to promote excellence and support in the legal profession.

The Secret to My Success:

The secret to my success before, during, and after law school is that my competition comes from within. I focus on my goals and strive to do my best at everything that I do. Focus on yourself and do not become easily distracted by anything else outside of your goals or dreams in school, work, or in your personal life. If you focus on what you need to do daily and put the time in, then you will slowly but surely get closer to achieving your goals. With God on my side, I strive to make my goals and my dreams a reality and you can do the same!!!!!

Practical Wisdom for Those on the Path to Lawyerhood

Scheril Antoinette Murray Powell, Esq.
Attorney at Law
Doumar, Allsworth, Laystrom, Voigt, Wachs, Adair, and Dishowitz LLP
Miami, Florida

"Lead with love, lead with compassion and you will never regret decisions."
– Scheril Antoinette Murray Powell

Success is . . . the ability to sustain the balance of mind, body, and spirit while maintaining a posture of service to your family and community.

PERSONAL FAVORITES

Favorite Quotes: "Injustice anywhere is a threat to justice everywhere." - Reverend Dr. Martin Luther King, Jr.

"If I can see further than others (before me)...it is because I stand on the shoulders of giants." - Sir Isaac Newton

"When you do the common things in life in an uncommon way, you will command the attention of the world." - George Washington Carver

"There is no shortcut to achievement. Life requires thorough preparation - veneer isn't worth anything." - George Washington Carver

Favorite Book: *Understanding the Purpose and Power of Woman* by the late Dr. Myles Munroe

Favorite Movies: *Silver Linings Playbook; Malcolm X; Mo' Better Blues*

Favorite Song: "The Conquering Lion" by Lauryn Hill

Favorite Law School Classes: Contracts; Wills and Trusts

Favorite Legal Case: *Loving v. Virginia* (legalized interracial relationships)

Favorite Hobbies: Karaoke; Poetry

Favorite Attorney Role Model: Charlotte E. Ray, Esq. She is the first Black woman licensed to practice law. I named the Florida International University College of Law Black Law Students Association's Charlotte E. Ray Scholarship after her.

FAMILY AND BACKGROUND

Where Born and Raised: Born - Long Island, New York; Raised - Long Island, New York until the age of 13 when my family relocated to Coral Springs, Florida

Family (Spouse/Partner and Children): Child - (son) Judah

Family Socioeconomic and Educational Background: My parents are Jamaican immigrants who worked hard for a middle-class lifestyle. I am a first-generation college graduate and first-generation law school graduate.

THE DECISION TO BECOME A LAWYER

When and Why I Decided to Become a Lawyer: I have been saying that I wanted to be a lawyer since the age of five, but I did not truly commit until the end of my first career as a wireless industry executive in 2011.

EDUCATIONAL ACHIEVEMENTS

High School: Coral Springs High School (Coral Springs, Florida)

College/University: Florida Atlantic University (Boca Raton, Florida)

Undergraduate Degree: Bachelor of Business Administration (B.B.A.)

Major: Business Management

College Honors, Achievements and Activities: *Senate Speaker,* Florida Atlantic University (for seven campuses for two years); *Chair,* Ways and Means, Delta Sigma Theta Sorority, Inc.; *2nd Vice President,* Delta Sigma Theta Sorority, Inc.

Law School: Florida International University College of Law (Miami, Florida)

Law Degree and Graduate Year: Juris Doctor/Doctor of Jurisprudence (J.D.) - Class of 2015

Law School Honors, Achievements and Activities: *First Place,* American Bar Association (ABA) Regional Negotiation Tournament (2012); *National Board Member,* National Black Law Students Association (NBLSA) (two years); *Charter President,* Palm Beach American Bar Association

Additional Education: Certificate, Human Resources Management, Florida Atlantic University; Certificate, Hospitality and Tourism Management, Florida Atlantic University; License, Florida Real Estate Agent

PROFESSIONAL ACCOMPLISHMENTS

State Bar Membership (Where Admitted to Practice Law): Florida

Other Professional Experience: *Founder and President,* Green Sustainable Strong, LLC; *Founder and President,* Canna Headhunters; *Founder and President,* Cannurban.com

Professional Organizations: *Member,* Broward County Bar Association

Post-Law School Honors, Achievements, Activities, and Community Involvement: *Awardee,* Cannabis MVP Award, Cannabis Business Awards; *Listed Honoree,* Top 12 Cannabis Attorneys in Florida; *Secretary,* Florida International University College of Law Alumni Association; *Executive Director,* Black Farmers and Agriculturalists of Florida; *Board Member,* U.S. Hemp Building Association; *Board Member,* Hemp Feed Coalition (University Outreach): *Member,* Broward County Medical Marijuana Advisory Board; *Member,* University of Florida Hemp Program Advisory Board; *Host,* Florida Agricultural and Mechanical University's Medical Marijuana Education and Research Initiative Videocast; *Executive Producer,* "Terps in the City" Talk Show

LESSONS LEARNED: MY RECOMMENDATIONS FOR YOUR FUTURE ACTIONS BASED ON MY PAST EXPERIENCE

Advice on Law School Preparation:

If you are interested in law school, I highly recommend going to a college that has a bachelor's in paralegal studies. The students that had a paralegal background had a clear advantage in law school.

Advice on Applying to and Selecting a Law School:

Do not let your Grade Point Average (GPA) or Law School Admission Test (LSAT) score keep you from applying to the schools you want to get into. Work to complete your law school applications BEFORE you take the LSAT, so that when the LSAT score is delivered to the school, it completes your application. Never say "no" to yourself!!!

Advice Regarding Academic Success, Co-Curricular and Extra-Curricular Participation, and Social Engagement in Law School:

I recommend just focusing on academics your first year of law school. Reach out to members of the Black Law Student Association (BLSA) for help, assistance, advice, etc. and participate in their mentor program during your first year, but your objective is to stay enrolled.

Advice on Preparing for and Taking the Bar Exam:

You are always going to think you are going to fail all the way until you get your results. Reject those thoughts and speak positivity. Remember to use the process of elimination on EVERY question. Also, take the bar prep course strategy lessons seriously; they tell you how the bar examiners test. Make sure that you do between 2,000 and 2,500 Multistate Bar Exam (MBE) questions by the time you take the bar. This helps you learn the law as well as how tricky the questions can be.

Advice on Choosing a Job and Career Path Inside or Outside of the Legal Profession:

Try to get diverse legal experience while you are in law school so that you figure out what areas of law you enjoy. I am now working at the same law firm where I clerked for two years. I learned so much from my supervising attorneys and learned that I loved estate planning, probate, and real estate law work.

Advice on Seeking Legal Job Opportunities and/or Creating One's Own Opportunities:

Start building your referral network while in law school. Don't wait until after you graduate to start setting up a LinkedIn profile and making connections. Try to establish mutually beneficial relationships with people in practice. Acquire mentors, but don't just use them where you are always asking for something from them.

Advice on Achieving Career Success and Advancement:

Advancement: Always have your notebook and pen so you can take notes when meeting with attorneys. Listen carefully and ask questions when you lack understanding. Your work should reflect your brand, so put 100% effort into every task.

Advice on Overcoming the Additional Challenges Black Law Students and Black Lawyers Face:

Make sure you have mentors from other demographics. Learn how to diplomatically respond to ignorance and prejudice. You don't have to tell people who you are - show them with your excellence.

The startup can be hard. If possible, try to join a firm so that some of your overhead can be taken care of such as your bar dues, copier, fax costs, rent, etc. Hang in there; it will get better financially, but do not be discouraged. Remember what you wrote on your law school application.

Best Advice I Received Regarding Law School and the Legal Profession:

If someone asks you to do something that makes you feel uncomfortable, think about whether it is worth your license to practice.

Worst Advice I Received Regarding Law School and the Legal Profession:

"Just aim for a C. Cs get degrees." Always, always aim for excellence.

Best Advice I Would Give to an Aspiring Black Lawyer:

Align yourself with people doing what you want to do so you can learn from them. Also, do not listen to anyone who says there are too many lawyers...there are not enough Black lawyers.

Thoughts About Why Earning a Law Degree Is a Powerful Credential for African Americans and Why There Is a Need for More African American Lawyers:

A law degree is very empowering. It allows you to help your family and help your community. Just being able to share recent cases and rulings on Facebook helps the community. You start to view current events through a legal lens.

Thoughts About Whether and Why Law School Is Worth the Financial Investment:

Law school is very much worth the financial investment. So often, we invest in material things, but the greatest investment is in yourself and your community. A law degree truly is the gift that keeps on giving. There are many affordable programs. Do not be discouraged by the cost of the most expensive ones.

LEGACY AND SUCCESS

My Most Outstanding Accomplishments:

Professional - 1) Being selected as the speaker for my law school commencement; and 2) Being selected to present at the National Association of Black Journalists (NABJ) Conference in August 2016.

Personal - Completing law school as a single mom of a high-performing son who has integrity and compassion.

The Legacy I Hope to Leave:

I want to be a social engineer and deliver a better world to my son through my knowledge of the law.

The Secret to My Success:

I do not believe that you can receive with a closed fist. I focus on giving and sharing, then the rest takes care of itself. I am constantly in pursuit of excellence. Most important, I put God first. Prayer is what got me through law school and created the opportunity for my attorney placement.

Marsha L. Ross-Jackson, Esq., M.P.A.

Senior Lecturer and Assistant Dean
Diversity, Equity, Inclusion and Student Professional Development
Executive Director
**Institute for Law and the Workplace
Chicago-Kent College of Law
Chicago, Illinois**

"If your voice is absent, so are you and the people you serve. Don't allow anyone or anything to cancel your existence."

– Marsha Ross-Jackson

Success is . . . when passion, purpose and opportunity meet.

PERSONAL FAVORITES

Favorite Quote: "Life's most persistent and urgent question is: 'What are you doing for others?'" - Dr. Martin Luther King, Jr.

Favorite Books: *Change Your Questions, Change Your Life* by Marilee Adams; *The Speed of Trust* by Stephen Covey; *The Traveler's Gift* by Andy Andrews; *White Fragility* by Robin DiAngelo and Michael Eric Dyson (Foreword); *The Color of Law* by Richard Rothstein

Favorite Movies: *The Pursuit of Happyness*; *Black Panther*; *Just Mercy*; *Marshall*; *Dreamgirls*

Favorite Songs: "I Have Nothing" by Whitney Houston; "The Battle is Not Yours" by Yolanda Adams; "What's Going On" by Marvin Gaye

Favorite Musical Artists: Yolanda Adams; Anita Baker; Whitney Houston; Marvin Gaye

Favorite Law School Classes: Constitutional Law; Employment Law; Food and Drug Law; Legal Writing

Favorite Legal Cases: *Brown v. Board of Education*; *Meritor Savings Bank v. Vinson*; *Grutter v. Bollinger*

Favorite Hobbies: Dancing (including line dancing, stepping, modern dance, praise dance, and Zumba)

Favorite Attorney Role Model: Thurgood Marshall

FAMILY AND BACKGROUND

Where Born and Raised: Chicago, Illinois

Family (Spouse/Partner) and Children: Spouse - Eric; Children - (daughter) Erica, (daughter) Myah, and (son) John

Family Socioeconomic and Educational Background: I grew up on the South Side of Chicago in the house with my parents, Marshall Ross, Jr. and Bettye Thigpen Ross, along with my two older sisters, Sherrill Ross and Beryl Ross-Randall. We have always been a very close family, with strong ties to our large circle of extended family members on both sides.

My parents migrated to Chicago from Mississippi, bringing their southern values and customs with them. My mother was the first in her family to earn a college degree, graduating from Tuskegee Institute in 1959 with a Bachelor of Science in chemistry. She went on to work one job as a laboratory technician for 34 years. My father was a machine mechanic at a food processing plant and later a stationary engineer for the United States Postal Service. In the 1970s, my father and a family friend opened a service station (now known as a gas station). Little did I know how significant that was. In later years, most of the businesses were no longer in existence.

Our family started out living in an apartment building. We knew all of the families in the two six-unit buildings that shared one common backyard. We all looked out for each other. When I was 10 years old, we purchased our first home – a three-bedroom, one-bathroom bungalow. Although it was relatively small, we were "moving on up" like the Jeffersons (TV sitcom). I attended Chicago Public Schools for both elementary and high school. In high school, I was a cheerleader, ultimately becoming the captain of our team. I also participated in dance, theater, choir, and a host of other activities. I maintained very high grades and graduated with honors. We didn't have a lot of money, but we were comfortable. I was fortunate to have an opportunity to take piano lessons and to study dance (ballet and tap) at Mayfair Academy of Fine Arts. I attended church every Sunday at Ebenezer Missionary Baptist Church in Chicago, where I was a member of the Sunday school and youth choir. It was at church where I continued to hone my leadership skills -- developing and leading several programs, as well as speaking at various events.

My mother was one of the most intelligent people I have ever met. She believed in education and excellence. She instilled in my sisters and me the desire to continue our education and become self-sufficient, which we all did. Our children are now following the legacy as well.

THE DECISION TO BECOME A LAWYER

When and Why I Decided to Become a Lawyer: I entered college at Hampton Institute (which became Hampton University while I was there) as a biology (pre-medicine) major. I thoroughly enjoyed my college experience. As I was finishing my junior year, I realized I did not want to become a doctor. However, I also did not want to get onto the five-year plan so I continued pursuing my biology degree. After graduation, I returned to Chicago. Within four months, I was hired by the City of Chicago Police Department Crime Laboratory as a criminalist. I started out analyzing clothing, hairs, fibers, etc. from crime scenes. Within six months, due to the war on drugs, I was transferred to the Chemistry Section where I analyzed drugs and testified in drug cases as an expert witness.

While being prepped by attorneys for my expert witness testimony, I often found myself advising attorneys on the best ways for me to offer testimony. It became increasingly clear to me that I had the passion and ability to practice law. I had never even considered the possibility of law prior to that experience. Although I became very interested in becoming a lawyer, I wasn't ready to take on law school at that time. I believed I needed to enhance my writing skills and raise my GPA to become more prepared and competitive. Therefore, I obtained a Master of Public Administration and taught English as a Second Language (ESL) at a City College in Chicago. Upon graduating with my master's degree, I applied and was accepted to several law schools in Chicago. I desired to continue working full-time as a criminalist while attending law school in the evening. This is one of the best decisions I have made thus far.

EDUCATIONAL ACHIEVEMENTS

High School: Percy L. Julian High School (Chicago, Illinois)

College/University: Hampton University (Hampton, Virginia)

Undergraduate Degree: Bachelor of Arts (B.A.)

Major: Biology

College Honors, Achievements and Activities: *Member,* Gospel Choir; *Member,* Biology Club/Ms. Biology; *Member,* Delta Sigma Theta Sorority, Inc.

Law School: DePaul University College of Law (Chicago, Illinois)

Law Degree and Graduation Year: Juris Doctor/Doctor of Jurisprudence (J.D.) - Class of 1996

Law School Honors, Achievements and Activities: *Member,* DePaul University Law Review; *Member,* Order of the Coif; *Awardee,* AmJur in Constitutional Law and Legal Writing II

Other Graduate or Professional Degree: Master of Public Administration (M.P.A.), Roosevelt University (Chicago, Illinois)

PROFESSIONAL ACCOMPLISHMENTS

State Bar Membership (Where Admitted to Practice Law): Illinois

Other Legal Work Experience: *Arbitrator,* Labor and Employment Law (2015-Present); *Senior Lecturer and Assistant Dean, Diversity and Inclusion, Multicultural Affairs and Professional Development; Executive Director of the Institute for Law and the Workplace,* Illinois Institute of Technology, Chicago-Kent College of Law (2012-Present); *Associate Attorney,* Lord, Bissell & Brook (1996-2004)

Other Professional Work Experience: *Contract Trainer - Leadership,* Liberty Mutual Insurance Company (2019-Present); *System Director of Labor Relations,* Cook County Health and Hospitals System (2010-2012); *Director of Workforce Engagement* (Labor and Employee Relations), Health Care Service Corporation (2005-2009); *Adjunct Professor,* Robert Morris University Morris Graduate School (2006-Present); *Deputy Director of Field Operations,* Illinois Department of Employment Security - Operations and Labor Relations (2004-2005); *Criminalist II,* Chicago Police Department Crime Laboratory

Professional Organizations: *Member,* American Bar Association; *Former Member,* The Black Women Lawyers' Association of Greater Chicago; *Former Member,* Cook County Bar Association; *Former Member,* Chicago Committee on Minorities in Large Law Firms

Post-Law School Honors, Achievements, Activities, and Community Involvement:

Member, Society of Human Resource Management; *Member*, Chicago Alumnae Chapter, Delta Sigma Theta Sorority, Inc.; *Featured Panelist and Moderator*, National HBCU Pre-Law Summit and Law Expo; *Featured Panelist and Moderator*, National Black Pre-Law Conference and Law Fair; *Honoree*, Legal Education Access & Diversity Champion Award

LESSONS LEARNED: MY RECOMMENDATIONS FOR YOUR FUTURE ACTIONS BASED ON MY PAST EXPERIENCE

Advice on Law School Preparation:

Preparation should begin as early as possible, in high school or even middle school. It is never too early to start honing your writing, speaking and analytical skills. You should seize any opportunity to run for an office and/or take on leadership roles. These experiences help you to build your confidence, ability to think on your feet, curiosity, and resilience. Opportunities to build these skills don't just emerge at school. Look for opportunities at your place of worship, in your community, or through youth organizations that provide leadership development and/or community service projects.

Upon entering college, choose a major that you are passionate about. I say this for three reasons. It is often difficult to manage social life and school work. Therefore, taking classes in which you are interested will likely result in better academic performance. When applying to law school, grades are important - often more important than choosing traditional law school feeder majors like history, political science or English. As a biology pre-medicine major, I was well-prepared for the rigor of law school. I quickly learned that my analytical and problem-solving skills from science were transferable to law. Second, in the event you decide that law school is not for you, it is good to have something that you enjoy to fall back on. Finally, given the breadth and diversity of legal practice areas, it is likely that you can use your law degree to compliment your undergraduate degree. When this happens, it is often the sweet spot – that place where passion, purpose and opportunity meet.

While in college, seek out opportunities to take on leadership roles, as well as to participate in programs that expose you to advocacy, networking, and professional development. You might consider working on political campaigns, volunteering at a public service organization, drafting articles or blogs on topics of interest, or advocating for changes to a policy or process that disadvantages certain groups or otherwise fails to further a particular interest. Additionally, take advantage of any opportunity to gain work experience, paid or unpaid.

Advice on Applying to and Selecting a Law School:

Take time to research law schools and maintain an open mind during your search. Students often look for schools with high name recognition or schools that are highly ranked. While there is nothing wrong with pursuing admission to such schools, don't overlook schools that might offer programs, classes, or a culture that is more aligned with your interests, finances and/or goals. Although many of the first-year classes are the same across most law schools in this country, there are often unique offerings beyond the core doctrinal courses. Some schools offer clinical education in different practice areas; have a greater pool of internship, externship and judicial clerkship opportunities; and/or provide more classes in distinct areas of the law. For example, if you are interested in litigation, consider schools with highly-ranked trial teams and other experiential learning classes and/or programs that focus on building litigation skills, strategies and opportunities to practice. If you are interested in a particular area of law, look for schools that offer a wide array of courses in that area, or maybe even a certificate. If diversity is important, learn about the school's diversity priorities, as well as the demographics of the faculty, staff and student body. Inquire about the school's involvement in social justice projects/programs, pipeline programs, and diversity and inclusion training. You can learn a lot about an institution by looking at where it invests its resources (time, staff and money).

Choosing a school in a desirable location is often important. A significant number of law students remain in the geographic area where they attend law school. This allows them to more easily continue enhancing relationships and building upon opportunities initiated during law school. Additionally, it is highly likely that many alumni from the school will work in the area and may have input into hiring decisions. These individuals will also be familiar with the school, as well as the quality of the professors and the learning experience, making them more open to hiring students from the school. Accordingly, I highly recommend selecting a school in a location with access to opportunities, and in which you would be willing to live for at least a few years after graduation.

Advice Regarding Academic Success, Co-Curricular and Extra-Curricular Participation, and Social Engagement in Law School:

There is no doubt about it, law school is difficult for most people, regardless of race, gender, ethnicity, sexual orientation, disability, etc. However, it can be even more difficult for those who are not prepared for, or committed to reading, analyzing and interpreting complex concepts. Therefore, in order to be successful, students must be organized, focused and willing to read the same material multiple times without throwing in the towel. Know that you are not out of your league because you have to read the same material multiple times. In fact, if you are not reading the same material multiple times, you are probably not adequately preparing for class and ultimately for finals. Further, you must attend class for yourself. Relying on notes from others who might learn differently than you is often not the best way to enhance your understanding of the material. It is important for you to find the listening, notetaking and content/concept organizing methods that work best for you. I listened very closely to the professor's way of analyzing issues and then organized my notes in the exact same manner. This helped me to create a course/professor-specific framework for my approach to analyzing issues presented.

Once you have a handle on how to manage your workload, I encourage you to get involved in extra-curricular activities. At most law schools, there are a number of student organizations that do great work. The members are often available to serve as mentors and tutors to help you navigate your coursework. Some organizations also provide opportunities for students from similar backgrounds to network, sponsor events aligned with their shared interests and to provide peer support. Depending on your interests and ability to manage your coursework, consider joining a law journal, moot court, trial team or other schoolwide programs.

Advice on Preparing for and Taking the Bar Exam:

Take a bar prep class and practice, practice, practice! Make sure to complete ALL of the class assignments, as the curriculum has been designed to provide you with the information needed to pass the bar. In preparation for the essay portion of the exam, consider writing out alternative ways of analyzing issues. Identify potential legal issues that could arise in the specific area of law. What is the legal standard or test that would be applicable for analyzing the issue? What specific parts of the standard or test does the issue implicate? What are typical defenses that might be asserted? What facts and arguments would cause the defense to be successful? To be unsuccessful? Are there any important public policy considerations? You have just completed a framework for analyzing one possible scenario. Now, choose another common issue and repeat. Please note, this is not a framework that I got from anyone or another source. Rather, it is the process I used to train my brain muscle to spot, interpret and analyze issues more quickly. Yes, neuroscience research confirms that we can train our brains how to process information in new and consistent ways. It worked; I passed on the first try!

Advice on Choosing a Job and Career Path Inside or Outside of the Legal Profession:

Reflection is the key to choosing your career path. Hopefully you will have the opportunity to participate in internships, externships, clerkships or jobs that allow you to work on different types of legal matters, in different sectors (i.e., law firm, government, corporate, court, etc.), in different industries (i.e., retail, technology, entertainment, finance, etc.), and performing different tasks (i.e., drafting discovery requests, writing memos or briefs, conducting research, interviewing witnesses, etc.). To the extent you can diversify your exposure and experience, you will accumulate data which can help you to identify your strengths, opportunities for improvement, likes and dislikes. You can also compare and contrast different work environments, styles of communication, levels of collaboration, political agendas, etc. Then, look inward and prioritize what you want. What type of work environment makes you feel as though you belong? What areas of the law interest you most? Which legal tasks/projects are you good at and/or do you enjoy? Once you have a good grasp of what you want, set up informational interviews with practitioners who are doing work you desire to do. Ask them about their career paths and if they can provide career advice. This information should assist you with choosing your career path.

Some law students and attorneys decide to use their legal knowledge and skills to pursue J.D. preferred or non-legal jobs. There is nothing wrong with this course of action. Many journalists, news anchors, human resource leaders, compliance officers, accountants, executives and other professionals have law degrees. It is no secret that the skills learned in law school are transferable to a variety of professions. Be open. Find your sweet spot.

Advice on Seeking Legal Job Opportunities and/or Creating One's Own Opportunities:

In addition to my comments above, I would add that if you are unable to find your dream job, consider jobs that help you to continue building your legal knowledge and skills. As long as you are continuing to learn and grow, you are making progress toward your goals. Focus on what you can learn from a job and not the job itself. Meanwhile, continue efforts to find the job/career you truly desire. To the extent that you are permitted, choose to work on projects, committees, company programs, etc. that will help you to build the type of resume you desire. In other words, work in reverse. First ask yourself, "What do I want my resume to reveal about me, including my knowledge, skills and abilities?" Then, find the experiences you need to create the desired narrative. Write your own story!

I am an advocate for creating your own opportunity if you have an entrepreneurial spirit or are unable to find another opportunity. Again, this is an opportunity to learn and grow. Schedule time to talk to other solo practitioners and pick their brains and/or seek advice. Many localities provide training and resources for small business owners; take advantage. Also, consider partnering with one or more classmates who you believe would be committed and great to work with. Always remember, you are not the first person to venture out on your own. There are many who have gone before you and are willing to mentor you through the process.

Advice on Achieving Career Success and Advancement:

Career success and advancement strategies vary depending on the job and the person. Learn the politics at your organization. Who makes things happen? How can you build relationships with those who are the influencers at your organization? How can you market yourself without appearing arrogant or selfish? These are some of the questions you must answer in order to create your pathway to advancement and success. In addition, you must produce excellent work - work that others can rely on when needed. Once people learn that you are a reliable source for trustworthy results, you will likely become a go-to person. If possible, you might consider becoming a subject matter expert in a discrete area of the law that would bring value to the organization and/or its clients. Finally, if there is an opportunity to work on projects that are important to the organization, or that would make you visible to influential leaders, seize the opportunity.

Advice on Overcoming the Additional Challenges Black Law Students and Lawyers Face:

Know your value, know your job, and know yourself. I direct you back to my advice on reflection. Don't let race-related challenges blindside you and throw you off your game. Instead, anticipate that such challenges will come and ensure that you have a strategy for responding. In order to develop your strategy, talk to other Black law students and lawyers to understand challenges they have faced. Read articles about challenges faced by minority law students and attorneys. Think about how you would like to respond if faced with similar challenges. This type of planning helps you to be less emotional and more strategic in the moment. Our brains are creatures of habit, looking for patterns in order to guide our behavior in certain situations. The good news is that we can control what we feed our brains. We do this by being more intentional about how we respond in certain situations. If, however, you determine that you are in fact being unfairly judged or denied opportunities because of your race, I suggest you first assess the pros and cons of potential responses. Then, respond in the manner you believe is best for you and your future. Try your best to avoid emotional responses in the moment. Finally, you do not have to navigate these challenges alone. There are many who have gone before you and would love to help you navigate these challenges. Don't be afraid to reach out.

Best Advice I Received Regarding Law School and the Legal Profession:

The best advice I received about law school was from myself. My famous words are, "Just start." I wasn't sure if I was ready to fully commit to law school after being out of college and working for five years. However, I told myself, "Just start studying for the LSAT." Then I said, "Just take the test to see what it is like." Finally, I stated, "If you get accepted, go; If not, try again later." I followed my advice, got accepted to several schools and started law school immediately thereafter.

The best advice I received about the legal profession was from my law school career counselor. I graduated from law school in the top 10% of my class and had no idea what I wanted to do. I wasn't pressed because I had a full-time job as a criminalist. However, when I met with my career advisor, he told me that given my academic accomplishments, I should attempt to work at a large law firm. He stated that even if I worked at the firm for 18 months to two years, I would have a great resume booster. Further, he stated that the large law firm work would set me up to be highly competitive for other opportunities. I followed his advice and started my legal career at a large law firm, where I worked for almost eight years. That experience definitely taught me a lot and opened many doors for me professionally and personally. Although I ultimately faced challenges when advancement discussions began, I do not regret my decision to start my legal career at a large firm.

Worst Advice I Received Regarding Law School and the Legal Profession:

The worst advice I received in law school was that evening students should focus on balancing work and school and avoid extra-curricular activities. In hindsight, I should have participated in student organizations and maybe even pursued the trial team. I had a pretty flexible job and could have found a way to be more active. Being more involved would have allowed me to build more relationships with my classmates. Because I was an evening student who did not get involved in anything other than law review, I have very few friends from law school. Accordingly, my legal network is not as far-reaching as it could be.

Best Advice I Would Give to an Aspiring Black Lawyer:

Be intentional; don't leave anything to chance. Decide how you want to show up and be intentional about developing the confidence and competence to make it happen. First impressions are generally lasting impressions – good or bad.

Thoughts About Why Earning a Law Degree Is a Powerful Credential for African Americans and Why There Is a Need for More African American Lawyers:

The Black community experiences unique issues and challenges that those outside the community will likely never be able to fully comprehend. As much as they may desire to be advocates for Black clients, lack of perspective often minimizes effectiveness. For example, if an attorney has a hard time believing that racism still exists, it might be difficult for him or her to making a convincing discrimination argument. Further, if a client in a criminal case admits that he ran from the police not because he was guilty, but because he was afraid the police would kill him, counsel who perceives the police as friends or protectors might doubt the veracity of his/her client's story. To be clear, I am not saying that only Blacks can effectively represent Blacks in all legal matters. Rather, I am saying that everyone deserves to be represented by an attorney who fully understands, appreciates and believes in them. Sometimes, this requires a person who has directly or indirectly had had similar experiences. Therefore, we need more Black lawyers to ensure that Black people are treated equitably and that their rights are protected.

Thoughts About Whether and Why Law School Is Worth the Financial Investment:

Anything you can do to make yourself more competitive in the job market is a benefit. A law degree says that you have survived a very rigorous course of study, and that you have mastered some of the most sought-after professional skills. Even if you decide not to practice law, your law degree will open the door to unlimited opportunities. Finally, the progress of the Black community is dependent upon those who advocate for changes to inequitable laws, policies and practices. You cannot put a price tag on human survival - survival meaning both total health and wealth. Black Lawyers = Black Lives Matter. I believe that when you invest in yourself in order to invest in others, you will be rewarded.

LEGACY AND SUCCESS

My Most Outstanding Accomplishment:

Graduating in the top of my law school class and becoming a labor and employment law arbitrator, a profession that has very few people of color.

The Legacy I Hope to Leave:

I want to be known as a person who passionately worked to increase diversity in the legal profession, and was successful. I also want to be known for transforming the lives of people from underrepresented communities who might not otherwise have even considered pursuing a legal education. Finally, I want to be remembered as one who opened the door for those who might not otherwise have been admitted to law school, not because they weren't capable, but because the barriers to entry often disproportionately impact students of color.

The Secret to My Success:

Strong faith in God, humility, excellence, and pride in my work.

Theodore M. Shaw, Esq.

Julius L. Chambers Distinguished Professor of Law
Director
The UNC Center for Civil Rights
University of North Carolina School of Law
Chapel Hill, North Carolina

"Hope is a choice. We choose hope even in the face of every reason to despair, and then work to make that hope reality."

"We have to fight. When we fight, we may lose and we may win. But if we don't fight, we cannot win."

– Ted Shaw

Success is . . . doing the best you can.

PERSONAL FAVORITES

Favorite Quote: "The moral arc of the universe is long, but it bends toward justice." - Dr. Martin Luther King, Jr.

Favorite Books: *Simple Justice* by Richard Kluger; *Invisible Man* by Ralph Ellison; *The Once and Future King* by T.H. White; *Race and Reunion* by David Blight; *Frederick Douglass* by David Blight; *The Fire Next Time* by James Baldwin; *Arguing Against Slavery* by William Lee Miller; *A Man for All Seasons* by Robert Bolt

Favorite Movies: *Do the Right Thing*; *Casablanca*; *Lawrence of Arabia*; *Dr. Zhivago*; *Imitation of Life*; *A Man for All Seasons*; *In the Heat of the Night*; *The Bridge on the River Kwai*

Favorite Songs: The songs on the album *Songs in the Key of Life* by Stevie Wonder (especially "As"); "Oh Freedom" by Harry Belafonte; "My Lord, What a Mornin'" by Harry Belafonte; "All My Trials" by Harry Belafonte; "Day O" by Harry Belafonte; "People Get Ready" by Curtis Mayfield and the Impressions; "Redemption Song" by Bob Marley; "Mercy, Mercy, Mercy" by Cannonball Adderly; "All Blues" by Miles Davis; "It Never Entered My Mind" by Miles Davis; "My Favorite Things" by John Coltrane; "Yes I'm Ready (If I Don't Get to Go)" by The Chi-Lites; "Ella's Song" by Sweet Honey In The Rock; "A Change Is Gonna Come" by Sam Cooke; "Viva La Vida" by Coldplay; "I've Been Buked" by Don Shirley; "For All We Know" by Donny Hathaway; "A Song for You" by Donny Hathaway; "Let's Do It" by Ella Fitzgerald and Louis Armstrong; "Come Thy Fount of Every Blessing" by The Mormon Tabernacle Choir; Any songs performed by Roberta Flack

Favorite Law School Classes: Trusts and Estates; Race and the Law

Favorite Legal Case: *Brown v. Board of Education*

Favorite Hobbies: Visiting used bookstores; Reading; Listening to R&B and jazz; Watching movies

Favorite Attorney Role Models: Real people - Charles Hamilton Houston; Thurgood Marshall; Historical figure - John Quincy Adams (for his role in fighting against the nineteenth-century congressional ban on debating slavery, and for his representation of enslaved Africans who rebelled against the crew of La Amistad); Television/movie characters - Atticus Finch and Perry Mason

FAMILY AND BACKGROUND

Where Born and Raised: New York, New York

Family (Spouse/Partner and Children): Spouse - Halona; Children - Amali and Isaiah; Winston and Zora

Family Socioeconomic and Educational Background:

I grew up first in Harlem, then in a public housing project in the Bronx. My mother died when I was just shy of three, and my grandmothers cared for my two sisters and me until my father remarried. They divorced a few years after having two children together. My stepmother did the best she could to raise five children, three of whom were not hers by birth. We attended an otherwise all-white parochial school in another neighborhood. We were poor but we got a good education. Many of my childhood friends from the projects did not. Eventually, my neighborhood succumbed to drugs and violence. College was not a forgone conclusion. The civil rights/black consciousness movements opened doors and opportunities; a leadership project for young black men, created in the aftermath of Dr. Martin Luther King's assassination, made the difference in my life.

THE DECISION TO BECOME A LAWYER

When and Why I Decided to Become a Lawyer:

I am certain that by the time I was in high school I wanted to become a lawyer, although I had no roadmap for how to get there. I may have decided I wanted to become a lawyer in grade school, inspired by a combination of Thurgood Marshall, Atticus Finch, and Perry Mason. In fact, I am sure I did.

Sometime in grade school, I came to the conclusion that the most important thing that was happening in my lifetime was the Civil Rights Movement, and I wanted to be part of that fight. I thought becoming a lawyer was the best way to do it.

So by high school, I was decided. But I think I came to it in grade school. My paternal grandmother was a domestic worker. Like many black women, she cleaned white people's homes on her hands and knees, washed their clothes, and cared for their children. She was poor, and everything she did was for her son and her grandchildren. She stood 4'9", was bow-legged, and was blind in one eye from splashing bleach while cleaning someone's house. She told me to get my education; it was the one thing they could not take from me.

One summer morning, she did not go to work. She took a city bus to the subway early that morning, went to a church near Penn Station, and boarded a bus to Washington, D.C. for the March on Washington. She wanted to take me with her, but there had been threats and rumors of violence and I was not allowed to go. I so wish I was with my Grandma Hattie that day. I have always been so proud of her.

Years later she gave me a package of papers from the March - mimeographed sheet music, the program for the day, the official handbill from the March, and one of the iconographic buttons. I treasure those gifts. Over the years, whenever I have seen photographs and newsreel footage from the March, I have always looked for my Grandma Hattie. Of course, I have never found her. There were 250,000 people there on that day, and she was only 4'9". But I have always been so proud of my grandmother. If she could march that day for the cause of civil rights, I could become a civil rights lawyer. And so I did.

EDUCATIONAL ACHIEVEMENTS

High School: Cardinal Spellman High School (Bronx, New York)

College/University: Wesleyan University (Middletown, Connecticut)

Undergraduate Degree: Bachelor of Arts (B.A.)

Major: Interdisciplinary Program of Government, Economics and History

College Honors, Achievements and Activities: Graduated with Honors; *Letterman/Team Member,* Wesleyan University Basketball (four years); *Team Member,* Wesleyan University Crew (two years)

Law School: Columbia University School of Law (New York, New York)

Law Degree and Graduation Year: Juris Doctor/Doctor of Jurisprudence (J.D.) - Class of 1979

Law School Honors, Achievements and Activities: Charles Evans Hughes Fellow; *National Board Member and Northeast Regional Director,* Black American Law Students Association (BALSA)

PROFESSIONAL ACCOMPLISHMENTS

State Bar Memberships (Where Admitted to Practice Law): New York; California

Other Legal Work Experience: *Of Counsel,* Fulbright & Jaworski, LLP/Norton Rose Fulbright; *Professor of Professional Practice,* Columbia Law School; *Full-Time Faculty Member,* University of Michigan Law School; *Director-Counsel and President,* NAACP Legal Defense Fund (fifth lawyer to serve in this role); *Trial Attorney,* Civil Rights Division, U.S. Department of Justice

Professional Organizations: *Member,* American Bar Association; *Member,* National Bar Association; *Member,* National Association for the Advancement of Colored People (NAACP); *Member,* Sigma Pi Phi Fraternity

Post-Law School Honors, Achievements, Activities, and Community Involvement: *Awardee,* Harlem Neighborhood Defenders Office W. Haywood Burns Humanitarian Award; *Awardee,* Office of the Appellate Defender Milton S. Gould Award for Outstanding Advocacy; *Awardee,* A. Leon Higginbotham, Jr. Memorial Award, National Bar Association Young Lawyers Division; *Honoree,* Lawrence A. Wein Prize for Social Justice, Columbia University; *Honoree,* Baldwin Medal, Wesleyan University Alumni Association; *Obama Transition Team Leader,* Civil Rights Division, U.S. Department of Justice; *Participant,* International Human Rights Law Group, Affirmative Action Affinity Group Conference, Rio de Janeiro, Brasilia, Sao Paulo (July 2003); *Participant,* International Human Rights Law Group,

Affirmative Action Affinity Group Conference, Montevideo, Uruguay (May 2003); *Participant,* Inaugural meeting of African Descendants and Afro-Brazilian Lawyers with African American, South African, Angolan, Cape Verdean, and Jamaican Lawyers, Rio de Janeiro, Brazil (December 2002); *Participant,* European Roma Rights Council Conference, Budapest, Hungary (May, 2002); *Participant,* United Nations World Conference on Racism, Racial Discrimination, Xenophobia, and Related Intolerance, Durban, South Africa (2001); *Speaker,* Roma Political Leadership Training Program, Blagoevgrad, Bulgaria (July 2000); *Speaker,* Conference on debates over group litigation in comparative perspectives, Geneva, Switzerland (July 2000); *Speaker,* Conference on the Rise of Racism in Europe, in Budapest, Hungary (July 2000); *Speaker,* National Employment Law Association delegation to joint symposium on employment discrimination in Tokyo and Osaka (February 1998); *Delegation Leader,* NAACP Legal Defense and Educational Fund delegations to conduct seminars on constitutional litigation in post-apartheid South Africa (in cooperation with the Black Lawyers Association of South Africa) (1994, 1995, 1999); *Consultant,* Senate judiciary committee of Spanish Parliament and select group of Spanish judges on consideration of adoption of juries in civil cases, Madrid, Spain (1994); *Participant,* Conference on Affirmative Action in Post-Apartheid South Africa, East London, South Africa (June 1993); *Salzburg Seminar Fellow,* Salzburg, Austria (Summer 1991); *21st Century Trust Fellow,* Seminar on Global Interdependence, Windsor Great Park, United Kingdom (July 1989); *Aspen Institute Fellow,* Seminar on Justice and Society, Aspen, Colorado (Summer 1987)

LESSONS LEARNED: RECOMMENDATIONS FOR YOUR FUTURE ACTIONS BASED ON MY PAST EXPERIENCE

Advice on Law School Preparation:

Even if you know that you want to attend law school, you don't need to take a "pre-law" curriculum. Take a major that is academically challenging - one which gives you an opportunity to demonstrate your intellectual capability. You want your major to provide strong writing experience, and your reasoning, problem-solving, and higher-order thinking ability.

Advice on Applying to and Selecting a Law School:

Apply to a range of law schools if you can. You know the strategy: choose a couple to which you think you have a good chance to be admitted. If you have a good Grade Point Average (GPA) and you do well on standardized tests, do not shy away from the best. Among the law schools to which you are admitted, all other things being equal, go to one you think has the best reputation. Law school is very expensive, so if you do not have a trust fund or parents paying your way, finances may be a big consideration. In spite of my advice, there are many good choices for law school; you do not have to go to a top ten institution to do well in a legal career.

Advice Regarding Academic Success, Co-Curricular and Extra-Curricular Participation, and Social Engagement in Law School:

I advise you to take a broad array of law school courses. You will learn your specialty by practice. Most law students do not start law school knowing exactly what they want to do. Even if you do know the area of law in which you think you want to practice, take a "liberal arts" legal education. I knew that I wanted to be a civil rights lawyer, yet I took federal income tax, trusts and estates, corporations, family law, evidence, and other courses that exposed me to legal education that served me well as a civil rights lawyer.

Advice on Preparing for and Taking the Bar Exam:

Go down to the courthouse and observe some trials. You might see a few obviously brilliant lawyers; you might not. You will see some lawyers who are pretty good, and you will surely see some who are mediocre. You will probably see some who will lead you to think, "If he or she passed the bar exam, I KNOW I can." The point is, the bar exam is a big cram. It does not tell you much, if anything, about how good a lawyer you will be. Respect the fact that you have to take it seriously, but do not be intimidated by it. You only have to pass it once. You will probably do it on the first try, but even if you don't, you will get it into your rearview mirror. Don't let performance anxiety derail you and you will do fine.

Advice on Choosing a Job and Career Path Inside or Outside of the Legal Profession:

Many people with law degrees do not practice law. Some practice for a while before being lured into other opportunities. Their law degrees are not wasted. On the other hand, unless you have money to burn, don't feel that you HAVE to go to law school. There are plenty of other things to do that have value and are rewarding. If you are going to go to law school, think about why you want to do it. Some people used to go to law school because they saw it as a finishing school of sorts. Maybe that was okay for some people before law school and college meant six-figure debt, but most people may want to think hard about that these days.

Advice on Seeking Legal Job Opportunities and/or Creating One's Own Opportunities:

When you seek legal (or any) jobs, remember, the interviewing process is a two-way street. You are checking the employer out as much as the employer is checking you out. You do not want any or every job. Having said that, make sure you present well. Use proper grammar. You know the old saying: You only get one chance to make a first impression. You may also keep in mind that law is a profession in which you can make your own way. It is not easy, but you do not have to work for someone else - at least not forever.

Advice on Achieving Career Success and Advancement:

If you are good at what you do, you cannot begin to imagine all the opportunities that will come to you. The most important thing is this: Jealously guard your reputation. Cultivate excellence. And always listen to that "little voice" when it talks to you. Call it conscience, your antenna, or whatever you want, but listen for it, and to it. It will not fail you, and if you do not develop and follow it, you will fail yourself. Know your strengths and your weaknesses. We all have them. Compliment your weaknesses by working with others who have strengths in the areas you do not.

Advice on Overcoming the Additional Challenges Black Law Students and Lawyers Face:

I wish I could say that there are no special challenges that Black lawyers face. I can't say that. I can say that it is important for all young lawyers to find good mentors. Be open to who they may be. If and when you come across someone who does not have your best interest at heart, go around them if you can. For every impediment, there is another way. But preserve your emotional and mental health. Protect it from those who would undermine it. Find people who will guide and mentor you.

Best Advice I Received Regarding Law School and the Legal Profession:

Do not, for one moment, doubt your right to be where you are. You have not gotten where you are so far by accident or happenstance. Don't be arrogant or condescending. Confidence is important, but so is a touch of humility.

Worst Advice I Received Regarding Law School and the Legal Profession:

Once, when I began to teach full-time after practicing for approximately a dozen years, a law professor (younger than I was), told me to never let students know that I did not know the answer to a question. I thought it was terrible advice. I thought about the times during my tenure at the Legal Defense Fund when a procedural question arose, for which I did not know the answer. Some of my favorite moments were the times, as rare as they may have been, when I walked down the hall to a colleague and raised the question, only to have my fellow lawyer say, "I don't know, let's ask so-and-so." If they knew the answer, asking is a way of learning, as much as is book research. But those rare moments when it became clear that the question seemed to be one of first impressions were the moments I live for in the practice of law. My point is one about not letting insecurity get in the way of learning from colleagues, but it is also one about how wonderfully intellectually challenging the practice of law can be.

Best Advice I Would Give to an Aspiring Black Lawyer:

When I was a law student, I heard it said that "The law is a jealous mistress." That saying is now outdated because of its sexist connotations. I beg pardon for using it. But here is the point: law is a demanding profession. It can exact a heavy toll on those who engage in its practice. It can be hard on relationships with spouses, loved ones, family members, children, and on one's self. Strive to find balance. It is not easy, but it is important.

Thoughts About Why Earning a Law Degree Is a Powerful Credential for African Americans and Why There Is a Need for More African American Lawyers:

Statistics tell us that only five percent of lawyers in the United States are Black. That is a stunning and deeply troubling statistic. Still, it underscores how important the credential of a law degree is, and how Black lawyers are needed. We need Black lawyers to be seen and heard in every corner of the profession. We need Black judges. We need Black lawyers to serve in communities that are underserved. We need people of all races and backgrounds to see Black lawyers doing all the things lawyers do. Law is a pathway to public service, to corporate, political, and civic leadership.

Thoughts About Whether and Why Law School Is Worth the Financial Investment:

I believe law school is worth the financial investment, but I know how much more expensive law school is with every passing year. I know that lawyers will disproportionately continue to be leaders in every sector of American life. I also know that many, if not most lawyers, make more money than the average person in the United States. Some do extremely well financially. Some even find that it is possible to do well and to do good. In the scheme of things, law is a profession that pays well.

LEGACY AND SUCCESS

My Most Outstanding Accomplishments:

Professional: It is hard to pick out one thing as the most outstanding accomplishment. Still, there is one thing that I think about that holds a life lesson. As a rising 3L law student, I was in the Supreme Court when the *Bakke* opinions were announced. I was deeply disappointed by the Court's betrayal, once again, of the Fourteenth Amendment's original purpose to protect the interests of African Americans. Yet, for forty years, a good part of my life was spent trying to preserve Justice Powell's diversity rationale, even though I considered it to be a second-best justification for conscious efforts to provide opportunities in higher education for black and brown students. Although I have been involved, in various ways, in cases that litigated affirmative action/diversity issues, the *Bakke* case marginalized or even eliminated the role of African American students and their lawyers in these cases.

Still, when I was teaching at Michigan Law School, I pressed the dean who had hired me, Lee C. Bollinger, to revisit the school's admissions policies and practices to bring them into alignment with the *Bakke* case, which was, at that time, the only existing governing law on race-conscious efforts to guarantee opportunities for black and brown students at selective institutions of higher education. I did so because I knew that right-wing lawyers and organizations were seeking cases with which to overturn *Bakke* and to have the Supreme Court declare affirmative action/diversity efforts to be unconstitutional. As a consequence of our conversations, he appointed a committee to rewrite admissions practices at Michigan Law. I served on that committee. But for those efforts, Michigan Law School would not have been in a position to win the *Grutter* case in 2003; its admissions practices before I arrived at the Law School were not *Bakke*-compliant. (I am aware of how self-aggrandizing this might appear to be, but it is the truth.)

I longed to litigate the rights of black and brown people in the most important cases in the Supreme Court and to win their victories. The *Bakke* case turned the affirmative action/diversity issues into contests between white applicants and white-controlled institutions. Black and brown people were turned into observers in these cases, even though they had the most at stake. I was involved in these cases and even argued in the Michigan undergraduate case in the Court of Appeals. But the Supreme Court refused to hear us. In the Law School case, I could not act as a lawyer because I had served on the Law School committee that designed the admissions plan and was a witness who was deposed. Back at the NAACP Legal Defense Fund (LDF), when the two Michigan cases were litigated, I was lead counsel for black and brown students in *Gratz v. Bollinger,* the undergraduate case. When *Grutter* reached the Supreme Court, LDF filed an amicus brief, of which I have remained proud.

Sometimes our roles in important matters are defined not by our plans, but by serendipity. I did not argue *Grutter* in the Supreme Court. But, casting modesty to the wind, without my efforts as a faculty member, the Michigan Law School admissions plan upheld by the Supreme Court, would almost certainly not have come into existence. (To be clear, many people, starting with Lee Bollinger, played vitally important roles in preserving educational opportunities for more than a generation of black and brown people, but I am proud of the role I played.)

Personal: I am most proud of my children. Each of them is extraordinary. They are not my accomplishments; they are my blessings, and in fact, they have accomplished the good things they have done in spite of, and not because of me.

The Legacy I Hope to Leave:

I think that the question of legacy is for others to decide. I won't be here to worry about it. As a general matter, I want to leave the world better than I found it. If I can do that, even to a small degree, that is as good a legacy as one can want.

* When Thurgood Marshall announced his retirement from the U.S. Supreme Court, a reporter at his press conference asked how he wanted to be remembered. By that time in his life, Justice Marshall was famously irascible and cranky. I thought his response was disappointing. He didn't talk about how *Brown v. Board of Education* broke the back of Jim Crow segregation, or any of the other landmark cases he had litigated, argued and won. Nor did he talk about being the first African American Justice (he would have said "Afro-American") to serve on the U.S. Supreme Court. Instead, his response was that he wanted it to be said, "I did the best I could with what I had." As disappointed as I was, as time passed, I came to understand that he could not have had a better response to the question of how he wanted to be remembered. It is all any of us could ask of ourselves. I don't know that anything I say will fit that bill, but I have come to believe that we do not hope because there is good reason to do so. Hope is a choice. We choose hope even in the face of every reason to despair, and then work to make that hope reality. AND we have to fight. When we fight, we may lose and we may win. But if we don't fight, we cannot win.

The Secret to My Success:

Any success I have had is the consequence of effort, hard work, the support and shared endeavors of colleagues, the patience and sacrifice of loved ones, and the grace of God.

Practical Wisdom for Those on the Path to Lawyerhood

Reginald T. Shuford, Esq.
Executive Director
American Civil Liberties Union (ACLU) of Pennsylvania
Philadelphia, Pennsylvania

"I consider it my responsibility and honor to be an advocate for the marginalized and a voice for those whose voices are ignored. I have been that person, and I know how it feels. I am determined to fight injustice until I can fight it no more."

*"We're humans, so we will all suffer self-doubt. The important thing is to battle through that self-doubt, get out of your own way; remember that you have earned the right to be where you are, at your job, in **that** room, at **that** table."*

– Reggie Shuford

Success is . . . being in a position to use one's resources, power, privilege, platform, status, social location or access to benefit others.

PERSONAL FAVORITES

Favorite Quote: "The arc of the moral universe is long, but it bends towards justice." - Dr. Martin Luther King, Jr.

Favorite Books: *The Warmth of Other Suns: The Epic Story of America's Great Migration* by Isabel Wilkerson; *The Bluest Eye* by Toni Morrison; *Sula* by Toni Morrison; *Another Country* by James Baldwin; *Go Tell It on the Mountain* by James Baldwin; *I Know Why The Caged Bird Sings* by Maya Angelou; *The New Jim Crow: Mass Incarceration in the Age of Colorblindness* by Michelle Alexander; *Where the Crawdads Sing* by Delia Owens; *The Color Purple* by Alice Walker; *Let the Dead Bury Their Dead* by Randall Kenan; Anything by Wally Lamb or Randall Kenan

Favorite Movies: *Moonlight*; *Imitation of Life*; *Black Panther*; *Call Me By Your Name*; *The Color Purple*; *Boyz n the Hood*; *Queen & Slim*; *13th*; *Fruitvale Station*; *School Daze*; *Do the Right Thing*; *Get Out*; *Precious*; *Pariah*; *Chinatown*; *Sparkle*; *Slumdog Millionaire*; *Brokeback Mountain*; *Bull Durham*; *No Way Out*; *Thelma and Louise*; *The Lion King*; *Titanic*; *American Beauty*; *Forrest Gump*; *The Godfather*; *Hidden Figures*; *Creed*; *12 Years a Slave*; *BlacKkKlansman*; *Waiting to Exhale*

Favorite Songs: "The Greatest Love of All" by Whitney Houston; "So Amazing" by Luther Vandross; "You Give Good Love" by Whitney Houston; "Human Nature" by Michael Jackson; "Alright" by Janet Jackson; "No More Tears" by Anita Baker; "Just Because" by Anita Baker; "The Best Things in Life Are Free" by Janet Jackson and Luther Vandross; "Quiet Time to Play" by Johnny Gill; "I'm So Proud" by Curtis Mayfield; "I Have Learned to Respect the Power of Love" by Stephanie Mills; "September," by Earth, Wind & Fire; "Just Fine" by Mary J. Blige; "This is America" by Childish Gambino

Favorite Musical Artists: Whitney Houston; Luther Vandross; Janet Jackson; Prince; Aretha Franklin; Michael Jackson; Anita Baker; Stevie Wonder; Fantasia; Heather Headley

Favorite Law School Classes: Race and Poverty; Employment Discrimination; Constitutional Law; Legal Research & Writing; Property; Trust & Estates; Contracts

Favorite Legal Cases: Brown v. Board of Education; Loving v. Virginia; Gideon v. Wainwright; Grutter v. Bollinger; Furman v. Georgia; U.S. v. Windsor; Roe v. Wade; Obergefell v. Hodges; Whitewood v. Wolf; Applewhite v. Corbett; Lawrence v. Texas; Romer v. Evans; Plyler v. Doe; Tinker v. Des Moines Independent Community School District; Abington v. Schempp

Favorite Hobbies: Running; Reading; Exercising; Writing; Traveling; Going to the beach; Taking long walks; Binge-watching TV

Favorite Attorney Role Models: Thurgood Marshall; Nelson Mandela; Bryan Stevenson; Barack Obama; Michelle Obama; Henry E. Frye; Hillary Clinton; Stacey Abrams; Sonia Sotomayor; Ruth Bader Ginsburg

FAMILY AND BACKGROUND

Where Born and Raised: Wilmington, North Carolina

Family Socioeconomic and Educational Background: My parents were Barbara Ann Shuford and Alfred James Berry. They never married, and my mother raised us as a single parent on welfare and food stamps, supplemented by work as a housekeeper. I was the third of five children, and attended public school until my junior year in high school, when I was awarded an academic scholarship to Cape Fear Academy, a local private school, where I graduated in 1984. I was the first African-American graduate of Cape Fear Academy and the first person in my family in a few generations to graduate from high school.

THE DECISION TO BECOME A LAWYER

When and Why I Decided to Become a Lawyer: I decided I would become a lawyer at age six. I was an inquisitive child. Whenever we received visitors at home, I would ask them lots of questions about themselves – their likes and dislikes, hobbies, favorite color, books, relationships with relatives, and so on. More than one person suggested that I sounded like a lawyer. It dawned on me that, if one could ask questions for a living, then I would do that. Of course, asking questions is just one part of being a lawyer! I also grew up in a very poor, racially segregated environment. Although I did not know it at the time, Wilmington, North Carolina, had been home to a race coup by White vigilantes in 1898. That legacy persisted, even if it was unspoken. It also impacted one's opportunities, or lack thereof. Given the social, economic and racial disparities I observed and experienced growing up, I decided I would commit my legal career to one of social justice, with Thurgood Marshall as my primary inspiration.

EDUCATIONAL ACHIEVEMENTS

High School: Cape Fear Academy (Wilmington, North Carolina)

College/University: University of North Carolina at Chapel Hill (Chapel Hill, North Carolina)

Undergraduate Degree: Bachelor of Arts (B.A.)

Major: Political Science

College Honors, Achievements and Activities: Johnson Scholar; Minority Advisor; Dormitory Representative; *Academic Recognition,* Dean's List; *Awardee,* Academic Achievement Awards; Campus Y; *Tutor,* Spanish Language

Law School: University of North Carolina School of Law (Chapel Hill, North Carolina)

Law Degree and Graduation Year: Juris Doctor/Doctor of Jurisprudence (J.D.) - Class of 1991

Law School Honors, Achievements and Activities: *Member,* International Law Journal; *3L Class President,* Student Bar Association; *2L Class Representative,* Student Bar Association; *Member,* Black Law Students Association; *Member,* Phi Alpha Delta Law Fraternity, International; *Teacher's Assistant,* Professor Robert Belton; *Independent Study,* Dean Judith Wegner

PROFESSIONAL ACCOMPLISHMENTS

State Bar Membership (Where Admitted to Practice Law): North Carolina

Other Legal Work Experience: *Law Clerk,* Supreme Court of North Carolina, Justice Henry E. Frye; *Associate,* Richard Schwartz & Associates Law Firm; *Staff Attorney,* American Civil Liberties Union (ACLU); *Senior Staff Attorney and Attorneys of Color Recruitment and Retention Officer,* American Civil Liberties Union (ACLU); *Director of Law and Policy,* Equal Justice Society

Professional Organizations: *Member,* Barristers' Association; *Member,* Philadelphia Bar Association; *Diversity Chair,* Philadelphia Bar Association; *Board of Governors,* Philadelphia Bar Association

Post-Law School Honors, Achievements, Activities, and Community Service:

Awardee, Michael Greenberg Community Service Award, LGBTQ Bar Association of Philadelphia (2019); *Magazine Recognition,* 2018 Icons, Innovators and Disruptors, The Advocate Magazine; *Awardee,* City of Brotherly Love Softball League Community Service Award (2017); *Honoree,* Most Influential African Americans, Philadelphia Tribune (2016, 2017, 2018); *Awardee,* David Rosenblum Public Policy Award, Pennsylvania Bar Association LGBTQ+ Rights Committee (2016); *Awardee,* Living Legend Award, Penn State Black Law Students Association (2016); *Awardee,* LGBT Business Advocate Award, Philadelphia Business Journal (2015); *Honoree,* Legal Intelligencer Diverse Attorney of the Year, Legal Intelligencer (2015); *Honoree,* Black History Month "Game Changer", KYW Newsradio/CBS Philly (2015); *Awardee,* Minority Business Leader Award, Philadelphia Business Journal (2014); *Honoree,* William Way LGBT Community Center Humanitarian of the Year (2014); *Fellow,* Wasserstein Public Interest Fellowship, Harvard Law School (2009-2010); *Honoree,* Distinguished Alumnus, University of North Carolina School of Law (2009); *Board Member,* Claneil Foundation (2019-Present); *Board Member,* Atlantic Center for Capital Representation (2018-Present); *Board Member,* Dance Iquail! (2017-2020); *Board Member and Vice Chair,* Free Speech TV (2017-Present); *Board Member,* Working Films; *President,* Working Films (2007-2015); *Executive Committee,* Public Interest Section, Philadelphia Bar Association (2012-16); *Member,* Board of Advisors, University of North Carolina Center for Civil Rights (2010-2017); *Diversity Chair and Board of Governors,* Philadelphia Bar Association (Present); *Committee Member and Current Chair, Steering Committee,* American Civil Liberties Union (ACLU) Executive Directors Council (2012-Present)

LESSONS LEARNED: MY RECOMMENDATIONS FOR YOUR FUTURE ACTIONS BASED ON MY PAST EXPERIENCE

Advice on Law School Preparation:

Take it seriously. Law school is challenging. There are no shortcuts to getting there or surviving, let alone thriving, once you are there.

Advice on Applying to and Selecting a Law School:

Getting into law school is very competitive. Unfortunately, old-school thinking about law school rankings applies to some employers. They also matter in terms of opening up the greatest number of opportunities postgraduation. My advice is to go to the best school you can and one that is as affordable as possible. While there, do as well as you can, which, again, broadens your options after graduation. At the end of the day, no matter where you go, your hard work, steadiness and resilience will determine your career trajectory and success.

Advice Regarding Academic Success, Co-Curricular and Extra-Curricular Participation, and Social Engagement in Law School:

Law school is not easy. Especially the first year. It certainly is not like college, where last-minute cramming is the norm. The work is voluminous and requires learning a whole new set of skills. Approach it like a job. Make time for yourself outside of school, for social activities and self-care, but most of your time should be spent studying. Regarding extra-curricular activities, I would minimize those until my 2L year.

Law school can be a stressful and isolating experience. Do what you can to keep it in perspective. Others are having similar experiences. Rely on whatever strategies that served you well before. Don't allow yourself to become isolated. Call on your village for support.

Keep perspective. It's three years. Three intense years, but you can get through it.

Advice on Preparing for and Taking the Bar Exam:

Make the bar exam your priority for the months you are studying for it. Approach it like a job. Get up in the morning, study all day, go home, have dinner, study some more. Take a bar exam prep course. Get a study partner. Schedule, take and learn from practice exams. Wash. Rinse. Repeat.

Advice on Choosing a Job and Career Path Inside or Outside of the Legal Profession:

Follow your heart. Know what you love and want to do. That may or may not be a practicing lawyer. It may require you to try many things before figuring out what fits. The legal education is excellent preparation for a wide variety of careers. Don't limit yourself.

Advice on Seeking Legal Job Opportunities and/or Creating One's Own Opportunities:

After figuring out exactly what you want, be persistent and creative in finding opportunities. Doing your own thing is a real option, too. Don't let fear stop you from trying.

Advice on Achieving Career Success and Advancement:

Find a mentor. Join some professional associations. Get involved. Network. Volunteer. Honor your commitments. Even if you are shy, as I am, putting yourself out there can be essential to career advancement and opportunities. You are a brand. Treat it with utmost care.

Advice on Overcoming the Additional Challenges Black Law Students and Lawyers Face:

You got this. Our ancestors went through worse. You stand on the shoulders of kings, queens, innovators, survivors, and creators. Do it for them; do it for yourself. Whatever the challenge is, it will not last forever.

To be human and alive is to necessarily experience life's ups and downs. It's important in those moments to treat yourself as you would your best friend: extend yourself grace and compassion.

Best Advice I Received Regarding Law School and the Legal Profession:

"No, there are not too many lawyers. There definitely are not too many Black lawyers. In fact, there are not enough of us."

Worst Advice I Received Regarding Law School and the Legal Profession:

"Don't take off any time between college and law school. You might not go back." It wasn't bad advice, *per se*, and certainly was meant to be encouraging, but taking time off between college and law school is precisely the right thing for some people. In fact, I recall that, generally speaking, the more successful law students tended to have taken some time off. They returned with perspective, enthusiasm, and real-life experiences to help inform their approach to law school.

Best Advice I Would Give to an Aspiring Black Lawyer:

Find mentors. Don't be afraid to ask someone to mentor you. Most people are flattered. Mentors can help you in more ways than you can imagine.

Go the way your blood beats. Live your life with authenticity, not in accordance with the expectations of others.

Don't let your well run dry. Make sure your reserves are replenished and always be working to shore up your foundation. For some people, that is faith and spirituality. For others, meditation, yoga or exercise. The more grounded you are, the better you will be able to respond to life's inevitable challenges.

Finally, I would quote Dr. King again: "Make a career of humanity. Commit yourself to the noble struggle for equal rights. You will make a greater person of yourself, a greater nation of your country, and a finer world to live in."

Thoughts About Why Earning a Law Degree Is a Powerful Credential for African Americans and Why There Is a Need for More African American Lawyers:

Lawyer jokes notwithstanding, a law degree is a well-respected credential that opens many doors and grants a seat at many tables. It also provides a platform and a voice that carries a lot of weight, in legal settings and beyond. For good (mostly) or ill, when lawyers talk, people tend to listen. Yes, there are a lot of lawyers. But there are not enough Black lawyers. We need more. Unfortunately, credentials matter, although our humanity - the fact that we are human beings - should be all that we need.

Thoughts About Whether and Why Law School Is Worth the Financial Investment:

In 2020, my answer is "probably". That is based on the uncertainty of our economy (at least in the short term) and the growing expense of law school. At the time that I graduated law school, in 1991, my answer would have been, "Absolutely!" If you believe a career in law to be your calling, my answer is, "Go for it!" Be deliberative about the decision-making process. It certainly is possible to make a good living as a lawyer, though I hope that won't be your motivation.

LEGACY AND SUCCESS

Most Outstanding Accomplishment:

Personal: Surviving a childhood of poverty, domestic abuse and limited opportunity with my spirit and dreams intact and having been able to achieve many of my professional goals, including my childhood decision to become a lawyer, which involve advocating on behalf of the marginalized or mistreated.

Professional: Pioneering racial profiling litigation and popularizing the term "driving while Black".

The Legacy I Hope to Leave:

That I was a good person who loved his family and friends and lived a life of honor, meaning and purpose.

I have already defied "the soft bigotry of low expectations". I want my legacy to be that I extended my mother's legacy and achieved my dreams when she was not allowed or encouraged to pursue hers. I further want my legacy to be one of having worked hard to fight for justice and equality and on behalf of the vulnerable, ignored, marginalized and disenfranchised.

The Secret to My Success:

Hard work, persistence, sound judgment, resilience, good deeds, good people, ethical behavior, self-belief, vision, determination, luck, favor, grace!

Practical Wisdom for Those on the Path to Lawyerhood

Grace E. Speights, Esq.
Global Leader
Labor and Employment Practice
Morgan, Lewis & Bockius, LLP
Washington, D.C.

"Don't look at everything that you may be requested to do because you are a diverse associate as a burden; think of these things as opportunities."

– Grace E. Speights

Success is . . . doing and engaging in something about which you are passionate.

PERSONAL FAVORITES

Favorite Quote: "I can do all things through Christ." - Philippians 4:13

Favorite Book: *I Know Why the Caged Bird Sings* by Maya Angelou

Favorite Movie: *Best Man Holiday*

Favorite Song and Musical Artist: Any song by Prince

Favorite Law School Class: Civil Procedure

Favorite Legal Case: *Roe v. Wade*

Favorite Hobbies: Running; Biking; Reading; Trying new restaurants

Favorite Attorney Role Model: Vincent Cohen (deceased). Vincent Cohen was one of the first Black lawyers in Washington to become a partner at a major law firm. He was a mentor and very helpful during my young years as an attorney.

FAMILY AND BACKGROUND

Where Born and Raised: Washington, D.C.

Family (Spouse/Partner and Children): Children - (daughter) Ashley and (son) Nathaniel "Hank"

Family Socioeconomic and Educational Background: I grew up in one of the roughest neighborhoods in South Philadelphia. I was raised by my mom, who raised me as a single parent because she and my dad separated when I was a very young kid. Mom only graduated from eighth grade and was a hard worker who worked very hard and long hours in a drapery factory in South Philadelphia. She did that because she was hoping for a better life for me; she was hoping for a way out for me from the poverty that surrounded us. The neighborhood that we lived in was a poor and undesirable neighborhood at that time. As a young kid, I had to walk over homeless folks and drug addicts to get to school or the local neighborhood playground. Even scarier, was that oftentimes I had to dodge bullets to get out of the neighborhood because there was always ongoing gang warfare when I was growing up there. I am not a betting person, but if I were, I would never have bet on me getting to the place that I am at today.

THE DECISION TO BECOME A LAWYER

When and Why I Decided to Become a Lawyer: I decided that I wanted to be an attorney after being exposed to the working conditions of my mother as a worker in a factory that made fiberglass draperies.

EDUCATIONAL ACHIEVEMENTS

High School: Philadelphia High School for Girls (Philadelphia, Pennsylvania)

College/University: University of Pennsylvania (Philadelphia, Pennsylvania)

Undergraduate Degree: Bachelor of Arts (B.A.)

Major: Political Science

College Honors/Achievements/Activities: Graduated *cum laude* "with distinction"; *Member,* Onyx Honor Society; *Member,* Alpha Kappa Alpha Sorority, Inc.

Law School: The George Washington University Law School (Washington, D.C.)

Law School and Graduation Year: Juris Doctor/Doctor of Jurisprudence (J.D.) - Class of 1982

Law School Honors, Achievements and Activities: *Member,* International Law Journal; Graduated in the Top 5% of class; *Member,* Order of the Coif (honor society for law students earning high grades); *President,* GW Black Law Students Association

PROFESSIONAL ACCOMPLISHMENTS

State Bar Memberships (Where Admitted to Practice Law): Pennsylvania; District of Columbia

Other Legal Experience: *Law Clerk,* the late Chief Judge Aubrey E. Robinson, Jr., United States District Court for the District of Columbia; *Associate,* Morgan Lewis

Professional Organizations: *Member,* American College of Trial Lawyers; *Member,* College of Labor and Employment Lawyers

Post-Law School Honors, Achievements, Activities, and Community Involvement:

Honoree, Lawyer of the Year, The Best Lawyers in America - Employment Law for Management, Labor Law, Litigation (2020); *Honoree,* Top 250 Women in Litigation, Benchmark Litigation; *Awardee,* M. Ashley Dickerson Award, National Association of Women Lawyers (2019); *Honoree,* Rainmaker, Minority Corporate Counsel Association (2019); *Special Recognition,* Leading Lawyer, Labor and Employment, The Legal 500 (2013-2019); *Honoree,* Attorney of the Year, American Lawyer (2018); *Special Recognition,* MVP (Most Valuable Player) Employment, Law 360 (2018); *Honoree,* Charles Hamilton Houston Medallion of Merit, Washington Bar Association (2018); *Awardee,* Justice Potter Stewart Award, Council for Court Excellence (2017); *Awardee,* George E.C. Hayes Memorial Award, Washington Bar Association (2016); *Special Recognition,* Top Woman Lawyer, The Best Lawyers in America, (2016-2019); *Special Recognition,* Most Powerful Employment Attorneys, Human Resource Executive (2008-2019); *Honoree,* Power List, Lawyers of Color (2014-2019); *Awardee,* Gavel for Good Corporate Citizen Award, The GWAC Foundation (Greater Washington Area Chapter Bar Association) (2016); *Awardee,* Thurgood Marshall Phenomenal Woman Award (2015); *Awardee,* Wiley A. Branton Award, National Bar Association (2013); *Awardee,* A. Leon Higginbotham Award, Young Lawyers Division, National Bar Association (2013); *Awardee,* Pathfinder Award, Diverse Partners Network of African American Managing Partners and General Counsels (2013); *Awardee,* Mabel Haden Trailblazer Award, Washington Bar Legal Foundation (2013); *Awardee,* Champion of Justice Award, National Association for the Advancement of Colored People (NAACP) (2013); *Honoree,* Outstanding Contribution to Public Service/Social Activism (Private Practice), Chambers USA Women in Law Awards (2013); *Awardee,* Women Who Mean Business Award, Washington Business Journal (2012); *Honoree,* "Good Scout" Award, National Area Council of the Boy Scouts of America (2012); *Awardee,* Charlotte E. Ray Award, Greater Washington Area Chapter, Women Lawyers Division, National Bar Association (2011); "Leading Lawyer" designation, Legal 500 U.S. Guide (2016); *Listed Honoree,* Lawyers of Color Power List (2014, 2015); *Listed Honoree,* Savoy Magazine's 2015 Most Influential Lawyers; Washingtonian Magazine's Best Lawyers in Washington, D.C. (2013-2016); *Listed Honoree,* Washington Post's Top 100 Lawyers in D.C. (2013-2016); *Listed Honoree,* Washington Post's Top 50 Women Lawyers in D.C. (2013-2016); *Listed Honoree,* The National Law Journal's 100 Most Influential Women Lawyers in Washington, D.C. (2010); *Listed Honoree,*Who's Who in Black Washington, D.C.; *Listed Honoree,* 2010 Washington Business Journal Minority Business Leaders; *Listed Honoree,* Minority Corporate Counsel 2009 Rainmakers; *Listed Honoree,* The Washingtonian Magazine's 100 Most Powerful Women in Washington, D.C. (2009); *Listed Honoree,* The Best Lawyers in America (2007-2016); *Listed Honoree,* Washington Super Lawyers (2007-2016); *Listed Honoree,* Super Lawyers Top 50 Women Lawyers in Washington, D.C. (2007); *Listed Honoree,* Human Resource Executive's Top 100 Most Powerful Employment Attorneys (2009-2016); *Listed Honoree,* Human Resource Executive's Top 50 Defense Employment Attorneys (2008-2016); *Listed Honoree,* The Legal Times Leading Labor and Employment Lawyers (2004); *Special Recognition,* Ranked by Chambers USA in Labor and Employment Law; *Fellow,* College of Labor and Employment Lawyers; *Fellow,* American College of Trial Lawyers; *Magazine Feature,* Featured in a cover story in the Washington Business Journal titled "A Few Good Women" (2016); *Magazine Feature,* Featured in "Powering Up: A Look at the First Generation of Minority Managing Partners," Diversity and the Bar Magazine, May/June 2011; *Member,* District of Columbia Judicial Nominations Commission; *Member,* District of Columbia Federal Judicial Nominations Commission; *President,* Greater Washington Area Chapter, Women Lawyers Division, National Bar Association; *President,* Washington D.C. Chapter of Jack & Jill of America, Inc.; *National President,* Jack & Jill of America Foundation; *Member,* District of Columbia Court of Appeals Committee on Admissions; *Member,* Board of Directors, Washington, D.C. Public Defender Service; *Member,* District of Columbia Judicial Tenure and Disabilities Commission; *Member,* Board of Trustees, George Washington University; *Secretary,* GWU Board of Trustees; *Chair,* Board of Trustees, The George Washington University (2019-Present); *Chairperson,* Board's Committee on Governance and Nominations

LESSONS LEARNED: MY RECOMMENDATIONS FOR YOUR FUTURE ACTIONS BASED ON MY PAST EXPERIENCE

Advice on Making the Choice to Apply to and Attend Law School:

Students should apply to and attend the best law schools that they can get into and from which they will graduate with the least amount of debt.

Advice on Law School Preparation:

Being able to read and write a great deal of material and being able to analytically do so is key. To prepare for law school, students should take as many courses as possible that will require them to read and write analytically.

Advice Regarding Academic Success, Co-Curricular and Extra-Curricular Participation, and Social Engagement in Law School:

The most important thing in law school is to get the best grades possible and to participate in classes or clinics that will allow you to get some practical experience while in law school. Also, students need to be careful about over-extending themselves in extra-curricular activities. It is very important that the bulk of a student's time be spent preparing for class and exams.

Advice on Preparing for and Taking the Bar Exam:

Preparing for the bar will require that you commit to intense focus for the six to eight-week period before the bar exam. Students just have to accept that during that period they will have no other life. Passing the bar is a must if they want to practice law.

Advice on Achieving Career Success and Advancement:

I have 10 pieces of advice regarding career success and advancement especially as it relates to Black lawyers.

First, you must have the right attitude and have a hunger and drive for success. Starting out as a summer associate in 1981 and then as an associate in 1984, I was hungry to be successful. A lot of that may have been because of my childhood background. Coming from the background that I had come from, I knew that I wanted to do a lot better than my folks. I saw how hard my mom had worked day in and day out. Having been given the opportunity to work at a place like my law firm, there was no way that I was going to blow the opportunity by being a slacker. I knew that things were not going to be handed to me on a silver platter. They never had been when I was growing up. I knew I had to work hard to earn everything that I got. Starting out, I had no ambition or thoughts about being a partner at my firm. It was a more short-term view than that. I had a real hunger and desire to be the best that I could be; the thought of partnership, at least at the early stages of my career, never really drove my actions.

Second, any chips that you have on your shoulder should be left at the door. When you start out as a new lawyer, you have a lot to learn, not just about the law, but also the environment and culture of the place that you are working. For some new lawyers, places like a large law firm are going to be a culture shock for you. You have to accept the fact that you are going to get criticism on some, or maybe most, of your work product. Sometimes as a woman or a Black lawyer you are going to be a minority in your workplace. Do not take the easy road of blaming any criticisms or stumbles that you may have within your workplace on the fact that you are a woman or Black lawyer. Even though you may have performed well in college and in law school, you have to expect that your legal job will be challenging, and you are not going to get everything correct right off the bat. The fact that you may get criticism does not necessarily mean that you are getting criticism because of your race or gender.

Third, there is no substitute for top quality and timely work product. You will need to check and double-check your work.

Fourth, focus on building internal and external relationships. As far as internal relationships, make sure that you start early to build relationships within your workplace. From an external standpoint, develop relationships with peers at other firms or legal organizations, lawyers who you met at bar activities, and even parents at your kids' schools. Clients or future employers can come from many sources. And most clients are going to send work to lawyers with whom they have developed a relationship. And once folks become a client, it's very important to develop relationships with them. Try to learn as much as you can about your client contacts including things they like to do in their spare time, whether they have children, the names of their children, etc. Relationships take time to nurture, so it's never too early to start developing relationships.

Fifth, having both internal and external mentors is crucial. Probably the most important factor in my career development and progression was the mentoring relationships that I had. Some of the mentoring relationships came through formal pairing at my firm, but most of my mentoring relationships were informal and were based on the natural development of relationships.

Sixth, be willing to get beyond your comfort zone. It is very easy to come to work, go into your office, close the door, work at your desk all day, and then go home. That is a very comfortable zone. And if you do leave your desk to go to lunch or get a cup of coffee, it's very easy and comfortable to do that with people who look like you. You are not going to be successful, however, if that's how you spend your days in the office. You have to venture outside of your office, learn to stop in and shoot the breeze with your colleagues, and welcome them to do the same thing with you.

Seventh, you have to be willing to stretch yourself to take on new work or new projects. Try to avoid saying "no" to a project, a new case, or event/activity unless you absolutely have too much work to do or taking on the new work/project will cause you to sacrifice the quality and timeliness of other work/projects. Some of the best projects that I worked on as a young associate were matters or projects that I took on when I was stretched to the limit and just thought I could not take on one more thing.

Eighth, try to look at things that you are asked to do as an opportunity rather than a burden. Coming up as one of the few diverse associates and later junior partners in my firm, I received numerous invitations from firm clients, outside organizations, and even partners at the firm to attend events and meetings focused on diverse attorneys. Most of these things were after normal working hours and some of them were even on the weekend. I also was called upon very often to interview and recruit diverse attorneys and to attend client pitches for clients or potential clients who had indicated that they wanted pitch teams to be diverse. Rather than view these kinds of activities or events as a burden on me and my time, I viewed each and every one as an opportunity. They were opportunities because they gave me chances to meet other associates and partners throughout the firm (all of these folks were potential internal clients), they gave me chances to meet clients and potential clients outside of the firm, and they gave me an opportunity to make a contribution to the firm. These kinds of opportunities were important to my progression and advancement at the firm.

Ninth, make sure that you invest in your future. You must take control of your own career and professional development. As a young associate at my firm, I made sure that I attended whatever training and professional development opportunities were offered by the firm. I also made sure that, on my own time, I kept up with new cases and other developments in my area of practice. I also tried to anticipate things that might come down the pike that would affect the clients that I worked for. I read everything that I could find about my clients and their industries. This meant that I had to do a lot of extra things that were not in the client billable category, but I did these kinds of things as my own personal investment in myself and my career.

Finally, probably one of the most important factors in my career success and advancement in my firm was that I figured out my value to the firm and my career, and once I figured that out, I ran with it and began to build a brand. I was in our firm's litigation practice group for about 15 years.

About 12 years into my practice in our litigation group, I was asked to work on some employment discrimination cases, which were not handled in our general litigation practice group but were handled in the firm's Labor and Employment Practice Group. My first reaction to this request was negative because I felt that I was only being asked to work on these cases because of my race and gender. I struggled with this issue for a little while. Fortunately, several mentors outside of the firm were able to help me understand that even if I was being asked to work on these cases because of my race and gender, it was a good thing. They helped me to understand that lawyers are hired every day because of some attribute or skill that they bring to the table. It just so happened that many clients believed that my race and/or gender were positive attributes that I could bring to the table in defending these kinds of cases. That thought was validated based on some of my very positive and rewarding experiences in the first few employment cases that I handled. That experience led me to transfer to the Labor and Employment Practice Group and was the start of my journey to becoming known and branded as one of the best employment lawyers in the country. Getting to this point was a very steep learning curve for me and required me to make a lot of sacrifices, especially when it came to my family and personal life. I now know that this was the best decision that I made concerning my career and it was well worth the temporary sacrifices.

Advice on Overcoming the Additional Challenges Black Law Students and Black Lawyers Face:

Always be prepared for class, volunteer to participate in class, get to know your professors, get help if you are struggling with a class, join study groups, and do not segregate yourself from students of other races and national origins.

Best Advice I Would Give to an Aspiring Black Lawyer:

Being successful as a Black lawyer requires a two-way street. The firms, companies, or other entities that you may work for will likely have many diversity efforts and initiatives for their diverse lawyers. However, if you as a Black lawyer do not shoulder some of the responsibility for your own success and do not invest in our own professional development and careers, there is no way that you are going to be successful. There is no dispute that Black lawyers should and can be successful in the legal profession. Just look at me. There are many paths to success in the legal profession. I challenge you to invest in your professional development and growth, find your path, and then run on that path like crazy!

LEGACY AND SUCCESS

My Most Outstanding Accomplishment:

Personal: raising two wonderful and responsible children.

Professional: rising through the ranks of summer associate, associate, partner, senior partner, and now leader in a major global law firm.

The Legacy I Hope to Leave:

I hope to leave a legacy of being a successful African American lawyer who never forgot from where she came and who was always available to mentor and sponsor Black students, law students, and lawyers.

The Secret to My Success:

Hard work, having a great deal of grit, never giving up, and having mentors and sponsors who were willing to invest in me.

Practical Wisdom for Those on the Path to Lawyerhood

Benjamin Taylor, Esq.
Partner Attorney
Taylor & Gomez Law Office
Phoenix, Arizona

"Justice is not just a legal matter; it's a human matter."

– Benjamin Taylor

Success is . . . not a destination. It is a series of achievements over the span of your life that occur. Occurrences that come with serious thought, hours of work, tons of sacrifice and a lot of faith.

PERSONAL FAVORITES

Favorite Quote: "Injustice anywhere is a threat to justice everywhere." - Dr. Martin Luther King, Jr.

Favorite Books: *King of Torts* by John Grisham; *Rich Dad, Poor Dad* by Robert T. Kiyosaki;

The Richest Man in Babylon by George S. Clason; *To Kill a Mockingbird* by Harper Lee

Favorite Movies: *Marshall; Coming to America; The Lion King; The Great Debaters*

Favorite Songs: Too many great songs to choose just one.

Favorite Musical Artists: Stevie Wonder; Luther Vandross; Sade; Temptations

Favorite Law School Classes: Contracts; Constitutional Law; Torts

Favorite Legal Cases: Roe v. Wade; Brown v. Board of Education; Miranda v. Arizona; Loving v. Virginia; Plessy v. Ferguson

Favorite Hobbies: Attending sporting events; Taking long walks at sunset; Volunteering in the community

Favorite Attorney Role Models: Barack Obama; Thurgood Marshall; Johnnie Cochran

FAMILY AND BACKGROUND

Where Born and Raised: Iceland (My family was in the U.S. Military.)

Family Socioeconomic and Educational Background:
I was born and raised in a military family. My parents were middle class and pushed a commitment to excellence early on. My dad was retired in the military after 20 years and my mom retired from teaching after 30 years of service. We were avid church goers. The importance of church, service and community were instilled in me at an early age.

THE DECISION TO BECOME A LAWYER

When and Why I Decided to Become a Lawyer: I was a finance major at Arizona State University in the Honors College. After working in finance, I felt a strong desire to switch to law. I began to observe the injustices in the nation and wanted to make a change. My connections in the community allowed me to understand the need for representation within the community. It was important for me to be the change that I wanted to see.

EDUCATIONAL ACHIEVEMENTS

High School: Sahuaro High School (Tucson, Arizona)

College/University: Arizona State University (Tempe, Arizona)

Undergraduate Degree: Bachelor of Science (B.S.)

Major: Finance

College Honors, Achievements and Activities: Honors College Graduate

Law School: University of Arizona James E. Rogers College of Law (Tucson, Arizona)

Law Degree and Graduation Year: Juris Doctor/Doctor of Jurisprudence (J.D.) - Class of 2004

Law School Honors/Achievements/Activities: *Recipient,* Arizona Black Bar Scholarship

PROFESSIONAL ACCOMPLISHMENTS

State Bar Membership (Where Admitted to Practice Law): Arizona

Other Legal Work Experience: *Attorney,* Maricopa County Public Defender's Office; *Intern,* Pima County Attorney's Office; *Intern,* Arizona State Legislature

Professional Organizations: *Member,* State Bar Board of Governors; *Member,* National Association for the Advancement of Colored People (NAACP); *Board Member,* Maricopa Bar Association

Post-Law School Honors, Achievements, Activities, and Community Involvement: *Honoree,* 40 Under 40, National Bar Association; *Honoree,* 35 Under 35 Arizona Republic Top Entrepreneur; *Honoree,* 40 under 40 Phoenix Business Journal; *Honoree,* Unsung Hero, Arizona Legislative Leadership Conference; *Statewide Officer,* Criminal Justice Section, Executive Council, The State Bar of Arizona; *Selected Participant,* State Bar Leadership Institute; *Member,* Maricopa County Bar Association; *Member and Legal Redress Committee Member,* Maricopa County Branch of NAACP; *Elected Member,* State Bar Board of Governors

LESSONS LEARNED: MY RECOMMENDATIONS FOR YOUR FUTURE ACTIONS BASED ON MY PAST EXPERIENCE

Advice on Law School Preparation:

Do your due diligence. Spend time speaking to law students and reading preparation books prior to attending law school. Law school is a massive commitment so make sure that you understand the sacrifice and expectations beforehand.

Advice on Applying to and Selecting a Law School:

Take your time and visit the law schools while applying. Make appointments to meet with the professors to understand the school culture, environment and resources available while a student and after graduation.

Advice Regarding Academic Success, Co-Curricular and Extra-Curricular Participation, and Social Engagement in Law School:

"You are the company that you keep." Align yourself with people who have similar goals as you and friends that you can trust. It is imperative to have a support network that understands your goals and commitment.

Advice on Preparing for and Taking the Bar Exam:

The bar exam is a beast. It is important to find a strategy for studying that works for you. Take the prep courses, consult with recent graduates who have taken the bar exam for advice and study hard. You cannot over study or prepare for the bar exam. Be transparent and prepared for the Moral Character Review. Again, you are the company that you keep.

Advice on Choosing a Job and Career Path Inside or Outside of the Legal Profession:

Accept as many clerkships as you can to learn. Use these experiences as building blocks to understand your likes and dislikes. There are various types of law that you can practice, and your relationships and network will take you a long way.

Advice on Seeking Legal Job Opportunities and/or Creating One's Own Opportunities:

Understand the power of your network before you need it. Begin building relationships early on. Fellow students, lawyers, judges, professors and co-workers will become your network. Spend some time understanding and building your network. This will serve as the basis for learning about job opportunities, getting the job and receiving client referrals.

Advice on Achieving Career Success and Advancement:

Remember that success is not one moment in time. It is a foundation based on hard work, time, patience, success and failure. Work hard, stay dedicated, learn from your failures, have unwavering belief in your abilities, and have faith that the stair is there even though you may not see it.

Advice on Overcoming the Additional Challenges Black Law Students and Lawyers Face:

You are not alone on this journey and nothing is fair. Do not get stuck on thinking that the world is fair. Go in with the understanding that it is not fair and that it hasn't been. Strategize how to excel in an unjust situation. Acknowledge your strengths and weaknesses and work to grow stronger in those areas. Do not be a loner. You will need a core group of attorneys for support and advice to lean on.

Best Advice I Received Regarding Law School and the Legal Profession:

The law will open up doors that you will never believe.

Worst Advice I Received Regarding Law School and the Legal Profession:

I have heard the most ridiculous advice from people who never attended law school. Do not limit yourself based on another person's inability to dream big. It will take an unwavering belief in your abilities and dreams to succeed. Do not listen to haters.

Best Advice I Would Give to an Aspiring Black Lawyer:

You are a lawyer who has the unique experience of being Black. Do not limit yourself by labels. Network with all races and types of people.

Thoughts About Why Earning a Law Degree Is a Powerful Credential for African Americans and Why There Is a Need for More African American Lawyers:

This is a pivotal time in our country's history. It is a crucial time for African Americans to become lawyers and judges. Representation is needed to have a more just system.

Thoughts About Whether and Why Law School Is Worth the Financial Investment:

Law school is an investment in yourself. There are cheaper degrees to attain and easier ways to earn a living. Please make sure that you are 100% sure that you want to be a lawyer before taking on the debt. A Juris Doctorate looks good on your resume but fighting for justice requires a passion and connection to humanity.

LEGACY AND SUCCESS

My Most Outstanding Accomplishment:

Being elected by fellow lawyers and judges to be on the State Bar Board of Governors to represent the State Bar.

The Legacy I Hope to Leave:

I would like to be known as an exceptional attorney that worked hard with integrity.

The Secret to My Success:

Be honest, be authentic and listen to understand.

David T. Taylor, Esq., M.B.A.
Trademark Attorney Advisor
United States Patent and Trademark Office
Alexandria, Virginia

"The moment you reach full contentment is the moment life loses its meaning and purpose."
— David T. Taylor

Success is . . . repeatedly setting new goals in each facet of your personal and professional lives and fighting through obstacles to accomplish them.

PERSONAL FAVORITES

Favorite Quotes:

"In the quiet crucible of your personal, private sufferings, your noblest dreams are born, and God's greatest gifts are given in compensation for what you have been through." - Wintley Phipps

"Dig the well before you're thirsty." - Unknown

Favorite Books: *Think and Grow Rich* by Napoleon Hill; *Who Moved My Cheese* by Spencer Johnson

Favorite Movies: *Airplane; Ray*

Favorite Songs and Musical Artists: "Before I Let Go" by Frankie Beverly; "Cosmic Slop" by Funkadelic

Favorite Law School Classes: Commercial Law; Torts; Property

Favorite Legal Cases: *Pierson v. Post; Palsgraf v. Long Island Railroad Co.*

Favorite Hobbies: Practicing martial arts; Drumming for an R&B band

Favorite Attorney Role Model: Edward Blackmon - Mississippi state legislator and private attorney.

FAMILY AND BACKGROUND

Where Born and Raised: Jackson, Mississippi

Family (Spouse/Partner and Children): Spouse - Wesla; Children - (daughter) Amelia and (daughter) Amber

Family Socioeconomic and Educational Background: My family evolved into a middle-class family from very humble beginnings. My mother and father were teen parents who went on to earn advanced degrees and recently retired after decades of service as college professors. I am a first-generation law school graduate.

THE DECISION TO BECOME A LAWYER

When and Why I Decided to Become a Lawyer: The legal profession was one of my top three options as early as high school. During my second year of business school, I discovered that the courses I found most interesting all had a foundation in business law. Thus, I saw law school as a logical next step.

EDUCATIONAL ACHIEVEMENTS

High School: Callaway High School (Jackson, Mississippi)

College/University: University of Southern Mississippi (Hattiesburg, Mississippi)

Undergraduate Degree: Bachelor of Science in Business Administration (B.S.B.A.)

Major: Business Administration

College Honors, Achievements and Activities: *Member,* Business Student Advisory Council; *Member,* Future Business Leaders

Law School: Thurgood Marshall School of Law, Texas Southern University (Houston, Texas)

Law Degree and Graduation Year: Juris Doctor/Doctor of Jurisprudence (J.D.) - Class of 1997

Law School Honors, Achievements and Activities: Graduated in Top 15% of law school class; *Academic Recognition,* Dean's List; *Awardee,* CALI Excellence for the Future Award® (The Center for Computer-Assisted Legal Instruction), Basic Federal Tax; *Awardee,* CALI Excellence for the Future Award®, Commercial Law; *Legal Writing Assistant* (for first-year legal writing class); *Member,* Black Law Students Association; Mediation Training

Other Graduate or Professional Degree: Master of Business Administration (M.B.A.), Mississippi State University (Starkville, Mississippi)

PROFESSIONAL ACCOMPLISHMENTS

State Bar Membership (Where Admitted to Practice Law): Maryland

Other Legal Experience: *Associate Attorney,* Williams, Birnberg, and Andersen, LLP; *Attorney Volunteer,* National Association for the Advancement of Colored People (NAACP) Legal Redress Program

Professional Organizations: *Member,* State Bar of Texas; *Member,* Maryland State Bar Association; *Member,* J. Franklyn Bourne Bar Association

Post-Law School Honors, Achievements, Activities, and Community Involvement:

Board Member, Project Healthy America; *Board Member,* World Academic Sports Team; *Advisory Board Member,* National Black Pre-Law Conference and Law Fair; *Member,* National Association for the Advancement of Colored People (NAACP); *Member,* Omega Psi Phi Fraternity, Inc.; *Awardee,* Leadership and Service Awards, Omega Psi Phi Fraternity, Inc.; *Awardee,* Alumnus of the Year Award, Future Black Law Students Association, University of Southern Mississippi; *Mentor,* Steve Harvey Mentoring Camp; *Mentor,* Manhood 101 High School Mentoring Program; *Guest Speaker,* Henley-Young Juvenile Justice Center; *Guest Speaker,* Fatherhood Program, Greater Mt. Calvary Church

LESSONS LEARNED: MY RECOMMENDATIONS FOR YOUR FUTURE ACTIONS BASED ON MY PAST EXPERIENCE

Advice on Making the Choice to Apply to and Attend Law School:

Interview as many lawyers as possible, and inquire about their day-to-day routines as well as their law school experiences. Do a self-assessment of your individual skills (i.e., critical thinking, writing, research) and interests to assure a match between your skill set, interests and the prerequisites for successful matriculation through law school. Law school is a tremendous sacrifice and many students do not have the proper foundation in their personal lives to allow them to satisfy the demands of full-time legal studies. Additionally, be aware that after graduation new lawyers are often disillusioned by the realities of legal practice that do not measure up to the Hollywood portrayals of high stakes legal dramas with courtroom showdowns, villains and heroes.

Advice on Law School Preparation:

Every student comes to the law school decision-point with a unique set of circumstances. For those who know early on that law school is the goal, there is no shortage of resources to assist in making oneself the best candidate for their target school or types of schools. Start early and find out what schools are looking for in an ideal candidate and find a way to fit that mold as you complete your undergraduate studies. Invest time in reviewing and/or taking practice tests and/or classes in preparation for the Law School Admission Test (LSAT) (technology-based or traditional prep). Identify a mentor in the law who can provide you sound advice, guidance and support. Those who decide to pursue law school late in undergraduate school or even later in life are at a slight disadvantage but should not be discouraged, as most schools take into account life experiences in the admissions process.

Advice on Applying to and Selecting a Law School:

The obvious and most often repeated mantra is to get into the best law school possible. I agree with this position with a few caveats. If there is a particular area of interest, the student should seek to identify and apply to schools that have a good reputation and/or special programs in that area of study. If there is a strong preference for a geographical location or region, consideration should be given to finding the most suitable schools in that area. Also, students should visit law schools at the top of their lists and get a feel for the environment from the perspective of current students. If there are special interest groups, be sure to reach out to the leadership of those groups and get as much insight into student life as possible. Three years can be an eternity to spend in an uncomfortable environment.

Advice Regarding Academic Success, Co-Curricular and Extra-Curricular Participation, and Social Engagement in Law School:

Law school will be an all-encompassing experience that should be treated as a full-time job, especially in the first year. While there will be plenty of opportunities for extra-curricular activities throughout the three-year program, the first-year course load coupled with the challenge of learning a new way of thinking require complete dedication to the task. Therefore, any structured activity that places consistent demands on the first-year student's time should be minimized or eliminated. There is no way around it - law school will be an incredible challenge for even the most prepared students. Those who find a way to maintain important areas outside of academia will be better equipped to cope with the inevitable stress. For instance, physical fitness routines must be incorporated into each day and social outings must be planned regularly, but must be managed in such a way that the distraction from studies is minimized. Time management is crucial - be creative. I recorded my notes and played them in the car on the way to and from social events, even if others were riding along. I took flashcards to family events. Relationships will be tested so getting the buy-in from your loved ones and others around you is important. The second-year student is far better equipped to strike a balance between academic requirements and law-related interests beyond the classroom. Most programs provide a wide range of opportunities such as legal clinics and community outreach programs to foster development as a lawyer while under the guidance of law school professors and legal practitioners. Participation in these programs is strongly encouraged.

Advice on Preparing for and Taking the Bar Exam:

Bar preparation takes a great deal of planning well in advance of your final semester of school. Take a deep breath after graduation and allow yourself to celebrate your accomplishment for a couple of days and don't think of anything law-related. Then enroll in a bar prep course and eliminate everything that does not enhance your chances of passing the bar exam. If you have planned properly, you will have enough money saved to allow you to study full-time for a couple of months leading up to the exam without having the distraction of a job commitment. Treat bar preparation as two full-time jobs. Resist the temptation to work for a firm during that time. Some firms or other employers will hire students just after graduation on the condition that they begin working full-time immediately and pass the bar exam within a number of months. This approach often sets the graduate up for failure. Devote 100% of your time to bar preparation and take as many practice tests as possible.

Advice on Choosing a Job and Career Path Inside or Outside of the Legal Profession:

This is likely the toughest challenge for most new lawyers. Some strive to maximize income and seek opportunities at large firms. Others are attracted to positions that offer immediate courtroom experience. Still others use their law degrees in entrepreneurial pursuits from establishing their own law practices to starting other businesses. With so many options, I would recommend pursuing those that present the most likely path to reaching your ultimate long-term goal as a practitioner. For instance, those who wish to develop courtroom experience early in their careers may be disappointed with the role of an associate at a large law firm, where it is rare for a young associate to be assigned such significant responsibilities. Similarly, the duties of a prosecutor may not align with the lawyer's interest in developing a technology firm. With the tremendous amount of debt often accumulated during law school, there is the temptation to pursue the job that provides the highest salary. While this is a reasonable approach, consideration should be given to the alignment of the prospect of a higher initial income versus the ultimate career goal.

Advice on Seeking Legal Job Opportunities and/or Creating One's Own Opportunities:

As with so many endeavors, start early. Summer internships can help set you apart from the competition. Be mindful of the types of personal relationships you are building. A personal recommendation from someone who knows and supports you gives you a tremendous edge over similarly qualified job applicants.

Always have a keen focus on your long-term goals. If you strive for middle management, then act the part of a middle-manager until you reach your goal. If the objective is to learn from others and apply it to your own business, then absorb everything possible and use it for your own benefit when the time comes.

Advice on Overcoming the Additional Challenges Black Law Students and Black Lawyers Face:

Focus on the study and practice of law and the rest will fall in place. However, it is crucial to appreciate the importance of sound financial decision making during the law school years. Black students often lack access to the financial resources required to attend law school without incurring significant student loan debt. While student loans help to create opportunities, they often lead to years or decades of loan repayments. Thus, careful consideration must be given to other means of defraying legal education costs, such as scholarships, grants, and paid internships. It is also important to recognize that discriminatory hiring practices can have an impact on employment opportunities upon graduation. These challenges are not unique to the practice of law. Understand that any challenges faced by Blacks in the law are the same challenges faced by Blacks in society generally, and we are familiar with them. Control those things you can control and be prepared to fight those fights that are worthy of your attention. Never compromise professionalism.

Best Advice I Received Regarding Law School and the Legal Profession:

Where you attend law school is not nearly as important as the skills you develop while there and the commitment you have for the profession. Enroll where you feel a level of comfort and have an opportunity to have an impact.

Worst Advice I Received Regarding Law School and the Legal Profession:

I was advised to delay law school attendance on the theory that I could benefit from a few years of experience in the workforce. While I believe this to have been bad advice, in fairness, I must also admit that I did indeed benefit tremendously from my brief stint with a major insurance company prior to entering law school. However, I quickly became very comfortable with my circumstances during that time, and the thought of leaving a place of relative comfort to confront the discomfort and uncertainty of law school nearly derailed my legal career before it began. From my observation, the risk of foregoing law school altogether after a period of full-time employment far outweighs any benefits gained from experience in the field.

Best Advice I Would Give to an Aspiring Black Lawyer:

Align yourself with organizations that are dedicated to the legal profession, and develop relationships with lawyers who are willing to serve as mentors. We need you, and we have a vested interest in your success. Also, participate in events like the annual National Black Pre-Law Conference where lawyers and law school representatives assemble to discuss topics relative to the law school experience from the Black student's perspective. Most importantly, understand that you have what it takes to be successful in law school and in the practice of law. Be bold, be confident, and refuse to be denied. With the help of a mentor, develop a plan and take meaningful steps toward your goal each day.

Thoughts About Why Earning a Law Degree Is a Powerful Credential for African Americans and Why There Is a Need for More African American Lawyers:

A law degree is a powerful credential in virtually any area of society and in any endeavor. More African American lawyers are needed in order to further level the playing field in our court systems and in corporate boardrooms. Lawyers, judges, and courts have historically acted to preserve citizens' rights when the broader society and elected officials fail to uphold the basic tenets of American citizenship. African American attorneys have led the charge in demanding equal rights and protection under the law. Although recent events illuminate the miles African Americans have yet to run, it has been the tireless efforts of these intellectual giants that has ushered our communities through decades of legalized and often weaponized discrimination, segregation, and racially-motivated mistreatment.

Lawyers like Thurgood Marshall, Charles Hamilton Houston, Constance Baker Motley, and Vernon Jordan used the power of the legal system and community activism to change laws and to bring about meaningful changes in key areas such as voter registration and discriminatory school and housing policies. Attorney Robert L. Carter served as lead counsel in *Sweatt v. Painter*, a U.S. Supreme Court case that successfully challenged the discriminatory admissions policies of the School of Law at the University of Texas. He would go on to play a major role in the landmark Supreme Court case *Brown v. Board of Education of Topeka*, which abolished legal segregation in public school systems. The hard work and dedication of these scholars led to change in the form of the Civil Rights Act, the Voting Rights Act, the Fair Housing Act and other significant advancements that have provided the foundation upon which we stand.

Fast forward to today's legal environment and lawyers such as Benjamin Crump continue the pursuit of justice in the field of civil rights. Lawyers like Billy Martin represent individuals and corporations in a wide variety of practice areas. In corporate America, Kenneth Chenault is the former CEO of American Express and currently serves on the board of Berkshire Hathaway, replacing Bill Gates. Countless other African American lawyers serve in various capacities of local, state, and federal governments, as well as in leadership roles of community-based organizations. In these varied roles, African American attorneys play a critical part in fighting for fairness and defending the rule of law in our courtrooms. They also advocate for policies that uniquely impact traditionally disadvantaged populations whose voices are often unheard by legislators, and whose perspectives are not often brought to the forefront for fair consideration by corporate leadership.

For these reasons, there is a clear and compelling need for African Americans to continue pursuing careers in the legal profession and to use those earned credentials in a way that reflects well on the profession and lays a foundation for the next generation of attorneys to continue molding the contours of our country's legal framework and to mount challenges where challenge is warranted.

Thoughts About Whether and Why Law School Is Worth the Financial Investment:

Law school is a worthy financial investment for those who have truly investigated the realities of the profession and have a defined purpose. I would not recommend law school as a method to delay entry into the workforce or to overcome a lack of opportunity in your chosen undergraduate field. The investment in time, energy, finances, and associated lost opportunities is enormous and should not be taken lightly.

LEGACY AND SUCCESS

My Most Outstanding Accomplishment:

I have granted federal intellectual property rights to thousands of domestic and international companies and have defended the rights of thousands more, including successfully arguing numerous appeals before a federal tribunal. I have been engaged with many companies during the start-up phase that have grown into some of the world's largest and most recognizable corporations.

The Legacy I Hope to Leave:

I hope to be remembered as a well-rounded, trustworthy advisor and confidant. My 20-plus year career in service of the United States federal government underscores a level of commitment and dedication that some may aspire to achieve.

The Secret to My Success:

If there is a secret to my success, it is commitment to a task, along with a healthy dose of competitiveness. For instance, during the first year of law school, many of us lived as neighbors in a small section of on-campus housing. I could not, in good conscience, close my books at the end of the night until I could look out of my window and verify that every one of the nearby fellow students had turned off their lights and gone to sleep. If even one of them was awake, I presumed they were studying and getting ahead. When you give that type of effort and energy to any endeavor you have no choice but to succeed.

Jerome Dennis Taylor, Esq.
Supervisory Attorney
Social Security Administration
Office of Disability Adjudication and Review
Chicago, Illinois

"Trust God and do your part."
– Jerome Dennis Taylor

Success is . . . having balance in every area of your life - spiritually, mentally, socially, physically, financially and emotionally.

PERSONAL FAVORITES

Favorite Quote: "Seek ye first the Kingdom of God, and His righteousness, and all these things shall be added unto you." - Matthew 6:33

Favorite Books: *Disciplines of a Godly Man* by R. Kent Hughes; *Marriage Matters* by Tony Evans; *Be In It to Win It* by Kirbyjon H. Caldwell

Favorite Movies: *ATL; Best Man Holiday*

Favorite Musical Artists: Tye Tribbett; Andy Mineo; Lecrae; Kurt Carr; Kem; Kool

Favorite Law School Classes: Critical Race Theory; Employment Law; Property II; Constitutional Law II

Favorite Legal Case: *Brown v. Board of Education of Topeka,* 347 U.S. 483 (1954)

Favorite Hobbies: Dancing; Watching movies; Reading; Traveling

Favorite Attorney Role Model: Samuel Mendenhall

FAMILY AND BACKGROUND

Where Born and Raised: Chicago, Illinois

Family (Spouse/Partner and Children): Spouse - Sondra; Children - (daughter) Zara and (son) Josiah

Family Socioeconomic and Educational Background:

I was raised in a single-parent home. My mother and father received their high school diploma but did not attend college. Education was not my mother's primary focus, as she spent most of her time trying to provide for her eight children. Of the eight children, I am the second oldest and the oldest male child. When I was two years old, my father was murdered.

I spent most of my childhood assisting my mother with my younger siblings. Due to domestic issues in our home, I moved with my grandmother once I graduated from eighth grade. Looking back, I know that my mother did the best that she could with what she had.

Although my mother did not encourage me to excel in school, I had prioritized my education because I saw it as my way of escape. We were living in a low-income, subsidized housing complex on the far South Side of Chicago. I knew that there had to be more to life than what we were experiencing. As a child, my education was the only thing I could control in my life. With chaos surrounding me on a daily basis, I wanted my grades to be excellent. My older sister was also focused on her grades, so I just naturally followed her lead. From grammar school through law school, academic excellence was my goal. My internal drive allowed me to press forward and work to beat the odds.

THE DECISION TO BECOME A LAWYER

When and Why I Decided to Become a Lawyer:

I decided that I wanted to become a judge at the age of five years old. When I realized that I would be fatherless the rest of my life because of the "bad guys" who murdered my father, I wanted to be the person who put the "bad guys" away. When I found out that person was a judge, from that point forward, I held on to my vision and worked towards making that dream a reality.

EDUCATIONAL ACHIEVEMENTS

High School: Morgan Park High School (Chicago, Illinois)

College/University: University of Illinois at Urbana-Champaign (Champaign, Illinois)

Undergraduate Degree: Bachelor of Arts (B.A.)

Major: Sociology

College Honors, Achievements and Activities: Graduated *magna cum laude* "with high distinction"; Edmund James Scholar; *Member,* Phi Beta Kappa (America's most prestigious honor society); *Member,* Phi Kappa Phi (honor society); *Member,* National Society of Collegiate Scholars (academic honor society); *Member,* Golden Key International Honor Society; *Founder,* Hip-Notic Dance Team (Fall 2003); *Graduate,* Scholarship Chicago, Class of 2007

Law School: University of Iowa College of Law (Iowa City, Iowa)

Law Degree and Graduation Year: Juris Doctor/Doctor of Jurisprudence (J.D.) - Class of 2010

Law School Honors, Achievements and Activities: Graduated with Highest Honors; *Awardee,* Boyd Service Award; *Fellow,* Minority Corporate Counsel Association (MCCA); *Recipient,* Lloyd B. Johnson Scholarship; *Awardee,* Faculty Award for Academic Excellence, Property II; *Awardee,* Most Outstanding Student Award, National Black Law Student Association (NBLSA) (2009); *President and Social Chair,* Alexander G. Clark Black Law Students Association (BLSA); *Regional Coordinator,* Midwest Black Law Students Association (MWBLSA); *Marshall,* Phi Alpha Delta Law Fraternity, Inc.; *2L Class Representative,* Iowa Student Bar Association; *Study Abroad Law Student,* University of Iowa-Bordeaux Summer Program in International and Comparative Law (Arcachon, France); *Study Abroad Law Student,* London Law Consortium (London, England)

PROFESSIONAL ACCOMPLISHMENTS

State Bar Membership (Where Admitted to Practice Law): Illinois

Other Legal Experience: *Adjunct Professor,* DePaul University College of Law; *Attorney Advisor - Regional Office,* Social Security Administration; *Attorney Advisor - Chicago Office of Disability Adjudication and Review (ODAR),* Social Security Administration; *Presidential Management Council,* Economic Development Administration, United States Department of Commerce; *Associate Attorney,* Gonzalez Saggio & Harlan LLP

Professional Organizations: *Member,* Illinois State Bar Association; *Vice President,* Board of Directors, Minority Legal Education Resources, Inc. (MLER); *Program Coordinator,* MLER Bar Process Management Program

LESSONS LEARNED: MY RECOMMENDATIONS FOR YOUR FUTURE ACTIONS BASED ON MY PAST EXPERIENCE

Advice on Law School Preparation:

I highly recommend that students take a Law School Admission Test (LSAT) test preparation course. Your LSAT score matters more than it should in my opinion, but it matters. Schools will make a determination about you and whether you are eligible for scholarships based on your LSAT alone. In addition, take courses in college that require a lot of analytical thinking and writing. My peers who were math majors and engineering majors in college had an easier transition to legal writing than those of us who had majors that did not focus on being able to synthesize information.

Advice on Applying to and Selecting a Law School:

I would recommend that if you have any other career avenue that you want to explore, do that before you apply to law school. Once you start the journey of law school and take the bar exam, you set yourself up to have to explain a lot if there are any gaps in your resume.

Make sure that your application is polished. Your personal statement should inform the admissions committee about things that your resume does not. It should tell your story. I spent four months working on my personal statement, and I had my freshman year English professor work on it with me.

Advice Regarding Academic Success, Co-Curricular and Extra-Curricular Participation, and Social Engagement in Law School:

The first year of law school is like learning a foreign language. You have to start with basic concepts, learn the vocabulary, learn how to use the words in sentences, and then learn how to speak the language. The more practice you have, the quicker you become fluent in the language. Reading your first case may not make sense and you will not know what to look for. By the time you finish your first year and have read thousands of pages, the language will make more sense.

The tough part is that your first-year grades really matter. I struggled my first year with not knowing what questions to ask my professors. I literally remember feeling like I just did not even know where to start. At that point, you have to dig deeper into the material so that you figure out what parts are not making sense. It needs to make sense to you so that you can issue-spot correctly and provide in-depth analysis using the case law to support your arguments.

As to extra-curricular activities, choose them wisely. Do not join a law journal if you are not interested in writing and reviewing scholarly articles written by other legal scholars. If you are interested in being a trial lawyer, then take Trial Advocacy and compete to join the moot court team. Whatever you do, do not sign up for things because your peers are doing it. Make sure that what you dedicate your time to is in alignment with your career goals.

Advice on Preparing for and Taking the Bar Exam:

Half of the battle when preparing for the bar exam is the "battle of mind". You have to decide early on in the process that you will be victorious and conquer the bar examination. There is no room for failure. I recommend that you make a study schedule for the summer and stick to it.

Additionally, I highly recommend that you do as many practice questions as possible. The exam tests your ability to know, comprehend, and regurgitate rules of law. It also tests your ability to understand what the questions are asking, which is a skill that can only be sharpened by doing as many practice essays and multiple-choice questions as possible.

Furthermore, I recommend that you treat each day like you are preparing for game day, i.e., the actual days that you prepare for the bar examination. Study in three-hour increments and always review your answers. It is better to get things wrong and understand why you got them wrong during the preparation phase.

Advice on Achieving Career Success and Advancement:

Develop a career plan, find a mentor, and work the plan. In this profession, you have to be flexible and willing to adjust your plan. It may not work out exactly how you thought it would but learn everything you can along the way because it all has purpose. Going into law school, I wanted to work at a big firm. After obtaining a summer associate position and working at a big firm for 12 weeks after my 1L year, I became more open-minded about different career paths. I am extremely blessed to be in the position I am in right now, where I am able to make a great salary and spend quality time with my growing family.

Advice on Overcoming the Additional Challenges Black Law Students and Lawyers Face:

Do not Be Afraid to Advocate for Yourself - In the legal profession, it is imperative that you learn to be an advocate for yourself and take advantage of every opportunity. Unfortunately, in some jobs, you are only as good as your last work product so everything that you produce needs to be great. When you get good feedback, make sure your supervisors know. If you get bad feedback, take complete ownership of the product and work to ensure that you do not make the same mistakes again.

Res Ipsa Loquitur (Latin word meaning "the matter speaks for itself") - Let your work speak for itself. You do not need to be validated. Your co-workers may always wonder how you got there, but your work must indicate that you belong exactly where you are.

Excellence Has to Be Your Standard - Your learning curve is different. You do not have room to make the same mistakes as your peers. Producing excellent work has to be your standard. Asking the right questions, appearing engaged, taking on the additional assignments that no one else wants are all ways to make yourself stand out in a positive manner. Be responsible and timely with your work assignments. Always meet your deadlines and communicate any deadline issues well in advance. Again, you do not have room to make the same mistakes when you are playing on a battlefield that is not always fair.

Set Career Goals That Are Not Driven By Money - Although money is important, you should also focus on gaining experience and developing your legal skill sets. If you want trial experience, find a job that will provide you that experience. If you want employment law experience, look for positions that will give you that experience.

Your Personal and Professional Image Matters - Protect your image. Make sure that you engage in behavior in law school and while practicing law that reflects the reputation you want. Your future jobs or potential client referrals depend on whether you are perceived as a hard worker or someone who does not really care about the quality of their work.

Best Advice I Received Regarding Law School and the Legal Profession:

"Your law school journey is yours. Do not try to emulate your peers. Do what is best for you." - Law School Mentor

"Stop crying about it not being fair. You know that already. Just do what you have to do to excel in a game that is not fair. You have to be twice as good as your peers." - Attorney Mentor

Best Advice I Would Give to an Aspiring Black Lawyer:

People trust lawyers to obtain justice, justice that may affect their Constitutional rights, their livelihoods, and maybe even their lives. Clients must never be just another case or file but deserve the very best their attorney has to offer. We can never lose sight of our ability to do tremendous good or devastating harm.

LEGACY AND SUCCESS

My Most Outstanding Accomplishments:

Personally - My most outstanding personal accomplishment is being a successful husband and father. My family is the center of my world, and anything that I achieve careerwise ultimately benefits them.

Professionally - The most outstanding accomplishment in my legal career has been my promotion to the supervisory attorney position. It was a competitive application process and I was selected based on my skill set. Higher-grade positions in the government are very selective and my labor relations background made me uniquely qualified for the position.

The Legacy I Hope to Leave:

To change lives one day at a time by providing hope, encouragement, and sharing the love of Christ. I also hope to increase diversity in the legal profession.

The Secret to My Success:

God. I honestly would not be where I am today without my faith in God. Every obstacle, every trial, every failure, every success…it was all part of God's plan for my life. When the vision got blurry and my first-year grades were not as good as I wanted them to be, I trusted God and worked to improve my grades. When I needed a job because my firm downsized and all the newer associates were laid off, I trusted God and did my part. I networked and God divinely connected me with someone who was able to assist me with the hiring process for a government attorney position.

Nydia D. Thomas, Esq.
Attorney and Director
RISE Transformative Justice Program
Lone Star Justice Alliance
Austin, Texas

"The lives we lead should be incontrovertible evidence of faith in action – faith in God, faith in the intrinsic goodness of mankind, and faith in our unique ability to transform the world around us."

– Nydia D. Thomas

Success is . . . when there is a divine alignment of spiritual, physical and fiscal well-being that enhances our ability to elevate and influence the lives of others.

PERSONAL FAVORITES

Favorite Quotes: "Be noble, for the nobleness that lies in other men - sleeping but never dead - will rise in majesty to meet thine own." - James Russell Lowell

"Success is the sum of small efforts, repeated day-in and day-out." - Robert Collier

Favorite Books: *Just Mercy: A Story of Justice and Redemption* by Bryan Stevenson; *How Six Black Golfers Won Civil Rights in Beaumont, Texas* by Robert J. Robertson; *Eyes on the Prize* by Juan Williams; *This Far by Faith* by Juan Williams; *The Prophet* by Khalil Gibran

Favorite Movies: *The Great Debaters; The Power of One; It's A Wonderful Life; Shawshank Redemption; Look for Me in the Whirlwind: The Marcus Garvey Story; Mama Africa: A Portrait of Miriam Makeba*

Favorite Music Genres: I enjoy a range of musical genres with encouraging lyrical content and a strong blend of jazz, classical, R&B, soft rock, funk, and gospel influences.

Favorite Songs: "I Wish I Knew How It Would Feel to Be Free" by Nina Simone/Emeli Sandé; "Strength, Courage and Wisdom" by India Arie; "On the Line" by Michael Jackson; "Free" by Stevie Wonder

Favorite Law School Classes: Constitutional Law; Entertainment Law; Contracts; Collective Bargaining

Favorite Legal Cases: Many of the transformative landmark cases that have changed the course of American life have emerged from the continuing struggles of people of color and other individuals who have been assigned to the margins of society. One noteworthy case that laid the foundation for diversity in the study of law is *Sweatt v. Painter* (1950). A recent series of cases in the area of juvenile law which include *Roper v. Simmons* (2005), *Miller v. Alabama* (2012) and *Montgomery v. Louisiana* (2016) also demonstrate and underscore the hope and potential for restorative, rehabilitative and even redemptive justice in the lives of youthful offenders.

Favorite Hobbies: Watching biographical documentaries and historical fiction films; Researching my family's genealogy; Playing the piano; Reading; Making short creative videos; Traveling

Favorite Attorney Role Model: Over the years, I have been most inspired by the clear and unwavering voice of advocacy of lawyer Marian Wright Edelman, president and founder of the Children's Defense Fund.

FAMILY AND BACKGROUND

Where Born and Raised: Born - Liberty, Texas; Raised - Cleveland, Texas

Family Socioeconomic and Educational Background:

My parents, William N. Thomas and Meta Garvey Thomas, were international students who immigrated to the United States from the Republic of Panamá in the late 1940s. They earned degrees from historically Black colleges Wiley College and Bishop College respectively, and graduate degrees from Prairie View A&M University. As educators and civic leaders, my parents were influential in shaping the lives of the people of Cleveland, a small town in Southeast Texas.

THE DECISION TO BECOME A LAWYER

When and Why I Decided to Become a Lawyer: I was inspired by the Honorable Barbara Jordan, lawyer and U.S. Congresswoman from Houston, Texas. Barbara Jordan's legal knowledge, oratory skills and superior understanding of the Constitution brought her to national prominence and also inspired me, as an impressionable teenager in a small town in Texas, to choose a career in law and to take up her challenge to work to "make America as good as its promise".

EDUCATIONAL ACHIEVEMENTS

High School: Cleveland High School (Cleveland, Texas)

College/University: Lamar University (Beaumont, Texas)

Undergraduate Degree: Bachelor of Science (B.S.)

Major: Government/Pre-Law

College Honors, Achievements and Activities: *Presidential Scholar,* Lamar University; *Member,* Pi Sigma Alpha, Zeta Lambda Chapter (National Political Science Honor Society); *Academic Recognition,* Dean's List; *Chair,* Forum Lecture Series; *Member,* Setzer Center Student Council; *Member,* Student Government Association

Law School: Howard University School of Law (Washington, D.C.)

Law Degree and Graduation Year: Juris Doctor/Doctor of Jurisprudence (J.D.) - Class of 1987

Law School Honors, Achievements and Activities: *Member,* Unemployment Poverty Action Council (Washington, D.C.)

PROFESSIONAL ACCOMPLISHMENTS

State Bar Membership (Where Licensed to Practice Law): Texas

Other Legal Experience: *Deputy General Counsel and Special Counsel,* Texas Juvenile Justice Department; General Civil Practice Attorney

Other Professional Work Experience: *Legal Education Program Coordinator,* Liberty County, Texas; *College Instructor,* Prairie View A&M University; *Non-Profit Foundation Development Associate,* Congressional Black Caucus Foundation; *Staff Assistant,* United States Congressman

Professional Organizations:

Chair and Section Council, Juvenile Law Section, State Bar of Texas; *Chair and Section Officer,* African American Lawyers Section, State Bar of Texas; *Member,* Texas Bar College, State Bar of Texas; *Member,* American Bar Association; *Member,* Houston Bar Association; *Member,* Liberty County Bar Association

Post-Law School Honors, Achievements, Activities, and Community Involvement:

City Council Member, City of Cleveland, Texas (1992-1998); *Mayor Pro-Tem,* City of Cleveland, Texas (1995-1998); *Gubernatorial Appointment,* Governor Anne Richards; *Attorney General Appointment,* Municipal Advisory Committee on Land Use; *Service Recognition,* Juvenile Law Section of the State Bar of Texas; *Service Recognition,* African American Lawyers Section, State Bar of Texas; *Awardee,* Barbara Jordan Lawyer - Legislator Award, Black History Committee, Cleveland, Texas; *Awardee,* Trailblazer Achievement Award, Cleveland, Texas; *Honoree,* Notable African Americans in Liberty County, Liberty County Historical Society; *Member,* Presidential Advisory Board, Wiley College Debate Program; *Legal Liaison,* Texas Violent Gang Task Force Advisory Board; *Member,* Interstate Compact for Juveniles State Council (Texas); *Member,* Statewide Disproportionality Task Force; *Member,* Board of Directors, Liberty County Children's Protective Services; *Member,* Board of Directors, Prosperity/Heritage Bank Business Development; *Member,* Board of Directors, Texas Association of Black City Council Members

LESSONS LEARNED: MY RECOMMENDATIONS FOR YOUR FUTURE ACTIONS BASED ON MY PAST EXPERIENCE

Advice on Law School Preparation:

Commit to doing your personal best now – wherever you are and whatever your current circumstance. Understand that preparation is an incremental endeavor (i.e., progress over time). Surround yourself with individuals, such as peer mentors or practicing lawyers who are pursuing or who have already achieved the key milestones and goals you have established for yourself.

Advice on Applying to and Selecting a Law School:

Motivational speaker Anthony Robbins says that "The only impossible journey is the one you never begin." Anyone who is spirited enough to pursue the study of law must take the first essential step of the journey – making the choice to apply to law school. Unlike other disciplines of study, a legal education touches every business and professional industry. The knowledge and experience gained will provide incredible opportunities in any field you choose.

I recommend three initial steps. First, assess your ultimate academic, financial and career objectives. Consider carefully what you want to get out of the law school experience and determine the key ingredients to your own individual success. Second, gather as much information about the law schools of interest. Third, align your personal goals and objectives with the strengths of the prospective law school. Find the best fit for you. You can learn a great deal by utilizing the law school recruitment infrastructure to network with current students. I also highly recommend participating in the National Black Pre-Law Conference. This well-known student networking conference is the perfect venue for an inspirational and informative 360-view of the law school application process.

Advice Regarding Academic Success, Co-Curricular and Extra-Curricular Participation, and Social Engagement in Law School:

Keep first things first – read, study, repeat. It will be necessary for many students to discard old study habits and refine their skills to meet the rigors of law school. One of the competencies you will need to master will be the art of synthesizing massive amounts of information in a meaningful way that complements your learning style. I believe that it is also critical to find a supportive team. My first introduction to the inner-workings of study groups came from the movie, *The Paper Chase*. Carefully select your "study buddies". These colleagues will be your winning team throughout the law school experience. Despite the demands of law school, participate in academic and co-curricular activities as well as service opportunities. An essential part of the law school experience is to fully engage in the greater community where you are studying. Finally, did I forget to say, "Have a little fun."? It will be important to keep your life balanced. Take care of yourself – eat well, sleep well, exercise and make time for spiritual fellowship and social interaction with friends.

Advice on Preparing for and Taking the Bar Exam:

Master key legal concepts and strengthen your writing and testing skills while you are in law school. Keep in mind that a bar preparation course is purely a supplemental tool to help you to become at ease with effective test-taking techniques, topic trends and subject review. Anyone attending a national law school should also become familiar with state-specific requirements and test subjects.

Advice on Achieving Career Success and Advancement:

Although your path toward career success and advancement will surely be unique, motivation can be derived from the life footprints of lawyers who have blazed trails ahead of us. Their professional choices can serve as inspiration and a template for your own success. There are numerous print and online journals and associational resources that contain biographical profiles of successful lawyers.

Advice on Overcoming the Additional Challenges Black Law Students Face:

Acknowledge the sacrifices that many have endured so that you can enjoy the special privilege of studying law at any institution that your talent and resources will allow. Do not take the experience for granted. Embrace our history of struggle and let it inform your level of commitment. Never forget that your life will always be transported in the direction of your interests, talent and energy. Embrace your own strength. Do not be deterred by the limited expectations of others, especially in the area of academic performance. To that end, continually strive to enhance your learning skills. Seek help early if you experience academic difficulties. Interface on a regular basis with law professors or student tutors and access helpful academic resources that may be available on campus.

Advice on Overcoming the Additional Challenges Black Lawyers Face:

African American lawyers often face public perceptions that are rooted in long-held racial and professional stereotypes. In the face of this dual burden, there is a corresponding individual responsibility to reshape and redefine these views - often one person at a time. In this effort, draw confidence in the fact that ours is a history of achievement in the face of struggle. We must embrace our unique role as lawyers and understand that the most compelling argument against any stereotype is excellence. Excellence in the legal profession is demonstrated through 1) the quality of our work; 2) a commitment to core values; 3) personal and professional integrity; 4) positive interactions with people of all backgrounds and experiences; and 5) a long-term commitment to public service.

Best Advice I Received Regarding Law School and the Legal Profession:

As I began the study of law, the advice I received took the form of encouragement and prayers of the people of my small hometown. When the challenges of the law school experience seemed overwhelming, I drew strength from the industrious elderly men and women of color in my community whose lives and career choices were limited only by history and the misfortune of timing. I will always remember the pride in their eyes as they encouraged me to "study hard and make us proud". Their encouragement and faith made my journey possible.

Worst Advice I Received Regarding Law School and the Legal Profession:

One of the biggest misconceptions relates to the so-called financial and material rewards of a career in law. The legal profession is a calling. Aspiring law students should have realistic expectations and work toward the greatest level of personal and professional satisfaction. Do what you love, and the rest will take care of itself.

Best Advice I Would Give to an Aspiring Black Lawyer:

As a lawyer in the new millennium, you are the inheritors and guardians of the proverbial "promised land" that Dr. Martin Luther King, Jr. spoke of in his famous final speech. Step forward and serve, not for accolades, but because it is the right thing to do. Recognize and embrace the new opportunities and challenges that will be presented in your lifetime.

Thoughts About Why Earning a Law Degree Is a Powerful Credential for African Americans and Why There Is a Need for More African American Lawyers:

As a life long student of the pivotal moments in American history, I have always drawn inspiration from the archival photographic images of Thurgood Marshall and his legal team standing victorious on the steps of the Supreme Court after the *Brown* decision; the former dean of my alma mater, Wiley A. Branton, Sr., whose work led to the successful desegregation of the University of Arkansas School of Law as well as images of other trailblazers such as Constance Baker Motley. At the height of their careers, these African American lawyers and others who are uncelebrated have transformed our nation and expanded opportunities for all people. Their achievements remind us of the ever-present need to cultivate a new cadre of lawyers who will do the day-to-day work as well as those who will rise up and take on the significant legal challenges that will come. Lawyers of the new millennium must recognize that you have a higher calling. Our rich heritage demands that we, within our sphere of influence, use the powerful credential of a law degree to realize the highest ideals of our global society.

Thoughts About Whether Law School Is Worth the Financial Investment:

The prevailing dictionary definition of the term investment is "the act of putting money, effort or time into an endeavor to make a profit, gain an advantage, or achieve a result." With respect to the law school experience, there will obviously be a financial investment as well as a significant personal expenditure of effort and time – three years of your life. As such, one of the first challenges that an aspiring lawyer must face will be to decide whether the life long benefits of a legal education outweigh the investment of funds, time and effort. You are the only person who is empowered to define and shape the particular advantages of the law degree you earn and how to best use the credential to change your life and the lives of others.

LEGACY AND SUCCESS

My Most Outstanding Accomplishment:

In 2018, I was awarded the Robert O. Dawson Visionary Leadership Award in Juvenile Justice by the State Bar of Texas, Juvenile Law Section. In many respects, this award was significant because it was an important culmination of my career. It is awarded to those who advocate for the state's juveniles and promote legislation advancing the juvenile justice system in Texas.

The Legacy I Hope to Leave:

There may never be a seminal existential moment when I will have absolute clarity on my purpose and legacy as a lawyer. Until then, my personal prayer is that my professional legacy will be characterized by untiring service to others. Most importantly, I hope that I will be counted among the lawyers who helped to bend, as Dr. King once said, the moral arc of the universe…just a little further toward justice.

The Secret to My Success:

Whatever I have accomplished in my life has been the sum total of my experiences as well as the culmination of the sacrifice, kindness, and wisdom of others - known and unknown - who have paved the way for me. In reality, there is no one "secret" to success. I can, however, think of one essential word that will help you to remember the key ingredient of success. Just remember the simple mnemonic concept of W-O-R-K to describe the fundamental characteristics needed to sustain your legal career: Wise - Seek wisdom and truth in all aspects of your life; Optimistic - Remain optimistic and know that all things work together for the good; Respectful - Respect the humanity of others - everyone has a story; and Knowledgeable - Strive to be a lifelong learner; knowledge is power.

Orlesia A. Tucker, Esq.
General Counsel
FBD Partnership, LP
San Antonio, Texas

"If I please God in all that I do, nothing else matters."

– Orlesia A. Tucker

Success is ... accomplishing goals that have been set, maintaining and nurturing those relationships that are important to me, and blessing others along the way.

PERSONAL FAVORITES

Favorite Quotes: "My mission in life is not merely to survive, but to thrive; and to do so with some passion, some compassion, some humor, and some style." - Maya Angelou

"Start where you are. Use what you have. Do what you can." - Arthur Ashe

Favorite Books: *The Woman Code* by Sophia Nelson; T.D. Jakes books; Self-help books

Favorite Movies: *The Color Purple; The Five Heartbeats; The Usual Suspects*

Favorite Musical Genres: Gospel music; R&B

Favorite Musical Artists: Yolanda Adams; Kirk Franklin; Prince; Stevie Wonder; Anita Baker

Favorite Law School Classes: Constitutional Law; Intellectual Property

Favorite Legal Case: *Brown v. Board of Education*

Favorite Hobbies: Traveling with family and friends; Cooking; Reading

Favorite Attorney Role Models: Justice Thurgood Marshall; Atticus Finch (fictional character in Harper Lee's *To Kill a Mockingbird*)

FAMILY AND BACKGROUND

Where Born and Raised: Born - Lackland Air Force Base, San Antonio, Texas; Raised - Houston, Texas (My dad was in the Air Force so we moved around a lot during my early years. We moved to Houston when I was 10 years old where I attended school through high school.)

Family (Spouse/Partner and Children): Spouse - Andre; Children - (daughters) Jordan, Amaris and Anaya

Family Socioeconomic and Educational Background: My parents have some college but did not graduate from college. I grew up with a single mom, lower middle class.

THE DECISION TO BECOME A LAWYER

When and Why I Decided to Become a Lawyer: I decided to become a lawyer my junior year in college after deciding I no longer wanted to pursue medical school with my biomedical engineering degree. At that time, a law degree was an alternative to a medical degree and the means by which I knew I could make a living after obtaining my degree.

EDUCATIONAL ACHIEVEMENTS

High School: Stratford High School (Houston, Texas)

College/University: Texas A&M University (College Station, Texas)

Undergraduate Degree: Bachelor of Science (B.S.)

Major: Biomedical Engineering

College Honors, Achievements and Activities: *Recipient,* President's Achievement Award; *Member,* Voices of Praise Gospel Choir; *Member,* Black Awareness Committee; *Member and Resident Advisor,* Xi Psi Chapter, Alpha Kappa Alpha Sorority, Inc.

Law School: South Texas College of Law Houston (Houston, Texas)

Law Degree and Graduation Year: Juris Doctor/Doctor of Jurisprudence (J.D.) - Class of 1997

Law School Honors, Achievements and Activities: *Recipient,* Aggie Bar Association Scholarship; *Regional Director,* Rocky Mountain Region, National Black Law Students Association; *Member,* Black Law Students Association, South Texas College of Law; *Member,* National Bar Association

PROFESSIONAL ACCOMPLISHMENTS

State Bar Membership (Where Licensed to Practice): Texas

Other Legal Experience: *Deputy General Counsel,* FBD Partnership, LP; *Of Counsel,* Alston Hunt Floyd & Ing, LLP; *Shareholder,* Graves Dougherty Hearon & Moody; *Associate,* Akin Gump Strauss Hauer & Feld, LLP

Professional Organizations: *Member,* San Antonio Bar Association; *Member,* Association of Corporate Counsel

Post-Law School Honors, Achievements, Activities, and Community Involvement: *Listed Honoree,* Super Lawyers, Litigation and Intellectual Property; *Class Member and Alumna,* Leadership Austin; *CASA Volunteer,* Court Appointed Special Advocates (CASA); *Board Member,* Volunteer Legal Services (VLS); *Board Member,* Reading Is Fundamental (RIF)

LESSONS LEARNED: MY RECOMMENDATIONS FOR YOUR FUTURE ACTIONS BASED ON MY PAST EXPERIENCE

Advice on Law School Preparation:

Work hard to maintain your grades while in college. If you don't like to write or don't consider yourself to be a good writer, take opportunities to write whether it's for the school newspaper or a student organization. Take on leadership roles in student organizations.

Advice on Applying to and Selecting a Law School:

Make your selection based on where you see yourself succeeding. I encourage you to talk to current law students to get a better understanding about the school. I also suggest taking a tour or shadowing a law student for a day.

Advice Regarding Academic Success, Co-Curricular and Extra-Curricular Participation, and Social Engagement in Law School:

Your law school experience will be very different from your college experience. During your first year, focus on mastering the concepts taught in those foundation classes (i.e., contracts, property). Take advantage of your professor's office hours. If you don't understand something, get help early.

Advice on Preparing for and Taking the Bar Exam:

Take a preparation course and practice taking exams under the same time constraints as the actual bar exam.

Advice on Seeking Legal Job Opportunities and/or Creating One's Own Opportunities:

While in law school, determine what area you want to pursue and meet lawyers who are practicing in that area. Whether it's a law firm, corporation, or non-profit organization, it's important that you find out what the expectations are of those employers as soon as possible so that your resume reflects those requirements. Never give up! When one door closes, another one will open. Most of my job opportunities came from knowing someone so I encourage you to meet the managing partner or general counsel of that law firm or corporation in which you are interested. In many cases, it does boil down to who you know and who knows you.

Advice on Achieving Career Success and Advancement:

Early on in your career, seek a mentor. That mentor doesn't necessarily have to be someone with whom you work. Don't rely on the mentor to nurture and grow the relationship. The relationship can only be what you make of it. Build relationships with those attorneys in your workplace and outside of your workplace by joining state bar committees or other organizations.

Advice on Overcoming the Additional Challenges Black Law Students and Black Lawyers Face:

Commit to yourself not to allow prejudice/discrimination/racism to stop you from accomplishing your goal of getting that law degree.

Know that at some point in your career, you will face some form of prejudice/discrimination/racism. It will be up to you to determine the best way to handle it.

Best Advice I Received Regarding Law School:

Work hard and always strive to produce quality work product.

Best Advice I Can Give An Aspiring Black Lawyer:

A career in law is full of so many possibilities. Before you pursue this path, make sure you have the ability to commit to the time that is required to succeed in law school.

Thoughts About Why Earning a Law Degree Is a Powerful Credential for African Americans:

A law degree can open so many doors whether you want to work for someone else or start your own business. There is a need for more African American lawyers because of our unique history and ability to empathize and relate to those in our community who need justice.

Thoughts About Whether and Why Law School Is Worth the Financial Investment:

Law school was a large financial investment, but it has paid off. I am pursuing the career I wanted, and I am being rewarded financially.

LEGACY AND SUCCESS

My Most Outstanding Accomplishments:

Personal: My supportive husband and two beautiful daughters.

Professional: Becoming the first African American shareholder at a firm where I was the only African American attorney at that time.

The Legacy I Hope to Leave:

I hope throughout my career, I have made a positive impact on the lives of others and motivated them to be better and do better.

The Secret to My Success:

My faith in God, hard work, and high ethical standards.

Practical Wisdom for Those on the Path to Lawyerhood

Twanda Turner-Hawkins, Esq.
Director
Global Litigation
Dematic Corp. and KION Americas
Atlanta, Georgia

"So many people want something; few will do what it takes to get it."
— Twanda Turner-Hawkins

Success is . . . being at peace in the center of God's will.

PERSONAL FAVORITES

Favorite Quote: "Injustice anywhere is a threat to justice everywhere. We are caught in an inescapable network of mutuality, tied in a single garment of destiny. Whatever affects one directly, affects all indirectly." - Dr. Martin Luther King, Jr., "Letter from the Birmingham Jail"

Favorite Books: *Underground Railroad* by Colson Whitehead; *Their Eyes Were Watching God* by Zora Neale Hurston; *Every Tongue Got to Confess* by Zora Neale Hurston; *I Know Why the Caged Bird Sings* by Maya Angelou; *The Five Love Languages* by Gary Chapman; *Why Nice Girls Finish Last* by Lois Frankel; *Man's Search for Meaning* by Viktor Frankl; *GRIT* by Angela Duckworth; *Marriage ROCKS for Christian Couples* by Harold L. Arnold

Favorite Movie: *Three the Hard Way*

Favorite Song: "You Say" by Lauren Daigle

Favorite Law School Class: Real Property Law

Favorite Legal Case: *Lee v. Macon County Board of Education*

Favorite Hobbies: Hiking; Dancing; Traveling abroad; Reading; Laughing with my family and friends; Cycling indoor and outside

Favorite Attorney Role Model: Fred Gray (Tuskegee, Alabama)

FAMILY AND BACKGROUND

Where Born and Raised: Born - Birmingham, Alabama; Raised - Boykin (also known as Gees Bend), Alabama

Family (Spouse/Partner and Children): Children - (son) Emerson Hawkins and (son) Christian Hawkins

Family Socioeconomic and Educational Background: My mother and father met in Birmingham, Alabama as my father hails from Talladega and my mother is from Gees Bend, Alabama. My mother was the daughter of a sharecropper who later became a farm owner. My mother was a teacher and my father worked at U.S. Steel while owning a taxi company with his identical twin brother. At the same time, my father owned and leased real estate. When I was five years old, my mother died from kidney disease. In fact, she was the first person to receive a kidney transplant from the University of Alabama Hospital in Birmingham, Alabama. When my mother died from complications due to pneumonia, my father received help raising us (five children) from my mother's parents. We lived on their 100-acre farm on the bend of the Alabama River and farmed during the school year and first part of summer. After each harvest, we lived with our father in Birmingham until school started each year. My grandfather was a powerful and smart man with only a grade school education. He was able to elevate himself from sharecropper to a farm owner and businessperson in the tumultuous, oppressive, and dangerous south. It was dangerous to be a successful Black man. He raised nine children before the five of us and my cousin came to live with them. We all went to college and my sister earned her doctorate. My father, mother, grandmother, and grandfather left an amazing legacy of strength and entrepreneurship. They valued education tremendously. My grandparents were married for more than 60 years; and raised 16 successful children while running a farm as a business.

THE DECISION TO BECOME A LAWYER

When and Why I Decided to Become a Lawyer: After undergraduate school, I was working as a claim adjuster and raising a family. I wanted more education; so as a result, I decided to go to law school at night solely for knowledge as power. I believed law would be the most impactful course of study for me because the law influenced every aspect of life. After law school, I continued my work as a claim adjuster; and later decided to practice law because I enjoyed law school so much!

EDUCATIONAL ACHIEVEMENTS

High School: Anne Manie Hill School (Anne Manie, Alabama)

College/University: Tuskegee Institute (Tuskegee, Alabama)

Undergraduate Degree: Bachelor of Science (B.S.)

Major: Dietetics

College Honors, Achievements and Activities: Graduated *cum laude* "with distinction"

Law School: Georgia State University College of Law (Atlanta, Georgia)

Law Degree and Graduation Year: Juris Doctor/Doctor of Jurisprudence (J.D.)

Law School Honors/Achievements/Activities: *Member,* Moot Court Society; *Member,* National Black Law Students Association; *Tutor,* Real Property Law

PROFESSIONAL ACCOMPLISHMENTS

State Bar Memberships (Where Admitted to Practice Law): Georgia; Illinois; Michigan; Pennsylvania

Other Legal Work Experience: *Corporate Defense Attorney,* Department Head and Leader, Allstate Insurance Company

Other Professional Work Experience: *Catastrophe Bodily Injury Claim Adjuster,* Allstate Insurance Company; *CEO and Founder,* The Executive Fitness Expert (coach busy professionals on how to live a healthy and fit lifestyle while excelling in a demanding career)

Professional Organizations:

Member, Coalition on Racial & Ethnic Justice, American Bar Association; *Executive Board Member,* National Bar Association; *Member,* Association of Corporate Counsel; *Chair,* Corporate Law Section, National Bar Association

Post-Law School Honors/Achievements/Activities/Community Involvement:

Honoree, Corporate Law Section of the Year, National Bar Association (2016 and 2019); *Honoree,* Outstanding Section of the Year, National Bar Association (2017); *Honoree,* Corporate Lawyer of the Year, Women's Lawyer Division, National Bar Association (2019); *Honoree,* Legal Education Access & Diversity Champion, National Black Pre-Law Conference and Law Fair (2019); *Awardee,* Cora T. Walker Corporate Partnership Award, National Bar Association (2017); *Awardee,* Distinguished Performance Award, Allstate Insurance Company (2010, 2011, 2012 and 2013); *Awardee,* Law and Regulations William C. Staszak Award for Teamwork and Leadership (2010); *Awardee,* Presidential Award, National Bar Association (2008, 2011, 2012, 2013, 2016, 2018 and 2019); *Board Member,* Chosen 300 (feeding the hungry); *Leader and Organizer,* True Rock Ministries (mentoring youth)

LESSONS LEARNED: MY RECOMMENDATIONS FOR YOUR FUTURE ACTIONS BASED ON MY PAST EXPERIENCE

Advice on Law School Preparation:

Prepare your family, friends, and your mind for law school. Before attending school, outline your current responsibilities; thereafter, determine how to share or eliminate some of them moving forward. Make creative plans to spend more quality time with your friends and family as the quantity will be limited somewhat. Prepare your mind and body by creating and following healthy plans. Incorporate a minimum of 30 minutes a day of working out. It will be tempting to skip working out because of your busy schedule. However, you owe it to yourself. Additionally, the workout will help your brain efficiently process and retain information. Finally, prepare to enjoy law school and get ready to settle into school with joy instead of thinking of your studies as a chore or task.

Advice on Applying to and Selecting a Law School:

As best you can, create your vision for post-law school. Your own personal vision will help you make decisions about which law school to attend. For example, if you want to work in an Am Law 100 law firm or a Fortune 100 corporation, what are the feeder law schools you should consider? If you want to serve on the U.S. Supreme Court, what should be your practice area after attending which law school?

Advice Regarding Academic Success, Co-Curricular and Extra-Curricular Participation, and Social Engagement in Law School:

Build a strong network with a couple of groups of your peers. They will be your colleagues of the future and you will need them in various industries, governments, and law practices. Participate in extra-curricular activities that will enhance your skills for your desired practice area and will start to build your network for post law school.

Advice on Preparing for and Taking the Bar Exam:

A prep course is a necessity; thereafter, try to plan a getaway to study for the bar with your study group.

Advice on Choosing a Job and Career Path Inside or Outside of the Legal Profession:

Ask practicing attorneys about career paths before attending law school and participate in bar association events to chart your path before attending law school. After setting your goals, aim even higher.

Advice on Seeking Legal Job Opportunities and/or Creating One's Own Opportunities:

Reach out to the networks you established in law school and mentors. Practice networking while still in school. Initially, attempting to network with seasoned attorneys and judges can be intimidating. However, many really love to help students and answer questions. Foster the relationships all the way through school and career development.

Advice on Achieving Career Success and Advancement:

Recognize from the onset that excellence is required; however, favor, branding, and internal advocates are equally important.

Advice on Overcoming the Additional Challenges Black Law Students and Lawyers Face:

Work hard, but smart; and always build coalitions.

Best Advice I Received Regarding Law School and the Legal Profession:

Seek great summer internships with organizations that will lead to a career with the organization.

Worst Advice I Received Regarding Law School and the Legal Profession:

There are too many lawyers and law school is too expensive.

Best Advice I Would Give to an Aspiring Black Lawyer:

Enjoy the journey while influencing lives in a positive way.

Thoughts About Why Earning a Law Degree Is a Powerful Credential for African Americans and Why There Is a Need for More African American Lawyers:

The world needs more African American lawyers in every practice of law and every industry as decision makers on policies and laws that will improve all communities, Black communities in particular.

Thoughts About Whether and Why Law School Is Worth the Financial Investment:

Law school is worth the financial investment. Knowledge is power. Your post law school goals will guide you in your decision-making on the law school tier to select and the cost.

LEGACY AND SUCCESS

My Most Outstanding Accomplishment:

My career as an attorney and leader. I have enjoyed the journey while influencing lives in a positive way.

The Legacy I Hope to Leave:

Courageous leadership while positively changing lives.

The Secret to My Success:

The ability to collaborate. The open and obvious reason for my success is God!

Artika R. Tyner, Esq., M.P.P., Ed.D.

Founding Director
University of St. Thomas Center on Race, Leadership and Social Justice
Clinical Faculty
University of St. Thomas
St. Paul, Minnesota

"A leader is a planter - a planter of ideas, seeds of change, and a vision for justice."

– Artika R. Tyner

Success is . . . the ability to make a positive impact on the lives of others and serve as a global citizen.

PERSONAL FAVORITES

Favorite Quote: "Service is the rent we pay to be living. It is the very purpose of life and not something you do in your spare time." - Marian Wright Edelman

Favorite Books: *Where Do We Go From Here: Chaos or Community* by Rev. Dr. Martin Luther King, Jr.; *Groundwork: Charles Hamilton Houston and the Struggle for Civil Rights* by Genna Rae McNeil; *Root and Branch: Charles Hamilton Houston, Thurgood Marshall, and the Struggle to End Segregation* by Rawn James Jr.; *Just Mercy: A Story of Justice and Redemption* by Bryan Stevenson; *Love Leadership: The New Way to Lead in a Fear-Based World* by John Hope Bryant; *The New Jim Crow: Mass Incarceration in the Age of Colorblindness* by Michelle Alexander; *The Sea Is So Wide and My Boat Is So Small: Charting a Course for the Next Generation* by Marian Wright Edelman

Favorite Movies: *Simple Justice; Just Mercy; Selma; Long Walk to Freedom; Great Debaters; Amazing Grace; Iron Ladies of Liberia; Slavery by Another Name*

Favorite Music Genres: Gospel music; Blues; Rhythm and blues (R&B)

Favorite Musical Artists: Mahalia Jackson; Soweto Gospel Choir; Luther Vandross; Whitney Houston; Koko Taylor; B.B. King; Muddy Waters; Motown Artists

Favorite Law School Classes: Real Estate Transactional Law; Tax; Race in the Law; Family Law Clinic

Favorite Legal Cases: *Dred Scott v. Sandford; Brown v. Board of Education; Plessy v. Ferguson*

Favorite Hobbies: Volunteering in the community; Baking; Traveling abroad; Learning about new cultures; Visiting museums; Studying civil rights history; Developing social enterprises and business ventures

Favorite Attorney Role Model: Justice Alan C. Page (Minnesota Supreme Court)

FAMILY AND BACKGROUND

Where Born and Raised: St. Paul, Minnesota

Family Socioeconomic and Educational Background: I am a first-generation college student and law school graduate. I grew up in a "poor" household that was filled with riches due to my mother's love.

THE DECISION TO BECOME A LAWYER

When and Why I Decided to Become a Lawyer: I decided to become a lawyer after my student teaching experience. As a student teacher, I recognized that education is the passport for the future (Malcolm X) but for far too many students of color this passport was permanently revoked. There was the young Black boy in my kindergarten classroom who struggled to read at grade level through no fault of his own. He never had access to early childhood education. He was not alone - 96% of eligible children never have the chance to attend programs like Head Start. When he struggled, we all struggled. Our children are broken.

It became clear to me at the intersection of race and poverty - our policies are broken. I had a choice to make. I could stand on the sidelines and observe the problems, or I could be a part of the solution. I believe all life is interconnected so I decided to be the change by becoming a lawyer. I recognized that the law is a language of power. I needed to learn this language in order to ensure that my community had access to their rights and a voice to shape their destiny.

EDUCATIONAL ACHIEVEMENTS

High School: Highland Park Sr. High School (St. Paul, Minnesota)

College/University: Hamline University (St. Paul, Minnesota)

Undergraduate Degree: Bachelor of Arts (B.A.)

Major: English

College Honors, Achievements and Activities: Page Education Scholar; *Member,* Phi Beta Kappa (America's most prestigious honor society); *Recipient,* Presidential Scholarship; *Writing Consultant,* Writing Center; *Events Editor and Staff Writer,* Oracle; *Internship,* Relational Perspectives on Conflict, Greenwich Mediation Center

Law School: University of St. Thomas School of Law (St. Paul, Minnesota)

Law Degree and Graduation Year: Juris Doctor/Doctor of Jurisprudence (J.D.) - Class of 2006

Law School Honors, Achievements and Activities: *Recipient,* Leonard Street Deinard Diversity Scholar (academic scholarship); *Mission Award Recipient,* Scholarly Engagement and Societal Reform, University of Saint Thomas (2006); *Mission Award Recipient,* Professional Preparation, University of Saint Thomas School of Law (2006); *Mission Award Recipient,* Living the Mission, University of Saint Thomas School of Law (2005); *Judicial Externship,* Judge Schellhas, Hennepin County District Court (2005); *Crime and Justice Externship,* Council on Crime and Justice (2005); *Certified Student Attorney,* Family Law Clinic, Interprofessional Center

Other Graduate and Professional Degrees: Doctorate in Leadership (Ed.D.), University of St. Thomas College of Education, Leadership and Counseling (St. Paul, Minnesota); Master of Public Policy and Leadership (M.P.P.), University of St. Thomas School of Education (St. Paul, Minnesota)

Additional Education: *Participant,* Economic Development and Urbanization in East China Seminar, East China Normal University (Shanghai, China); Mini-Masters in Investment Real Estate, University of St. Thomas Opus College of Business; Certificate, Fundraising and Development, University of St. Thomas Opus College of Business

PROFESSIONAL ACCOMPLISHMENTS

State Bar Membership (Where Licensed to Practice Law): Minnesota

Other Legal Experience: *Law Professor, Clinical Law Fellow,* University of St. Thomas School of Law

Other Professional Work Experience: *Assistant Professor,* University of St. Thomas College of Education, Leadership and Counseling; *Associate Vice President of Diversity and Inclusion,* University of St. Thomas; *Director of Diversity,* University of St. Thomas School of Law; *Commercial Banker,* US Bank; *Optician,* Target Optical; *Museum Exhibit Development,* Science Museum of Minnesota

Professional Organizations: *Fellow,* American Council on Education; *Facilitator,* World Academy for the Future of Women (China); *Advisory Board Member,* Children's Defense Fund-Minnesota; *Member,* Emancipation Proclamation Committee, Minnesota African American Museum; *Board Member,* ABA Council for Racial and Ethnic Diversity in the Educational Pipeline, American Bar Association; *Member,* GP|Solo Committee, Solo, Small Firm and General Practice Division, American Bar Association; *Member,* Diversity Committee, American Bar Association; *Member,* Publications Committee, American Bar Association; *Member,* Pro Bono Committee, American Bar Association

Post-Law School Honors, Achievement, Activities and Community Involvement: *Awardee,* Minnesota Lawyer Diversity and Inclusion Award (2018); *Awardee,* Women in Business Award, Minneapolis/St. Paul Business Journal; *Awardee,* International Educator Citizenship Award, International Leadership Institute (2018); *Awardee,* Difference Maker Award, American Bar Association (2018); *Good Neighbor Honoree,* WCCO (2018); *Friend of Community Finalist,* Mshale African Award (2017); *Listed Honoree,* Top 100 Under 50, Diversity MBA (2017); *Awardee,* Denise A. King Award, Wilder Foundation (2017); *Honoree,* American Small Business Champion, SCORE Mentors/Sam's Club (2017); *Awardee,* Kay Pranis Restorative Justice Award, Dispute Resolution Center (2016); *Emerging Scholar,* Self-Sufficiency Research Clearinghouse (January-March 2015); *Writing Fellow,* Ms. JD (2015); *Fellow,* American Bar Foundation (2014); *Awardee,* Community Service Award, Mentoring Young Adults (2014); *Awardee,* Outstanding Commitment Award (Diversity), University of St. Thomas (2013); *Honoree,* Minnesota African American Heritage Society (2013); *Honoree,* Hall of Fame, Highland Park Senior High School (2011); *Awardee,* First Decade Alumni Award, Hamline University (2010); *Awardee,* Dean's Award for Outstanding Teacher, University of St. Thomas School of Law (2010); *Awardee,* Up and Coming Attorney Award, Minnesota Lawyer (2009); Faculty/Staff Award, Black Law Student Association (2007); *Member,* The Woman's Club of Minneapolis; *Senior Mentor and Founding Member,* Alumni Society, Page Education Foundation; *Advisory Board Member,* African American Baby Project Coalition; *Volunteer,* Law and Democracy Initiative, Books for Africa

LESSONS LEARNED: MY RECOMMENDATIONS FOR YOUR FUTURE ACTIONS BASED ON MY PAST EXPERIENCE

Advice on Making the Choice to Apply to and Attend Law School:

Law school will provide you with the opportunity to make a difference in the world. You will gain the practical skills needed to problem solve and create practical solutions to some of the most pressing social justice issues of our time.

Advice on Law School Preparation:

I would recommend finding a mentor who is a lawyer. I also recommend taking courses which provide you with the opportunity to develop core legal competencies such as research, writing, analytical, and oral advocacy skills. You should also take an LSAT test preparation course.

Advice on Applying to and Selecting a Law School:

Narrowly tailor your personal statement to each individual school based upon your interest in this particular school. Participate in a tour of each law school, meet the admissions team, and attend a class session. Build a connection with the diverse student associations.

Advice Regarding Academic Success, Co-Curricular and Extra-Curricular Participation, and Social Engagement in Law School:

During your first year, focus on your academics, invest time in learning the new content and develop your test-taking skills. Remember, law school classes are like building blocks. For example, in contracts class if you do not understand the concept of an "offer", then you will have difficulty in evaluating whether a contract is valid. Therefore, understanding each key concept is essential for developing your working knowledge of a given subject area.

Seek the guidance of your professors early and often. As a professor, I can attest to the fact that most students do not maximize office hours. This is a great opportunity to receive additional support with learning new concepts and applying your knowledge.

Advice on Preparing for and Taking the Bar Exam:

Take a test preparation course. Practice taking exams under the actual time constraints.

Advice on Achieving Career Success and Advancement:

Mentorship - Your mentor will aid you in gaining a deeper understanding of your organizational culture and professional identity.

Coaching - Consider enlisting the support of a coach in order to strengthen your professional platform. A coach will assist you with discovering your full potential and implementing your professional development plan.

Networking - It is important to build a strong network of colleagues across sectors and disciplines.

Advice on Overcoming the Additional Challenges Black Law Students and Lawyers Face:

Know your self-worth: Your self-worth will provide the intrinsic motivation to excel in your career. Your self-worth is defined by your strengths, talents and drive.

Develop your signature brand: In building your brand, you will discover the "value-added" that you bring to your organization, the legal profession, and the world, at large.

Best Advice I Received Regarding Law School and the Legal Profession:

Develop your Mission Statement: Every organization has a mission statement or statement of purpose. It is also important to have your personal statement of purpose at the forefront of your daily agenda. What do you seek to accomplish? What does career success look like? By answering these questions, I gained new insights into how to advance my personal mission of empowering the next generation of students to serve and lead.

Create a Personal Board of Directors: The Board of Directors protect the prosperity of an organization. They have a fiduciary duty to provide oversight and exercise due diligence. This same type of support is needed in your personal life. You need people in your life who will offer encouragement, correction and guidance.

LEGACY AND SUCCESS

My Most Outstanding Accomplishments:

During my TEDx Talk, I opened with the question: What is in your hands to make a difference in the world? I challenge my students to explore this question while also challenging myself to take action. As a result, I discovered my power as a lawyer, entrepreneur, author, and speaker. I developed a nonprofit which focuses on promoting literacy and diversity in books. As a result, our team developed and produced a children's book on leadership and social justice entitled "Justice Makes a Difference: The Story of Miss Freedom Fighter, Esquire"; Launched a "Leaders are Readers" Campaign and donated 1,000 copies of our book "Justice Makes a Difference"; Partnered with local retailers and donated over 1,500 books and cases of school supplies; Inspired 5,000+ children around the world through our school visits.

The Legacy I Hope to Leave:

I build my legacy each day through the lives of my students. I seek to provide them with the tools to discover the leader within and make a positive impact in the world.

The Secret to My Success:

Faith - My role as a lawyer is deeply rooted in my faith. I was blessed with gifts and talents. It is my responsibility to use these gifts to leave the world a better place than how I found it. My motto is found in Micah 6:8: Act justly, love mercy and walk humbly with your God.

My village - I have a strong network of supporters (family, friends, colleagues) who have empowered and inspired me to serve and lead in the global community.

Gerald L. Walden, Jr., Esq., M.B.A.
Head of Legal
The Fresh Market, Inc.
Greensboro, North Carolina

"Don't talk about what you're going to do . . . go do it!"
– Gerald L. Walden, Jr.

Success is . . . having (i) a relationship with God, (ii) family and friends who love and support you, (iii) a fulfilling career, and (iv) the desire to share how you've attained all of the above to help someone else achieve the same.

PERSONAL FAVORITES

Favorite Quote: "Life's most persistent and urgent question is, 'what are you doing for others?'" – Dr. Martin Luther King, Jr.

Favorite Book: *The Audacity of Hope* by President Barack Obama

Favorite Movies: *The Color Purple; Boomerang;* All Marvel Comics movies

Favorite Music Genres: Essentially all 90s R&B and Neo-Soul; Modern R&B; Gospel; Pop; Rap; Country; Soul; Smooth jazz

Favorite Musical Artists: Fantasia; Tasha Cobb-Leonard; LeAndria Johnson; Marvin Sapp; Maroon 5; P!nk; Jay-Z; Biggie Smalls; Carrie Underwood; Sade

Favorite Law School Classes: Contracts; Civil Procedure; Fundamentals of Taxation; Appellate Advocacy; Civil Litigation

Favorite Legal Cases: Brown v. The Board of Education; Loving v. Virginia

Favorite Hobbies: Mentoring minority students; Dancing; Traveling; Binge watching TV series on Netflix, Hulu, etc.

Favorite Attorney Role Models: Thurgood Marshall; Mary E. Wright and Thomas M. Ringer (my former law school professors); The Honorable Patricia Timmons-Goodson (former North Carolina Supreme Court Justice); The Honorable Henry E. Frye (former North Carolina Supreme Court Chief Justice)

FAMILY AND BACKGROUND

Where Born and Raised: Hampton, Virginia

Family (Spouse/Partner and Children): Spouse - Saranah; Child - (daughter) Emily

Family Socioeconomic and Educational Background: I grew up in a lower middle-class household with tremendously supportive parents and extended family members. Both parents were college-educated, as well as much of my extended family (many of whom were educators). As a result, there was never any doubt that I would attend college.

THE DECISION TO BECOME A LAWYER

When and Why I Decided to Become a Lawyer: The idea of becoming a lawyer first materialized for me in eighth grade when my language arts teacher, Ms. Whitaker, had our class put certain characters in a Shakespearean play on trial. I was assigned the role of the prosecuting attorney and did so well that I made one of the "witnesses" cry! Years later, after graduating from college with a mechanical engineering degree and starting my career in that field,

I soon realized that I did not see myself as an engineer for the rest of my life. Thus, I recalled that eighth grade experience, as well as more recent stories from friends who were in law school and enjoying it, and decided . . . why not!

EDUCATIONAL ACHIEVEMENTS

High School: Phoebus High School (Hampton, Virginia)

College/University: North Carolina Agricultural & Technical (A&T) State University (Greensboro, North Carolina)

Undergraduate Degree: Bachelor of Science (B.S.)

Major: Mechanical Engineering

College Honors, Achievements and Activities: Graduated *summa cum laude* "with highest distinction"; *Academic Recognition,* Dean's List; General Electric Scholar; NASA Scholar; *Awardee,* National Collegiate Engineering Award; *Member,* Tau Beta Pi Engineering Honor Society; *Member and Vice President,* Pi Tau Sigma Mechanical Engineering Honor Society; *Member and President,* Virginia Aggie Club

Law School: North Carolina Central University (NCCU) School of Law (Durham, North Carolina)

Law Degree and Graduation Year: Juris Doctor/Doctor of Jurisprudence (J.D.) – Class of 2001

Law School Honors, Achievements and Activities: Honors Graduate; *Academic Recognition,* Dean's List; *Comment Editor,* NCCU Law Journal; NCCU Scholar; *Awardee,* 2001 NCCU Law Leadership & Scholarship Award; *2L and 3L Class President,* Student Bar Association; *Listed Honoree,* Who's Who: American Law Students; *Awardee,* Floyd B. McKissick Excellence in Leadership Award; *Law Student Recruiter,* Admissions Office, North Carolina Central University School of Law; *Recipient,* George H. White Bar Scholarship

Other Graduate or Professional Degree: Master of Business Administration (M.B.A.), Elon University Martha and Spencer Love School of Business (Elon, North Carolina)

PROFESSIONAL ACCOMPLISHMENTS

State Bar Membership (Where Admitted to Practice Law): North Carolina

Other Legal Work Experience: *Director of Externships and Adjunct Clinical Professor,* General Externship Program, North Carolina Central University (NCCU) School of Law; *Judicial Law Clerk,* The North Carolina Court of Appeals

Other Professional Work Experience: *Manufacturing Engineer & Production Supervisor,* Siemens Automotive

Professional Organizations: *Board Member,* Elon University School of Law Advisory Board; *Board Member,* Greensboro Bar Association; *Former President and Treasurer,* Guilford County Association of Black Lawyers; *Board Member,* National Employment Law Council; *Former Board Member,* North Carolina Bar Association (NCBA) Board of Governors; *Former Board Member,* Corporate Counsel Section, North Carolina Bar Association (NCBA); *Former Chair,* NCBA's Minorities in the Profession; *Board Member,* North Carolina Central University School of Law Board of Visitors

Post-Law School Honors, Achievements, Activities, and Community Involvement: *Awardee,* Outstanding Legal Advocate Award, Guilford County Association of Black Lawyers (2018); *Listed Honoree,* 50 Most Influential African Americans in the Piedmont Triad, Black Enterprise Ink Magazine (2018); *Honoree,* Corporate Counsel of the Year Hall of Fame, Legal Elite, Business North Carolina Magazine; *Honoree,* Leader in the Law, North Carolina Lawyers Weekly (2015); *Honoree,* Citizen Lawyer Award, North Carolina Bar Association (NCBA) (2013); *Member,* Elon University Black Life Advisory Council; *Member,* Greensboro Rotary Club; *Board Member,* Guilford College Board of Visitors; *Former Chair and Member,* Guilford County Juvenile Crime Prevention Council; *Member,* Burlington Alumni Chapter, Kappa Alpha Psi Fraternity, Inc.; *Board Member,* North Carolina A&T State University Board of Visitors; *Former Board Member,* Triad Health Project Executive Board

LESSONS LEARNED: MY RECOMMENDATIONS FOR YOUR FUTURE ACTIONS BASED ON MY PAST EXPERIENCE

Advice on Law School Preparation:

- Seek an undergraduate major and/or opportunities that will allow you to obtain a strong background in reading comprehension and writing.

- Talk to current law school students and practicing attorneys to obtain realistic short-term and long-term expectations regarding the rigors of law school and the practice of law itself.

- Take a Law School Admission Test (LSAT) preparation course and take that course seriously!

Advice on Applying to and Selecting a Law School:

- Have a general idea of the type of law you'd like to practice, in what type of environment (i.e., firm, in-house, government, etc.) and the geographic location. While one or all of these things may change in the years to come, your answers to those questions can help you narrow down a vast list of law school choices.

- Research each school's bar passage rate and career service placement statistics to get a sense of how the school may prepare students for bar passage and the ability of students to find employment.

- Gain insight into the school's alumni network to determine if there are alumni in locations and/or working in areas of law that are of interest to you. Networking should start early and those alumni can play a major role in helping you obtain future mentors and/or employment opportunities.

Advice Regarding Academic Success, Co-Curricular and Extra-Curricular Participation, and Social Engagement in Law School:

Law school requires tremendous dedication, focus and perseverance, especially during the first year as you learn ideas and concepts that are completely foreign. Therefore, do not try to overexert yourself during that first year by taking on a number of other activities. You should however, identify one or two things that will allow you to "escape" and prevent burnout (i.e., reading, exercising, etc.). Your second and third years will provide greater opportunities to engage in activities outside of the classroom, and I would suggest taking advantage of them particularly, with respect to activities that could reap future benefits (i.e., joining the law journal, moot court or the local bar association; attending attorney-law student mixers and networking events, etc.).

Advice on Preparing for and Taking the Bar Exam:

- Sign up for a bar preparation course that will complement your learning style (i.e., do you need live classes or will online videos suffice?).
- Take practice exams (preferably, actual past bar exams) under timed conditions and consider asking your law school professors or attorney mentors to review your sample essay responses.
- Treat the bar preparation like a job; commit to studying for a certain number of hours (at least eight) every day blocking out all distractions during that time.

Advice on Choosing a Job and Career Path Inside or Outside of the Legal Profession:

Any legal experience is good experience and will assist you with honing your craft. However, if there is a goal you are seeking, such as being an in-house counsel, the employment opportunities sought should be in areas that are most beneficial to being in that role (i.e., contracts experience would be very valuable, but criminal law experience would be less valuable). While jobs outside the legal profession are not as preferred if you want to be a practicing attorney, opportunities that provide a legal component or exposure (i.e., compliance or licensing roles) allowing you to continue growing in the law could be strong alternatives until you are able to secure that attorney position.

Advice on Seeking Legal Job Opportunities and/or Creating One's Own Opportunities:

Be informed. There are pros and cons regarding seeking legal job opportunities with others (as an employee) or creating your own opportunities (as your own boss). Weigh those against your goals and/or current life challenges/situations and seek the opportunities that most closely align with them.

Advice on Achieving Career Success and Advancement:

- Take on tasks that are unfamiliar, unknown, or even in areas that you believe you may not like. Do not rule something out before trying it first.
- Learn to self-promote (without being cocky . . . there is a fine balance). If you do not advocate for yourself, you cannot expect others to do it for you.

Advice on Overcoming the Additional Challenges Black Law Students and Lawyers Face: Seek out opportunities – make it your mission to find (or even make) opportunities for yourself with your employer, in your community, on boards, etc. Learn to be resourceful like the generations of African Americans who came before us who had far fewer opportunities than we have today.

Best Advice I Received Regarding Law School and the Legal Profession:

- In Law School: If possible, become a sales representative for a bar preparation entity because those individuals are often able to obtain the courses for significantly discounted rates or for free.
- In the Legal Profession: Be malleable. A significant number of attorneys are not practicing the type of law they originally intended due to (i) a limited number or lack of opportunities, (ii) the needs of their employer, and/or (iii) the needs of the economy.

Worst Advice I Received Regarding Law School and the Legal Profession:

"You'll hate it! Law school is no fun, and you'll work continuously as a lawyer with no work-life balance." I personally enjoyed my law school experience immensely. I had wonderful professors and amazing classmates who are some of my best friends over 20 years later. Also, while the hours can sometimes be grueling as a practicing attorney, there is such variety in the types of legal jobs and work environments available that it is certainly possible for attorneys to find the right work-life balance mix that is ideal for them.

Best Advice I Would Give to an Aspiring Black Lawyer:

Do not let someone else decide your quality as a lawyer based on your race, your background or what law school you attended. You are good enough so be the author of your own story and let the naysayers read it!

Thoughts About Why Earning a Law Degree Is a Powerful Credential for African Americans and Why There Is a Need for More African American Lawyers:

A law degree is a powerful credential for anyone but most definitely African Americans. As a people who have historically had the law used against us resulting in all too frequent disastrous outcomes, knowing our rights and being able to navigate and understand the legal landscape is invaluable. Also, as in all professions, having racial diversity present in the room changes the conversation and causes individuals/professions to consider ideas, positions and alternatives they may have otherwise never considered.

Thoughts About Whether and Why Law School Is Worth the Financial Investment:

Law school is one of the ultimate long games. While it happens for some, a vast majority of law school graduates do not leave law school and immediately secure a six-figure salary. However, as legal acumen grows over time, so do the available professional and financial opportunities which make that initial financial investment worthwhile. Further, if the desired career path is one that historically pays a lower salary as a lawyer, that should be taken into consideration when evaluating the tuition costs of prospective law schools.

LEGACY AND SUCCESS

My Most Outstanding Accomplishment:

Professionally, my most outstanding accomplishment is achieving the position of head of legal at my current place of employment. It was not a position I was even sure I wanted for several years (or thought I would be considered for), but I put in the work, intentionally diversified my legal experiences and areas of practice within the company, and built relationships that would position me for the role in case the opportunity presented itself. Knowing I had done all of the above, I ultimately was not afraid to <u>ask</u> for the position when it became available (because a "closed mouth does not get fed" as the old saying goes). It is not an easy role, but I enjoy the work and the challenges.

The Legacy I Hope to Leave:

While I am very pleased to have obtained a certain level of success and recognition as an attorney, the legacy I hope to leave is related to the law students I have taught, mentored or advised over my legal career. I've had the pleasure of personally mentoring at least 20 students through law school and beyond, teaching over 300 law students during my tenure as an adjunct clinical law professor, and speaking to thousands of aspiring and current law students as a keynote speaker, panelist, or moderator for numerous programs. Throughout these opportunities, I hope I have encouraged these students to do all the things I've tried to do and more, and then ultimately give back to those coming after them.

The Secret to My Success:

The secret to my "success" is being my own brand ambassador. Unfortunately, I have never had an official "mentor" or "sponsor" as an attorney – someone to help guide me along my journey in the law or promote me to others. However, I believe I possess a keen sense of what works and what doesn't, as well as identifying a path to get there. For me, that included: working in several areas of the law to secure a diverse knowledge base; joining numerous volunteer organizations and boards that were truly of interest to me (while **simultaneously** offering great networking opportunities); and working as hard on them as I did my full-time job; securing leadership roles in those organizations and boards; going outside of my comfort zone to serve on panels and as a keynote speaker; becoming comfortable talking about myself and my accomplishments without being boastful; and seeking nominations and even being selected for awards and recognitions where I believed I met the qualifications. A close friend of mine said it best, "Who is this product called *you*?" I know who I am and what I want my brand to be; therefore, I am in the best position to serve as my own ambassador.

Asha White, Esq.
Deputy Chief of the Criminal Bureau
Massachusetts Office of the Attorney General
Boston, Massachusetts

"Power is as much an illusion as it is real. Stare your fears in the eye, never allow others to impart their own fears onto you, and the strength of your character will be as powerful as any title, position or possession."

– Asha White

Success is . . . the freedom and ability to protect your family, have the career you want, and live your life in the way you choose.

PERSONAL FAVORITES

Favorite Quotes: "It is not light we need but fire; it is not the gentle shower, but thunder. We need the storm, the whirlwind and the earthquake." - Frederick Douglass

"Nothing discloses real character like the use of power. It is easy for the weak to be gentle. Most people can bear adversity. But if you wish to know what a man really is, give him power." - Robert Ingersoll

Favorite Books: *Night* by Elie Wiesel; *Black Boy* by Richard Wright; *The Odyssey* by Homer; *The Autobiography of Malcolm X* by Alex Haley; *Things Fall Apart* by Chinua Achebe; *Animal Farm* by George Orwell; *The Godfather* by Mario Puzo; *Dreams from My Father: A Story of Race and Inheritance* by Barack Obama

Favorite Movies: *Star Wars*; *Casino*; *The Godfather*; *The Godfather Part II*; *Usual Suspects*; *Coming to America*; *Hoop Dreams*

Favorite Musical Artists: Nas; KRS-ONE; Slick Rick; Sam Cooke; Marvin Gaye; Buju Banton; Bob Marley; Leon Bridges; J.Cole

Favorite Law School Classes: Criminal Procedure; Criminal Advocacy Clinic; Negotiation; Constitutional Law; Race and American Law; Moot Court; Trusts and Estates

Favorite Legal Cases: *Miranda v. Arizona*; *Dred Scott v. Sandford*; *Mapp v. Ohio*; *Marbury v. Madison*; *Crawford v. Washington*

Favorite Hobbies: Reading; Watching boxing; Teaching Trial Advocacy; Exercising; Coaching my kids in basketball and baseball

Favorite Attorney Role Models: Thurgood Marshall; Johnnie Cochran; Barry Scheck; Ronald Sullivan

FAMILY AND BACKGROUND

Where Born and Raised: Born - St. Thomas, U.S. Virgin Islands; Raised - Providence, Rhode Island

Family (Spouse/Partner and Children): Spouse - Fabiola; Children - Amari, Avani and Ahsir

Family Socioeconomic and Educational Background: I was born on the island of St. Thomas in the U.S. Virgin Islands to two loving parents and a large extended family. At the time, both of my parents were high school teachers who were legendary in the local community for their commitment to the growth of local youth on the island. From the start, they instilled in my older brother and me a love of education and an understanding that those who can, must serve their communities.

When I was three years old, my family and I moved to Providence, Rhode Island, where both my parents attained graduate degrees from Brown University. What was intended to be a short stint in the United States became a lifelong stay. I can vividly recall watching both my parents cross the stage to receive their doctoral degrees and the pride they had in being the first people in both their families to accomplish such a feat. The chance to watch my parents work their way up to better lives left an indelible imprint on me as to what can be achieved when opportunity is combined with effort.

However, the most important part of my childhood was the opposing worlds I saw inside my home and outside my home. This dual existence gave me a special insight into how the lives of individuals are shaped by the people, groups, ideas, and institutions that surround us. Since my parents had limited income as they tried to finish school with two children, we lived in poor and working-class neighborhoods in the city. While my home life was stable, the homes of many of my friends were not. When I left my house every day, I saw children who wandered the streets with no supervision, constant confrontations between young people, and a general disorganization that marred the lives of so many of my peers. Bearing daily witness to the differences between my circumstances and those of my peers had a dizzying effect on me. This led many people to become involved with the legal system later in life.

THE DECISION TO BECOME A LAWYER

When and Why I Decided to Become a Lawyer: I decided to become a lawyer at about 13 years old after learning about the Supreme Court in civics class. That decision was solidified at 16 years old when I enrolled in a Law & Society class during my junior year in high school and watched the O.J. Simpson trial. My desire to become a lawyer was based on one overarching goal: ensuring a just society through equal access and fair treatment in our legal system. Ideally, a just society is one that conforms to evolving standards of fairness, reason, equality and morality. It has been, and continues to be, my life's goal to help provide the same access to resources and justice to all people regardless of their starting point in life.

EDUCATIONAL ACHIEVEMENTS

High School: Classical High School (Providence, Rhode Island)

College/University: Boston College (Chestnut Hill, Massachusetts)

Undergraduate Degree: Bachelor of Arts (B.A.)

Major: Sociology

College Honors, Achievements and Activities: *Assistant Director of Social & Cultural Issues,* Undergraduate Government, Boston College; *Executive Staff Member,* Undergraduate Government, Boston College; *Member,* AHANA (People of African, Hispanic, Asian, and Native American Descent) Leadership Council

Law School Degree: Northeastern University School of Law (Boston, Massachusetts)

Law Degree and Graduation Year: Juris Doctor/Doctor of Jurisprudence (J.D.) - Class of 2004

Law School Honors, Achievements and Activities: *Team Member/Winner,* Northeast Regional Best Brief Award, Frederick Douglass Moot Court Competition; *Team Member/Winner,* Northeast Regional Champions, Frederick Douglass Moot Court Competition; *Team Member/Winner,* National Third Place, Frederick Douglass Moot Court Competition; *Team Member/Winner,* National Best Brief Award, Frederick Douglass Moot Court Competition

PROFESSIONAL ACCOMPLISHMENTS

State Bar Membership (Where Admitted to Practice Law): Massachusetts

Other Legal Work Experience: *Assistant Clerk Magistrate,* Boston Municipal Court-Dorchester Division; *Attorney,* The Law Office of White & White; *Attorney,* The Law Office of Asha Z. White; *Assistant Corporation Counsel,* City of Boston Law Department; *Assistant District Attorney,* Suffolk County District Attorney's Office

Other Professional Work Experience: *Adjunct Professor,* Suffolk University (Subject Taught: Intro to Criminal Justice)

Professional Organizations: *Member,* Massachusetts Black Lawyers Association; *President-Elect,* Massachusetts Black Lawyers Association

Post-Law School Honors, Achievements, Activities, and Community Involvement: *Honoree,* Prosecutor of the Year, Suffolk County District Attorney's Office (2005)

LESSONS LEARNED: MY RECOMMENDATIONS FOR YOUR FUTURE ACTIONS BASED ON MY PAST EXPERIENCE

Advice on Law School Preparation:

There is not one definitive single path to law school. You can major in any subject and go to law school. Almost everyone starts from scratch on day one. However, if you can, write as much as possible. Learning to write well will be an invaluable benefit for any first-year law student.

Advice on Applying to and Selecting a Law School:

Law schools are very selective so it is important to apply to as many as possible. Like the college [selection] process, consider the academic reputation and region of each school and the financial resources that they offer. Also consider clinical, externship and other "real world" opportunities each school has.

Advice Regarding Academic Success, Co-Curricular and Extra-Curricular Participation, and Social Engagement in Law School:

The first year of law school is difficult and is the equivalent of learning a foreign language. Moreover, you are taught a whole new way to think. In your first year, focus on your studies full time and only join activities that support you academically. Once you get acclimated to the demands of law school, there are several great traditional opportunities. I advise you to do a clinic before you graduate.

Advice on Preparing for and Taking the Bar Exam:

Do as many practice questions as possible under time constraints. The key with the bar exam is learning the material but also getting in condition to finish 200 questions in six hours.

Advice on Choosing a Job and Career Path Inside or Outside of the Legal Profession:

Always keep in mind that we all have to make a start. Where you begin doesn't always have to be your dream job. Follow your interests and strengths. Also, find a good mentor who is caring, patient and honest. They exist!

Advice on Seeking Legal Job Opportunities and/or Creating One's Own Opportunities:

It is difficult, but not impossible, to practice on your own right out of law school. Ideally, your first couple years as a lawyer should be spent learning in a firm or an agency. After that, it is great to give your own practice or business venture a try.

Advice on Achieving Career Success and Advancement:

The most important habit in anything is preparation. Networking is important but it pales in comparison to having a reputation as an attorney who is always well prepared. Also, always be willing to try new things and move to new opportunities. In order to reach your potential, you must take risks in your career. The success of your legal career will be based on your ability to simultaneously master a small group of skills while simultaneously broadening your skill set.

Advice on Overcoming the Additional Challenges Black Law Students Face:

Be prepared, be patient and be persistent. It doesn't always matter where you start your first year, it matters how committed you are to improving. You will inevitably deal with condescension from your professors and classmates. It is important for Black students to support each other academically and socially. Form study groups, take classes together and continue to support one another for all three years.

Best Advice You Received Regarding Law School and the Legal Profession:

"Don't try and 'out-scream' or 'out-talk' them, but instead, out-think them."

Worst Advice You Received Regarding Law School and the Legal Profession:

"It's not what you know but who you know."

Best Advice You Would Give to an Aspiring Black Lawyer:

Believe in yourself and commit to improving a little bit every day.

Thoughts About Why Earning a Law Degree Is a Powerful Credential for African Americans and Why There Is a Need for More African American Lawyers:

African Americans have faced injustice in this country for 400 years. Our plight has been at the center of the development of American Law. Becoming a lawyer puts you on the front lines of the fight for a better society.

Thoughts About Whether and Why Law School Is Worth the Financial Investment:

Law school, in my opinion, is a good financial investment for those who want to practice law. For those who have a law degree but do not practice, I think it is a closer question.

LEGACY AND SUCCESS

My Most Outstanding Accomplishment:

My biggest accomplishment is the opportunity to advocate on behalf of the most vulnerable individuals every day.

The Legacy I Hope to Leave:

I hope that my legacy is that I was a good attorney who fought to make society more fair and just; that I was always honest, ethical, prepared and competent; and that I helped those who came after me and respected those who came before me.

The Secret to My Success:

There is no secret to anyone's success. I committed to becoming a competent attorney and then tried to improve year after year.

Paul S. Williams, Esq.
Partner Emeritus and Advisor
Major, Lindsey and Africa
Chicago, Illinois

"We're limited only by the constraints we place on ourselves. Unshackle yourself and you will soar!"

– Paul S. Williams

Success is . . . being content most of the time.

PERSONAL FAVORITES

Favorite Quote: "Setting goals is the first step in turning the inevitable into the visible." - Tony Robbins

Favorite Book: *Awaken the Giant Within* by Tony Robbins

Favorite Movie: *The Color Purple*

Favorite Song: "That Girl" by Stevie Wonder

Favorite Law School Class: Corporations

Favorite Legal Case: *Pennoyer v. Neff*

Favorite Hobbies: Working out; Watching movies; Reading

Favorite Attorney Role Model: Thurgood Marshall

FAMILY AND BACKGROUND

Where Born and Raised: Born - San Francisco, California; Raised - Los Angeles, California area

Family (Spouse/Partner and Children): Spouse - Laura (Yale Law School Class of 1982); Children - (son) Scott and (son) Ryan

Family Socioeconomic and Educational Background: My dad was a physician, and my brothers and I grew up in an affluent household.

THE DECISION TO BECOME A LAWYER

When and Why I Decided To Become a Lawyer: When I was young, I decided to become a lawyer because I enjoyed debating so much.

EDUCATIONAL ACHIEVEMENTS

High School: Harvard School (North Hollywood, California)

College/University: Harvard University (Cambridge, Massachusetts)

Undergraduate Degree: Bachelor of Arts (A.B.)

Major: Government

College Honors, Achievements and Activities: Graduated *cum laude* "with distinction"

Law School: Yale Law School (New Haven, Connecticut)

Law Degree and Graduation Year: Juris Doctor/Doctor of Jurisprudence (J.D.) - Class of 1984

Law School Honors, Achievements and Activities: Met my wife!

PROFESSIONAL ACCOMPLISHMENTS

State Bar Memberships (Where Admitted to Practice Law): Ohio; California

Other Legal Experience: *Chief Legal Officer and Executive Vice President and Secretary,* Cardinal Health, Inc.; *General*

Counsel, Information Dimensions Inc.; *Group Counsel,* Borden; *Associate Attorney,* Vorys, Sater, Seymour and Pease LLP; *Associate Attorney,* Gibson, Dunn & Crutcher LLP

Other Professional Work Experience: *Corporate Director,* State Auto Insurance; *Corporate Director,* Bob Evans Farms, Inc.; *Corporate Director,* Essendant; *Managing Director,* Allegis Partners; *Corporate Director,* Compass Minerals; *Corporate Director,* Capital Group

Professional Organizations: *Member,* National Bar Association; *Member,* National Association of Corporate Directors

Post-Law School Honors, Achievements, Activities, and Community Involvement: Included on lists of the most influential diverse lawyers and corporate directors in the U.S.; *President and Chair,* Chicago Chapter, National Association of Corporate Directors (NACD); *Trustee,* George Jackson Academy

LESSONS LEARNED: MY RECOMMENDATIONS FOR YOUR FUTURE ACTIONS BASED ON MY PAST EXPERIENCE

Advice on Making the Choice to Apply to and Attend Law School:

Make sure you understand what practicing law is like before you apply to law school. Too many people apply because they can't decide what else to do.

Advice on Law School Preparation:

Take as many political science and government classes as you can.

Advice on Applying to and Selecting a Law School:

Be sure to apply to a "stretch" school. Since law is a very rankings-conscious profession, consider attending a highly-ranked school if you're admitted.

Advice Regarding Academic Success, Co-Curricular and Extra-Curricular Participation, and Social Engagement in Law School:

Keep your head up and keep moving ahead even if the first year or two of law school seem boring or too abstract. The actual practice of law is much more interesting!

Advice on Preparing for and Taking the Bar Exam:

Definitely take a prep course.

Advice on Choosing a Legal Job and Career Path Inside or Outside of the Legal Profession:

Figure out what your passion is and make sure your job is aligned with that.

Advice on Seeking Legal Job Opportunities and/or Creating One's Own Opportunities:

Be perseverant in searching for a job. Sometimes it takes a while to find one with the right fit.

Advice on Achieving Career Success and Advancement:

If you work hard consistently, you will inevitably rise and succeed in your organization.

Advice On Overcoming the Additional Challenges Black Law Students and Lawyers Face:

Never think that your status as a Black person will prevent you from succeeding.

Best Advice I Received Regarding Law School and the Legal Profession:

Make sure you know what practicing law is like by speaking with many lawyers before you apply to law school.

Worst Advice I Received Regarding Law School and the Legal Profession:

The worst advice was that law consists only of trial law and litigation. There are many other types of law.

Best Advice I Would Give to an Aspiring Black Lawyer:

Talk to lawyers who can be your role models and mentors.

Thoughts About Why Earning a Law Degree Is a Powerful Credential for African Americans and Why There Is a Need for More African American Lawyers:

There is a tremendous need for more Black lawyers. The legal profession safeguards much of what keeps our society stable and civil.

LEGACY AND SUCCESS

My Most Outstanding Accomplishments:

My family is my most outstanding personal accomplishment.

Professionally, being general counsel of a Fortune 20 company (Cardinal Health) was my greatest achievement.

The Legacy I Hope to Leave:

The legacy I hope to leave is the many new diverse lawyers who consider me a positive and influential role model.

The Secret to My Success:

The secret to my success is my tenacity and optimism.

Sherry D. Williams, Esq.

Senior Legal Executive
Former Vice President, Deputy General Counsel & Global Chief Ethics & Compliance Officer
Jabil Inc.
Former Senior Vice President, Global Chief Ethics & Compliance Officer
Halliburton Company
Tampa, Florida

"Leadership means creating and adding value in your work and your community; and cultivating an environment where people feel valued and empowered."
– Sherry D. Williams

Success is . . . using your gifts, whatever they may be, to have a positive impact on the lives and successes of others.

PERSONAL FAVORITES

Favorite Quote: "Our deepest fear is not that we are inadequate. Our deepest fear is that we are powerful beyond measure. It is our light, not our darkness that frightens us most." - Marianne Williamson

Favorite Books: *Beloved* by Toni Morrison; *All Quiet on the Western Front* by E. Maria Remarque; *Invisible Man* by Ralph Ellison; *Madame Bovary* by Gustave Flaubert; *So Long a Letter* by Mariama Bâ; *The First 90 Days* by Michael Watkins; *Faces at the Bottom of the Well* by Derrick Bell; *And We Are Not Saved* by Derrick Bell

Favorite Movies: I have varied movie tastes, from romantic comedies like *Brown Sugar* and *When Harry Met Sally* to heavy, important movies like *Hotel Rwanda, Schindler's List* and *Amistad*. I am also a huge fan of the Marvel Cinematic Universe!

Favorite Music Genres: I love all kinds of music.

Favorite Musical Artists: Etta James; Prince; Lizz Wright; Run DMC; LL Cool J; Kem; Melody Gardot; William McDowell; Shekinah Glory Ministry

Favorite Law School Classes: Litigation Skills; Evidence; Criminal Procedure; Civil Procedure

Favorite Legal Cases: Brown v. Board of Education, 347 U.S. 483 (1954); Gideon v. Wainwright, 372 U.S. 335 (1963); Miranda v. Arizona, 384 U.S. 436 (1966); Loving v. Virginia, 388 U.S. 1 (1967); Roe v. Wade, 410 U.S. 113 (1973); and Griswold v. Connecticut, 381 U.S. 479 (1965)

Favorite Hobbies: Cooking; Traveling; Reading; Writing; Public speaking

Favorite Attorney Role Models: Practical role models - Albert O. Cornelison, Esq.; Benjamin Wilson, Esq.; Charisse R. Lillie, Esq.; Joseph K. West, Esq.; Sally Yates, Esq.; the Honorable Judge Mary Ellen Hicks, Esq.

"Famous" role models - The Honorable Barbara Jordan, Esq.; Justice Thurgood Marshall; Justice Ruth Bader Ginsberg; Justice Sonia Sotomayor

FAMILY AND BACKGROUND

Where Born and Raised: Fort Worth, Texas

Family (Spouse/Partner and Children): Child - (daughter) Sloane

Family Socioeconomic and Educational Background: My mother had a sixth-grade education, and my father was functionally illiterate. They were both born at the height of Jim Crow, and worked in blue collar jobs. Our family was considered "working-class poor", but I had a loving and fun childhood, despite its hardships. My parents were wonderful and hardworking people. I am the youngest of my mother's nine biological children. I was the first to attend both college and graduate school.

THE DECISION TO BECOME A LAWYER

When and Why I Decided to Become a Lawyer: I decided that I wanted to be a lawyer when I was nine years old. My parents were extremely strict about TV, but amazingly, one of the shows I could watch was Perry Mason. I thought he was wonderful. Skilled, serious, honest. But the two things I could never figure out was one, why only the "boys" could ask the witness questions and talk to the judge; and two, why it was only the "White boys"? The women were always getting coffee or crying; and there were no diverse people standing or speaking in the court. So, one day I announced to my family that when I grew up, I was going to be a lawyer like Perry Mason, except I was Black, and I was a girl!

EDUCATIONAL ACHIEVEMENTS

High School: The High School for Finance Professions at Polytechnic (Fort Worth, Texas)

College/University: The University of Oklahoma (Norman, Oklahoma)

Undergraduate Degree: Bachelor of Arts (B.A.)

Major: English

College Honors, Achievements and Activities: *Academic Recognition,* President's List (Spring 1992); *Academic Recognition,* Dean's List (Fall 1990, Fall 1991); *Awardee,* Melvin B. Tolson Award for Outstanding Journalism (1992); *Honoree,* Outstanding Senior Woman, Black Student Association (1992); *Opinion Columnist,* The Oklahoma Daily college newspaper (At that time, I was the first African American to write for the Opinions & Editorial Page in the University of Oklahoma's 100-year history.)

Law School: University of Miami School of Law (Coral Gables, Florida)

Law Degree and Graduation Year: Juris Doctor/Doctor of Jurisprudence (J.D.) - Class of 1995

Law School Honors, Achievements and Activities: *Scholar of the Year,* Miami Chapter, American Board of Trial Advocates; *Member,* National Mock Trial Team; *Semifinalist,* Southern Region, National Mock Trial Competition; *Chair,* Minority Affairs Commission, Student Bar Association; *Chair,* Fundraising Committee, Black Law Students Association

PROFESSIONAL ACCOMPLISHMENTS

State Bar Memberships (Where Admitted to Practice Law): Florida; New Jersey; New York

Other Legal Work Experience: *Consulting Counsel - Strategic Projects,* Greathouse Holloway McFadden PLLC; *Business Litigator,* K&L Gates

Professional Organizations: *Member,* American Bar Association; *Member,* National Bar Association; *Member,* Association of Corporate Counsel; *Member,* Minority Corporate Counsel Association; *Member,* Society for Corporate Governance; *Member,* Corporate Counsel Women of Color

Post-Law School Honors, Achievements, Activities, and Community Involvement: *Magazine Recognition,* Minority Business News Texas, Cover: "Halliburton's Sherry Williams on Leadership and Achieving Success", October 2007 Issue; *Magazine Recognition,* Capital Thinking Magazine, "Cherry-picking Global Talent", Fall 2008; *Magazine Recognition,* "Women on the Rise", Mayes & Baysinger, Courageous Counsel: Conversations with Women General Counsel in the Fortune 500, Leverage Media 2011; *Magazine Recognition,* Named "Women Worth Watching in 2009", Profiles in Diversity Journal, October 2008 Issue; *Magazine Recognition,* Named "Top Chief Compliance Officer" Ranked 74 of 1500 by ExecRank, the leading ranking service for corporate executives, 2012; *Magazine Recognition,* Named "R-3 100" InsideCounsel, Female lawyers named by the publication as ready to be a Fortune 500 General Counsel within 3 years, August/September 2013; *Listed Honoree,* "Power 100" 100 Most Powerful Black Lawyers in America, On Being a Black Lawyer (February 2013/February 2014); *Listed Honoree,* Houston's 50 Most Influential Women of 2013, Houston Woman Magazine (January 2014); *Honoree,* Success to Significance Award, Girl Scouts of San Jacinto (April 2014); *Listed Honoree,* Inaugural "Nation's Best" List, Lawyers of Color (2019); *Honoree,* 2004 TRIO Achiever, Oklahoma Division of Student Assistance Programs (2004); *Honoree,* 2006 National TRIO Achiever, Council for Opportunity in Education, Washington, D.C. (2006); *Honoree,* Magna Stella Award for Diversity in Law, The Texas General Counsel Forum, San Antonio, Texas (November 2010); *Honoree,* Women Looking Ahead Magazine's Law and Justice Awards: "Houston's Most Powerful and Influential Female Attorneys", Houston, Texas (September 2011); *Corporate Representative,* Testimony before Senate Subcommittee on Interstate Commerce, Trade and Tourism, Washington, D.C. (April 2007); *Member,* Board of Directors, Brown Girls Do Ballet (2016-Present); *Member,* Board of Trustees, Wheeler Avenue Christian Academy; *Former Director and Chair,* Nominating & Corporate Governance Committee, Wheeler Avenue Christian Academy (2014-2016); *Member,* Board of Directors, Alley Theatre (2007-2014); *Advisory Board Member,* Alley Theatre (2014-2016); *Chairwoman,* Halliburton Supplier Diversity Executive Advisory Board (2008-2011); *Member,* Board of Directors, Women's Business Enterprise National Council (2007-2010); *Member,* Board of Directors, Women of Tomorrow, Inc. (1999-2005); *Executive Board Member,* University of Miami Law Alumni Association (1992-1999)

LESSONS LEARNED: MY RECOMMENDATIONS FOR YOUR FUTURE ACTIONS BASED ON MY PAST EXPERIENCE

Advice on Law School Preparation:

Despite what lawyers will lead you to believe, there are no "special" prerequisite majors that will make you successful in law school. I have colleagues who majored in math, history, psychology, engineering, journalism, and many other disciplines. Each was successful in law school and has become a successful attorney. Therefore, I think a candidate for law school can be successful as long as they have the ability to read and digest large amounts of information, can sit and read for extended periods of time, have strong analytical reasoning skills, and have better than average writing skills.

Advice on Applying to and Selecting a Law School:

Lawyers will differ significantly on their advice in this regard, therefore, take any advice you receive with a grain of salt! My philosophy is to be realistic about your credentials - meaning your grades, Law School Admission Test (LSAT) scores, personal statement, letters of recommendation and how much you can financially contribute to your law school education. Given your assessment of your qualifications, apply to the best schools that you can and attend the best school to which you are admitted. There are those who say your law school does not matter that much, but I generally disagree. I have sat on law firm hiring committees and overseen hiring for corporate law departments. I can tell you from personal experience that candidates from better ranked law schools have a higher probability of getting an interview. Of course this opinion is tempered if you attend law school in a city in which you plan to practice, because the "hometown" law school can absolutely be an advantage for those staying "local".

Advice on Preparing for and Taking the Bar Exam:

The bar exam creates a great deal of stress on law students. It feels like an all-or-nothing endeavor, and no one wants to face failure. I recall that feeling very well, despite the fact that my bar exam days are far in the rearview mirror of my career.

The advice I would offer regarding the bar exam and preparation for it would be:

a. *Reading Comprehension Is Key*: The bar exam is a glorified reading comprehension test! Think about it, all law students have spent fifteen weeks sitting through torts, property, contracts, and other classes. You have learned the elements of the laws and statutes; now you are going to be tested on information you mostly know. So, the bar exam is less about what you learn during the bar review, and far more about reading the questions carefully, understanding what is being asked, and answering quickly.

b. *Bar Review Courses*: You must absolutely take a bar review course and actively engage and participate. It is the best way to obtain all relevant materials and have them at your fingertips.

c. *Study Schedules*: Set a study schedule and stick with it. But you do not have to always study at the library. I studied at the pool, the coffee shop, at diners, the food court in the mall and even in restaurants over a meal because I simply found it difficult to stay in one location the whole eight to nine hours a day. And although my location changed, my study hours were consistent – 9:00 a.m. to 6:00 p.m. every day. I took a break from 6:00 p.m. to 9:00 p.m., then spent another hour doing multiple-choice questions from 9:00 p.m. to 10:00 p.m., then bed. Every single day!

d. *Review Mistakes*: Take the time to review the substantive law in your bar review materials if you find yourself missing the same questions repeatedly.

e. *Study Groups*: Join a study group **only** if the people in the group have your same commitment to preparation and time management.

P.S.: I sat for and passed bar exams for three different states.

Advice on Choosing a Job and Career Path Inside or Outside of the Legal Profession:

In the absence of knowing a candidate personally, I think it is extremely hard to provide advice on this topic because the saying "Man plans, and God laughs" is absolutely true. My general advice is if possible, choose a practice area that you genuinely enjoy, even if it is not your "passion". Consider alternative practice areas. Everyone cannot be in employment and labor, corporate or litigation. Look into other practice areas such as bankruptcy, intellectual property, cyber-security, privacy, or education law. Read about emerging business trends and take those trends into consideration when you look at legal practice areas.

Be nimble, flexible, and opportunistic. It is unlikely that your career will move in a straight linear fashion. It will twist and turn, and that is okay as long as you are learning and growing in the process. Think less about your title or practice area, and more about what is going into your legal "toolbox" that makes you a better and more skilled lawyer and advocate.

Advice on Seeking Legal Job Opportunities and/or Creating One's Own Opportunities:

When you first graduate from law school, your opportunities are varied because you have not yet set yourself on a specific practice path. Nevertheless, you want to follow the tenets of all job seekers as follows:

1.) Develop a networking strategy.

2.) Communicate professionally.

3.) Follow up on all discussions, offers of assistance and introductions.

4.) Understand that "politics" matter; and

5.) Do not be afraid of self-promotion.

Advice on Achieving Career Success and Advancement:

Own your career. Take true ownership of your career from the beginning. Rather than handing over responsibility for your development to your superiors or the firm, become the CEO of your own career, even if that means paying for important training or coaching with your own money. If you do this, you will sustain a higher level of confidence over time, and you will always understand that you are often better and more skilled than you have been led to believe.

Advice on Overcoming the Additional Challenges Black Law Students and Lawyers Face:

As Black lawyers, we must understand that firm and corporate politics matter. Do not neglect internal firm or department politics under the misguided belief that good work speaks for itself. The law is a service business. There are many competent professionals who are a part of it. Access to quality work and expanded opportunities is based almost exclusively on personal relationships, so it is imperative that Black lawyers figure out the internal politics of their firms or companies and execute them well.

Best Advice I Received Regarding Law School and the Legal Profession:

The best advice I ever received was from a partner at K&L Gates, my former law firm. He told the associates at a firm retreat, "You have five years to get good. I mean really good - at research, writing, procedure, advocacy, politics, developing executive presence and showing good judgment. After that period, you lose the 'benefit of the doubt' and partners will move to associates who meet those criteria, and thus are more useful to clients and profitable to the firm." I have never forgotten his words, and I have shared those words with students, young lawyers and my protégés for over 20 years.

Thoughts About Why Earning a Law Degree Is a Powerful Credential for African Americans and Why There Is a Need for More African American Lawyers:

Almost without exception, the institutions that impact our lives in the United States are all governed by laws, statutes, and legal principles. Unfortunately, few of those institutions are led, governed, or managed by diverse teams. As a result, much of the racism that was built into these institutions many years ago still exists and continues to negatively impact the lives of people of color in general and African Americans in particular. That institutionalized racism is why Black lawyers are needed and necessary. We need great legal minds everywhere – in law enforcement, prosecutor's offices, public defender offices, on the bench as judges, in the federal, state, and local government, in non-profits, higher education, Fortune 1000 companies, in law firms (large, medium and small), as entrepreneurs and in elected office. Our voices and legal skills are necessary to continue to liberate our community and force the United States to live up to its promises of "all men are created equal" and "liberty and justice for all".

Thoughts About Whether and Why Law School Is Worth the Financial Investment:

Over the course of my career, I have often counseled law students on the cost-benefit analysis of attending law school, including the depth of the financial investment. At the end of the day, this is a deeply personal decision. What I can say is that you need to be certain that law school and practicing law are what you want to do, because achieving this goal means that you are taking out *a mortgage on your life*. I personally borrowed over $150,000 to complete my undergraduate and law school education. For me it has been more than worth it. We can all invest in anything we want, and most times we have no real control over how profitable an investment will be. However, in the case of law school, the investment is in YOU! As a result, you control the ROI [Return on Investment]; and you can always control 100% of the return because it is YOU investing in YOU!

LEGACY AND SUCCESS

My Most Outstanding Accomplishment:

Endowing The Hattie Williams Memorial Scholarship at the University of Oklahoma in honor and memory of my mother, and all of the sacrifices she made for my education. It is a maximum five-year, $5,000 per year scholarship for first-generation college students from financially disadvantaged backgrounds who demonstrate financial need and embody the resilience and perseverance necessary to succeed in college.

The Legacy I Hope to Leave:

I hope that my legacy is that I have contributed in a meaningful way to my family and community. That the women and men I have managed and trained feel that their career opportunities were enhanced because of their work with me. And finally, that I did the best I could with the time I was given.

The Secret to My Success:

I think a few of the keys to my success have been my willingness to be unapologetically myself, my willingness to "take up space" in a room, and my willingness to speak truth to power, even when it comes at personal or financial cost.

Suntrease Williams-Maynard, Esq., M.P.A.
Special Counsel
Adams and Reese LLP
Mobile, Alabama

"All it takes is dedication, determination and drive."
– Suntrease Williams-Maynard

Success is . . . self-defined. Set high goals for yourself and let your God-given talent and hard work take it from there.

PERSONAL FAVORITES

Favorite Quotes: "For I know the plans I have for you," declares the LORD, "plans to prosper you and not to harm you, plans to give you hope and a future." - Jeremiah 29:11

"A true leader has the confidence to stand alone, the courage to make tough decisions, and the compassion to listen to the needs of others. He does not set out to be a leader, but he becomes one by the equality of his actions and the integrity of his intent." - General Douglas MacArthur

"I can do all things through Christ who strengthens me." - Philippians 4:13

Favorite Books: *The Bible* is my guiding source. It is because of God I am who I am and where I am today; Topics of self-improvement; Terry McMillan's books

Favorite Movies: Comedy; Romance; Horror; Drama; A fan of the Lifetime Movie Network

Favorite Music Genres: Gospel music has been my source of foundation and saw me through some challenging times; Jazz at nighttime; R&B of the 90s

Favorite Songs: "Fire and Desire" by Rick James and Teena Marie; "You for Me" by Johnny Gill; "Can't Give Up Now" by Mary Mary; "Never Would've Made It" by Marvin Sapp

Favorite Musical Artist: Whitney Houston

Favorite Law School Classes: Clinics; Constitutional Law; Education Law; Civil Rights in Politics; Wrongful Conviction

Favorite Legal Case: *Brown v. Board of Education*. This case hits home literally being a native of Farmville, Virginia, where the schools were closed for five years from 1959-1964 because of the town's refusal to integrate. Some may be unaware, but Farmville was a part of the *Brown v. Board of Education* case. In our community, the students led a strike to speak against the unequal treatment in education.

Favorite Hobbies: Spending time with family (i.e., playing board games, traveling, spending hours on the boat, spa day with daughter); Restorative yoga; Helping others; Developing youth programs and conducting outreach

Favorite Attorney Role Models: Charles Hamilton Houston is someone I always admired for his accomplishments in the legal realm and the community. However, as a child I was always drawn to the legal prowess and sheer fearlessness of Johnnie Cochran.

FAMILY AND BACKGROUND

Where Born and Raised: Farmville, Virginia

Family (Spouse/Partner and Children): Spouse - Stephen; Children - (son) Dareon and (daughter) Destiny

Family Socioeconomic and Educational Background: I am a first-generation college student and law school graduate. I am a product of "humble" beginnings. However, I was reared by my loving grandmother, who was filled with wisdom.

THE DECISION TO BECOME A LAWYER

When and Why I Decided to Become a Lawyer: Since the age of four, I have wanted to be an attorney. The injustices and racial tension in my hometown of Farmville, Virginia was evident to me even at that tender age. Seeing my family members and those within my community suffer from the after-effects of the unprecedented and highly controversial Massive Resistance (where Prince Edward County shut down public schools to resist integration) influenced me to be an advocate. Charles Hamilton Houston said that lawyers are either social engineers or social parasites. I chose to be the former.

EDUCATIONAL ACHIEVEMENTS

High School: Prince Edward County High School (Grades 9-11); Randolph-Henry (Grades 11-12) (Farmville, Virginia)

College/University: Shaw University (Raleigh, North Carolina)

Undergraduate Degree: Bachelor of Arts (B.A.)

Majors: Sociology and Criminal Justice

College Honors, Achievements and Activities: *Founding Member and First President,* Social Sciences Club; *Secretary,* Alpha Kappa Alpha Sorority, Inc.; *Public Relations Chair,* Student Government Association; *Vice President,* Criminal Justice Club; *Honoree,* Honorary Student of the Year 2004 (Highest GPA in discipline); *Member,* Alpha Chi National Honor Society; *Recipient,* Tom Joyner Scholarship; *Academic Recognition,* National Dean's List

Law School: North Carolina Central University School of Law (Durham, North Carolina)

Law Degree and Graduation Year: Juris Doctor/Doctor of Jurisprudence (J.D.) - Class of 2008

Law School Honors, Achievements and Activities: *Member,* North Carolina Central University Law Review; *Publicist,* Women's Law Caucus; *Law Week Committee Member,* Student Bar Association; *Founding Member/Director of Membership,* Public Interest Law Organization; *1L Representative,* Black Law Students Association; *Vice President,* Black Law Students Association; *Clerk,* Phi Delta Phi International Legal Fraternity; *President,* American Association for Justice (formerly ATLA); *Member,* National Bar Association; *Member,* American Bar Association; *Member,* Sports & Entertainment Law Society; *Member,* North Carolina Bar Association; *Recipient,* NCCU Public Interest/Judicial Clerk Stipend; *Recipient,* Richard D. Hailey Scholarship; *Research Assistant,* Legal Reasoning & Persuasion; *Recipient,* Willie E. Gary Scholarship

Other Graduate or Professional Degree: Master of Public Administration (M.P.A.), Pennsylvania State University (World Campus)

Additional Education: Graduate Certificate, Public Sector Human Resource Management, Pennsylvania State University (World Campus)

PROFESSIONAL ACCOMPLISHMENTS

State Bar Memberships (Where Licensed to Practice Law): Maryland; District of Columbia

Other Legal Experience: *Assistant United States Attorney,* Southern District of Texas and Southern District of Alabama; *Trial Attorney,* U.S. Equal Employment Opportunity Commission; *Assistant Staff Judge Advocate,* United States Air Force Reserve, Judge Advocate General Corps; *Law Clerk,* Legal Aid of North Carolina; *Legal Intern,* Child Advocacy Center

Other Professional Work Experience: *Teen Court Judge,* Escambia County, Florida (2019-Present); *Adjunct Professor* (Subjects Taught: Sociology, Criminology, Criminal Law and Procedure, Juvenile Delinquency), Spring Hill College (2017-Present)

Professional Organizations: *Member,* National Bar Association (2020-Present); *Member,* American Bar Association (2020-Present); *Southern District Representative,* Alabama Lawyers Association (2019-Present); *Member,* National Conference of Bar Presidents (2016-Present); *Executive Council Member,* National Conference of Bar Presidents (2018-Present); *Co-Chair,* Diversity & Inclusion Committee, National Conference of Bar Presidents (2017-Present); *Member,* Program Committee, National Conference of Bar Presidents (2018-Present); *Member,* Membership Committee, National Conference of Bar Presidents (2016-2017); *Member,* Government Relations Liaison Committee, Alabama State Bar (2019-Present); *Member,* Leadership Forum Alumni Section, Alabama State Bar (2016-Present); *President,* Mobile Bar Association's Women Lawyers (2016-2017); *Vice President,* Mobile Bar Association's Women Lawyers (2015-2016); *Chair,* Ad Hoc Diversity Committee/Diversity & Inclusion Committee, Mobile Bar Association (2016-Present); *President,* Vernon Z. Crawford Bay Area Bar Association (2018-Present); *President-Elect,* Vernon Z. Crawford Bay Area Bar Association (2017-2018); *Recording Secretary,* Vernon Z. Crawford Bay Area Bar Association (2016-2017); *Chair,* Expungement Committee, Vernon Z. Crawford Bay Area Bar Association (2016-Present); *Chair,* Community Affairs, Vernon Z. Crawford Bay Area Bar Association (2016-Present); *Member,* Paul W. Brock Inn of Court (2016-Present); *Vice President of Programs,* National Black Prosecutors Association (2014-2015); *Regional Director,* Southern Region, National Black Prosecutors Association (2011-2014); *Director,* Pro Bono and Community Outreach, Laredo Webb County Bar Association (2013-2014); *Board Member,* Advisory Board, Safe Haven (2011-2012); *President,* Webb County Women's Bar Association (2011-2012); *President-Elect,* Webb County Women's Bar Association

(2010-2011); *Treasurer,* Webb County Women's Bar Association (2009-2010); *Touch 10,000 Ambassador,* American Bar Association (2010-2011); *Member,* Alliance of Black Women Attorneys (2008-2009)

Post-Law School Honors, Achievements, Activities, and Community Involvement:

Honoree, Top 40 Under 40, The National Black Lawyers (2020); *Honoree,* Nation's Best Advocates 40 Under 40, National Bar Association (2020); *Awardee,* Community Service Award, U.S. Equal Employment Opportunity Commission (2019); *Recipient,* Diversity Scholarship, Diversity & Inclusion Committee, National Conference of Bar Presidents (2016 and 2018); *Featured Reservist,* The Judge Advocate General's Corps Reserve (TJAGR) Publication (2014 and 2018); *Awardee,* Student Involvement Starts with Us Award, Mobile County Public Schools System (2016); *Honoree,* Top 40 under 40, Mobile Bay Magazine (2016); *Honoree,* Top 40 Under 40, North Carolina Central University (2016); *Recipient,* Air Force Commendation Medal, United States Air Force (2015); *Awardee,* Dedicated Service Award, United States Attorney's Office, SDTX (2014); *Recipient,* Inaugural Community Service Award for Outstanding Service, Judge Advocate Staff Officer Course (JASOC) (2014); *Honor Flight,* Commissioned Officer Training, United States Air Force (2014); *Awardee,* Best Regional Director of the Year Award, National Black Prosecutors Association (2013); *Listed Honoree,* Hot List, Lawyers of Color (2013); Awardee, Best Regional Director of the Year Award, National Black Prosecutors Association (2012); *Awardee,* Exemplary Leadership Award, Webb County Women's Bar Association (2012); *United States Attorney General's Honors Program Attorney,* United States Department of Justice (2009); *Board Member,* Bishop State Community College Foundation (2020-Present); *Member and Sergeant-at-Arms,* Links, Incorporated, Greater Mobile Chapter (2019-Present); *Chair,* Diversity and Inclusion, Junior League of Mobile (2019-Present); *Member and Chair,* Legislative Committee, Jack & Jill of America, Inc., Mobile Chapter (2016-Present); *Member,* Rotary Club of Mobile (2016-Present); *Member,* South Alabama Chapter, Military Officers Association of America (2016- Present); *Member,* Big Brothers Big Sisters of South Alabama (2015-Present); *Member,* Junior League of Mobile (2015-Present); *Member,* Marriage Ministry, Macedonia Missionary Baptist Church (2015-Present); *Member,* Alpha Kappa Alpha Sorority, Incorporated (2003-Present); *Host,* (First) Bullying Awareness Walk (Laredo, Texas); *Host,* (First) Multi-Cultural Festival (Laredo, Texas); *Host,* (First) Community Fair (to restore voting rights and expunge eligible state convictions in Mobile, Alabama) (2016, 2017, 2018); *Creator,* S.T.Y.L.E. (Successful Tips for Youth on Law Enforcement Encounters) for the Department of Justice

LESSONS LEARNED: MY RECOMMENDATIONS FOR YOUR FUTURE ACTIONS BASED ON MY PAST EXPERIENCE

Advice on Law School Preparation:

Everyone is going to be at a different place in regards to preparation. Everyone will also have different resources in terms of financial ability to pay for prep course and familial support while studying. When I was preparing for the Law School Admission Test (LSAT), I had neither the time nor money to properly prepare for several reasons. For starters, I had anticipated another semester in undergraduate school as I was originally pursuing a double major. However, I changed my second major to a minor. This change allowed me to graduate with my peers that I started my undergraduate career with but left little time for me to adequately study for the LSAT. Not only did I lack the financial resources, but I had little to no parental support. As a result, I became the Google queen. I also asked as many questions from as many lawyers as I could find, and I made use of the free resources available at the local and university libraries. Therefore, the best advice that I can give is to always remember to make the most out what you have. It is imperative to remain resourceful. Don't be afraid to ask questions and never underestimate the power of Google. I learned early on that you can do a lot with a little.

Advice on Applying to and Selecting a Law School:

Attending law school is a serious time and financial commitment. Therefore, the decision to apply should not be based on the fact that one's family members are lawyers or the promise of financial gain. In the words of my husband, "If you are following the money, then you are already lost." Applying for law school, as well as the practice of law, has to stem from one's own passion to make a difference and/or represent one's clients to the fullest.

Take the appropriate time and care when writing your personal statement. Don't be afraid to be "personal" because you have to sell *you*. Also, take time to explain anything negative on your records. Once again, don't be afraid to ask questions. For example, applying for law school can be an expensive venture. However, I was able to waive most of my application fees because I asked about fee waivers.

In terms of selecting a law school, don't overly concern yourself with rankings. Instead, learn what the law school has to offer and compare it to your needs. For instance, if your interest is to be a litigator, you should look at schools with this emphasis that offer various clinical opportunities. Additionally, I am a firm believer that it is not the school that is extraordinary, but the student. As my grandmother would say, "It is not where you graduate from, it is the graduate." It is about applying yourself and performing at the highest level despite your alma mater. Make the most out of the education provided to you by your law school. Lastly, I am a huge proponent of touring schools of interest.

Advice Regarding Academic Success, Co-Curricular and Extra-Curricular Participation, and Social Engagement in Law School:

Law school is challenging and there may be times when you want to throw a few books out of a window. I know I have had those times. Stick with it. The three years are simply a means to an end, and they will go by faster than you think. If you are having trouble understanding a concept, reread and reread again until you understand. The sacrifice you make will yield a great return.

Also, DO YOUR OWN WORK. Create your own outlines. Do not be one of those students who accepts hand-me-down notes. There is value in hard work. Finally, don't be afraid to seek help from your professors. They actually encourage this.

In regard to the extra-curricular activities, you have to do what works for you. You know your limitations. People may tell you not to become involved in activities during your first year. However, I made the choice to sacrifice my social life for extra-curricular activities. I later learned that my diverse experiences as a law student opened the doors for various career opportunities.

Advice on Preparing for and Taking the Bar Exam:

Take a test preparation course, if you can afford it. If you cannot afford one (like me), don't get discouraged. There are various self-aid books. Also, don't be afraid to borrow study materials from a friend. Lastly, put in the time to study. However, I don't believe in an unbalanced life, so take time for yourself. Address your needs (i.e., physical, spiritual, emotional, etc.). In short, take breaks. If you followed my previous advice regarding doing your own work as a law student, this is where it will pay off!

Advice on Choosing a Legal Job and Career Path Inside or Outside of the Legal Profession:

At the end of the day, follow your passion. When you are doing something that you enjoy, you will always give it your best.

Advice on Seeking Legal Job Opportunities and/or Creating One's Own Opportunities:

I believe in following the opportunity. Don't be afraid to move. Too many of us develop a reluctance to leave what is familiar. Do not miss an opportunity because of fear. When it comes to applying, be sure to sell yourself and distinguish yourself from your peers. Be able to say more than "I was an excellent student."

Advice on Achieving Career Success and Advancement:

I am an advocate of hard work. Having a strong work ethic goes a long way even if you think no one notices. Networking and creating professional relationships are also essential to career growth and development. Lastly, seek out mentors. They don't have to look like you or share similar professional backgrounds. Everyone can add value.

Advice on Overcoming the Additional Challenges Black Lawyers Face:

There may be stereotypes and barriers because of one's skin color or socioeconomic background, but you have to remain steadfast in your conviction and your professionalism. Break those stereotypes and barriers and do not feed them. Also realize that those who look like you can also present challenges. Do not be the "crab in the barrel". Lift as you rise.

Best Advice I Received Regarding Law School and the Legal Profession:

There were times when I wanted to give up. However, my grandmother would simply say, "You can do it." I know that the simplicity may seem lackluster, but as I said before, my grandmother was such a wise woman. By simply rebutting my "I can't" with "You can", it constantly reminded me that those who achieve their dreams didn't have a magic formula or a secret they guarded like a precious treasure. There was no genie in the bottle. They simply said, "I *can* do it."

Worst Advice I Received Regarding Law School and the Legal Profession:

I was told to not participate in extra-curricular activities during my first year of law school. However, it was my diverse experience that allowed me to be selected for the United States Attorney General's Honors Program. Therefore, I was able to join the United States Attorney's Office at the age of 25, making me one of the youngest federal prosecutors in the nation.

Best Advice I Would Give to an Aspiring Black Lawyer:

In the words of the greatest, Muhammad Ali, "If your dreams don't scare you, then they aren't big enough." Don't let fear command your life. YOU CAN DO IT!

Thoughts About Why Earning a Law Degree Is a Powerful Credential for African Americans and Why There Is a Need for More African American Lawyers:

A Juris Doctorate is such a versatile degree. So don't close the doors on countless opportunities.

LEGACY AND SUCCESS

My Most Outstanding Accomplishments:

Professionally - I created a program that I named Successful Tips for Youth on Law Enforcement Encounters (S.T.Y.L.E.), which started as part of my civil rights outreach for the United States Attorney's Office for the Southern District of Alabama (Mobile). In light of the tragic incidents we have faced as a nation, this program seeks to bridge the gap and foster positive relationships between our youth and law enforcement communities. Students participating in the program experience a simulated traffic stop, home encounter and street encounter. Furthermore, they are given an opportunity to understand the split second decision making that law enforcement officers face in the line of duty. Additionally, the students are provided with a brief legal overview of use of force. In my collaboration with the Mobile Police Department and the FBI, the program was provided to hundreds of students in the Mobile area and contributed to the significant reduction of school arrests in the Mobile County Public School System. This program has been adopted by the FBI for national implementation under the name Bridging the Gap.

Personally - There is nothing like being a mother and a wife. Being able to create the family that I always desired is an ultimate blessing. Molding and shaping the two little lives that God has chosen for me is the greatest honor. Finally, having a husband that supports me in all that I do and encourages me to reach my full potential has left me with such a sense of gratitude for the multitude of blessings in my life.

What Legacy I Hope to Leave:

As a fellow Rotarian said, "It is nice to be important, but it is important to be nice." At the end of the day, I just want to treat people right, be the best mother and wife I can be, and live a life that is pleasing to God.

The Secret to My Success:

My **four** secrets include: not being afraid to think outside of the box; being tenacious and persistent; not being afraid to go where the opportunity is; and keeping God first, for He directs my life.

Patricia Wilson, Esq.
Professor of Law
Baylor University Law School
Waco, Texas

"There are few skills more useful than the ability to ask a good question and listen to the answer. Questions sate curiosity; they confront injustice; and they provide the information needed to be effective."

– Patricia Wilson

Success is . . . being satisfied and at peace with the decisions one has made, the paths one has taken.

PERSONAL FAVORITES

Favorite Quotes: "I learned that courage was not the absence of fear, but the triumph over it. The brave man is not he who does not feel afraid, but he who conquers that fear." - Nelson Mandela

"Success consists of going from failure to failure without loss of enthusiasm." - Winston Churchill

Favorite Books: *To Kill a Mockingbird* by Harper Lee; *Their Eyes Were Watching God* by Zora Neale Hurston; *I Know Why the Caged Bird Sings* by Maya Angelou

Favorite Movies: *Courage Under Fire*; *A Few Good Men*; *Hollywood Shuffle*; *The Godfather*; *Star Wars* (the original episodes)

Favorite Musical Genre: 1970s Soul

Favorite Songs: "Natural Woman" by Aretha Franklin; "The Ground" by Ola Gjeilo

Favorite Musical Artist: Aretha Franklin

Favorite Law School Classes: Employment Discrimination; The Law and Social Change

Favorite Legal Cases: *Loving v. Virginia*; *Brown v. Board of Education*

Favorite Hobbies: Reading; Quilting; Learning new things

Favorite Attorney Role Models: Thurgood Marshall; Constance Baker Motley; Barbara Jordan

FAMILY AND BACKGROUND

Where Born and Raised: Fort Wayne, Indiana

Family (Spouse/Partner and Children): Spouse - Michael

Family Socioeconomic and Educational Background: I was raised by a widowed mother who had only a ninth-grade education, but she possessed great wisdom. She taught me the importance of integrity, compassion, education, and hard work. We were poor by every measure, but I never felt poor or lacked for any of the necessities. Although my mother could not have afforded to pay for my college education, she never wavered in her promise and her expectation that I would attend college.

THE DECISION TO BECOME A LAWYER

When and Why I Decided to Become a Lawyer:

I decided to apply to law school one lovely fall day of my senior year of college because it seemed like a good idea and there was nothing else I wanted to do as a career.

EDUCATIONAL ACHIEVEMENTS

High School: Concordia Lutheran High School (Fort Wayne, Indiana)

College/University: Purdue University (West Lafayette, Indiana)

Undergraduate Degree: Bachelor of Arts (B.A.)

Major: Sociology

College Honors, Achievements and Activities: Graduated "with distinction"; Completed Sociology Honors Program; *Member,* Alpha Lambda Delta Honor Society

Law School: Northwestern University Law School (Chicago, Illinois)

Law Degree and Graduation Year: Juris Doctor/Doctor of Jurisprudence (J.D.) - Class of 1985

Law School Honors, Achievements and Activities: John Henry Wigmore Scholar; *Editorial Board,* Journal of International Law and Business; *Member and Secretary,* Black Law Students Association; *Chair,* Special Events, Black Law Students Association

PROFESSIONAL ACCOMPLISHMENTS

State Bar Membership (Where Admitted to Practice Law): Texas

Other Legal Experience: *Volunteer Lawyer* (Pro Bono Legal Service - Family Law); *Staff Attorney,* American Airlines, Inc.; *Associate,* Johnson & Swanson; *Associate,* Bracewell & Patterson (now Bracewell & Giuliani)

Professional Organizations: *Member,* State Bar of Texas; *Member,* American Bar Association; *Member,* Competitions Committee, *Law Student Division,* American Bar Association (ABA); *Chair,* Client Counseling Subcommittee, Competitions Committee, Law Student Division, American Bar Association (ABA) (Served three times)

Post-Law School Honors, Achievements, Activities, and Community Involvement: *Honoree,* "Outstanding Professor for Contributions to the Academic Community", Baylor University (2016); *Director,* People's Law School (2006-Present); *Member,* Governing Board and Coordinating Council, National Cooperative Baptist Fellowship (2008-2015); *Chair,* Legal Committee (2010-2015); *Member,* Governing Board, Texas Cooperative Baptist Fellowship (2005-2015); *Moderator,* Texas Cooperative Baptist Fellowship (2013); *Member,* Brazos Valley Public Broadcasting Board of Trustees (2003-2011); *Vice-Chair,* Brazos Valley Public Broadcasting Board of Trustees (2009, 2010); *Member,* Vanguard College Preparatory School Board of Trustees (2003-2009)

LESSONS LEARNED: MY RECOMMENDATIONS FOR YOUR FUTURE ACTIONS BASED ON MY PAST EXPERIENCE

Advice on Law School Preparation:

Do what is hard. Law school is hard, so prepare yourself by taking courses that force you to engage in complex critical reading, thinking, and writing. Venture outside of your comfort zone because at first law school is outside of everyone's comfort zone.

Advice on Applying to and Selecting a Law School:

Law schools have different missions and strengths. Know what is important to you and seek a school that is best for you. If it's important to you, consider the racial and ethnic makeup of the student body, but don't let it limit your choices or keep you from going to the school that is best for you.

Advice Regarding Academic Success, Co-Curricular and Extra-Curricular Participation, and Social Engagement in Law School:

Strive for balanced involvement. Studying must be a student's first priority, but I encourage my students to get acquainted with their classmates and to get involved in extracurricular activities - everyone needs a break from studying and the law from time-to-time. Finally, ignore anyone who questions your right to be there. Like Jon Snow in *Game of Thrones*, "They know nothing."

Advice on Preparing for and Taking the Bar Exam:

Study, study, study . . . and start early!

Advice on Choosing a Legal Job and Career Path Inside or Outside of the Legal Profession:

Any job worth having is likely to be competitive, regardless of the pay or whether it is in the private or public sector. When contemplating your first career move, go where you can get the best experience, without regard to location, type of work, or even pay, as long as you can survive. Experience is marketable and will let you move toward your dream job.

Advice on Seeking Legal Job Opportunities:

Your efforts should start early, as in the first month of law school. Make the placement office your second home; get to know the personnel there and let them know you. Don't expect the placement office to find you a job - you must take an active interest in your future. But make the placement people there your allies and partners in creating and seeking job opportunities.

Advice on Achieving Career Success and Advancement:

Work hard. Take the road less traveled - it's not as crowded and therefore, it's easier to excel and be noticed.

Advice on Overcoming the Additional Challenges Black Law Students Face:

Develop a supportive circle of law school friends as well as friends not in the legal field. Set clearly defined goals and then work hard. Ignore the naysayers. Let nothing deter you from your goals.

Advice on Overcoming the Additional Challenges Black Lawyers Face:

You probably will have to be twice as good to get half as much. Yes, it's unfair (and maybe even illegal), but it's a reality. But know that with each successful step, you make it easier for yourself and those who follow in your path.

Best Advice I Received Regarding Law School and the Legal Profession:

Being assertive doesn't mean you have to be mean or rude. Maintain your professionalism at all times - assume that everything you write, do, or say may come before a jury.

Best Advice I Would Give to an Aspiring Black Lawyer:

People trust lawyers to obtain justice - justice that may affect their constitutional rights, their livelihoods, and maybe even their lives. Clients must never be just another case or file but deserve the very best their attorney has to offer.

Thoughts About Why Earning a Law Degree Is a Powerful Credential for African Americans and Why There Is a Need for More African American Lawyers:

A law degree automatically gives the holder a measure of prestige and credibility. Membership in the bar is a privilege extended to only those who have proven themselves worthy, and with that privilege, lawyers are able to advocate for the weak and vulnerable. For those of us who prove ourselves worthy, law is our superpower.

Thoughts About Whether and Why Law School Is Worth the Financial Investment:

If one wants only to make lots of money, law school is probably not worth the financial investment. There are many ways to make money with less financial outlay. One should not be blind to the cost of a legal education, but it is an investment in oneself, and opens many opportunities that are not available to non-lawyers.

LEGACY AND SUCCESS

My Most Outstanding Accomplishments:

Personal - being mom to our four children. Professional - earning tenure at Baylor University.

The Legacy I Hope to Leave:

My legacy is the students I have taught. I hope that beyond the legal concepts they learned in class, they will be touched by the lessons on integrity, professionalism, and compassion I tried to instill.

The Secret to My Success:

I have tried to take my work seriously, but not take myself too seriously. I have tried to find the good in every situation.

Adrien K. Wing, Esq., M.A.

Bessie Dutton Murray Professor of Law
Associate Dean for International and Comparative Law Programs
France Summer Abroad Program Director
University of Iowa College of Law
Director
University of Iowa Center for Human Rights
Iowa City, Iowa

"Whether I live only until tomorrow or until I am 100, I want to give my heart and soul to the cause of justice."
— Adrien K. Wing

Success is . . . raising, mentoring children and young people; serving people around the world.

PERSONAL FAVORITES

Favorite Quote: "Service is the rent we pay to be living on the planet." - Marian Wright Edelman

Favorite Books: *Just Mercy: A Story of Justice and Redemption* by Bryan Stevenson; *Long Walk to Freedom* by Nelson Mandela

Favorite Movies: Spike Lee movies; *It's a Wonderful Life; The Lord of the Rings; Star Wars; Star Trek*

Favorite Music Genres: Smooth jazz; R&B

Favorite Musical Artists: Michael Jackson; Prince; Luther Vandross; Whitney Houston; Al Jarreau

Favorite Law School Classes: International Law; Externship at the United Nations

Favorite Legal Cases: Brown v. Board of Education; Loving v. Virginia

Favorite Hobbies: Reading biographies; Mentoring; Writing poetry; Traveling (over 100 countries)

Favorite Attorney Role Models: The late Justice Thurgood Marshall; Justice Sonia Sotomayor; Professor Bryan Stevenson; the late Professor Derrick Bell

FAMILY AND BACKGROUND

Where Born and Raised: Born - Oceanside, California; Raised - Orange, New Jersey (primarily)

Family (Spouse/Partner and Children): Partner - James (20+ years); Children - two biological children - (son) Che and (son) Nolan Melson, and five surrogate children - Dr. Willie Barney, Brooks Barney, Charles Johnson, Lome Adam, and Shebere Adam

Family Socioeconomic and Educational Background: My father died tragically when I was nine years old. My single mom raised three of us. I am a third-generation college graduate on my mother's side.

THE DECISION TO BECOME A LAWYER

When and Why I Decided to Become a Lawyer: It was just after the civil rights era and I was very inspired. Plus, I had a family that was involved in that movement and on the local level in Bronx, New York community engagement. I ended up being the first lawyer on either side of my family. Now we have two generations of lawyers in my extended family. When I was in college, I also considered whether I should get a Ph.D. instead of or in addition to a law degree. I did get a M.A. in African Studies, but it seemed that there were more options for lawyers than for Ph.D.s. That is even more true today than then. I definitely made the right choice, and I became a professor too. There are more jobs for law professors, and they have more earning capacity than liberal arts professors.

EDUCATIONAL ACHIEVEMENTS

High School: Newark Academy (Livingston, New Jersey)

College/Undergraduate: Princeton University (Princeton, New Jersey)

Undergraduate Degree: Bachelor of Arts (A.B.)

Major: Politics

College Honors, Achievements and Activities: Graduated *magna cum laude* "with high distinction"; *Honoree,* Frederick Douglass Award (Graduation 1978); *Honorable Mention,* Afro-American Studies Thesis Prize; Senior Thesis: New Jersey Governmental Policy Analysis of Equal Educational Opportunity; *Resident Advisor,* Princeton University (Worked all four years, 10 to 20 hours per week); *Activist,* Anti-Apartheid Movement; *Trustee,* Princeton University Store; *Founder,* Forum for Interracial Communication; *Founder,* Paul Robeson Association; *Member,* Student Government: *Chair,* Residential Life Committee; *Member,* Undergraduate Life Committee; *Member,* Wilson College Council; *Reporter,* WPRB Radio Black Montage news show; *Member,* Politics Department Committee

Law School: Stanford Law School (Stanford, California)

Law Degree and Graduation Year: Juris Doctor/Doctor of Jurisprudence (J.D.) - Class of 1982

Law School Honors, Achievements and Activities:

Articles Editor, Stanford Journal of International Law and published article; *Southern Africa Task Force Chairperson,* National Black American Law Students Association (NBALSA); *Co-Founder and Director,* East Palo Alto Community Law Project; *Intern,* United Nations Council for Namibia (1981); *Summer Associate,* Rosenfeld Meyer & Susman (1980); *Summer Associate,* Curtis, Mallet-Prevost, Colt & Mosle (1981); *Honoree,* Who's Who Among American Law Students (1982); *Awardee,* Stanford African Students Association Award (1982); *Honoree,* Outstanding Young Women of America (1980)

Other Graduate or Professional Degree: Master of Arts (M.A.) in African Studies, University of California at Los Angeles (UCLA) (Los Angeles, California)

Graduate School Honors, Achievements and Activities: Graduate Division Academic Fellow (4.0 GPA); *Articles Editor,* UFAHAMU: A Journal of African Studies; *Teacher/Counselor,* UCLA Upward Bound summer program

PROFESSIONAL ACCOMPLISHMENTS

State Bar Membership (Where Admitted to Practice Law): New York

Other Legal Experience: *Associate,* Rabinowitz, Boudi, Standard, Krinsky, Lieberman; *Associate,* Curtis, Mallet-Prevost, Colt & Mosle LLP

Professional Organizations: *Member,* American Bar Association; *Member,* National Bar Association; *Member,* American Association of Law Schools; *Member,* American Society of International Law; *Member,* Society of American Law Teachers; *Member,* Council on Foreign Relations (Since 1993)

Post-Law School Honors, Achievements, Activities, and Community Involvement: *Counsellor,* American Society of International Law (2014-2020); *Co-Chair,* Blacks of the American Society of International Law (2014-2020); *Board Member,* International Law Student Association Board (2018-Present); *Awardee,* Newark Academy (NJ) Alumna Award (2014); *Awardee,* Regents Award for Faculty Excellence (State of Iowa) (2012); *Member,* American Law Institute (2009); *Awardee,* Clyde Ferguson Award, Association of American Law Schools Minority Section (2009); *Awardee,* Lena O. Smith Award, Minnesota Black Women Lawyers Network (2007); *Awardee,* Distinguished Achievement Award, University of Iowa (2007); *Awardee,* Juliette Gordon Low Award, Mississippi Valley Girl Scouts (2007); *Awardee,* Gertrude Rush Award, Iowa National Bar Association and Iowa Women's Bar Association (2006); *Awardee,* Newark Academy Distinguished Alumni Award (2004); *Awardee,* Diversity Award, University of Iowa African Student Association (1998); *Awardee,* Haywood Burns & Shanara Gilbert Award, Northeastern Law Professors of Color (1997); *Recognition,* "Author of the Month", New York University Press Author of the Month (October 1997); *Listed Honoree,* Outstanding Young Women of America; *Vice President,* Princeton Class of 1978 (1993-1998); *Member,* Board of Trustees, Princeton University (one of three alumni chosen to run on At-Large ballot) (1995); *Listed Honoree,* Who's Who in America; *Listed Honoree,* Who's Who in Finance and Industry; *Listed Honoree,* Who's Who Among African Americans; *Listed Honoree,* Who's Who in American Education; *Listed Honoree,* Who's Who of American Women; *Listed Honoree,* Who's Who Among Young American Professionals; *Listed Honoree,* Who's Who in the Midwest; *Term Member,* The Council on Foreign Relations (1985-1990); *Listed Honoree,* Who's Who in American Law; *Listed Honoree,* Who's Who in the World; *Awardee,* Hope Stevens Award, National Conference of Black Lawyers (1988); *Participant,* Old Gold Summer Research Fellowship, University of Iowa (1988-1990); *Listed Honoree,* World Who's Who of Women; *Listed Honoree,* Who's Who in the East International Youth in Achievement (1984); *Awardee,* Special Mention Award, Best Paper, Inter-American Bar Association (1985); *Appointee,* Iowa Commission on the African American Prison Population by Governor Vilsack (1999-2001); *Member,* American Bar Association Middle East/North Africa Council (2011-2014); *Member,* American Bar Association Accreditation Committee (2012-2018); *Vice President,* American Society of International Law (2007-2009); *Member,* American Society of International Law Executive Council (2014-2020, 2007-2010, 1996-1999, 1986-1989); *Member,* Advisory Committee, African Division, Human Rights (2007-2010); *Member,* Princeton University Maclean Society (2004-Present); *Member,* Princeton African American Studies Advisory Council (2000-2012); *Site Inspector,* American Bar Association (2002-Present); *Member,* Princeton University Alumni Service Awards Committee (2002-2005); *Member,* Princeton Alumni Council Executive Committee (2002-2004); *Member,* American

Association of Law Schools Africa Section (2000-2003); *Member,* American Friends Service Committee, Middle East Programs (1998-2004); *Member,* Minority Section, American Association of Law Schools (1997-2002); *Chair,* Minority Section, American Association of Law Schools (2002); *Member,* Princeton Committee to Nominate Alumni Trustees (1997-2000); *Member,* Princeton Alumni Council (1996-2000); *Member,* International Third World Legal Studies Association (1996-2000); *Member,* Princeton University Class of 1978 Foundation (1985-1987, 1993-2003); *President,* Princeton University Class of 1978 Foundation (1993-1998); *Member,* Stanford Law School Board of Visitors (1993-1996); *Member,* Iowa Peace Institute Board (1993-1995); *Member,* Transafrica Forum Scholars Council (1993-1995); *Member,* Iowa City Foreign Relations Council Board (1989-1994); *Member,* Association of Black Princeton Alumni Board (1982-1987); *Consultant,* American College Testing, Iowa (1993); *Consultant,* Amer-I-Can Program, Inc. (1994-1996); *Consultant,* Motion Picture Corporation of America (1997); *Member,* Board of Editors, American Journal of Comparative Law (1993-Present); *Reviewer,* University of Pennsylvania Press, Middle East Journal, New York University Press, University of Nebraska Press, Oxford University Press

LESSONS LEARNED: MY RECOMMENDATIONS FOR YOUR FUTURE ACTIONS BASED ON MY PAST EXPERIENCE

Advice on Making the Choice to Apply to and Attend Law School:

Be sure to consult with a lot of people concerning your particular situation. Make sure you really want to do it rather than it just being something you fell into because you did not know what else to do!

Advice on Law School Preparation:

Choose a major you like; get high grades; be involved in a lot of college activities; get several professor mentors.

Advice on Applying to and Selecting a Law School:

Take a Law School Admission Test (LSAT) prep course; have several people look at your personal statement; seek out advice regarding particular schools to apply to based on your profile, rankings, and debt loads.

Advice Regarding Academic Success, Co-Curricular and Extra-Curricular Participation, and Social Engagement in Law School:

Aim to maximize your Grade Point Average (GPA); get faculty and staff mentors; join a law journal; join the Black Law Students Association (BLSA) and other groups; do stress-relief activities.

Advice on Preparing for and Taking the Bar Exam:

Take a bar prep course; do not get distracted by other activities or people.

Advice on Choosing a Job and Career Path Inside or Outside of the Legal Profession:

Try a legal job at the beginning of your career as it can be very difficult to try to get one later; ask advice from many people regarding your options; taking time off for child-rearing and other activities may make it very difficult to reenter the profession.

Advice on Achieving Career Success and Advancement:

Keep consulting and developing mentors; develop emotional intelligence and other characteristics that will help you succeed in the workplace; make sure to acknowledge and befriend the support staff wherever you work. Many of them may be people of color in certain cities, and they can make or break you.

Advice on Overcoming the Additional Challenges Black Law Students and Lawyers Face:

Find mentors; find stress relief; get family support.

Best Advice I Received Regarding Law School and the Legal Profession:

It was the 1970s. I did not have people giving me great advice. I was on uncharted ground in my family and in that I did not know any lawyers, law professors, judges, etc. Thank goodness the situation is different now.

Worst Advice I Received Regarding Law School and the Legal Profession:

I did not get advice of any type.

Best Advice I Would Give to an Aspiring Black Lawyer:

Seek out lots of people for advice!

Thoughts About Why Earning a Law Degree Is a Powerful Credential for African Americans and Why There Is a Need for More African American Lawyers:

The law degree is one of the most powerful tools you can have in any society. The law enables you to speak truth to power and to aim for justice. Do not let anyone tell you there are too many lawyers - there are certainly not too many Black lawyers. Blacks are only about 4% of the lawyers yet nearly half the prison inmates! This situation cannot continue. The law may or may not be the career path for you, but we certainly need lots more of us involved.

LEGACY AND SUCCESS

My Most Outstanding Accomplishments:

- My children and grandchildren
- Being in a loving relationship for over 20 years with James Sommerville
- Working at the University of Iowa College of Law for over 30 years
- Authoring or editing over 140 publications
- Assisting in the drafting of three constitutions (South Africa, Palestine, and Rwanda)

The Legacy I Hope to Leave:

My legacy is my children, grandchildren, students, and some small contributions to the cause of justice.

The Secret to My Success:

My secret is family support and faith.

Ruqaiijah Yearby, Esq., M.P.H.
Professor of Law
Member
Center for Health Law Studies
Co-Founder and Executive Director
Institute for Healing Justice and Equity
Saint Louis University School of Law
Saint Louis, Missouri

"You cannot retain your humanity, while you deny mine."

– Ruqaiijah Yearby

Success is . . . working to uplift the voices of the marginalized and changing the systems that oppress them.

PERSONAL FAVORITES

Favorite Quotes: "Whatever affects one directly affects all indirectly. … [for] I can never be what I ought to be until you are what you ought to be. And you can never be what you ought to be until I am what I ought to be." - Dr. Martin Luther King, Jr.

"Every life is capable of greatness." - Condoleezza Rice

"My mission in life is not merely to survive, but to thrive; and to do so with some passion, some compassion, some humor, and some style." - Maya Angelou

Favorite Books: *The Broken Earth* Series by N.K. Jemisin; *Wild Seed* by Octavia Butler; *Nobody Knows My Name* by James Baldwin

Favorite Movie: *The Matrix*

Favorite Songs: "Don't Feel Right" by The Roots; "Something Bigger" by Mary Mary; "Somewhere I Belong" by Linkin Park

Favorite Law School Class: Administrative Law

Favorite Legal Case: *Canterbury v. Spence*

Favorite Hobbies: Swimming; Running; Biking; Basketball; Hiking; Reading

Favorite Role Models: The Reverend Martin Luther King, Jr.; Sonia Sanchez; Angela Davis; bell hooks; Malcolm X

FAMILY AND BACKGROUND

Where Born and Raised: Born - Detroit, Michigan; Raised - We moved a lot, but most of my childhood was spent in Michigan in Highland Park or Detroit.

Family (Spouse/Partner and Children): Spouse - Jim; Child - (son) Malcolm

Family Socioeconomic and Educational Background:

My parents are from working-class families. My parents were first-generation college graduates. I was the first to graduate from law school.

EDUCATIONAL ACHIEVEMENTS

High School: Southfield High School (Southfield, Michigan)

College/University: University of Michigan (Ann Arbor, Michigan)

Undergraduate Degree: Bachelor of Science (B.S.)

Major: Honors Biology

College Honors, Achievements and Activities: *Recipient*, Academic Scholarship (1992-1996); Class Honors (1993); *Awardee*, Sophomore Honors Award (1994); *Research Assistant*, University of Natal (South Africa)

Law School: Georgetown University Law Center (Washington, D.C.)

Law Degree and Graduation Year: Juris Doctor/Doctor of Jurisprudence (J.D.) - Class of 2000

Law School Honors, Achievements and Activities: *Academic Recognition,* Dean's List (1999); *Staff Editor,* Georgetown Journal on Poverty Law & Policy (1998-2000); *Research Assistant,* Institute for Health Care Research and Policy (1999-2000)

Other Graduate or Professional Degree: Master of Public Health (M.P.H.) in Health Policy & Management, Johns Hopkins School of Public Health (Baltimore, Maryland)

PROFESSIONAL ACCOMPLISHMENTS

State Bar Memberships (Where Admitted to Practice Law): Maryland; District of Columbia; Illinois

Other Legal Experience: *Professor of Law, David L. Brennan Professor of Law* (Chair), and *Associate Dean of Institutional Diversity and Inclusiveness,* Case Western Reserve University School of Law (2011-2018); *Visiting Professor,* University of Connecticut School of Law (2011); *Associate Professor,* University at Buffalo Law School, The State University of New York and University at Buffalo School of Public Health and Health Professions (2008-2011); *Assistant Professor,* Loyola University Chicago School of Law and Loyola University Chicago Stritch School of Medicine (2003-2008); *Law Clerk,* Honorable Ann Claire Williams, U.S. Court of Appeals, Seventh Circuit (2002); *Health Care Associate,* Duane Morris, LLC (2001-2002, 2002-2003); *Assistant Regional Counsel,* U.S. Department of Health and Human Services (2000-2001)

Professional Organizations: *Chair,* American Association of Law Schools, Law, Medicine, and Health Care; *Member,* Advocacy Advisory Committee, Generate Health STL; *Member,* Advisory Board, American Public Health Association, Aging and Public Health Book Project; *Member,* Norman S. Minor Bar Association; *Member,* American Association of Law Schools; *Member,* Administrative Law Section, American Association of Law Schools; *Member,* Minority Section, Association of Law, Medicine and Ethics

Post-Law School Honors, Achievements, Activities, and Community Involvement: *Co-Principal Investigator,* Are Cities and Counties Ready to Use Racial Equity Tools to Influence Policy?, Robert Wood Johnson Foundation Policies for Action grant (December 2018-August 2020); *Mayor's Proclamation Recipient,* Proclamation issued by Mayor of the City of Cleveland celebrating appointment as Associate Dean (January 2016); *Awardee,* Women Achievement Award, Case Western University Reserve School of Law (October 2012); *Awardee,* Performance Award, Job Rating of Excellent, U.S. Department of Health and Human Services, Office of the General Counsel (August 2001); *Awardee,* Secretary's Award for Distinguished Service, U.S. Department of Health and Human Services (June 2001); *Awardee,* Norman Amaker Award of Excellence, Loyola University Chicago (January 2007)

LESSONS LEARNED: MY RECOMMENDATIONS FOR YOUR FUTURE ACTIONS BASED ON MY PAST EXPERIENCE

Advice on Law School Preparation:

Focus on the positive and do not let people limit you. Get the best grades you can by working hard, studying, and being prepared for class. If you need help, don't be afraid to get a tutor. Network with your professor by going to office hours and asking questions. Ask your professor and the teaching assistant how you can do well in the class, then do what they say, and let them know you are doing it.

Advice on Applying to and Selecting a Law School:

Do well in school and participate in extra-curricular activities. Take a Law School Admission Test (LSAT) prep class and do the work necessary to get a good LSAT score. Have someone review your personal statement and resume before you submit it to law schools. Once you are admitted, select the school based on the following factors: scholarship money; whether the school is known for the area of practice you are interested in; whether they have diverse faculty and students; and whether you plan to stay in the city in which the school is located.

Advice Regarding Academic Success, Co-Curricular and Extra-Curricular Participation, and Social Engagement in Law School:

Build a community while in law school including a study group and a support group. Find support outside of law school as well. Spend some time working separately from other students to ensure you do your best. Do not believe others when they say law school is easy; IT IS NOT. Work hard and be professional: show up on time for class (in fact, show up early); be prepared; don't miss class; go see professors with questions; and turn in your best work all the time.

Advice on Preparing for and Taking the Bar Exam:

Study. Study. Study. This is a full-time job and it should be your priority. Do not let anything get in the way of studying. You should plan for some break time about two hours a day, otherwise you should be studying, sleeping, or eating.

Advice on Choosing a Legal Job and Career Path Inside or Outside of the Legal Profession:

When you go to law school, you should have an idea of what areas of practice you are interested in and what your career path will be after you graduate law school. During law school, you should work and/or volunteer in these areas of practice to determine whether this is really going to be your career path. Once you decide what you want to do for your legal career, identify a person who is doing what you want to do and ask them questions about their career path. Use this information to draft your own career plan. Every year reread your career plan and revise it as necessary.

Advice on Seeking Legal Job Opportunities:

Work hard and network. You create opportunities for jobs when you work hard because people will talk about how great your work product is at your job and to their friends. That is the best recommendation you can get.

Advice on Achieving Career Success and Advancement:

Never stay stagnant. You should have a career plan that includes long-term and short-term goals. Every year you need to review your career plan to identify what you have accomplished and what new goals you need to add. You also need to assess whether your current job will allow you to reach your goals. If not, then it is time to find a new job that will allow you to accomplish your goals.

Advice on Overcoming the Additional Challenges Black Law Students Face:

Stay positive. Work hard and always strive for excellence even when those around you are settling for less.

Advice on Overcoming the Additional Challenges Black Lawyers Face:

I always felt the need to work hard because in law, in science, in most jobs, women and minorities are viewed as less qualified. In addition to working hard, I tried to connect with people who were senior to me. I used music, sports, TV shows, travel, etc. I always remained me, but I focused on the things that we had in common. Hard work and connections paid off because I can and do still go back and visit people at every job I have had since law school.

Best Advice I Received Regarding Law School and the Legal Profession:

Work hard; be professional; and network with law professors and those in the legal profession.

Worst Advice I Received Regarding Law School and the Legal Profession:

My honors counselor made fun of my dream to go to law school and I was told that I would not get into any law school by counselors in the academic support program. However, I still believed in myself enough to apply to Michigan, Georgetown, Northwestern, Boston University, and Wayne State. Not only did I get into every school, but also the dean of Georgetown wrote a note on my admittance letter saying he hoped I would come to Georgetown. This was one of the reasons I chose to go to Georgetown.

Best Advice I Would Give to an Aspiring Black Lawyer:

Don't always think diversity is the problem; sometimes people are just mean and insecure. Therefore, the key is to do the work of building relationships with those who look like you and those that don't because law, like every other field, is about relationships. Keep focused on yourself and your goals. My goal was to help people, so I always did this even when my job was not focused on it. Keep your integrity and be honest. Do not let other people bring you down with their own insecurities. Be YOUR own STAR, no matter what people say.

Thoughts About Why Earning a Law Degree Is a Powerful Credential for African Americans and Why There Is a Need for More African American Lawyers:

A law degree is a powerful credential for African Americans because it allows you to have independence in your career. Even if you do not practice law, having a law degree provides some level of respect. Law school also teaches you to think critically and come up with a solution to any problem using the law to support your solution. Thus, it teaches you to think in a way that will allow you to address any obstacle that is placed in your way.

Thoughts About Whether and Why Law School Is Worth the Financial Investment:

Law school is worth the investment. Once you have a law degree and pass the bar, you have the capacity to always have a job because someone always needs a lawyer. The key is to not overspend in law school. Go to a law school offering scholarship support. Work during the summers and during the school year when allowed. During your first year, see if you can work at the school in the library or within another office at the law school. Keep your personal expenses down by serving as a resident advisor or director in the dorms.

LEGACY AND SUCCESS

My Most Outstanding Accomplishments:

Presenting my work concerning the exploitation of children in medical research studies at the 2015 Oxford Global Health and Bioethics International Conference, Oxford, England. Also having my article "Reducing Errors Key to Reform" that was printed in the Rochester Democrat and Chronicle on October 3, 2009 and reprinted in USA Today Magazine, November 1, 2009); My article "Striving for Equality, But Settling for the Status Quo in Health Care: Is Title VI More Illusory Than Real?", 59 Rutgers L. Rev. 429-496 (2007), which discusses the continuation of racial bias in health care was cited under the Law Review Commentaries of Title VI of the Civil Rights Act of 1964 (42 U.S.C.A. § 2000d), the federal law that prohibits racial bias in health care.

The Legacy I Hope to Leave:

The need to speak for those who are ignored (the poor, minorities, women, children, LGBT) is why I went to law school, became a law professor, and why I am the Co-Founder and Executive Director for the Institute of Healing Justice and Equity. Thus, my legacy will be to make where I live and work more diverse, more inclusive, and fair for everyone and to empower others to do the same.

The Secret to My Success:

The secret to my success is working hard, staying positive, and using others' negativity to fuel my resolve to succeed.

Pre-Law Resources for African Americans

EVENTS

National Black Pre-Law Conference and Law Fair - www.blackprelawconference.com

National HBCU Pre-Law Summit and Law Expo - www.hbcuprelawsummit.com

INFORMATIONAL/RESOURCE WEBSITES

Black Pre-Law - www.blackprelaw.com

HBCU Pre-Law - www.hbcuprelaw.com

VIDEO/FILM

Becoming Black Lawyers: African Americans and the Law School Experience (Documentary Series) - www.becomingblacklawyers.com

MENTORSHIP PROGRAM

The Bridge Builders Esq.: National Mentorship Program for Aspiring Black Lawyers - https://bridgebuildersesq.org

Also by Evangeline M. Mitchell

The African American Pre-Law School Advice Guide: Things You Really Need to Know *Before* Applying to Law School

Profiles & Essays of Successful African American Law School Applicants

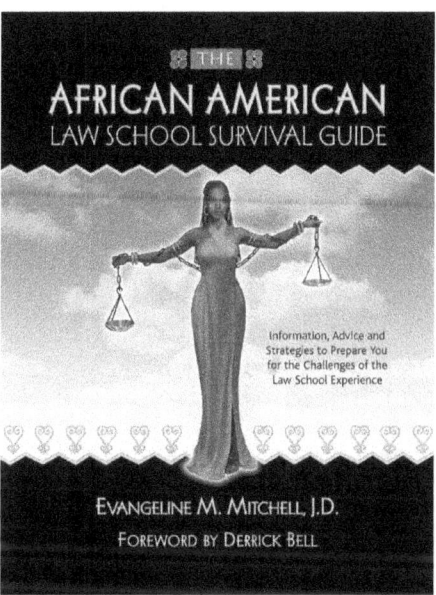

The African American Law School Survival Guide: Information, Advice, and Strategies to Prepare You for the Challenges of the Law School Experience

Conquering the Bar Exam: Personal Stories and Practical Advice for Overcoming the Final Hurdle to Becoming a Full-Fledged Licensed Lawyer

Creating Your Personal Strategic Action Plan for Law School Admission Success: A Planning Workbook for College Students

www.ingramcontent.com/pod-product-compliance
Lightning Source LLC
Chambersburg PA
CBHW080515090426

42734CB00015B/3057